ARCHITECTURE
IN THE 20TH CENTURY

Udo Kultermann

VNR VAN NOSTRAND REINHOLD
New York

All rights for all countries with
DuMont Buchverlag GmbH & Co.,
Kommanditgsellschaft, Koln,
Bundesrepublik Deutschland.
Under the title:
Die Architektur im 20. Jahrhundert,
von Udo Kultermann

Copyright © 1993 by Van Nostrand Reinhold

Library of Congress Catalog Card Number 92-26734
ISBN 0-442-00942-9

I(T)P   Van Nostrand Reinhold is a division of International Thomson
Publishing. ITP logo is a trademark under license.

Printed in the United States of America

Van Nostrand Reinhold
115 Fifth Avenue
New York, New York 10003

International Thomson Publishing
Berkshire House
168-173 High Holborn
London, WC1V 7AA, England

Thomas Nelson Australia
102 Dodds Street
South Melbourne 3205
Victoria, Australia

Nelson Canada
1120 Birchmount Road
Scarborough, Ontario
M1K 5G4, Canada

16 15 14 13 12 11 10 9 8 7 6 5 4 3 2 1

Library of Congress Cataloging-in-Publication Data

Kultermann, Udo.
    [Architektur im 20. Jahrhundert. English]
    Architecture in the 20th century / Udo Kultermann.
        p.   cm.
    Includes bibliographical references and index.
    ISBN 0-442-00942-9
    1. Architecture, Modern—20th century. I. Title. II. Title:
Architecture in the 20th century.
NA680.K7913 1993
724'.6—dc20   92-26734
                                                          CIP

Contents

Preface vii

I Puristic Tendencies: Architecture, Science, and Industry
   and the Attitude Towards the Machine
   The Necessary Synthesis 1
   Frank Lloyd Wright and the Aesthetics of the Machine 3
   Thomas Alva Edison and Industrial Production of Houses 9
   Alexander Graham Bell and Lightweight Construction 12
   Expressionism in America — The Second Phase of the Skyscraper . . 14
   The Early Modern Movement in California 15
   Tony Garnier and the Vision of the Industrial City 20
   Changes in Construction with Reinforced Concrete 22
   Le Corbusier and the Aesthetics of the Machine in France 26
   Peter Behrens and "Industrial Design" 29
   The Early Work of Walter Gropius 31
   Idea and Form of the Bauhaus 34
   The Ideology of Industrialization — The Contribution of
   Mies van der Rohe 38
   Hans Poelzig and Expressionism 42
   Bruno Taut and the "Glass Chain" 46
   Bruno Taut and Social Housing 47
   Organic Architecture — Hugo Häring and Rudolf Steiner 52
   Perfection of Shell Construction 54
   Futurism in Italy 57
   De Stijl and the School of Amsterdam 60
   Synthesis in Russia 65

II Empiristic Tendencies: Organic Architecture and Technology
    Serving Man and Nature
    The Change Towards the Organic 73
    New Beginnings in the Work of Frank Lloyd Wright 75
    Architecture and Architectural Engineering in America
    Around 1930 79
    New Beginnings in Latin America 82

Beginnings in South Africa, India, Australia, and Japan 83
Alvar Aalto and the Contribution of Scandinavia 84
The Conservative Avant-Garde in England 87
A New Flourishing of Architecture in Holland 88
Swiss Architecture After 1930 89
Spain During the 1930s and 1940s 91
Fascist Architecture in Italy 91
National Socialist Architecture in Germany 95
Stalinistic Architecture in Russia 100
France Between 1930 and 1950 103

III Syncretic Tendencies: Urbanistic Architecture and Building
     Within a Context

The International Situation After 1950 107
Architecture in the United States After 1950 108
Louis I. Kahn and the Young Generation 122
Canadian Architecture Between 1950 and 1970 127
European Architecture After World War II 130
City Planning and Educational Buildings in England 130
Model Case—Finland and Scandinavia 134
Continuation of a Tradition in the Netherlands 137
France After 1950 138
German Architecture Between 1950 and 1970 141
Swiss Architecture Between 1950 and 1970 145
Building in Austria 147
Postwar Architecture in Italy 147
Spanish and Portuguese Architecture Between 1950
and 1970 149
Architecture in the Soviet Union . . . . , . . 150
Architecture in Eastern Europe Between 1950 and 1970 152
Architecture of the Third World 153
The Revolution in Latin America 155
Mexican Architecture After 1950 155
Building in Central America 157
Architecture in South America After 1950 157
The Rebuilding of the State of Israel 161
Contemporary Architecture in the Arab Countries 163
New Architecture in Africa 166
Architecture in India, Pakistan, and Bangladesh 172
Architecture in Australia and New Zealand 175
Postwar Architecture in China 176
Japanese Architecture Between 1950 and 1970 177

IV Autonomous Architecture Since 1970: Regional Identity and the Regaining of Tradition

Transformations Around 1970 185
American Architecture Since 1970 186
The Continuation of a Tradition 187
Further Lessons from Louis I. Kahn 190
New Structural Tendencies in American Architecture 192
Redefining American Architecture 196
The Young Generation 198
Contemporary Architecture in Canada 199
European Architecture Since 1970 200
English Architecture Since 1970 200
Architecture in Finland and Scandinavia Since 1970 202
Dutch Architecture Since 1970 204
Architecture in Belgium Since 1970 204
Contemporary Architecture in Germany 205
Architecture in Austria Since 1970 209
Swiss Architecture Since 1970 210
Architecture in France Since 1970 210
Contemporary Architecture in Italy 212
Contemporary Architecture in Spain 212
Architecture in Portugal Since 1970 213
Eastern European Architecture Since 1970 214
Contemporary Polish Architecture 220
Contemporary Architecture in the Czech and Slovak Republics 221
Hungarian Architecture Since 1970 221
Contemporary Architecture in Rumania 223
Contemporary Architecture in Bulgaria 223
Architecture in the Former Yugoslavia 224
Architecture in the Southern Hemisphere 226
Architecture in Mexico After 1970 227
Contemporary Architecture in Central America 227
South American Architecture Since 1970 228
New Architecture in South Saharan Africa 229
Architecture in the North African Arab States Since 1970 229
Architecture in Iraq, Syria, Jordan, and Lebanon 231
Recent Architecture in Saudi Arabia and the Gulf States 232
Architecture in Israel Since 1970 235
Recent Developments of Architecture in Iran 236
Architecture in Pakistan Since 1970 236
Architecture in India Since 1970 237
New Architecture in Bangladesh 239
Architecture in Southeast Asia 239

    Architecture in Australia and New Zealand 241
    Architectural Alternatives in China 242
    Contemporary Architecture in Korea 244
    Japanese Architecture Between 1970 and 1990 244
    Conclusion 248
Notes 251
Critical Bibliography 277
Photo Credits 287
Index of Names 289
Index of Places 301

Preface

This book evolved from a teaching experience of about 25 years at an American school of architecture and was conceived as a textbook with the focus on practical usefulness. In spite of the multitude of publications concerning architecture of the twentieth century, none of the available works has been fully accepted as handbook or textbook. This book seeks to close that gap, yet like any textbook it cannot be more than an outline of dates and facts, interpretations and hypotheses whereby use and expansion must be left up to the individual. However, one thing is certain: knowledge before actual observation is useful with regard to art, to life in general, as well as to the concerns of the history of architecture. If one admires the west facade of the cathedral in Florence or the nave in the cathedral of Cologne without knowing that these elements were built during the nineteenth century, one is not able to realize the emotions adequately, since an error and a false viewpoint make a fair perception impossible.[1]

However, methods as such are neither right nor wrong; their use alone can determine the qualification and stand the test. A particular example during the last few years is the effort concerning a semiology of architecture, which up to now is limited to controversy and apology.[2]

In contrast to the numerous publications concerning architecture in the twentieth century, the attempt will be made here to overcome the existing partiality of the varying views. The art of building, in the narrow sense, the construction of cities and architectural engineering, even three-dimensional structures not erected by architects or engineers, are here to understood as contributing elements of the total constructed environment and are included. The total environment, which influences the entire human being, was taken as theme of this presentation, since the ideals, hopes, and limitations of the individual, as well as of social groups, can best be recognized through such integrated views.

The categories for evaluation and the resources for the historian of architecture are subject to his own time period with its architectural culture. The observer must have had this contemporary experience, if he is to arrive at an aware relationship with tradition. Siegfried Giedion postulated for the historian: "Only if he is filled with the spirit of his own time period, is he able to uncover the trends of the past."[3] The facts concerning the history of art and the observer who describes them are to be seen as connected flexible, variable poles, and they must be integrated into the system of observations. It can be said, with a slight modification of a quotation by Karl Marx, that history has to be viewed anew before the reality can be changed.

Just as life is not the question of cosmetics that advertising constantly suggests, so architecture of the twentieth century is rather more than a phenomenon of photogenic facades and striking surface details. Therefore, it is here viewed in regard to truth and relevance to changing sociological and political transformations. The questions of likes and dislikes, forms, symbols, ornaments or materials, or the expressions of beautiful, ugly, or functional are irrelevant. Only involvement with truth, as it can be found in a building, is singularly relevant. Architecture can therefore not be perceived from the viewpoint of taste or as a personal means of expression of the architect. It is part of a larger human and social fabric from which it evolves and finds its place.

Therefore, it is relevant to recognize that parts of a system can be understood only by means of a larger framework and only when the elements are viewed in their context. The same applies with regard to the lapse of time. Just as a painting or sculpture must be seen as true and complete throughout the various stages of its production, so also the organization and of structure material of a historical depiction must be seen in its entirety, as a totality permanently subject to a changing process. Beyond the scientific considerations, esthetic ways of seeing also retain their relevance, as they explain man's relation to his changing reactions to his environment. In particular, the alteration of the human environment, the theme of architecture, evolves in a complex and ambivalent way, more so than the historical sciences have learned to understand. Such a development, based on permanent changes, requires personal involvement and vigorous participation in a manner that heretofore has been merely theoretical in nature.

I

Puristic Tendencies: Architecture, Science, and Industry and the Attitude Towards the Machine

The Necessary Synthesis

The basis for architectural development in the twentieth century is the integration of science and technology into the construction area. Around 1900, industrial production was for the first time viewed as a given in modern society, and architecture was newly looked upon in this aspect. Although Gottfried Semper (1803–1879) had been able to speak of "Science, Industry, and Art" (1852),[1] a systematic coordination and the highest degree of development of the existing potential were possible only after 1900. The close relationship between history and architecture, which had existed earlier, was to a great degree dissolved and the question of the relationship to tradition became a problem for more than half a century.[2]

Rational methods, technical building materials, and an ideal determined by the production of machines are decisive for the development of architecture during the first three decades of the twentieth century. Ludwig Hilberseimer wrote in 1924: "The architect must agree with the principles of the engineers as their creations — machines and ships, cars and planes, cranes and bridges — are always connected through the spirit of unity and the expression of a common purpose."[3]

Modern means of transportation have in this sense been considered to be exemplary by Henry van de Velde, Walter Gropius, Le Corbusier, Moholy-Nagy, Tatlin, Sant'Elia, and numerous other architects. Moholy-Nagy wrote in 1929: "The ocean liners, which were built since the 1890s, are

1

the forerunners of contemporary architecture."[4] E. Gibbs-Smith visually demonstrated the technical development of the airplane, which was analogous to the architecture of the time and reached surprising conclusions. In particular, new insight was gained through the parallel development of the brothers Wilbur and Orville Wright and the architect Frank Lloyd Wright.[5]

The significance of the airplane with regard to the general development of modern civilization and the modern view of the world was recognized early by the art historian Bernard Berenson (1865–1959). After once viewing one of the airplanes of the brothers Wright, he commented: "I cannot tell you how I hate this innocent monster which is going to destroy the world I love. It will destroy my beloved world, the world of level vision or vision from below upwards, in other words, the whole way of looking at things that the artist has been taught to expect, all the rules of perspective, the sense of looking at solid objects from one fixed point on earth. . . ."[6]

Agreement between engineers and industrial production includes the simplification of form as well as standardization. In the Wiener Werkstätte, founded in 1903, forms of architecture and interior design were developed, geared to simple and clear structures. Josef Hoffmann's sanatorium in Purkersdorf near Vienna (1904–1905) is one of the most prominent examples in architecture of this process of simplification. In 1908, Hendrik Petrus Berlage imagined a universe, "based on and designed according to laws of geometry." He concluded: "Indeed, one can go still further and maintain that symmetry, present in all forms in nature, is pointing to certain basic primordial laws of creation, which totally conform to the laws of geometry, the basic geometric forms of the polygons, or the divisions of the circle."[7]

The ideas of Le Corbusier, as well as Hoffmann, Berlage, Mondrian, Kandinsky, and Mies van der Rohe are deeply rooted in symbolism: "Le Courbusier's work was to be characterized most essentially by a search for generalization, universality, and absolute formal truths which would put man in touch with a harmony underlying nature—a divine 'axis,' as he called it, which 'leads' us to assume a unity of direction in the universe, and to admit a single will at its source."[8]

J. J. P. Oud adds:

Analogous was the purpose in building: an architecture which should be most universal. No more small works of art for the individual, no more precious country houses with beautiful handcrafted work and luxurious decoration, but mass production and standardization with the intent of creating good dwellings for many. The detail as end in itself would disappear in favor of the whole. The products of the machine should be accepted on the basis of the uniqueness of the machine, and no longer as substitute for handcrafted work. The preciseness of the purely technical products which we admire (automobile, ship, instruments, etc.) should be an example for reorganization in architecture in the sense that the demands made on a structure should be as precisely fixed, and realized with the latest materials, construction, and work technology. . . .[9]

Even earlier, the machine had been discovered as a determining factor for form.[10] Riuox de Maillou wrote in 1895 about the relationship between decorative art and the machine: "If a machine does the work, it should be allowed to leave its mark, to imprint its mode of expression on the things it produces."[11] Somewhat later, Frank Lloyd Wright, Sant'Elia, and Le Corbusier referred to the house as a machine to be lived in, Paul Valéry (1871–1945) understood: "a book as a machine for reading," I. A. Richards (1893–1979) considered a book to be a thinking machine, and numerous metaphors of the time embraced the image of the machine, so that one could truly speak of the age of the machine.[12]

Theo van Doesburg characterized the meaning of the machine: "If it is correct, that culture means in the broadest sense independence from nature, then we should not be surprised, if the machine dominates with regard to cultural wishes concerning style."[13] And Gino Severini saw the machine as completely analogous to the work of art: "All elements of matter, for example the components of a machine are assembled by one mind, the mind of the inventor. . . . The process of developing a machine is analogous to the creation of a work of art."[14]

The programs of the Futurists, the Bauhaus, the circle around Le Corbusier, and the Russian Constructionists all have a common view regarding the machine, technology, and subsequent industrialization. Moholy-Nagy's teaching at the Bauhaus explains perhaps most clearly the concept, which was geared towards a program of integration and synthesis: "his teaching principle aspires to, in his words 'the closest union of art, science and technology.'"[15]

Frank Lloyd Wright and the Aesthetics of the Machine

The earliest transcending of the boundaries existing between the various connected areas of architecture, technology, and industry was achieved by Frank Lloyd Wright (1867–1959) in the Midwest of the United States of America.[16] This was achieved by an architect who, after instruction by Louis Sullivan (1856–1924) regarding high-rise office buildings and after his construction of predominantly one-family houses using traditional building materials, developed from a basic view of the Romantic tradition (Fig. 1). When

1 Louis Sullivan: The Carson, Pirie & Scott department store, Chicago (1898–1899, 1903–1904)

Wright gave a talk at Hull House in Chicago on the 6th of March, 1901, titled "The Arts and Crafts of the Machine," he laid down a basis for a new evaluation of technology and architecture, which must have seemed revolutionary at the time. While Victor Hugo, John Ruskin, William Morris, and — under their influence, the young Frank Lloyd Wright, also — had previously seen the machine as a necessary evil, which had no place in architecture, he now discovered this instrument and with it the notion that modern technology is a beneficial tool in the hands of the architect: "Standardization was either the enemy or a friend to the architect. He might choose."[17]

Simplicity was the goal of these architectural endeavors, similar to the views, which governed the French painter Paul Cézanne, that nature itself is organized by means of cubes, cylinders, and spheres.[18] While European architects Peter Behrens, Josef Hoffmann, Otto Wagner, and Tony Garnier had similarly arrived at new technical conditions to simplify and reduce elements, it was Wright who created the basic integration of machine aesthetics, economy of construction, and the tradition of architecture. This synthesis cannot be valued too highly, and it represents one of the fundamentals of the architecture of the twentieth century.

One of the early Wright houses in the vicinity of Chicago, for example, the Warren Hickox house in Kankakee, Illinois, of 1900 (Fig. 2) shows clearly the trend towards simplifica-

2 *Frank Lloyd Wright: Warren Hickox house, Kankakee, Illinois (1900)*

tion of basic forms, in the same manner as Wright's experiences as a child when playing with the toys of Froebel.[19] Economical conditions were also solved in an exemplary manner, later seldom achieved.[20]

Wright's early houses, deeply rooted in the American architectural tradition, were perceived by contemporaries as being unusual and revolutionary. However, it would be a misunderstanding to view Wright as an isolated genius. Rather, he evolved from a cultural climate along with numerous other architects, such as George W. Maher (1864–1926), Robert C. Spencer (1865–1953), Dwight H. Perkins (1867–1941), George Elmslie (1871–1952), Marion Lucy Mahony (1871–1962), and Walter Burley Griffin (1876–1937), who all strove for similar goals and often worked in close contact with Frank Lloyd Wright.

It is not at all surprising that Wright's houses were connected at that time with other technological inventions, especially with the flight experiments of the Wright brothers and the production of vehicles.[21] The E. A. Gilmore house in Madison, Wisconsin, of 1908 was called the "Airplane House," probably due to the elevated main living room and the placement of the house on the tip of a hill. Also, the structure of the building itself and its wide overhanging roof, as well as the nearly streamlined contour of the walls, may have contributed to the development of the metaphor.

The major work in Wright's early years was the Robie house in Chicago of 1909 (Figs. 3, 4). By contemporaries, it was named "The Battleship."

3 *Frank Lloyd Wright: Robie house, Chicago (1909) plan*

4 *Frank Lloyd Wright: Robie house, Chicago (1909)*

The centrally located chimney was interpreted as being a mast, the long, horizontal balconies as decks and the living room as bridge. The common analogy of houses and ships that was already used during the nineteenth century — Horatio Greenough (1805–1852), as well as James Ferguson (1808–1886), used it in a positive sense — symbolized an altered perception of a house. In contrast to the earthbound, firm linkage to the ground, it is now being compared with the vehicles considered to be functional in form and dependent upon the power of the machine. Beyond that, more and more technical equipment was integrated into the to-

tality of the living space, for example, necessary mechanical installations, such as a heating system, lighting, and —maybe for the first time in the history of architecture—a garage.[22]

Wright's inventive spirit was also demonstrated by the creation of new building tasks, such as the housing estate, which had only existed in a rudimentary or a totally different form up to that time. The Francisco Terrace housing complex in Chicago of 1895 (demolished in 1974), was one of the earliest experiments to bring social necessity and economical restrictions into harmony with creative architecture.[23] Wright placed 44 small apartments in a two-story structure around an open courtyard, which guaranteed privacy of the individual occupant, but at the same time affording the best possible communication among the residents. Secluding isolation and connecting through communication were thus recognized, and realized not mutually exclusive, but complementary.[24]

In addition to the houses, there are two outstanding examples typical of Wright's basic thought. The Larkin Administration Building was erected for a mail-order company (Figs. 5, 5a), an internally well-organized, well-functioning operation whose principal function was office work. Wright's solution of designing the total area from floor to ceiling as open space furnished with air-conditioning demonstrates his architectonic view. The uppermost floor contained a restaurant

5a Frank Lloyd Wright: Administration Building of the Larkin Soap Company, Buffalo (1904) view of the exterior

and a conservatory, while the roof itself was built as terrace, which could be used as recreation space.

Wright clearly defined the meaning of his work within the new architecture: "The Larkin Administration Building was a simple cliff of brick hermetically sealed (one of the first air-conditioned buildings) to keep the interior space clear of the poisonous gases in the smoke from the New York Central Trains that puffed along beside it."[25] The architect was also able to design the total interior environment of this modern workplace, from the steel furniture to the small details of the firm, in a comprehensive

◁ 5 Frank Lloyd Wright: Administration Building of the Larkin Soap Company, Buffalo (1904) view of the interior

6 Frank Lloyd Wright: Unity Church, Oak Park, Illinois (1906)

6a   Frank Lloyd Wright: View of the interior of
the Unity Church, Oak Park, Illinois (1906)

plan. Wright, himself, in his biography makes the comparison to a modern vehicle. The construction was for him a "genuine expression of power directly applied to purpose, in the same sense that the ocean liner, the plane or the car is so."[26] Reyner Banham rightfully considered the Larkin Building as "a bridge between the history of modern architecture as commonly written — the progress of structure and external form — and a history of modern architecture understood as the progress of creating a humane environment."[27]

Two years later, Wright went yet a step further when designing and constructing the Unity Church in Oak Park (Figs. 6, 6a). He created, as he himself proudly announced, "the first concrete monolith in the world."[28] Limited financial means — only $45,000 dollars were available for the construction of the church and the community house — led Wright to the choice of reinforced concrete as building material. The laws for the use and form of reinforced concrete led to the basic form of the square as the module for all parts of the building.[29] The squares of the skylight in the church interior are a symbolic expression of the technical necessity of the principle of the simplified square form. The integration of architecture, technology, and industry thus led to a new form of architecture as it was developed similarly during the same time period by Peter Behrens and Tony Garnier in Europe — although in a different tradition.

Thomas Alva Edison and Industrial Production of Houses

The history of twentieth-century architecture must include the work of a man who has hardly been mentioned up to now, yet who made a contribution as decisive as that of Frank Lloyd Wright: Thomas Alva Edison (1847–1931). He had an influence on the synthesis of science, technology, and architecture and was, like Wright, without a complete education in the field of architecture. Beside his epochmaking inventions (incandescent lightbulb, phonograph record, microphone), there were his mostly overlooked experiments with Portland concrete and the subsequent mass production of prefabricated houses made of concrete (Figs. 7, 8).[30]

The base for the typical experiments of the time was the Edison Portland Cement Company in Orange, New Jersey, founded in 1899 by Edison, which in a short time became the fifth largest concrete manufacturing plant in America. In 1907, Edison progressed one step further and started production of houses made of poured concrete, which could be cast at the construction site and which represented a remarkably economic solution to the construction and housing problem.

In cooperation with the architects Mann and McNaillie, a prefabricated house was developed with a room for the heating system, a laundry room and a coal cellar in the basement, hall, living room, and kitchen, as well as two verandas on the slightly elevated first floor, two bedrooms, bathroom, and hall on the second floor, and two additional bedrooms on the third floor.[31]

The price reduction for the completed prefabricated house, possible due to the automatic manufacturing process, was the sensation of the period: The final price, including heating and electricity systems, was $1,200 dollars. Also included were fire safety, which was most important for that time period, the modern sanitary installations, guaranteed heat in winter and cooling in summer, which were enhanced by the building material. The *Daily Mail*, a mass circulation newspaper, printed this headline in its edition of the 11th of December, 1907, "Nine-Roomed Houses for Dollar 1200. Mr. Edison's Plan for Cheap Dwellings, — Has He Hit Upon a Practical Scheme?" The question had not been posed unjustly by the newspaper, as was demonstrated by the subsequent development, which did not lead to the mass production as planned. Nevertheless, a large number of houses was produced by Edison's system and built in New Jersey, among them in Union and Philippsburg.

7 *Thomas Alva Edison: Model of prefabricated
concrete house (1907) view of the rear*

The technology of the casting was achieved through a system of scaffoldings, which allowed for variations and alterations: "No street of Edison Cement Houses will be a dull thoroughfare in uniform color and design. One house will be built on one plan, the next on another. One house will be gray, another red or light green, while a third may be yellow. Everybody can choose his color. Tinting the cement before it is poured is easy."[32] The erection of the scaffolding was achieved in about four days, the casting took only six hours, and the disassembly of the scaffolding required four additional days per house. The scaffolding was made of metal and could therefore be reused. The manufacturing capacity at Edison's plant at New Jersey was projected to be 144 houses per year.[33] Edison had secured a special patent for his production concerning the color variations of the cast concrete, which was to prevent a monotony of the multiple houses.[34]

The social consequences, in particular, played a central role for Edison and his public. When Edison was interviewed by Allan L. Benson in 1909, he emphasized this aspect intensively and gave prominence to "what inventiveness can do for the poor."[35] He considered these to be most important among his more than thousand inventions, "because it will solve the problem of housing."[36] These houses were very suitable for the creation of housing colonies for workers: They were inexpensive, secure, flexible, hygienic, and free of profit speculation, due to Edison's special provisions in this regard. It may be this latter aspect that stood in the way of a successful continued development of the project and that actually prevented its further development.

Edison's hopes are expressed in a brochure, which he published himself in Orange, New Jersey, around 1910, with the title "Edison Cast Concrete House": "I think the age of concrete has started and I believe that I can prove that the most beautiful houses that our architects can conceive, can be cast in one operation in iron forms at a cost, which by comparison with present methods, will be surprising. Then even the poorest man among us will be able to own a house of his own —a home that will last for centuries with no cost for insurance or repairs, and be as exchangeable for other property as a United States Bond."[37]

The complex historical reality did not favor early development of mass production of prefabricated houses, as in the case with automobiles. Henry

8 *Thomas Alva Edison: Model of prefabri-* ▷
cated concrete house (1907)

Ford was a close friend of Edison, but the resistance was obviously too strong against an invention that could eliminate numerous occupations in the construction industry. Henry J. Harm, a collaborator of Edison, passed the invention on to the Dutch architect Hendrik Petrus Berlage, who supposedly constructed a prefabricated concrete house in Sandpoort.[38] However, again this time, the fruitful development was nipped in the bud, and the social implications were thus not expanded. It was a chance to decisively change the total environment of the twentieth century.

Alexander Graham Bell and Lightweight Construction

The works of Frank Lloyd Wright and Thomas Alva Edison showed clearly that the interpenetration of science, technology, and industry influenced the early years of modern architecture decisively. In addition to Wright, Edison, and several other architects, engineers, and inventors, Alexander Graham Bell (1847–1922) had a significant influence on the necessary synthesis, though in a different area. As outsider and nonarchitect, his influence was nevertheless important regarding the principles of a certain kind of construction, which was only taken up and expanded during the subsequent phases of twentieth-century architecture.

Alexander Graham Bell had experimented since 1899 on his houseboat on the Potomac with flying objects — which were laughed at. Bell, however, did not allow himself to be troubled and continued with his experiments

undisturbed, knowing that a "successful flying machine was a possibility in the near future."[39] This was proven by the Wright brothers in 1901.

Bell, however, went his own way. He invented a cell system consisting of tetrahedrons, which he considered suitable for his aeronautical experiments, since according to him, they made a "three-dimensional strength" possible. During the early experiments, these tedrahedron systems were constructed with rods made of spruce, which were no stronger than splinters. Soon they were replaced by hollow aluminum pipes, which combined the greatest possible lightness with the greatest possible strength.[40]

In 1907, Bell transferred these results, which mainly stemmed from experiments with kites, to architectural applications, and he erected a tower with a height of 72 ft (22 m), which was to demonstrate the new structural possibilities. J. A. D. McCurdy (1886–1961), F. W. Baldwin (1882–1948), G. H. Curtiss (1878–1908), and T. E. Selfridge (1882–1908) were his collaborators.[41] The whole substance of the building (Fig. 9) had been reduced to a minimum in this structure, and the efficiency of skeleton construction (the Chicago school, Gustave Eiffel), which had developed up to this time, was greatly increased. The reduction of material corresponded also to the development of the model of the atom at this time, which replaced matter through a dynamic system of strength and energy. Bell's principle analogously replaced static building material with a system of energy lines, made effective only through their connections.

9 Alexander Graham Bell (in cooperation with F. W. Baldwin): Tetrahedral tower, Beinn Bhreagh, Canada (1887–1907)

Bell had demonstrated possibilities with regard to architecture with an exemplary new principle, just as Gustave Eiffel had done with his tower for the 1889 world's fair in Paris (Fig. 9a), and going far beyond this result. Not just a new material had been tested for its quality and effectiveness, but a new system had been established that derived its strength from the placement of single parts. This system could be transferred to other materials, so that wood, steel, or light building materials could be used. Richard Buckminster-Fuller was able to draw on these and their inherent possibilities with his geodesic domes several decades later.[44]

The tower, clearly invented by F. W. Baldwin, is described by Parkin: "The tower was, itself, a 72-foot tetrahedron, comprising three 72-foot legs rising from foundations at the base of a 72-foot equilateral triangle. Each leg was constructed of four-foot tetrahedral cells made of half-inch galvanized wrought-iron pipe threaded into corner connectors of cast iron. Some 260 of these cells were used in the construction of the three legs and the observation platform where the three legs met at the top. The whole structure weighed less than five tons."[42] The tower was erected in a few hours by unskilled laborers without scaffolding. It could be taken down and rebuilt in a different location.[43]

9a Gustave Eiffel: Eiffel Tower (started 1887) for the Paris world's fair, 1889

Bell's subsequent experiments in the area of aerodynamics are a further organic development of the earlier experiments in constructing tetrahedrons. A synthesis of science, technology, and industrial production had become necessary to airplanes as well as to architecture. Bell's collaborators, Selfridge and Baldwin, initiated commercial air service on March 12, 1908, in America. Other aviation pioneers in Europe were Gabriel Voisin, Louis Bleriot, Alberto Santos Dumont, and Henry Farman.[45] Gustave Eiffel had proceeded similarly with the construction of his airplane model Breguet II, following a construction principle for structures and flying machines. These tendencies were expressed convincingly through the flying experiments of Wilbur Wright (1867–1912) and Orville Wright (1871–1948) as well as through the early prairie houses of Frank Lloyd Wright,[46] which at that time had been compared with airplanes. Aerodynamics, machine aesthetics, light construction, and industrial standardization had moved onto the same level and showed distinctly, through their peak performance, the structures of a new era.

Expressionism in America—The Second Phase of the Skyscraper

Gustave Eiffel, as well as the architects and engineers of the Chicago school, had during the 1880s developed forms of skeletal structures, which made possible building heights never known before.[47] Steel and reinforced concrete were the materials necessary for these high rises, which were erected in large numbers within a short time. It was William Le Baron Jenny (1832–1907), who for the first time used steel[48] on an experimental basis instead of cast iron for the five uppermost floors of the Home Insurance Building in Chicago in 1885. Such architects as Louis I. Sullivan, Burnham, and Root as well as Holabird and Roche rapidly advanced the construction of skyscrapers using the steel-skeleton technique during the following years.

There was a significant change during the early part of the twentieth century with a development towards historical styles. The Woolworth Building of 1911–1913 in New York, by Cass Gilbert (1859–1934), received neo-Gothic ornamental form, which caps the utilitarian framework of the office skyscraper and resulted in an amalgam of gothic verticality as well as the most highly developed form of skeleton construction. The skyscrapers, for example, by McKenzie, Voorhees, and Gmelin (Barclay Building of 1926 in New York, Fig. 10) and by Horace Trumbauer (1869–1938), (*New Evening Post* Building of 1925 in New York) continually intensified the tendencies of a construction principle geared towards expression which finally culminated with the construction of the Chrysler Building by William van Alen in 1930 (Fig. 12).[49]

The situation at the time regarding architecture of high-rise buildings can best be determined by the submissions to a contest announced by the *Chicago Tribune*.[50] A confusing number of architectural ideas from many countries came together—for instance, designs by Walter Gropius, Max and Bruno Taut, Bijvoet and Duiker, and Eliel Saarinen. The American architect Raymond Hood (1881–1934) received first prize and pointed toward the development, as well as the relationship, of technology and architecture which had been reached around 1922. The subsequent work of Raymond Hood can be seen as typical for development in America,[51] as he realized in cooporation with John Mead Howells, the *Chicago Tribune* Building between 1923 and 1925 as well as other high-rise buildings in New York (American Radiator Company Building of 1924). The *Daily News* Building, erected in 1930, and the McGraw-Hill Building of 1929–1931 (Fig. 11) were the climax. Both had been constructed by Hood in cooporation with other architects and equalled the then-current results of the "International Style."[52] Naturally, the development progressed to far-greater projects such as the Chrysler Building by William van Alen (1930, Fig. 12) and the Empire State Building by Shreve, Lamb, and Harmon (1929–1931), which reached the remarkable height of 1,250 ft. (375 m) and a total weight of 300,000 tons. Hood turned his attention towards the coordination of several disk-shaped high-rise buildings within the city in the planning and execution of Rockefeller Center in New York (1931–1939, Fig. 73) during the following years.[53]

10 *McKenzie, Voorbees, and Gmelin: Barclay Building, New York (1926)*

The Early Modern Movement in California

There was also a visible change taking place in California, parallel to the tendencies of development in the East and Midwest of the United States of America, with a bent towards a stronger inclusion of East-Asian and Spanish traditions[54] due to the geographic location. This development had been visible since 1894 in San Francisco and was called the Bay Area Style.[55] The strongest manifestation

11 Hood, Godley, and Fouilhoux: McGraw-Hill Building, New York (1929)

12 *William van Alen: Chrysler Building, New York (1930)*

13   Willis Jefferson Polk: Hallidie Building, San Francisco (1918)

was in the buildings of Bernhard Maybeck (1862–1957), with his Christian Science Church of 1910 in Berkeley, a major example of the eclecticism of the time as it combined Gothic and East Asian elements.[56] Maybeck's subsequent development lead to classical structures (Fine Arts Building in San Francisco of 1915) and mixed classical and romantic elements.

The work of Willis Jefferson Polk (1867–1924) sought to introduce the industrial architecture of the Midwest to California. His Hallidie Building in San Francisco of 1918 (Fig. 13) repre-

sents a variant of the successful type of high-rise office building of the firm Burnham and Root, where Polk had worked several years before.[57]

The architecture of Southern California is strongly inspired by Spanish-Mexican and East-Asian influences.[58] Irving Gill (1870–1936) started with the Spanish colonial style and arrived at reducing the buildings to basic stereometric forms, superficially similar to the European structures of Adolf Loos, but with different criteria regarding interior organization.[59] Gill erected the Wilson Acton Hotel in 1908 in La Jolla and the Dodge house in 1916 in Los Angeles (Fig. 14), which created an important bridge to subsequently constructed buildings by the young Austrian immigrants Rudolph M. Schindler (1890–1953) and Richard J. Neutra (1892–1970), who were influenced by Loos.[60]

The buildings by the brothers Charles Sumner Greene (1868–1957) and Henry Mather Greene (1870–1954) show a stronger dependence on a variant of East-Asian wood architecture. The two brothers came to California from the East Coast in 1894 and began with patio houses, which were suitable to the climate of southern California (Bandini house in Pasadena in 1903, Hollister house in Hollywood in 1906). However, their masterpieces are the Blacker house of 1907 and the Gamble house of 1908–1909. Both are in Pasadena, exquisite examples of the complete integration of structure, surroundings, and inte-

14   Irving Gill: Dodge house, Los Angeles ▷ (1916)

15 Simon Rodia: Watts Towers, Los Angeles (1921–1954)

rior on the basis of laws developed for the use of wood as a building material.[61]

The subsequent development of California architecture is chiefly determined by the settlement of Frank Lloyd Wright in Los Angeles and through his houses constructed from cast concrete blocks—one for Mrs. Millard in Pasadena (1923) and another for Charles Ennis in Los Angeles (1924, Fig. 16). The work of the immigrants Schindler and Neutra, who had first worked for Wright, and soon followed their own imagination, enriched the scene with buildings that incorporated more industrial compo-

nents into building technology (house for Dr. Lovell in Los Angeles by Neutra, 1927–1929).[62] The early work of Lloyd Wright (1890–1978) developed certain forms of his father's work and arrived at a romantic excess in his construction with cast concrete blocks. Early influenced also by Irving Gill, Lloyd Wright's achievement was a synthesis of Gill's cubic architecture and Frank Lloyd Wright's middle phase of his California career.[63]

Concrete as building material was designated for early official buildings in California, for example, the Public Library in Los Angeles (1927) by Bertram Grosvenor Goodhue (1869–1924) and C. M. Winslow, Grauman's Chinese Theater in Hollywood by Meyer and Holler of 1927, and the Aztec Hotel in Monrovia by Robert Stacy Judd of 1925.[64] Characteristic of distinctive Californian style are buildings such as San Simeon by Julia Morgan (1872–1957), the William Randolph Hearst residence (1919–1947),[65] the Watts Towers (1921–1954, Fig. 15) by Simon Rodia, and the numerous hamburger stands, which were forerunners of later Pop Art.[66]

Tony Garnier and the Vision of the Industrial City

During the first three decades of the twentieth century, American as well as French architecture was defined by the interpenetration of architecture, technology, and science. This was demonstrated in its purest form by the Cité Industrielle by Tony Garnier (1869–1948).[67] Garnier, like his contemporary Frank Lloyd Wright in

16 *Frank Lloyd Wright: Charles Ennis house, Los Angeles (1924)*

America, combined the isolated paths of development into one synthesis that demonstrated the principles of architecture during the twentieth century. The social and political concerns are, in this sense, of equal significance with those elements looked upon in a formal manner.

Garnier began his work on the industrial city in 1899 at the École des Beaux Arts in Paris. He had won the Grand Prix de Rome in 1899, and completed the greatest part during his stay at the Villa Medici in Rome between 1901 and 1904.[68] The plan started with the urban reality, although it was created within the framework of a French institution, which was perceived as traditional. Tradition and the present melded into a new unity. Modern technology was one of the decisive elements for all-inclusive planning, which not only included concrete as principal building material, but also modern remedial treatments — such as sun therapy and hydroelectric plants.

The city was planned for a population of approximately 35,000 inhabitants, but flexible enough for possible enlargement. Garnier considered the citizens of his city to have equal rights with regard to land use, in contrast to the planning ideas of Ebenezer Howard in England (1850–1928) and Arturo Soria y Mata in Spain (1844–1920), which were still class-oriented. No priviledged groups existed for Garnier in society, as was still the case, for example, in the planning of the linear city and the location of the houses by Soria y Mata, as well as Howard's English garden city.[69] According to their plans, the houses along the arterial roads were given to the more affluent citizens, while the financially weaker had to be content with the side streets. In Garnier's concept a governing body, which managed the land and beyond that, took care of social services, such as the distribution of bread, meat, and milk, as well as free medical care. The basically humanist idea of Garnier's political attitude was manifested in such concepts as the programmatical absence of police, judiciary buildings, and churches.

The various functions of the city organism were carefully separated: living in a central area with administrative and cultural buildings in the center (Fig. 18), working in a separate zone, reserved for industry in the north of the residential area (Fig. 17),[70] with a special area set aside, away from the rest, for recreation and recuperation. The divergence of the functions of a city, which was expressed for the first time at this point, will play an important role later on, especially concerning Le Corbusier's plans, which were strongly influenced by Garnier; even though the ever-present schematic character of Garnier's work was more and more misunderstood as a basis for realistic, up-to-date planning.

Garnier had designated concrete as building material for the community buildings and had legitimized its use as economical, similar to experiences in America at the same time by Frank Lloyd Wright. In Garnier's words it reads: "The simpler the molds, the easier will be the construction, and consequently the less the cost."[71] Garnier was sure that the elementary nature of the means would also be followed by a simplicity of expression. The reduction of the architectural means towards geometric, regular forms was the result of a complex process, just as Wright had experienced.

The relation to tradition is also clearly visible. Wright had started a new way to view the old American and East-Asian architecture through his buildings. If one compares Garnier's Heliotherapeutic clinic with the suburban living quarters of the old Egyptian city of Tel-el-Amarnah, as it was reconstructed during Garnier's time, one can detect surprising similarities. The simplification and reduction to geometric, basic forms in modern architecture goes hand in hand with the development of new areas of architecture of the past that comes closer to this contemporary vision.[72]

Changes in Construction with Reinforced Concrete

During the first part of the twentieth century, the development of architecture was determined by the synthesis of various tendencies in America as well as in France: the most important, the architectural tradition of the École des Beaux Arts, the technoscientific development of reinforced concrete, and modern industrial reality. François Hennebique (1842–1924) had already used monolithic concrete for the construction of his numerous silos, factories, hospitals, and hotels, and in 1896 for prefabricated houses

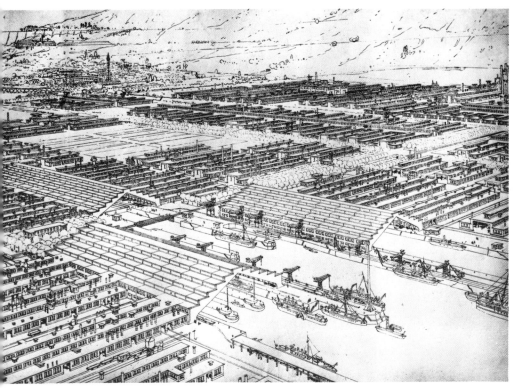

17 Tony Garnier: Cité-Industrielle, the factories (1901–1904)

to be used by gatekeepers and which could be transported easily, with 2 in. (5 cm) wide walls.[73] Siegfried Giedion was successful in pointing to a great number of pioneering achievements in France with regard to reinforced concrete and he particularly emphasized the work of Anatole de Baudot (1834–1915), who was a member of the École des Beaux Arts and who had achieved results with this material, which was of significance during this particular epoch.[74]

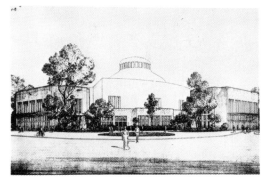

18 Tony Garnier: Cité Industrielle, theater (1901–1904) project

This development formed the basis for the work of Auguste Perret (1874–1955), who conducted research for decades in technical building methods, which resulted in the world-wide use of reinforced concrete. Perret used in his apartment house of 1902–1903, a skeleton of reinforced concrete in its most perfected form, which was clearly visible on the exterior of the building (Fig. 19). The walls with flower-enhanced ornamental areas no longer play a supporting role, thus rather creating the impression that the lower floors were lighter than the upper ones, with the protruding first floor giving an antistatic character to the building.[75]

Perret, who had developed reinforced concrete for architectural use for almost 50 years, arrived at innovative forms, for instance, with regard to the docks at the North African cities of Casablanca, Tiaret, and Sidi-Bel-Abbes, where he found new structural and immanent possibilities for the material in the method of shell construction. Another form of using reinforced concrete was established with the two church structures, one in Raincy (1922–1923) and the other in Montmagny (1924–1925),[76] where the building task was resolved by having the walls appearing to dissolve into a transparent skeletal grid system, which was filled with colored stained-glass windows.

The development of reinforced concrete continued with the structures and research of Eugène Freyssinet (1879–1962). In 1913 he planned, and between 1916 and 1924 constructed, the first eight hangars at the airport at Avord (Cher), bringing together the trend in development of architectural engineering and flight technology, which went far beyond the more metaphorical relationships in the works of Frank Lloyd Wright, Alexander Graham Bell, and Gustave Eiffel. Beyond that, these structures made a new architectural concept possible with regard to space.[77]

A commission for 31 more hangars followed the first 8 at Avord, securing extensive success for this type of building (Fig. 20).[78] Modern technology lead to a new concept of construction, where there is no longer a causal relationship between support and weight, and the supported and the supporting part, but where each part of the parabolic form of the roof becomes an active vehicle of energy. Here, the traditional architectural form of the box has been overcome in favor of a dynamic form of open space and in a totally different way than was the case with earlier houses by Frank Lloyd Wright—a new form of dy-

20 Eugène Freyssinet: Airport hangar, Paris-Orly (1916)

◁ *19 Auguste Perret: Apartment house, 25bis Rue Franklin, Paris (1902–1903)*

21 Henri Sauvage: Terrace housing (1929) project

namic open space had replaced the traditional limitations of architecture.

Le Corbusier and the Aesthetics of the Machine in France

After Garnier and Perret, a younger generation of French architects was searching for realistic change in the environment, on a larger scale. Suggestions for solving urban and architectural concerns went hand in hand. In 1912, Henri Sauvage (1873–1932) built an apartment house in Paris, 25 Rue Vavin, with receding terracelike upper floors and balconies which make possible opening up the living space.[79] These ideas of Sauvage were further developed after World War I and another apartment house of 1924 showed a refined execution compared to the former solution. After 1920, Sauvage tried to continue to articulate his ideas in the form of integrated planning, as was demonstrated

with a terraced housing development plan (Fig. 21) and a series of blocks of residential houses that were also based on a pyramid formed of terraced units.[80]

In addition to his individual residences in the Rue Mallet-Stevens of 1927, Robert Mallet-Stevens (1886–1945) endeavored to obtain a similar expansion and integration of several houses into the street network and in this sense an integration into a small urban unit. Eugène Beaudouin (* 1898) and Marcel Lods (1891–1978) finally created in 1933, in the Cité de la Muette near Bordeaux, one of the early European housing estates with an integrated concept of high rises in linear-geometric rows, combined to form an urban unit.[81]

The work of Le Corbusier (1887–1965) which is based equally on urban coordination, skeleton construction of reinforced concrete, and the classical teachings on proportion of the École des Beaux Arts, shows a lasting expression of this combined effort.[82] Le Corbusier absorbed the tradition of Auguste Perret, Tony Garnier, Eugène Freyssinet, Josef Hoffmann, Peter Behrens, and Frank Lloyd Wright in an individual conglomeration of ideas that clearly shows the components of technology and of a standardized mass production of cellular residential areas—either separate as an individual house or as apartments.[83]

To Le Corbusier, order based on the laws of geometry was central. In his eyes, the right angle possessed an axiomatic character, but not for its own sake: "The frame of a building or buildings is like the laws that govern society—without these laws there is

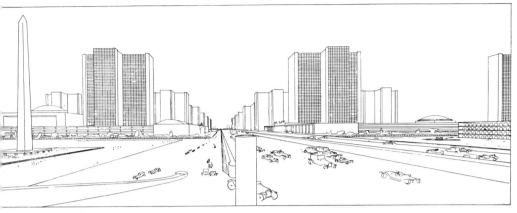

21a Le Corbusier: Plan of a city (1922)

anarchy, and without the frame there is visual anarchy."[84]

Yet in regard to the basic urban concept, Le Corbusier's attitude can also be viewed differently: "And Le Corbusier's conception of the city transformed into a technical machine differs totally from Garnier's desire to emancipate the inhabitants of the city by means of the machine."[85] Indeed, Garnier's aspiration of the union of a garden city and linear city was — by Le Corbusier — transformed into a monumental and abstract scheme that did not take the inhabitants into consideration (Fig. 21a).

Le Corbusier was led to the highest conclusion and possibly to exaggeration by the analogy of buildings and machines used by Wright, Garnier, and Henry van de Velde. In his first book, *Vers une architecture,* in 1923, he demands "the right to health, logic, courage, harmony, and perfection in the name of the ocean liner, airplane, and the automobile." Aesthetics of engineering and the art of building are considered by him to be a unity, and consequently he suggests the construction of mass-produced residential houses with industry as producer: "The major industries must be involved in architecture and must mass produce the various elements for building."[86]

Projects — called Citrohan — for industrially produced houses by Le Corbusier, influenced by the automobile manufacturer Citroën, designed during the years 1920–1922, the embodiment of what he termed a dwelling machine. This was a cell with minimal requirements as to a residence, and was built in a separate area without topographical concerns, or could be integrated into the system of a residential block. The basic idea of this architect always was a cell, which could be produced industrially and to which he paid the greatest attention in its varied applications.[87]

Peter Serenyi emphasizes the iconological relevance: "It must be remembered that Le Corbusier likes to consider the home a monastic cell, created ideally at least, for the single individual; the family, as a small, intricate social group, has no place in Le Corbusier's art or mind."[88] Le Corbusier confirmed this emphatically in his lectures in South America in 1929: "The family has been eliminated. Sons and daughters, father and mother—each one goes separately every morning to his workplace or his office."[89] Le Corbusier's thought becomes entirely clear when his position regarding the family is compared to that of Frank Lloyd Wright, who basically considered the family to be the most important form of social organization.[90]

Le Corbusier consequently saw his projects of apartment buildings under the aspect of the multiplication of cells. In the case of the Immeuble-Villas of 1922, 120 cell blocks were stacked on top of each other, having merely a service function in common. The Salvation Army residential ship of 1929 represents the idea of a vehicle for transportation. The house for Swiss students at the Cité Universitaire in Paris built in 1930–1932, follows this principle in the same manner; and also the newly realized Unité d'habitation of 1947–1952 at Marseille is a monumentally transformed manifestation of the industrial residential cell.

Le Corbusier's basic concept of the residential cell is transcended in the few large-scale structures that he could plan or realize during the latter part of the 1920s. Among these projects of major significance, developed in 1927, is the design of the Palace of the League of Nations in Geneva (Fig. 22). Yet it is remarkable that this bril-

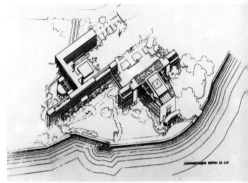

22 Le Corbusier and P. Jeanneret: Design of the Palace of the League of Nations in Geneva (1927)

liant design for the world organization of nations, with wings stretching into the landscape, came from an architect who could work at the same time for the Supreme Soviet in Moscow, for the Salvation Army in Paris, and for the Swiss government, and who had the French Fascist Dr. Franz Winter as friend.[91] Dr. Franz Winter could glorify the residential settlement in Pessac of 1925 openly in a publication as an example of the new architecture of Fascism.[92] Alfred Roth, Le Corbusier's former pupil and colleague, wrote the following when trying to understand the relation between an architect and politics: "He identified with the intellectual, cultural, and the political efforts of the 'grande nation' as well as with its glorious past. This explains his conviction of rightful personification with regard to supreme power, which was expressed in his later life through a certain unconcealable admiration of a dictatorial head of state."[93]

As to Le Corbusier's Palace of the League of Nations, as well as other designs of these years, the planned Mundaneum of 1929, the building for the Centrosojus in Moscow of 1931, his concerns were always the articulation of the circumstances of the individual and the community, of ruler and the ruled. Yet there are traditional ideas, for instance, axiality and a counterpoint order "like a baroque castle,"[94] even though integrated into a framework consisting of different levels and transparent composition.[95] It is significant that the basic idea of the cell could serve as a point of departure, although gathered around a group of assembly halls and community institutions, which were initially required. The Palace of the Soviets of 1931 (Fig. 23) shows that for the first time the structure of the total complex is no longer ruled by the character of an enlarged box, but instead by the sculptured form of the interior as well as by the fascination of the monumental parabolic arch, from which is suspended the ceiling of the largest of the proposed halls with a capacity to hold 15,000 people.[96] The parabolic arch is a construction element of architectonic accentuation; it possibly repre-

sents an homage to constructivism, which was widespread in Russia during the 1920s, yet it can also be interpreted as being a metaphoric symbolization of higher energy.[97]

Le Corbusier's design of the Palace of the Soviets was rejected by Stalin in favor of the figurative-monumental design of Jofan, Shchuko, and Helfrich, but it can nevertheless be viewed as a symbol of power architecture. It is without a doubt a forerunner of an idea developed later by Corbusier of an urban nucleus.[98] Le Corbusier conceptualized architecture as integrated, although partly physically isolated. There exists a deeper relevance, when the architect presents an analogy of a sketch of Pisa of the 11th of June, 1934, of the magnificent group of structures consisting of the cathedral, baptistry, and campanile and the proposed building complex in Moscow, consisting of several halls, foyers, and municipal rooms.[99]

Peter Behrens and "Industrial Design"

At the beginning of the twentieth century, German architecture arrived at a synthesis of technology, science, and

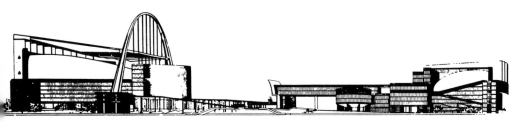

23 Le Corbusier: Palace of the Soviets, Moscow (1931) project

industry, as in America and France. Industrialists, politicians, and architects formed the German Werkbund in 1907, which was chiefly a managerial arm expressing the tendencies of the time. The program of 1910 of the German Werkbund formulated as its goal: "The Werkbund wants to choose the best with regard to art, industry and trade, as well as the best craftsmen; it wants to coordinate quality of work with the world of labor; it is the rallying point for all who are willing and able to achieve quality work."[100]

For nearly a whole generation, the most important architectural achievements were achieved due to the ideas of the Werkbund. It was the basis for buildings by Hans Poelzig, Walter Gropius, Ludwig Mies van der Rohe, Bruno Taut, and Hans Scharoun, and many vital key works were erected for exhibits of the Werkbund.

Numerous ideas from foreign countries merged with these thoughts: English residential architecture was introduced by Hermann Muthesius (1861–1927);[101] Bruno Schmitz passed on the knowledge of H. H. Richardson; publication and exhibition of the work of Frank Lloyd Wright in Berlin in 1910 brought a new concept of space; and the architecture of Art Nouveau with its disciplined structures was introduced by Henry van de Velde of Belgium and Joseph Maria Olbrich of Austria.[102]

Peter Behrens (1868–1940) was the leading personality in Germany during those years. His career mirrors the developments of this time period.[103] Behrens started out as painter and craftsman and gained recognition as an architect for the first time with his

house at an exhibition at Darmstadt in 1901. Behrens developed, like Wright, more and more toward a geometrically founded standardization, which specifically meant an industrialization of the basic utilitarian objects.[104]

While at Darmstadt, still spellbound by symbolic notions, which culminated in the symbol of a diamond,[105] this conception changed step by step into well-designed industrial goods, which he produced after 1907, in his function as technical director at AEG in Berlin, in the form of industrial products and buildings.[106] These works are no longer crafts in the traditional sense, no mere ornamentation of objects, but new forms dependent on the laws of machine production. This realization is decidedly significant in regard to architecture. In a programmatic article, "The Influence of Time and Space on the Development of Modern Forms," Behrens spoke against the static concept of modern structures, espousing a new rhythm dictated by technology.[107]

The turbine hall for the AEG in Berlin-Moabit — on the corner of Hutten Street und Berlichingen Street — of 1909 (Fig. 24) represented the culmination of his efforts to give architectural dignity to a workplace, similar to the achievement of Wright with the Larkin Building in Buffalo.[108] Glass and iron took over the function of a roof over a workshop of an industrial plant, with an enormous span (28.16 yd.; 25.6 m). Behrens achieved a plastic effect and a dynamic form of construction by means of the supporting construction of the trusses, which were pulled towards the outside, as well as through the tapering iron trusses and the glass areas which were drawn towards the inside.[109] In particular, the monumental shape of the façade with corner pylons, which could not be considered a necessity for construction, and which were built with a thin ferro-concrete shell, caused criticism among younger architects. Ludwig Hilberseimer wrote: "Peter Behrens is led astray by the imperialistic power consciousness of the prewar years and restrained by classical influences, and he thinks to add a façade to his turbine hall of the AEG at Moabit; an otherwise terse structure. . . ."[110] And Erich Mendelsohn criticized the building: "He pastes over the expression of tension, which the hall creates, with the rigidity of a repeatedly broken temple tympanon. . . ."[111] Le Corbusier, however, admired the structure as being a charged center, "which represents the integral architectonic creations of our time — rooms with admirable moderation and cleanness, with magnificent machines, which set solemn and impressive accents, as the center of attraction."[112]

By no means did Behrens try to solve industrial problems by excluding the continuity of the architectural tradition, but he was concerned about the integration of past and present, just as he had worked earlier on the conversion of the coal symbol to the diamond symbol, which showed his life as being integrated with art.[113] The Romanesque church S. Miniato al Monte in Florence and early Christian mosaic art were the inspiration for the Crematorium in Hagen of 1909, although its clarity was still further simplified

24 Peter Behrens: The turbine factory for the AEG, Berlin-Moabit (1909)

through geometrical reduction. The designs for a church in Hagen and for the pavilion of the AEG for the Ship Guild exhibition in Berlin of 1908 are derived from the model of the chapel of Charlemagne in Aachen, which thus combines the national heritage with the necessities of German production of industry.[114]

The building of the German Embassy in St. Petersburg, which Peter Behrens had erected in 1911 (Fig. 25), became the total expression of the German national consciousness. The classical form admired by Albert Speer later influenced the architecture of the National Socialist period. Ludwig Mies van der Rohe — like Walter Gropius and Le Corbusier working at the time in the offices of Peter Behrens — had a decided influence on the design for the structure.[115]

The Early Work of Walter Gropius

Walter Gropius (1883–1969) played an important role during the development of the Werkbund and the increasing integration of industry, archi-

25 *Peter Behrens: German Embassy in Leningrad (1911–1912)*

tecture, and design; and, in a wider sense, his works and activities had an influence on the integration of art and politics.[116] Even before joining the office of Peter Behrens, the young architect Walter Gropius had been occupied (1906) with dwellings for farmworkers at his uncle's estate at Dramburg in Pomerania and came upon the necessity of standardization and mass production.[117]

Gropius was in charge of the offices of Peter Behrens from 1908 to 1910, and during that time he had sufficient opportunity to deal with current questions and solutions concerning industrial architecture and "industrial design." It was a time of learning that

influenced him the rest of his life.[118] In 1909, he submitted a plan to the subsequent foreign minister Emil Rathenau. It was a plan for a factory with specific details for the mass production of apartment houses from standardized elements.

Gropius's first large building, the Fagus Shoe-Last Factory in Alfeld on the Leine in 1911 (Fig. 26), was materialized due to his connection with Peter Behrens—and in cooperation with Adolf Meyer (1881–1929), as had been the case with most of his early structures.[119] The starting point for the young architect was the already existing site plan, the ground plan, and construction plans of the architect

Eduard Werner, as well as the foundation, which had already been laid. A loan from the American United Shoe Machinery Corporation made the continuation of the construction possible in 1911, and continued until 1912 step by step under the new concept of Walter Gropius. The whole operational procedure was newly thought through, according to the inner functions, and then articulated in a three-dimensional form.[120] The client's wish for an attractive façade was solved by Gropius in a special way: by means of a projected steel skeleton, which pulled the function of support to the inside, thereby making possible a broad dissolution of the exterior envelope into glass walls; the idea of the "curtain wall" was at this point first expressed in a consistent manner.[121]

The second large structure by Walter Gropius was built in connection with the Werkbund exhibition at Cologne in the summer of 1914.[122] The commission was for a model factory with office space. In particular, the shape of the model office areas with the two towers with stairways on both sides, enveloped by glass, and the roofgarden to be used for dance events (Fig. 27), attracted the attention of contemporaries, who had the opportunity to visit the exhibition prior to the beginning of World War I. Hermann Scheffauer published his impressions in 1923 and called the office wing "a laymen's temple of symphonic symmetry, a hall in which machine and structure — one of the two totally out of metal, the other only partly — were celebrating a new kind of reconciliation."[123] Scheffauer, the American, surprisingly overlooked the obvious

26 *Walter Gropius: Fagus factory, Alfeld/Leine (1911)*

dependence of the façade on an office wing of a building by Frank Lloyd Wright in Mason City, Iowa, of 1909 (Fig. 27a), which became known to German architects in Berlin through a publication by Wasmuth in 1910.[124]

Indeed, it took great courage for the young German architect to acknowledge such a superior example, as was here documented in a programmatic manifesto. A. Busignani had recently arrived at this conclusion: "It would, indeed, seem to suggest that Gropius, with great moral courage, was admitting the insufficiency of the European tradition when it came to producing new architecture, and that therefore he was turning to something (the

27 *Walter Gropius: Model factory at the Werkbund exhibition, Cologne (1914)*

27a *Frank Lloyd Wright: City National Bank Building and hotel in Mason City, Iowa (1909)*

American tradition as it appeared in Wright), that in many ways was still, even historically, original and unexplored. . . ."[125]

Idea and Form of the Bauhaus

The Bauhaus itself founded in Weimar in 1919, can be considered as a further phase of the integration, of architecture, science, and technology, since it was chiefly an alliance of the Art Academy and Academy for Arts and Crafts, which had separately existed in Weimar up to then, and which symbolically meant the union of art and crafts.[126] Gropius placed the idea of synthesis at the beginning of his explanation: "This idea of basic unity of all creative work was my guide when founding and realizing the Bauhaus." And he expands this idea: "I combined these two institutes to form one school for creative construction with the name of 'Staatliches Bauhaus in Weimar.' As basis for instruction, and as goal throughout the institute, I arranged to make life comprehensive in its cosmic totality by educating the student, and at the same time taking his natural abilities into consideration —a goal which is unobtainable through the generally divided instruction of specialized subjects."[127]

The efforts of Walter Gropius as well as of the German Expressionists and Frank Lloyd Wright were based upon the English plans for reform, where already during the middle of the nineteenth century, modern civilization defined by machines was to be united with the tradition of architecture. John Ruskin (1819–1900) and William Morris (1834–1915) were searching to change the totality of modern life, including industry, economy, and politics, into the ideals formed during the Middle Ages. A woodcut by Lyonel Feininger, created for the first Bauhaus publication of 1919, leaves no doubt that the Bauhaus also still felt this tradition: a Gothic cathedral with three stars in heaven is the ruling symbol, representing the three disciplines of architecture, sculpture, and painting (Fig. 28). A modern civilization without the unification of these three disciplines was, in the opinion of Walter Gropius, unthinkable.[128]

The first few years of the Bauhaus were characterized by bringing together the original institutions step by step. The new instructors, invited by

28 *Lyonel Feininger: Cathedral, woodcut for the title of the first Bauhaus publication (1919)*

Gropius, for several years taught parallel with the master craftsmen, before the new integrated concept could be implemented. Artists such as Wassily Kandinsky, Paul Klee, Oskar Schlemmer, Gerhard Marcks, and Lyonel Feininger therefore became pioneers in forming a new vision of art and craft and tried to use the material free of any preconceived opinions of academic teaching. Johannes Itten (1888–1967) created the preliminary course (Vorkurs), which each student

Die Reihe wird in schneller Folge fortgesetzt.
IN VORBEREITUNG:

BAUHAUSBÜCHER

BAUHAUSBÜCHER

W. Kandinsky:	Punkt, Linie, Fläche
	Violett (Bühnenstück)
Kurt Schwitters:	Merz-Buch
Heinrich Jacoby:	Schöpferische Musikerziehung
J. J. P. Oud (Holland):	Die holländische Architektur
George Antheil (Amerika):	Musico-mechanico
Albert Gleizes (Frankreich)	Kubismus
F. T. Marinetti und	
Prampolini (Italien):	Futurismus
Fritz Wichert:	Expressionismus
Tristan Tzara:	Dadaismus
L. Kassàk und **E. Kàllai**	
(Ungarn):	Die MA-Gruppe
T. v. Doesburg (Holland):	Die Stijlgruppe
Carel Teige (Prag):	Tschechische Kunst
Louis Lozowick (Amerika):	Amerikanische Architektur
Walter Gropius:	Neue Architekturdarstellung ● Das flache Dach ● Montierbare Typenbauten ● Die Bauhausneubauten in Dessau
Mies van der Rohe:	Über Architektur
Le Corbusier-Saugnier	
(Frankreich):	Über Architektur
Knud Lönberg-Holm	
(Dänemark):	Über Architektur
Friedrich Kiesler	
(Österreich):	Neue Formen der Demonstration
	Die Raumstadt
Jane Heap (Amerika):	Die neue Welt
G. Muche und **R. Paulick:**	Das Metalltypenhaus
Mart Stam	Das „ABC" vom Bauen
Adolf Behne:	Kunst, Handwerk und Industrie
Max Burchartz:	Plastik der Gestaltungen
Martin Schäfer:	Konstruktive Biologie
Reklame und **Typographie**	
des Bauhauses	
L. Moholy-Nagy:	Aufbau der Gestaltungen
Paul Klee:	Bildnerische Mechanik
Oskar Schlemmer:	Bühnenelemente
Joost Schmidt:	Bildermagazin der Zeit I
Die neuen künstlichen	
Materialien	

Die BAUHAUSBÜCHER sind zu beziehen einzeln oder in Serien durch jede Buchhandlung oder direkt vom

VERLAG

ALBERT LANGEN

MÜNCHEN Hubertusstr. 27

Bestellkarte liegt diesem Prospekt bei.

BAUHAUSDRUCK MOHOLY DIN C5

29 A list of the Bauhaus books, as seen in an advertisement

had to attend before he could make a decision about his career.[129]

The first phases of the Bauhaus were mainly oriented towards crafts, but around 1922–1923 there appeared a clearly visible shift in emphasis within the curriculum: industrial production became increasingly the focal point, and a revision of all values occurred during this phase, which took place because of outside influences — mainly due to Theo van Doesburg (1883–1931) — as well as through the addition of Laszlo Moholy-Nagy (1895–1946) to the faculty in the year 1923 (Fig. 29).[130]

The result was a much broader universality in the curriculum, which now also embraced theater, photography, and film, as well as music, dance, and literature, due to the personal initiative of Moholy-Nagy. From now on, the Bauhaus was internationally oriented and able to absorb heterogeneous artistic works from Italy, Holland, France, and Russia, unlike the nationalistically determined efforts of the German Werkbund. However, the internationalization of the Bauhaus started to evoke the hatred of nationalists, as well as of the National Socialists.[131]

It was vital for the existence of the institute to launch a direct contact with industrial firms, with particular attention to the airplane manufacturer Junkers in Dessau and various other firms, which also increased the budget for students, due to the licensed mass manufacture of Bauhaus designs (furniture, lamps, textiles, dishes). The structure of the new school built in Dessau in 1925–1926 was an example of these new contacts.[132] It was de-

signed by Walter Gropius in 1925 and constructed in 1926, with all departments of the school participating.

The Bauhaus building provides an important landmark of architectural history, even though it was dependent on earlier projects of the architect (the Philosophy Academy in Erlangen in 1923), as well as on the basic outlines and concepts of Frank Lloyd Wright.[133]

It consists of three connected wings for school, workshop, and student dormitories, each of which is a separate entity, but is also connected through wings or bridges (Fig. 30). School and workshop are connected through a two-story bridge, which spans the approach road from Dessau. The administration was located on the lower level of the bridge, and on the upper level was the private office of the two architects, Walter Gropius and Adolf Meyer, which could be compared to the ship captain's "command bridge" due to its location.[134] The dormitories and the school building are connected through a wing where the assembly hall and the dining room are located, with a stage between.

The basic structure of the Bauhaus consists of a clear and carefully thought-out system of connecting wings, which correspond to the internal operating system of the school. The technical construction of the building (Fig. 31) is demonstrated by the latest technological development of the time: a skeleton of reinforced concrete with brickwork, mushroom-shaped ceilings on the lower level, and roofs covered with asphalt tile that can be walked upon. The construction area consisted of 42,445 yd.^{3} (32,450 m^3) and the total cost amounted to

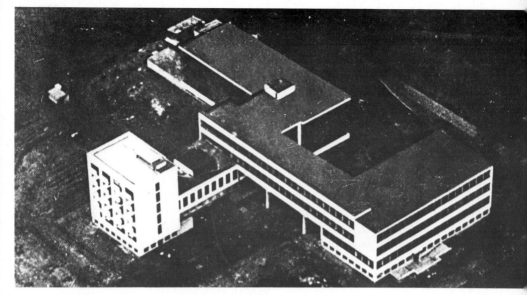

30 Walter Gropius: The Bauhaus in Dessau (1925–1926) general view

31 Walter Gropius: The Bauhaus in Dessau (1925–1926)

Walter Gropius resigned from the Bauhaus in 1928 and placed the directorate in the hands of the Swiss architect Hannes Meyer (1889–1954) who managed the Bauhaus until 1930 in a more product-oriented manner.[135] Mies van der Rohe became his successor, and was forced by political pressure to move the Bauhaus to Berlin in 1932, where it was, however, closed by the just-installed National Socialist government on January 30 1933.[136]

The Ideology of Industrialization — The Contribution of Mies van der Rohe

While theorists and architects at the beginning of the century had been trying to attain a balance between the various elements of architecture, science, and technology, industrial production had a place beside science and the tradition of architecture. Two decades later, with the wake of radicalization, all former views were pushed into the background and industrializa-

902,500 marks. Such an economical achievement was possible only due to the assistance of the Bauhaus teachers and students, which at the same time, of course, could be viewed as an ideal means of education.

tion became the dominating issue. The spokesman for these tendencies, directed towards Elementarism and Purism, was Ludwig Mies van der Rohe (1886–1969) and his agent was the magazine *G*, which he co-founded in 1923 with Werner Graeff (*1901) and Hans Richter (1888–1976).[137] In an article about "Industrial Building" in the issue of June 10th, 1924, Mies van der Rohe went so far as to expect industrialization to be a kind of panacea for all problems: "I consider the industrialization of building to be the main concern of our time. If we succeed with this industrialization, consequently the social, economical, technological and artistic questions will be easily solved."[138]

A complete reversal of all values had taken place at this point. The integration of technology, governed by humane and social values, still attempted by Peter Behrens, was now reduced to technical solutions of the industrialization of building. After a short time, this view was still further intensified demanding the dictatorship of the machine: Hans Schmidt (1893–1972) and Mart Stam (*1899) wrote in 1928 in the magazine *ABC*:

. . . the machine is not a servant, but a dictator—it dictates how we think and what we are to comprehend. As leader of the mercilessly united and dependent masses, it demands year by year more urgently a change in our economy and culture. It knows no rest on the philosophical bench, no compromise through pacifist phrases. It does not allow a peaceful pleasurable view, nor an aesthetic distance to the demands of life. Reality shows how far we have followed the dictates of the machine: we

have sacrificed crafts, we are about to relinquish the farmer. We had to admit to consolidation of our most important public conveyance and our large industries. We were pressured into developing new methods for standardized and mass production. Because of the machine we have had to hand over more and more the power to the state organization and we even had to internationalize our most holy national goods.[139]

Typical for the time in various countries, especially in the Soviet Union, is the vocabulary reaching into politics.[140]

The early projects of Mies van der Rohe's office building of steel and glass (Fig. 32) are still between an Expressionism inspired by Paul Scheerbart (1863–1915) and the technical requirements of the modern, industrial world of the big city.[141] His single-family houses in Guben of 1926 and in Krefeld of 1928 followed the disciplined clarity of Hendrick Petrus Berlage (1856–1934), with regard to the choice of brick as the main building material, without touching the theoretically postulated goals of industrialization.[142] Even the German pavilion at the 1929 world's fair in Barcelona (Fig. 33) and the Tugendhat house in Brno of 1930 are refined and spatially more dynamic developments of earlier houses (Figs. 34, 35). Only at a Werkbund exhibition at the Weissenhof in Stuttgart in 1927, organized by Mies van der Rohe, does the thought of industrialization become a practical focal point.[143] He was able to create an internationally comparable level of industrialized buildings through the inclusion of such architects as Le Corbusier, Mart Stam, J. J. P.

32 L. Mies van der Robe: Design for a glass high rise in Berlin, Friedrich Street (1919)

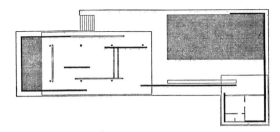

*33 L. Mies van der Rohe: German pavilion at
the Barcelona world's fair (1929)*

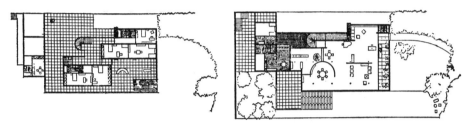

*34 L. Mies van der Rohe: Tugendhat house, Brno (1930) plan of the second floor (l) and
the main floor (r)*

35 L. Mies van der Rohe: Tugendhat house, Brno (1930) view from the garden

Oud, Walter Gropius, Hans Scharoun, Max and Bruno Taut, and Peter Behrens. The crowning achievement of the housing settlements was the apartment block, which Mies van der Rohe himself contributed to the exhibition, where in addition to new construction techniques, a new, more flexible placement of the inner walls of the apartment was tested on an experimental level.

Condemnation for this ensemble of "modern architecture" in Germany was expressed through a photographic satire, which interpreted the settlement as an "Arabic village," renouncing the flat roof for its supposedly oriental origin and propagating a new nationalistic line, as demanded a few years later by the ideologists of the National Socialistic movement and realized by the architects in the years after 1933. But the exhibition also evoked criticism by Kurt Schwitters, who rejected the formal style by considering it questionable and not in harmony with the site.[144]

Hans Poelzig and Expressionism

The situation in Berlin at the beginning of the twentieth century was in no way restricted to architectural efforts geared to standardization and industrialization alone. This complex situation left room for counter movements and alternatives, which developed partly due to the reaction to too

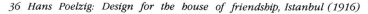

36 Hans Poelzig: Design for the house of friendship, Istanbul (1916)

37 Hans Poelzig: Grosses Schauspielhaus in Berlin (1919)

strong a rationalization, and which became creatively corrective for the subsequent development.[145] The work of Hans Poelzig (1869–1936) can be seen as being especially representative of this tendency, and his excellent performance as teacher led to worldwide consequences.[146]

Poelzig's buildings before World War I remained within the framework of the industrial architecture of those years: the water tower in Posen of 1911 and the chemical plant in Luban of 1911 to 1912 show individualistic results, while adapting to the power of technology. The office building in Breslau of 1911 is an early adaptation of the skeleton construction technique with reinforced concrete in Germany.[147] However, a radical change is noticed in the year 1919 due to the designs developed during the war years (Fig. 36): In an early form of recycling, Poelzig developed the Grosses Schauspielhaus in Berlin (Fig. 37) from the Market Basilica, which already had been transformed into the Circus Schumann and which had been constructed during the middle of the nineteenth century by Friedrich Hitzig. Poelzig achieved the best possible conversion under the circumstances, in spite of numerous handicaps due to the lack of material during the postwar period, when he created exceptional forms, more emotionally pleasing than the earlier industrial structures.

38 Erich Mendelsohn: Einstein Tower, Potsdam (1920–1921)

In contrast to the rational, functional theories during these years, Poelzig could say: "It is always better, if one forces the issue and creates a genuine work of art, than to let the objective, i.e., the cold intellect be triumphant."[148] Thus Poelzig became the speaker of an alternative concept, to which other architects also belonged, such as Fritz Höger (1877–1949), Wilhelm Kreis (1873–1955), and most of the young generation, who had an openly contrasting relationship with the rational architects of the time, who focused on the machine and technical functionality.[149]

The work of Erich Mendelsohn (1887–1953) carries further this visionary emotionalism of Poelzig, which step by step adjusted to the practical and utalitarian necessities.[150] Mendelsohn's early drawings from the years of World War I—partly influenced by Art Nouveau and Futurism—culminated in the structure of the Einstein Tower in Potsdam (Fig. 38), erected in 1920–1921, which best demonstrated the excitement of the time, as well as clearly showing its technical problems.[151] Conceptionalized as a reinforced concrete structure, due to a shortage of building material the structure was built out of brick, with the added plaster simulating a monolithic material. Yet the inner organization of the observatory consists of a fixed layout, defined by a scientific program, while the expressive outer form has a dynamic, streamlined, and monument-like character. Gustav Adolf Platz went so far as to connect the conceptionalized building material with the name of Einstein (one-stone): "Mendelsohn created the dynamic total form from the main motive of the turnable, astronomic cupola. Ascending terrasses prepare for the tower, which looks with numerous windows as 'One-Stone' defiantly into the landscape. A swaying movement combines all building elements into a circular rhythm."[152] Later on, international reaction returned negative verdicts: the English architect Reginald Blomfield viewed the structure in 1934 as being "that notorious observatory at Potsdam by Herr Eric Mendelsohn, which looks like the gun turret of some nightmare battleship, with the lower part of it shaped like a ram, and windows designed to resemble the embrasure of eight-inch guns. . . ."[153]

The subsequent works of the successful architect Erich Mendelsohn focused on structures for factories and department stores. Both building tasks were, however, dependent in a sense on the earlier expressively modeled form of the Einstein Tower, yet reduced to more crystalline and controllable laws. The structures are, however, continually expressive in showing emotional values; indeed, they are frequently used in connection with advertising. The Schocken department store in Stuttgart of 1926–1928 (Fig. 39), as well as other structures for the same firm (Chemnitz and Nürnberg), created evidence of practical functionality, with the relation to the user not being reduced to rational considerations, but addressing the total personality.

39 Erich Mendelsohn: Schocken department store, Stuttgart (1926–1928)

Mendelsohn's structures are therefore units of totality, conceptionalized in their entirety just as are buildings by Borromini and Gaudi, and are therefore subject to different laws than those of Gropius or Mies van der Rohe. Bruno Zevi tried to make this clear: "The eloquence of the art of Mendelsohn revives goals, which Borromini and Gaudi also knew: the structure is to be understood as unified mass, almost as if derived from a terra-cotta form, swelling in a lava-like substance, formed in one casting."[154] In a building complex on the Kurfürstendamm corner of Cicero street, Mendelsohn combined in 1926 to 1928 (Fig. 40) several functions, such as a cinema, cabaret, hotel, and apartments, which were subordinated to each other through superior, spatial-rhythmic, artistic-architectural laws to develop a uniformly conceptionalized urban unity.

Bruno Taut and the "Glass Chain"

Architecture in Berlin around 1910–1920 was enhanced through the activity of Bruno Taut (1880–1938), who accentuated foremost the socio-political and social necessities, beside the industrial and spatial-artistic aspects of architecture.[155] Under the influence of the poet Paul Scheerbart (1863–1915), whose novels and short stories proclaimed a visionary unity of architectural imagination and social necessity, Taut arrived—after early works in the Art Nouveau (pavilion of the Wasmuth firm at the world's fair in St. Louis in 1904)—at forms of an industrial architecture, which culminated in the pavilion of the steel industry in Leipzig (1913) and in the pavilion of the glass industry at the Werkbund exhibition in Cologne (1914, Fig. 41).[156] Paul Scheerbart had published his book, *Glass Architecture*, dedicated to

40 Erich Mendelsohn: Universum Cinema, Berlin, Kurfürstendamm (1926–1928)

41 Bruno Taut: Glass pavilion for the Werkbund exhibition in Cologne (1914)

ect, called "Hufeisen" (horseshoe), where the first segment of construction was executed in cooperation with Martin Wagner 1925–1927, in open confrontation with the building authorities and even the interference of the police (Fig. 43).[162] The extraordinary form of the housing development and its exceptional social function, cannot be overvalued, even today:

The so-called horseshoe consists of a three-story closed front of houses, which curve around a far-reaching hollow with a small pond. The strong impression of the project not only develops due to the courageous use of obviously sensible principles of modern construction of housing and cities, but mostly due to high artistic quality. Ground and structure, the lower area of the environment, and the circle of the buildings are melded together over an extensive area, where the structure and the trees of the gardens in front of the first-floor apartments seemed like a carefully inserted connecting link between the flat lawn and the tall wall of the building.[163]

42 Wenzel Hablik: Flying housing (1920) etching

was given the opportunity to transform his architectural ideas into reality. He worked at this challenge, which he had hoped for a long time, three years, but which he gave up in 1924, due to the unlikelihood of large-scale realization, because of the entire economic situation.[160] It was a suitable environment for the realization of his visions, when he entered his new position as consulting architect with "Gehag" in Berlin. The large housing developments in and around Berlin, created or proposed by Bruno Taut for the "Gehag" over the next years, represented one of the most important and extensive solutions of architecture of the twentieth century.[161]

One of the most magnificent housing developments of Bruno Taut within the framework of planning with "Gehag" is the Berlin-Britz proj-

The housing developments in Berlin, proposed by Bruno Taut, consist of a group of masterpieces, which can hardly be found within the framework of modern architecture. Social programs were realized, previously a mere dream, with the cooperation of Otto Bartning, Fred Forbat, Hugo Häring, Walter Gropius, and Otto Rudolf Salvisberg. The large Berlin-Siemensstadt development by Hans Scharoun (1893–1972), built 1929–1931 (Fig. 44) and called "The Battleship" by the

43 Bruno Taut: Extensive housing development, Berlin-Britz (1925–1927)

44 Hans Scharoun: Housing development Haselhorst in Berlin-Siemensstadt (1929–1931)

people, still seems exemplary today —even within the framework of recent social housing developments.[164] Structures for living and working co-existed in a harmonious way, and an urban unity was accomplished due to the added integration of shops, restaurants, and public institutions. Isolated parts were integrated as never before into a comprehensive system, which included the space for streets and parking areas.

A high standard of construction of the public housing developments was also achieved in other cities. Ernst May (1886–1970), superintendant of the office for construction and housing of the city of Frankfurt-on-Main, built the housing developments Römerstadt and Niederrad (Fig. 45), and

45 *Ernst May: Housing development Niederrad, Frankfurt (1930)*

46 *Karl Ehn: Large housing development, Karl Marx Hof, Wien (1927–1930)*

47 *Walter Gropius: Housing in Dessau-Törten
(1926–1928)*

48 *J. J. P. Oud: Row houses of the Weissenhof
housing development in Stuttgart (1927)*

Karl Ehn built the large housing area Karl Marx Hof in Heiligenstadt (1927–1930, Fig. 46) in Vienna for approx. 50,000 inhabitants in 14,000 apartments with a main facade, which Scully called "A proud, dark banner of socialist solidarity."[165] Engelsplatz housing (1930, R. Perco, architect) was also developed in Vienna, as well as the Werkbund housing complex (1930–1931), coordinated and planned by Josef Frank. Frank gathered the most significant architects of the time—Haerdtl, Hoffmann, Holz-

meister, Lichtblau, Loos, Niedermoser, Plischke, Sobotka, Strnad—as well as prominent foreign visitors—Häring from Berlin, Lurçat and Guevrekian from Paris, and Rietveld from Utrecht. Walter Gropius built housing in Dessau-Törten (1926–1928, Fig. 47)[166] and Karlsruhe-Dammerstock (1927–1928), and Otto Haesler built the Rotenberg housing in Kassel (1930–1932). The Weissenhof housing in Stuttgart (Fig. 48), already mentioned before in the context of the Werkbund, built under the direction of Mies van der Rohe in 1927, attempted a unity in planning and achieved a total concept despite the diversity of the participating architects: "It was surprising, that a uniform, total completeness was achieved in spite of diversity; uniformity in spite of diversity."[166] German housing of the 1920s, along with housing developments in Holland, represent the most important steps towards the recognition of the architect's function in society. They created alternatives to the central task of architecture, which is still unresolved in its diversity even today.

Organic Architecture—Hugo Häring and Rudolf Steiner

The work of Hugo Häring (1882–1958) can be seen as a continuation of the organic architecture of Louis Sullivan and Frank Lloyd Wright, even though immediate relations are difficult to prove. Häring saw the house as an "organic form," as "the second skin of a human being" and concluded: "A new technology, working

49 *Hugo Häring: Farm development Garkau near Lübeck (1924–1925)*

with light construction, elastic and pliant building materials will not demand a right-angled or cubic house, but will allow or realize all shapes of the house as 'housing organ.'"[168]

One of Häring's few realizations is the Garkau farm near Lübeck of 1924–1925 (Fig. 49), where the inner functions of the farm operation have been given an outer form. The building materials — brick, reinforced concrete, and wood — were used in harmony with a traditional bond to the landscape and thus gave the total construction a unique "design." In no way was Häring concerned with a new principle of an organlike fixation during the design process: "Organic construction has of course nothing to do with the imitation of organic works of the human environment. The decisive demand, derived from the organic point of view, is that the form of the objects is no longer determined from the outside, but that it has to be found in the nature of the object."[169]

Häring's perception, diametrically opposed to that of Le Corbusier, can be understood in this context as a bridge between the American architects Sullivan and Wright and the later ideas of Alvar Aalto and Louis I. Kahn.

Similar principles, which stem from a different basis, find a powerful expression in the thoughts and structures of Rudolf Steiner (1861–1925).[170] He also, in cooperation with the architect Ernst Aisenpreis and others, arrived at forms of construction with reinforced concrete, where the form was created with regard to the inner functions and their symbolism, founded on the teachings on metamorphosis by Goethe and the subsequent anthroposophical interpretation of the arts. Especially in regard to the second "Goetheanum" in Dornach (Fig. 50), built in 1924–

50   Rudolf Steiner: Goetheanum II in Dornach (1924–1928)

1928, as the central meeting place of the Anthroposophical Society, as well as the numerous surrounding buildings, the concept in combination with the technology and imagination, forms a powerful expression, so that the complex could be called "one of the most magnificent spatial, architectural inventions, which the twentieth century has to offer. . . ."[171] The large, integrated, spatially articulated, total form includes numerous inner units, which were kept flexible to such a degree, that a continuous change of the structure of the inner area was possible, since its completion in the year 1928. The "Goetheanum," which is still in use today, was completely adapted to the tendencies of the expressionistic style and serves as central building of the Anthroposophical Society in its complex function. It is in this sense a sign of a — certainly esoteric — society, yet it articulates the relation between individual and community, as was searched for at that time.

Perfection of Shell Construction

In America, France, as well as in Germany, construction with concrete shells was further developed during the first decades of the twentieth century. The architects Heilmann and Littmann had already used reinforced concrete for the Tietz department store and the anatomy building at the University of Munich (1907–1908).

*51   Max Berg: Hall of the Century in Breslau ▷
(1911–1913)*

ready of 43¾ yd. (40 m), with the thickness of the shell only 2⅜ in. (6 cm). This ratio could be increased to 1/666, when constructing the planetarium in Jena (Fig. 52a), whereby the natural relative values—for example, that of a chicken to an egg (1/100)—are greatly exceeded.[175]

The results of Dischinger and Finsterwalder were used in numerous planetariums (for instance, in Mannheim, Nürnberg, Dresden, Berlin, Düsseldorf, Milan, and Moscow), but also in connection with powerful utilitarian structures, such as the market halls in Frankfurt-on-Main in 1926–1927.[176] The responsible architect in cooperation with Dyckerhoff and Widmann in Frankfurt was Martin Elsässer. The new market hall in Leipzig by H. Ritter and H. Ruesch in 1927–1929 reached a span of 82 yd. (75 m) with the three powerful cupolas on a square ground plan, the weight of the cupolas being 2,000 tons, whereby the weight of the Hall of the Century in Breslau was already reduced by a third. The market hall in Basel, erected in 1929 by the architects Gönner und Rhyner according to a Dyckerhoff and Widmann system, finally covers 3,588 yd.² (3,000 m²) with a span of 65½ yd. (60 m) and a shell thickness of 3⅛ in. (8 cm). The ratio of span to shell thickness obtained in Basel is 1/700. The new possibilities gained in the use of reinforced concrete were considered to be of a pioneering nature in regard to international development, just as the simultaneous results of the Swiss engineer Robert Maillart could only later be further developed through more refined methods.

Futurism in Italy

At the beginning of the twentieth century, Italy remained more than America, France, and Germany under the dictates of traditional values, as shown in all the more intensive revolutionary outbursts. Filippo Tommaso Marinetti (1876–1944) became the spokesman of a young antitraditional generation of painters, sculptors, and architects, who drew international attention in 1909 in Paris, due to the published manifesto of Futurism.[177] Big city, machines, and dynamism were the slogans of the antihistorical and antibourgeois group.[178] The political agenda of Futurism, in the manifesto of the 11th of October 1913, states: "Everything is allowed, except to be a coward, pacifist, or anti-Italian. A larger fleet, and a larger army, a people proud to be Italian, for the war, the only hygiene of the world, and for a great Italy with intensive agriculture, industry, and commerce.—Economic protection and patriotic training of the proletariat.—A cynical, cunning, and aggressive foreign policy—colonial expansion—free trade."[179] The subsequent Fascist system, which Marinetti supported, and which he served several years as minister of education, had been prepared for concerning its most important points and established the close relation between art and politics during the twentieth century. Marinetti's book *Futurismo e fascismo* of 1924 was to be distinct proof.[180]

The architectural statement of Futurism was minted by Antonio Sant'Elia (1888–1916), who encountered the group in the spring of 1914, though it had already existed for five years, grouped around Marinetti.[181] Sant'Elia had not been able to build anything, except the Villa Elisi in Como, in 1911, and he had only become known through his publication *Le case populare e la citta giardino* of 1911 and his drawings, imagining a modern city with typical individual structures.[182]

The sketches by Sant'Elia, as well as the manifestos, which were signed by him, were concerned with the design of the modern city and the integration of industry, electricity, and speed (Fig. 53). He went so far as to glorify noise and industrial pollution, a view which in its limitations and dangers was recognized only half a century later:

We must plan and build the city of the future as a huge, noisy construction site,

flexible and dynamic in all its parts, and the house of the future like a giant machine. The elevators are not allowed to hide in the stair wells, like lonely worms, but the stairs, which are no longer necessary must be abolished, and the elevators must wind upwards on the facades, like snakes of iron and glass. This house without cement, glass or iron, without paintings or sculptures, which was only adorned with lines and forms of natural beauty, and which is extremely ugly in its mechanical simplicity, and as high and wide as necessary, not as required by the building authorities, this house has to rise at the edge of a noisy abyss: the street, which no longer spreads like a rug on the level of a lodge, but which reaches several storys deep into the ground, and these levels are connected through metal-runways and very fast escalators for the necessary passage.[183]

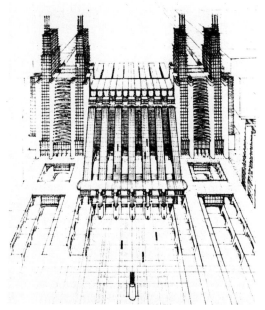

53 Antonio Sant'Elia: Design for the main railroad station in Milan (1914)

Sant'Elia dealt with some significant singular arguments, in the tradition of Otto Wagner and Tony Garnier, before subsequent architectural development: the integration of vertical and horizontal circulation within the city organism, the utilization of basement and attic for new functions, the inclusion of synthetic building materials, textiles, and light construction materials: "I insist: The new architecture is an architecture of cool calculation, daring boldness and simplicity: an architecture of reinforced concrete, iron, glass, textiles, and all synthetic materials in place of wood, stone, and brickwork, which contribute to the achievement of maximum elasticity and lightness."[184]

Due to the death of Sant'Elia in 1916, none of his futuristic ideas were realized. Nevertheless, his sketched plans of power plants and airplane hangars had a considerable influence on the new architecture. In a group of drawings for the main railroad station in Milan (Fig. 53), Sant'Elia had focused his attention on a concrete task, yet he had banished it at the same time into a visionary sphere, due to the coordination of land, rail, and air traffic. Characteristically, Sant'Elia gave a few of his projects the more or less utopian title "Milano 2000."

After 1918, a decisive change occurred. Antonio Gramsci, in a letter to Trotsky on September 9th, 1922, about the changed situation after the World War, writes: "The most significant spokesmen for Futurism from pre-war times became Fascists."[185]

Besides Sant'Elia, one has to refer to projects by Mario Chiattone (1891–1957), who sketched interrelated high-rise city complexes and modes of transportation in 1924 in Milan, and to Ottorino Aloisio and his sports center project (1926–1928), as well as to Virgilio Marchi (1895–1960), who rebuilt the Casa d'arte and the Teatro degli Independente in Rome, in a bizarre, romanesque, cavelike style.[186] However, the architectural scene in Italy continued to be dominated by historical concepts, which reached a high standard, especially through the works of Marcello Piacentini (1881–1960) and Armando Brasini (1879–1965). The most important realization of Futuristic thoughts were those by Giacomo Mattè-Trucco

54 G. Mattè-Trucco: Fiat works near Turin (1919–1923) ramp

(1869–1934) and his building of the Fiat factory in Lingotto near Turin (1919–1923). A huge complex of workshops and offices, connected to a test track for car races on the roof via a huge ramp, became a visionary and real unity (Fig. 54). The utopian visions of Sant'Elia and Chiattone were here turned into commercial reality, a reality that fused structure and street, technical architecture and the speed of machines.[187]

De Stijl and the School of Amsterdam

Examples of Dutch architectural work of the early twentieth century are works by Hendrik Petrus Berlage (1856–1934) and Petrus Josephus Hubertus Cuijpers (1827–1921), as well as the varied influences through the work of Frank Lloyd Wright.[188] Berlage's influence on the young generation of European architects came mainly through his Exchange Building in Amsterdam, but also through his plans for housing and city projects, which were concerned with social questions. Bruno Taut considered Berlage as source of the whole new movement of solving housing problems: "His fundamental conviction seems obviously to have been based on the contention that construction and material, i.e., iron, stone, and wood, were to remain thoroughly pure—that is to say, they were to be left naked and unadorned. A puritanical principle which, as opposed to other constructive conditions, exacted the ethical claims of unconditional truthfulness and an implacable animosity towards all decorative ambiguity."[189]

The School of Amsterdam, a group of architects around Theo van de Wijdeveld, the editor of the magazine *Wendingen*, are all partly in direct contact with Berlage. Many are involved with the construction of the project in South Amsterdam, planned by Berlage. Michel de Klerk (1884–1923), Paul Kramer (1881–1961), and Johan Melchior van der Meij (1868–1949) transferred Berlage's principles into a different era and intensified the emotional values of brick. De Klerk's housing (Fig. 55) corresponded to the Romantic or Expressionistic ideal through addressing equally the characteristics of intimate seclusion and social communication.[190]

Willem Marinus Dudok (1884–1974) takes a middle-of-the-road, more conservative stand; as city planner for public construction in Hilversum since 1915, he executed public buildings like the bathhouse (1921), the slaughterhouse (1923), and the town hall (1924–1928) in a style also influenced by Wright.[191]

The painter and art theoretitian Theo van Doesberg (1883–1931) had an influence on the entire European situation (Fig. 56) with his ideas and the group "De Stijl," founded in 1917.[192] In the first edition of the *De Stijl* magazine, he writes programmatically: "There is an old and a new conscientiousness at this time. The old one is directed towards individualism. The new one is geared towards universalism. The fight of the individual versus the universal is manifested equally with regard to the world war and the art of our time period."[193] The principles of the De Stijl group were demonstrated in their complexity by

55 Michel de Klerk: Housing area in South Amsterdam (1921)

van Doesburg, in cooperation with Hans Arp and Sophie Täuber-Arp, through the entire new design of an inner room of the "L'Aubette" Café-Restaurant, built in Strasbourg 1926–1927.[194]

The principles of the De Stijl group find their architectural expression in the work of Gerrit Thomas Rietveld (1888–1964), who had started his career as a cabinetmaker.[195] Rietveld had discovered and used the new principles of spatial freedom introduced to architecture by Wright, as early as 1918, with his Red-Blue chair. They are all applied in different ways, with regard to the Schröder house in Utrecht in 1924 (Fig. 57).[196] Color and space, areas joined at a right angle, and flowing areas of space are intertwined and constitute a dynamic whole (Fig. 58).

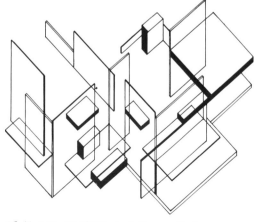

56 T. van Doesburg and C. van Eesteren: Study of a residence (1923)

57 *Gerrit Thomas Rietveld: Schröeder house in Utrecht (1924)*

58 *Gerrit Thomas Rietveld: Schröeder house in Utrecht (1924) study on the upper floor*

Jacobus Johannes Pieter Oud (1890–1963) belonged to the founders of the De Stijl group, but he detached himself from the goals of the group, after being called to be Rotterdam city planner in 1918, where he concentrated on the significant communal tasks of Rotterdam.[197] His housing projects, such as Tusschendijken of 1919 (Fig. 59), influenced by Frank Lloyd Wright, are bringing the type of row-house for people with a low income to a climax, also the Kiefhoek

village for workers (built 1928–1930, Fig. 60), and the housing development in Hoek van Holland of 1926 to 1927. Already in 1929, Hitchcock considered Oud's housing project in Hoek van Holland to be the most beautiful example of modern architecture ever.[198] For an extraordinarily low rent, these individual houses consist of three rooms and a kitchen, the corner houses having a larger living area. Leonardo Benevolo wrote about Kiefhoek: "This area is one of the most convincing works of the so-called functionalism; this time it is true in the sense of the word, because here we have not a rather elegant expression of a function, but a technical, truly profitable solution."[199]

Dutch architecture came in contact with the movements of the rest of Europe through Mart Stam (* 1899). He worked together with El Lissitzky on the Wolkenbügel project (Fig. 61),[200] with Ernst May in Frankfurt and Bruno Taut in Berlin, regarding the concept of housing projects. He was invited by Mies van der Rohe in 1927 and participated in the development of exemplary row houses at the Weissenhof project. With W. Brinkmann and L. C. van der Vlugt, Stam created the probably most significant industrial structure of the time (Fig. 62), the van Nelle Tobacco factory in Rotterdam (1928–1929). He was also interested in the integration of city planning and architecture: his project for the Damrak in Amsterdam in 1924 had the power to reach far into the future. The magazine *ABC — Contributions for Construction*, which was published by him, was one of the most radical publications of these years, and men-

59 J. J. P. Oud: Housing development Tusschendijken in Rotterdam (1919)

60 J. J. P. Oud: Kiefhoek, housing for workers, Rotterdam (1928–1930)

61 *El Lissitzky and Mart Stam: The Wolken-bügel project (1924)*

tioned demands for a "Dictatorship of the Machine."[201]

The buildings by Johannes Duiker (1890–1935) and Bernard Bijvoet seemed in a sense to come from a different futuristic concept and were the preparation for the architectural view of the 1930s. Duiker and Bijvoet first stood out in 1918 with a project for an academy. They took part in the international competition by the *Chicago Tribune* in 1922 and opened up original and previously unknown possibilities for rhythmical organization of the volume of construction, as currently rediscovered, through the residential structure in Aalsmeer of 1924. Bernard

62 *W. Brinkmann, L. C. van der Vlugt, and M. Stam: Van Nelle Tobacco factory, Rotterdam (1928–1929)*

GRAND HOTEL GOOILAND

63 J. Duiker and B. Bijvoet: Gooiland Hotel, Hilversum (1935–1937)

Bijvoet left the partnership in 1926 and settled in Paris. Johannes Duiker produced, on his own, masterpieces of outstanding quality: the Zonnestraal Sanatorium (1926–1928), the open-air school in Amsterdam (1930–1932), and the Gooiland Hotel in Hilversum (1935–1937, Fig. 63). These buildings show new and exceptional possibilities of the sensible and open use of technical systems in a comprehensive totality, determined by a humane value system.[202]

Synthesis in Russia

The various results of the architectural development in Italy, Germany, France, and Holland found a synthesis in Russia, yet also an integration into a sociopolitical reality took place, in contrast to other Western-European countries.[203] Lenin (1870–1924) had recognized the significance of science and technology early on, in regard to the development of the Soviet state and was from the beginning interested in the basic reorganization of industry.[204] Even before 1917, there was a revolutionary group of artists occupied with projects, while serving the state for a number of years after 1917; they were Kasimir Malevich, Vladimir Tatlin, and Alexander Rodtschenko.[205]

However, the new basis from which the new development of the state could proceed was necessary. Bruno Taut wrote in 1929 after a visit to Russia: "In Russia all thoughts are ruled by the industrialization and development of huge areas of land, which are rich in natural resources yet poor with regard to technical resources."[206] After the cessation of private property with regard to land ("Constitutional rights of the working and exploited people of the 13th of January, 1918") and due to the prohibition of any speculation with land (decree of the 14th of December, 1917), a freedom for planning and new construction was created, as in no other country before. Beyond that, a new group of clients provoked experimental solutions, as articulated in housing communes (project of N. Ladowski of 1920), in clubhouses for workers, sports centers, and recreational areas, which

64 *El Lissitzky: Design of the main entrance of the Soviet pavilion at the* Pressa, *Cologne (1927)*

were no longer erected for private interest or financial profit, but for the good of the entire society.[207] However, the central government was given a tremendous amount of power in order to solve these tasks.

During the first few years after the revolution, visionary designs, as in Germany, were the main focal point; Naum Gabo's design for a broadcasting station in 1919–1920, Vladimir Tatlin's tower for the international in Moscow in 1920, and the designs by Kasimir Malevich of Suprematist houses, cities, and forms of housing in space, called planites.[208]

El Lissitzky (1890–1941) became the personality whose ideas and works produced the strongest effect on the West. He developed Lenin's grandstand for mass meetings in 1924, and, together with Mart Stam, created projects for new kinds of high rises (Cloud Hangers, Fig. 61), stronger in regard to city construction and the visions of the Futurists of Italy, with the structure-giving function in an urban context, and who started a new phase of dynamic city construction (Fig. 64). Architects soon also had the opportunity to build, in spite of initial economic difficulties and in addition to their fruitful and innovative occupation of teaching. Victor Vesnin (1882–1950), Alexander Vesnin (1883–1959), and Leonid Vesnin (1880–1933) constructed office buildings and department stores (Fig. 65),[209] the Panteleimon Golosoff brothers (1883–1945) built the Soviet club in the Lesnaja in Moscow and the *Pravda* building, which however was only completed in 1934 (Fig. 66). The architects S. Serafimov and S. Kravez built the House of Industry in Charkow (1929), in a semicircle and in a bridgelike connection of parts of the upper stories; M. Korchev constructed the stadium in Moscow (1926); and Ivan Leonidov (1902–1960) stood out with brilliant designs, such as for the Lenin Institute in 1927 (Fig. 67), the Palace of Culture of 1930, and for the Ministry of Heavy Industry of 1933, which are considered to be among the highest achievements of international architecture of that time.[210] Other architects with extraordinary qualifications are A. S. Nikolski (1884–1953), M. J. Ginsburg (1892–1946), and G. B. Barchin (1880–1969), who erected the *Izvestia* structure in Moscow in 1927.

The outstanding personality of Russian architecture of the 1920s was Konstantin Melnikov (1890–1969), who went his way independently of the existing groups.[211] His pavilion at the arts and crafts exhibit in Paris in 1925 created dynamic areas of convincing boldness with the traditional building material wood, and brought the new Russian architecture into contact with West European architects. In his clubhouse for streetcar workers in Moscow of 1927–1929 (Fig. 68), he achieved a cooperative architecture of such a new design form that Western critics are seldom able to see the architectural quality, even today.[212] The residence of the architect, which was built in 1929 in Moscow, is developed from a circular form and creates an unusual, yet flexible, new kind of interior. Melnikov's design for the Palace of the Soviets of 1931 finally surpasses all domestic and foreign projects with the symbolic exaggerated spatial

65 *V. Vesnin and A. Vesnin: Design of a department store in Moscow (1927)*

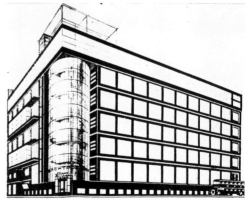

66 *I. Golosoff: Design of the Elektrobank in Moscow (1927)*

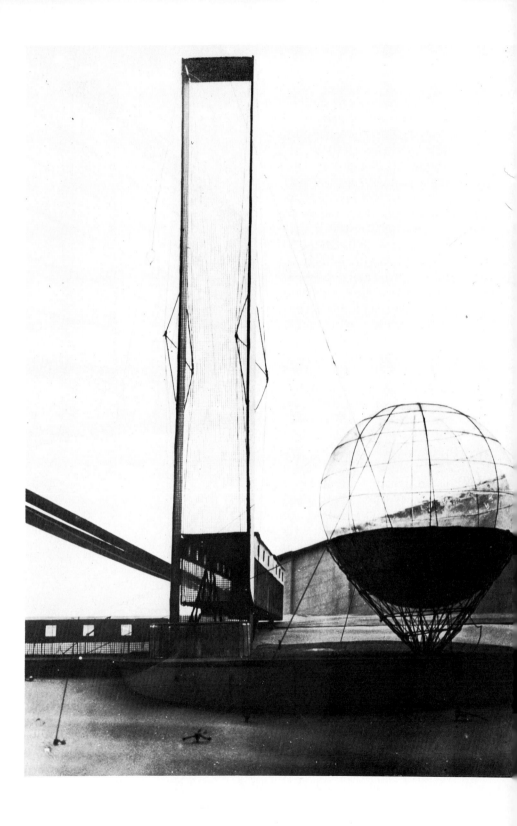

power of a dynamic architecture.[213] In 1933 Melnikov designed the headquarters for the Ministry of Heavy Industry, a bold and innovative spatial expanse. After these projects no further developments by the brilliant architect were published, and his work had to be rediscovered after the years of Stalinist regime.

City planning in Russia during the 1920s attained a central meaning due to necessity, and Russian planners like N. A. Miliutin, T. Warjenzov, and B. Lawrov developed ideas, which were congruent with the ideas of a communist city.[214] Ernst May and a team of German architects planned and constructed the industrial city of Magnitogorsk partly with Milintin's newly revised concept of the linear city. Additionally other foreign architects were invited to execute important structures, for example, Le Corbusier, Mart Stam, Hannes Meyer, Erich Mendelsohn, and André Lurcat. Peter Behrens, Hans Poelzig, Auguste Perret, Walter Gropius, Marcel Breuer, H. P. Berlage, J. J. van Loghem, and Norman Bel Geddes participated in the contests, which were organized by the government, so that the general situation in Russia conveyed a picture of many rich and complex possibilities.

68 *Konstantin Melnikov: Clubhouse for street-car workers, Moscow (1927-1929)*

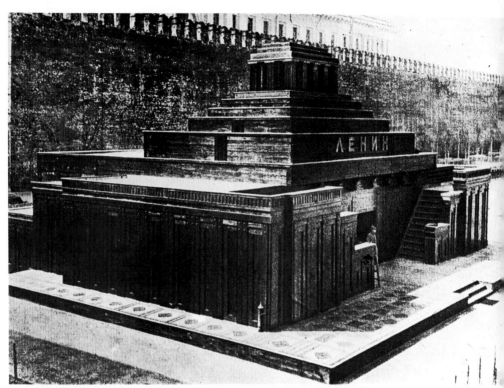

69 Alexej Witkorowitsch Shchusev: Lenin's Tomb in Moscow, first version, built of wood (1924)

Yet this perspective is incomplete, as parallel and contrary to the emphatically constructive strengths, there exists an equally rich development of conservative architecture. It is marked by such architects as Ivan Wladislawowitsch Sholtovski and Alexej Witkorowitsch Shchusev (1874–1949). Sholtovski's magnificent central heating plant in Moscow of 1917 was integrated harmoniously into the total picture of Russian architecture, in spite of the attachment to historical form elements. Shchusev's Tomb of Lenin on Red Square in Moscow became the cult building of the young state. The structure was at first built of wood, after Lenin's death on January 21st, 1924 (Fig. 69), and only reached its final form in 1929 (Fig. 69a). The early development of the architect Shchusev, who was given this central task, shows the opposite of constructivism and modernism with greater correspondence to the official character of Russian architecture, binding it to the tradition: the Kasan Railroad Station in Moscow of 1913 represents late czarist architecture, and the Meyerhold Theater in Moscow of 1932 has the clearly visible signs of the Stalinistic architecture. Lenin's Tomb thus found its precise historical place, as well as its architectural form.[215]

Through the award of the first prize at the contest for the Palace of the So-

69a   Alexej W. Shchusev: Lenin's Tomb in Moscow in its final form (1929)

viets in Moscow in 1931 to the team of Jofan, Vladimir A. Shchuko (1878–1949), and Helfreich, the conservative side of Russian architecture had gained predominance. The Theater of the Red Army in Moscow by the architects K. S. Alabyan and W. Simbirzev (Fig. 100, 1934–1940) shows a programmatic five-pointed star as plan and allows a comparison with the structure of the Pentagon in Washington, D.C., by G. E. Bergstrom and D. J. Wittmer, completed in 1934 (Fig. 101). In both buildings, development of the construction is replaced by symbols of the state's authority and a figurative, symbolic language was put in place of the previously experimental function.[216]

II

Empiristic Tendencies: Organic Architecture and Technology Serving Man and Nature

The Change Towards the Organic

The development of architecture in various areas between 1900 and 1930 was significantly influenced by the interpenetration of science, technology, and industry. Industrial structures were the focal point and rational principles dominated.[1] The machine had become a symbol; standardization and mechanization were the inescapable results. The major achievements of such leading architects as Walter Gropius, Mies van der Rohe, and Le Corbusier must be seen in this light. Hans Schmidt and Mart Stam went so far as to demand the "dictatorship of the machine" in 1928.[2]

However, around 1930, a recognizable change took place with regard to the machine or technology in general and industrial building methods. Eric de Maré expressed it thus, in retrospect: "In general, it is a reaction against too rigid formalism. . . . There is a feeling that buildings are made for the sake of human beings rather than for the bold logic of theory."[3]

Frank Lloyd Wright articulated the new ideas, with which he had been familiar for a long time, during his lectures in Princeton in 1930: "Oh yes, young man, observe by all means, that a house is a machine to be lived in, yet in the same sense as a heart is a suction pump. Man's feeling begins where the imagination of the heart ceases. Recognize that a house is a machine in which one lives, but architecture begins where this perception of the house ends. All of life is machinery in the rudimentary sense, and yet machinery is the life of nothing. Machines are only machines because of life."[4] In 1937, Wright expressed his general view in this simple formula: ". . . it seems to me that what the cause of Architecture needs most, to put into plain, homely English, is love . . ."[5]

This change in emphasis around 1930 is an international phenomenon and is not limited to any one country. Therefore, in no way can this period be defined as the time "of the great setback of 1930 to 1940" as has been done quite often.[6] Hugo Häring noticed a general "shift of structure from geometrical to organic" in 1932, and even Mies van der Rohe, the most radical theoretician of an industrialization of architecture, wrote in 1930: ". . . the question of mechanization, of the establishment of types, and standardization should not be overrated." Now he also focused on the question of value: "We have to set new values, show the latest reasoning in order to establish standards."[7] The engineer Eugène Freyssinet was even able to consider the subconscious as "the constant, the calmness in us," without negating the greatness and beauty of mathematics.[8]

The parallels to the efforts of Surrealism which are geared towards total integration of life and art cannot be overlooked.[9] The interference of the group of Surrealists with the political situation in France in the 1930s, and their stand regarding Communism and Fascism, show a changed situation. Not only were science, technology, and culture viewed as one, but also the inclusion of politics and culture has to be considered typical during the time between 1930 and 1950.

In the wake of these basic changes, humanistic and architectural tasks in relation to nature were focused upon more strongly.[10] Sanatoriums, open-air schools, sports stadiums, and health centers took the place of the former exemplary tasks such as factories, power plants, and exhibition halls. In place of standardized small apartments, there appeared terrace houses and housing in a green environment. Indeed, a renaissance of the idea of a garden city is clearly visible. Konstantin Melnikov's "Green City" of 1930 and Wright's "Broadacre City" of 1934 show the direction of a new development. Even Le Corbusier suggested the reorganization of buildings for agriculture in 1934.

As already mentioned, in no way is the tendency of the shift and the accentuation towards the organic, nature, and humanization limited to countries such as Scandinavia, Switzerland, or America. In Russia, Germany, and Italy, also, the ideology is moving in comparable tracks of anti-urban, anti-technology and anti-rational concepts. Protests against the large city are also found during those years in the thoughts of D. H. Lawrence, Max Ernst, and Frank Lloyd Wright in their new residences in the desert of the American West, as well as in the program of a lifestyle connected with the soil. From National Socialism evolved the parallel ideology of blood and soil.

In the same vein also, the variants of Neoclassicism cannot solely be interpreted as expressions of dictatorial power-architecture. Albert Speer was surprised in 1937 to find Neoclassicist structures in Paris also and he wrote: "There was a subsequent insistence that this style has been a characteristic of the art of construction of totalitarian states. This is not the case. It is rather a characteristic of the epoch and it influenced Washington, London, or Paris in the same way as Rome, Moscow, or our own planning with regard to Berlin."[11] R. R. Taylor arrives at this conclusion, like many other historians: "In the thirties, in fact, neo-classicism was the official style of many countries."[12] The opposition of official and nonofficial architecture is, of course, obvious.

Hitler's architectural and urbanistic programs were founded on native traditions, as was the case with other governments and significant architects. Natural materials frequently replaced the formerly dominating synthetic building materials. Alfred Rosenberg gave architecture a central position in his book *Der Mythos des 20. Jahrhunderts,* and wrote: "The change from a technology which adored material to a genuine feeling for style has taken place today. The still unbroken occidental personality will not try to escape from the earth in eternal longing, but will respect, form, and 'spiritualize' the earth. . . . Architecture is today (in spite of the School of Architecture at Dessau) the first art form, which is on its way to becoming honest again."[13] Rosenberg saw first signs of this new sentiment, like the architects before him, around 1910, with regard to the "corn silos of California," the "steamships of the Norddeutscher Lloyd," and the "bridges of the Tauernbahn."[14]

Landscape planning and construction in harmony with the given topography was expressed in the American cloverleaf and parkway systems as well as in the German Autobahn. The expression "Biological Engineering," coined by Dr. Todt, gets to the core of the new view. The accomplishments of the architects were generally integrated into a far-reaching renewal plan, whether it concerned the construction of the dams of the Tennessee Valley Program in America, erected within the framework of Franklin D. Roosevelt's (1882–1945) "New Deal" (Hoover Dam, 1931–1935),[15] the Ural dams near Magnitogorsk (1931), or the dams at Beni-Badhal in Algeria (1935–1940); it is a new combination of standardization and irrationalism, as Siegfried Giedion has incomparably articulated, for example, in the sense that "standardization shall no longer be master, but servant."[16]

New Beginnings in the Work of Frank Lloyd Wright

After a prolonged phase of personal crises and relative idleness, a new period of productivity began for Frank Lloyd Wright after 1930, manifested in a large number of visionary proposals and several completed structures of unusual quality. In 1932, his book *The Disappearing City* was published, in which Wright expressed openly his anti-urban stand that coincided with the general situation of the time. In 1934, the publication of *Broadacre City* followed, in which Wright presented to his people, shaken by the economic crisis, a preference for the combination of city and country, based on the ideas of Ralph Barsodi.[17] The efforts of Clarence Stein in favor

70 *Frank Lloyd Wright: The Kaufman house, "Falling Water," Bear Run, Pennsylvania (1936)*

of the New Town Movement in America (Greenbelt in Maryland of 1935 in collaboration with Henry Wright) are based upon similar concepts, yet are more easily integrated into the tradition of English garden cities, which Ebenezer Howard had promulgated three decades earlier.[18]

The most important works of Wright in the 1930s are at the same time key works towards the integration of nature and architecture, which are demonstrated in a inimitable manner in the Kaufman house, "Falling Water," of 1936 in Bear Run, Pennsylvania (Fig. 70),[19] in the complex of the Johnson Wax Company in Racine, Wisconsin, of 1936–1939, in Florida

Southern College in Lakeland, Florida, of 1938 to 1959, as well as in Wright's residence and architecture office in Taliesin West near Phoenix, Arizona, of 1938–1959.

The role that technology played in Wright's structures is most visible in the building for the Johnson Wax Company in Racine, (Figs. 71, 72), for which Wright had developed a supportive column system of reinforced concrete, which had not been known before, and which was rejected by the construction authorities and the engineers because of its unusually slender form. Finally, the safety of this construction system was to be determined through a public contest, a procedure described by Wright himself with obvious pride during an interview:

The crane kept swinging and dumping, swinging and dumping, until the sun went down. We were still there waiting for collapse. Long ago any requirement by the commission had been passed and doubled. Still the heap up there on top kept growing.

The sight was incredible. The police had taken charge and roped the populace from the vicinity of that heroic slender stem, standing up there a graceful thing on tiptoe, standing straight and true, until sixty tons, instead of the twelve tons required were on top of a shaft nine inches in diameter at the tip of the ground. No more load could be put on without sliding off, so I gave the word to break it. . . . A lateral push against the shaft brought the enormous overload tumbling to the ground causing a tremor felt to the surrounding streets. The shaft, still unbroken, lay on the ground. The spreading had been broken off. The commissioners disappeared. Their silence gave consent.[20]

71 *Frank Lloyd Wright: Johnson Wax Company factory building, Racine, Wisconsin (1936–1939). Tower of the research laboratory (1949–1950)*

72 *Frank Lloyd Wright: Johnson Wax Company factory building, Racine, Wisconsin (1936–1939) interior*

Architecture and Architectural Engineering in America Around 1930

American architecture developed partly in open opposition to Wright's ideas — the National Gallery in Washington, D.C., (completed in 1941) by John Russell Pope (1874–1937) is a typical example — partly in retrospect of a tradition committed to an articulation of form, which nevertheless coincided with the new urban necessities. Alongside, there developed a construction method imported by European emigrants, which was characterized by the expression "International Style."[21] The large skyscrapers in New York, such as William van Alen's Chrysler Building (Fig. 12) of 1930 and the Empire State Building of Shreve, Lamb, and Harmon (1929–1931), and in Philadelphia, the Philadelphia Savings Funds Society Building of George Howe (1886–1955) and William Lescaze (1896–1969) of 1931–1932 gave an architectonic and urban articulation to changing economic development.[22] In a cooperative effort in regard to Rockefeller Center in New York (1931–1939), a first-time integration of building blocks and city organism was achieved (Fig. 73), due to the coordinated planning of Raymond Hood (1881–1934), who in his earlier works had pioneered the development of the skyscraper as a building type.[23]

◁ 73 *Reinhard and Hofmeister; Corbett, Harrison, and MacMurray; Hood and Fouilhoux: Rockefeller Center in New York, (1931–1939)*

Development in California followed its own direction and developed special new forms of architecture for recreation and the entertainment industry.[24] The early work of Richard Neutra (1892–1970), for example, the Lovell house in Los Angeles (1927), the Corona-Bell school in Los Angeles (1935), and the housing development for workers, Channel Heights (1942), expressed clearly the new situation. Typical for the international movement are also the open-air school in San Francisco (1931–1940), as well as the farm workers' commune in Chandler, Arizona, (1936–1937), by Vernon de Mars (* 1908). Architecture in Chicago in the thirties was determined by George F. Keck (* 1895), Andrew N. Rebori (1886–1966), and Howard T. Fisher.

Besides the domestic architects, emigré architects from Europe took part decisively in the renewal of American architecture. Eliel Saarinen came from Finland, William Lescaze from Switzerland, Schindler, Neutra, and Victor Gruen (* 1903) from Austria, Konrad Wachsmann, Marcel Breuer, and Ludwig Hilberseimer from Germany, and Antonin Raymond from Czechoslovakia. Yet the European component developed a stronger effect, due to Walter Gropius, who was originally from Germany, came from England in 1937 and settled in Cambridge, Massachusetts, and became active in education as head of the Department of Architecture at Harvard University. His graduate center at Harvard of 1949–1950 is the architectural expression of these efforts (Fig. 74).

Of even greater significance was the influence of Ludwig Mies van der

74 *Walter Gropius and TAC: Harvard University Graduate Center, Cambridge, Massachusetts (1949–1950)*

Rohe, who emigrated to Chicago in 1938 and took over the directorship of the Illinois Institute of Technology as well as the entire planning and construction of the new campus. The expanse of the university area, which was divided into rectangular complexes (Fig. 75), with the various buildings for the institute and for housing, represents a continuation of Mies van der Rohe's earlier ideas, which were realized at this point for the first time on a large scale and in a comprehensive unified plan. With the work of Ludwig Hilberseimer, as well, extensive areas of American construction were to be influenced for decades to come by this concept of architecture geared to industrialization and standardization.

Industrialization was by no means a negative word in America during the 1930s, it was merely used in a different way than had been customary earlier. Konrad Wachsmann (1901–1980), in cooperation with Walter

75 *L. Mies van der Rohe: Campus design for the Illinois Institute of Technology, Chicago (1939)*

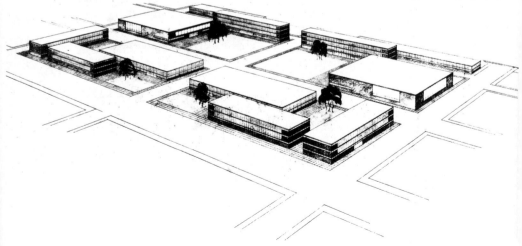

Gropius, developed in 1940 an industrial system for prefabricated houses (General Panel Corporation) and Richard Buckminster-Fuller (1895–1983) sought in his concept of the Dymaxion House an optimal use of technical possibilities. After the first publications in the year 1927, and after the establishment of the Fuller Houses, Inc., in the year 1944, the first Dymaxion house was constructed in 1946 in Wichita, Kansas (Fig. 76).[25]

The dominating expression of the time was found in the work of the great bridge builders, of whom Othmar H. Ammann deserves special mention.[26] Among his bridges are the Bayonne Bridge across the Kill van Kull (1928–1931), with a span of 551 yd. (504 m), the George Washington Bridge across the Hudson in New

76 *Richard Buckminster-Fuller: Dymaxion house, Wichita, Kansas (1946)*

York (1927–1931) with a span of 1,148¼ yd. (1,050 m), as well as the Golden Gate Bridge in San Francisco (1933–1937) with a span of 1,400 yd. (1,280 m) (in cooperation with Joseph B. Strauss, Fig. 77).

77 *O. H. Ammann in cooperation with J. B. Strauss: Golden Gate Bridge in San Francisco (1933–1937)*

At this time, masterpieces of technology were developed that show a harmonious linkage with nature, as well as the necessary connection of traffic. They thus bring together technology and the organic into a new unity.

New Beginnings in Latin America

The years around 1930 showed, for the first time, expansion of the new ar-

78 *L. Costa, C. Leao, J. M. Moreira, O. Niemeyer, A. E. Reidy, and E. M. da Vasconcelos: Ministry for Education and Welfare in Rio de Janeiro (1937–1943)*

chitecture, which had been previously restricted to Central Europe and America, to the countries of Latin America, Africa, and Asia and thus overcame a lack of development. Brazil especially attained an early assimilation of the European results through the structures of Gregori Warchavchik (1896–1972), Lucio Costa (* 1902), and Oskar Niemeyer (* 1907), yet these were variations according to a specific regional way and new time phase.[27] The Ministry for Education and Welfare in Rio de Janeiro (1937–1943, Fig. 78) — the name alone is a sign of the new development — which was influenced by Le Corbusier, is the cooperative result of the architects Lucio Costa, Carlos Azevedo Leao (* 1906), Jorge Machado Moreira (* 1904), Oskar Niemeyer, Affonso Eduardo Reidy (1909–1964), and Ernani Mendez da Vasconcelos (* 1911).

Other structures by the young architect Oskar Niemeyer changed the initially decisive influence of Le Corbusier — who visited Brazil in 1936 and was received with enthusiasm — with the additional influence of Erich Mendelsohn into an independent regional, Brazilian vocabulary of articulation.[28] Niemeyer's Yacht Club (1942), the island restaurant (1942), and the theater (1947) in Belo Horizonte showed an up-to-now unknown freedom of anti-rectangular forms as well as the intertwining of open and closed areas. His church of San Francisco in Pampulha of 1943 is the manifestation of a new antistatic articulation of space.

Probably the most convincing expression of the new Brazilian culture is shown by the gardens of Roberto Burle-Marx (* 1909), who also executed wall treatments and fountains, in cooperation with Niemeyer. These gardens are derived from regional local traditions, yet at the same time are typical for the tendencies of the 1930s, which are targeting organism and a new feeling for nature.

In neighboring Argentina, Amancio Williams (* 1913) and Eduardo Catalano must be singled out. Their work is more directed towards technical and urban tasks and shows trends of the coming development.[29] Mexico, also, was arriving at a new architecture during the 1930s, which, however did not fully develop until after 1950.[30]

Beginnings in South Africa, India, Australia, and Japan

After a long independent development, the countries of the Southern Hemisphere were under European influence during the 1930s and only slowly separated themselves from the models. In South Africa, it was Le Corbusier's influence manifested in the works of housing and cultural institutions of Rex Martienssen (1905–1942), Fussler and Cooke, as well as Gordon McIntosh.[31]

The beginnings of new Indian architecture were determined by the transplantation of English architectural forms. Edwin Lutyens (1869–1944) planned and built the new capital, New Delhi (begun in 1914), the central administration structures, as well as the monumental palace of the viceroy (1920–1931).[32] Subsequent prominent structures in India stem from Herbert Baker (1862–1940), who before had planned and executed the capital of Pretoria in South Africa and Walter Burley Griffin (1876–1937), who had earlier built the Australian capital of Canberra.

In Australia for the first time during the thirties, modern architecture is introduced with structures by Harry. A. Norris (Mitchell House in Melbourne, 1938), Stephenson and Turner (Royal Melbourne Hospital in Parkville, Victoria, 1939–1943), Leighton Irwin (Hospital in Heidelberg, Victoria, 1942), and Harry Tompkins (The Meyer Emporium in Melbourne, 1937).[33]

As in South Africa and Australia, signs of a modern conviction are also expressed for the first time in Japan, during the thirties. Among the important foreign contributions in Japan are works by Frank Lloyd Wright, Bruno Taut, and Antonin Raymond. Also the major Japanese architects were under Western influence. Sutemi Horiguchi (* 1895) was impressed by Dutch architecture during a trip to Europe. This is clearly expressed in his Nakaza house in Tokyo of 1939. Mamaru Yamada (1894–1966) with his welfare hospital in Tokyo of 1937 and Tetsuro Yoshida (1894–1956) with the structures for the post office in Tokyo (1937) and Kyoto (1939), all show similarities to examples in Europe.[34] Junzo Sakakura (1904–1969), working in the office of Le Corbusier in Paris at that time, built the Japanese pavilion for the world's fair in Paris in 1937, and transferred the new spirit of Japan to the West. These various structures determine the beginning of a new Japanese architecture with subsequent phases, leading to revolutionary results, which have in retrospect an influence on the West. The National Museum in Tokyo by Hitoshi Watanabe of 1937 (Fig. 79), on the other hand, demonstrates the development toward the militaristic system in Japanese government and is thus a parallel to other international tendencies of the same years in other countries.[35]

Alvar Aalto and the Contribution of Scandinavia

As in Brazil and also partly in Japan, architecture undergoes a significant development around 1930 in Finland, as well. Although at first under the influence of central Europe, Finland soon attains a significant independence and its own unmistakable identity.[36] The return to natural living conditions, reintroduction of natural building materials, and integration of structures within the interdependence of landscape and vegetation are especially Finnish characteristics, but are also those of the general development of the time. Alvar Aalto's (1898–1976) early works are in between the influences from Central Europe and the awareness of his Finnish identity. His workers' club in Jyvaskyla of 1924 is in its task comparable to the con-

79 Hitoshi Watanabe: National Museum, Tokyo (1937)

temporary solutions in Russia, but lacks their spatial imagination. Also, Aalto's buildings for the Sanomat firm in Turku of 1930 remain, in their focussing on the façade, within the Central European tradition. His tuberculosis clinic in Paimio of 1929–1933 is therefore the key building (Fig. 80). It represents the change in direction in the international development of architecture.[37] The structure, with its various wings, which reach far into the landscape, is a symbol: nature and sun, trees and air are part of the function, serving technology and mechanical installations, integrated into the total concept. The international development of hospital architecture had found its model for decades to come.

The early work of Aalto is marked by further masterpieces: the library in Viipuri (1930–1935) with the wavy undulating ceiling design of the lecture hall out of reddish Scotch pine, his own house in Munkkiniemi (1936), the Villa Mairea (1938), and the factory with housing for workers in Sunila (1936–1939).[38]

When constructing the workspace, Aalto considered the same criteria as with the sanatorium: a feeling for the presence of the landscape, a synopsis of working and living, and areas for recreation and social establishments as part of the entire complex.[39] Finally, in the community center of Säynätsalo (planned in 1949, executed in 1950–1952), Aalto succeeded in articulating from a regional plan, the living center of a small community of about 3,000 people, with a town hall, library, and apartment for the custodian, as well as commercial establishments around an elevated

80 Alvar Aalto: Sanatorium in Paimio, Finland (1929–1933)

inner courtyard, completely architectural and urban (Fig. 81), so that this complex of buildings can be viewed as a transitional example of a new developmental phase of architecture after 1950.[40]

Aalto and other Finnish or Scandinavian architects of the 1930s were building more or less in harmony with nature, not against it. They sought to humanize technology, to have it serve humanization of the constructed environment. Thus we find comparable architectonic results in the work of

81 Alvar Aalto: Community center in Säeyn-
äetsalo, Finland (1950–1952)

◁ 82 Arne Jacobsen: Tennis hall in Gentofte,
Denmark (1935)

83 Arne Korsmo: Villa Damman, Oslo (1930)

Arne Jacobsen (1902–1971) in Denmark (Fig. 82)[41]; and in Sweden, Erik Gunnar Asplund (1885–1940), Sven Markelius (1889–1972), Hellden, Lallerstedt, Lewerentz (Theater in Malmoe, 1934), and Olof Thunstrom (housing development near Stockholm, 1932); and in Norway, Arne Korsmo (1900–1968, Fig. 83).[42] The given climatic situation was seen as a deciding factor and regional traditions were respected, in contrast to the standard solutions for construction of the international style, which could be transplanted anywhere. The new viewpoint in Scandinavia corresponded to the changed conditions of architectural development itself and found here a valid expression. It was to reach worldwide expansion.[43]

The Conservative Avant-Garde in England

The turning point around 1930 brought new impulses to the mostly conservatively oriented English architecture through the new impulses of immigrants from Russia and Germany and thus created the MARS association (Modern Architectural Research), which was founded in 1931 and became the basis for a new development.[44] Berthold Lubetkin (1901–1990), who immigrated from Russia in 1930, created structures for the Zoo at Regent's Park in London (gorilla house and penguin basin of 1933, Fig. 84), as well as exemplary high rises (Highpoint I and II in London, 1936–1938).[45]

84 Berthold Lubetkin: Penguin pool for the zoo in Regent's Park, London (1933)

Serge Chermayeff (* 1900) came from Russia and entered into a partnership with Erich Mendelsohn (1887–1953), who had come from Germany. Together, they erected the beach pavilion De La Warr in Bexhill-on-sea (1935), one of the most significant structures of the time, with walls of glass, balconies, and a curved plan. Walter Gropius and Marcel Breuer came from Germany and joined the English architects for several years. In collaboration with E. Maxwell Fry (* 1899), Gropius built the Village College in Cambridge (1939); Marcel Breuer in collaboration with F. R. S. Yorke (1906–1962), single-family houses and designed the project of a cultural center.[46] Other architects who were active in England during those years were William Lescaze (1896–1969), Well Coates (1895–1958), John Burnet (Raven's Court Park Hospital, London, 1934), and Charles Holden (1875–1960). The underground stations by Holden, such as Wood Green Station and Southgate Station of around 1934, especially correspond to the empiristic tendencies of the time, with their round walls and traditional building materials.

English architecture of the 1930s culminated in the structures by E. Owen Williams (1890–1969). Architectural engineering and architecture became one. The chemical factory in Beeston (1930–1932), the Empire Pool in Wembley (1934), the Pioneer Health Center in Peckham (1935), the Dollis Hill Synagogue (1937), and the Finsbury Health Center (1939) embody the technical components of architecture in their role of serving as organic functions.[47]

A New Flourishing of Architecture in Holland

Through the pioneering achievements of Hendrik Petrus Berlage and the architects who followed him in Amsterdam, Rotterdam, Hilversum, and Utrecht, Holland had reached a high level in construction around 1930, which gave this small country a certain significance, which had only been achieved in Finland. This development was continued after 1930 without diminishing quality. This is mainly due to the achievements of Johannes Duiker (1890–1935). The Sonnestraal Sanatorium in Hilversum of 1928, like the structure by Alvar Aalto in Paimio, pointed towards a new integration of nature and a rhythm of forms, in the sense of a physical care given to the structure.[48] Duiker's open-air school in Amsterdam of 1930–1932 was another key work (Fig. 85): an elementary school for about 240 children—only later surrounded by housing blocks. The reinforced-concrete skeleton construction in its pure and openly visible form made possible the clear placement of closed and open classrooms. Duiker's and Bijvoet's Goiland Hotel in Hilversum of 1935–1937 was developed with an open combination of hotel, restaurant, café, and theater, which included such natural elements as a water basin and plants. Private and public areas are intertwined and create an ensemble of new social imagination.[49]

Especially in the construction of housing, exceptional results were achieved in Holland. Willem van Tijen (* 1894) developed examples for

85 Johannes Duiker: Open-air school in Amsterdam (1930–1932)

high-rise housing, which were constructed as variants in cooperation with H. A. Maaskant (* 1908), namely the high-rise Bergpolder (1933–1934) and Plaslaan (1937–1938).[50] Exceptional, up-to-date central sport constructions were the stadium in Amsterdam by Jan Wils (1928) and in Rotterdam by Johannes Andreas Brinkman (1902–1949) and L. C. van der Vlugt (1896–1936) in 1940, as well as the indoor pool in Haarlem by J. J. van Loghem in 1932.

Typical structures in neighboring Belgium are the clinic in Charleroi by Marcel Leborgue (1935), the sanatorium in Tombeek by Maxime Brunfaut (1935), as well as the home for convalescent children in Antwerp by L. Stijnen of 1938.[51]

Swiss Architecture After 1930

A new phase of architectural development is visible in a tradition, bound to the country and its specific characteristics in the Scandinavian countries and in England, as well as in Switzerland, around 1930.[52] The housing estate Neubühl near Zürich of 1930, which was planned and constructed by the Swiss Werkbund, is a cooperative effort by the architects Werner M. Moser (* 1896), Emil Roth (* 1893), Alfred Roth (* 1903), Max Ernst Häfeli (1901–1976), Carl Hubacher (* 1897), Rudolf Steiger (* 1900), Paul Artaria (* 1892), and Hans Schmidt (1893–1972).[53] Subsequent buildings, which were characteristic of the situations of the 1930s, are the ones erected by Alfred and Emil Roth, in cooperation with Marcel Breuer for Siegfried Giedion, namely the Doldertal houses in Zürich of 1935–1936 and sports structures by Karl Egender (Stadium in Zürich of 1939), the Congress and Concert Buildings in Zürich by Häfeli, Moser, and Steiger (1939), the School of Arts and Crafts in Bern by Hans Brechbühler (1937–1939), and the Canton Hospital in Zürich, also by Häfeli, Moser, and Steiger (1943–1951).

In architectural engineering, Switzerland is represented by the work of Robert Maillart (1872–1940), who continued the great Swiss tradition of bridge construction.[54] Maillart at-

86 Robert Maillart: Schwandbach Bridge near Bern (1933)

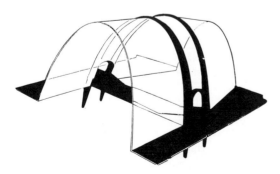

87 Robert Maillart: Design of a cement hall for the National Swiss exhibition in Zürich (1939)

tained construction possibilities and achievements never before accomplished with reinforced concrete. With his Salginatobel bridge of 1929–1930, with a free span of 100 yd. (92 m), a complete integration of technology and nature is reached; the Schwandbach bridge near Bern of 1933 (Fig. 86) even follows the curves of the street and thus brings the technical necessity of the work into visual harmony with the flowing lines of the street.[55] The construction is identical with the street; there is nothing unnecessary that can be deducted from the work. Siegfied Giedion rightfully considered Maillart a symbol of the new cultural effort of around 1930: "It is significant that Maillart made the calculations a servant instead of the master. His bridges satisfy the emotions through their poetic expression and the senses through their delicate balance."[56]

In addition to a number of Maillart's subsequent bridges, there is the cement hall at the Zürich exhibition of 1939 (Fig. 87), which was a pioneering task in international shell architecture. Maillart succeeded in achieving a ceiling thickness of only 2⅜ in. (6 cm) in this hall, which was erected for exhibits, and at the same time in creating an open dynamic spatial form, of basic importance for the subsequent works of Felix Candela (* 1910) in Mexico as well as for engineers in Germany, France, and Rumania.

Spain During the 1930s and 1940s

Candela's homeland, Spain, had achieved imaginative solutions with Antoni Gaudi (1852–1926) and Catalan Art Nouvea, but this high-quality work was not continued at the same level.[57] The painter Salvador Dali (1904–1989) spoke in 1932 of an "edible beauty" in regard to Gaudi's architecture and also expressed in his work the new concept directed towards the organic and the irrational. Spanish architecture after Gaudi's death is marked by early structures of José Luis Sert (1902–1983), as well as the buildings of Eduardo Torroja (1899–1961).[58] Torroja's market hall in Algeciras of 1934 reached a span of 51½ yd. (47.20 m) with the help of the scientific use of reinforced concrete and an octagonal cupola.[59] The major work of Torroja was the roof of the grandstand of the Hippodrome La Zarzuela near Madrid of 1935, which reached a free projection of 13¾ yd. (12.57 m), through the shell-like expanse of the material in hyperbolic paraboloids. Numerous other exemplary structures, as well as a far-reaching occupation of teaching and research at the Research Institute for Concrete in Costillares, were instrumental in making Torroja for decades an international authority in construction with concrete.[60]

Fascist Architecture in Italy

Italy had a Fascist government following 1923. Benito Mussolini (1883–1945), in contrast to other dictators, expressed himself clearly in favor of the modern architecture: "It would be unthinkable, not to be in favor of the rational and functional architecture of our time."[61] Large areas of Italian ar-

88 *Giuseppe Terragni: Casa del Popolo, Como*
    (1934)

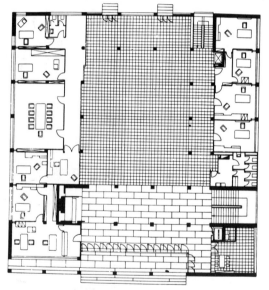

89 *Giuseppe Terragni: Casa del Popolo, Como*
    (1934) plan

chitecture remained, however, at the point of the reestablishment of historical style forms, for example, the buildings and plans by Armando Brasini (1879–1965),[62] which were admired by Mussolini. Also, the views of Marcello Piacentini (1881–1960) determined the opinion of the Fascist Party and were always present as an alternative to rational architecture.[63]

The culmination of twentieth-century Italian architecture was reached in the work of Giuseppe Terragni (1904–1942). His building for the Fascist Party in Como of 1934 (Fig. 88, 89) is an administration building of clearly calculated function and harmonious proportions, precisely placed around a glass-covered courtyard.[64] G. E. Kidder-Smith rightfully called it the most beautiful public building in the country.[65] With the design of the Fascist Party headquarters in Rome of 1934, Terragni progressed to bold spatial forms, which were also self-confident and independent alongside such antique masterworks as the Colosseum and the Basilica of Maxentius.

A view existed that placed rational effectiveness and adequate use of modern materials ahead of symbolic values and decorative provisions as in the epoch-making transportation structures of the Florence railroad station, completed in 1934 by the architects Baroni, Berardi, Gamberini, Guarneri, Lusanna, and Michelucci, as well as of the main Rome railroad station, begun in 1938.[66] The structures engineered by Pier Luigi Nervi (1891–1979) achieved technical ingenuity united with the political will of the regime (Fig. 90). His airplane hangers in Orbetello, Orvieto, and Torre del Mare (1939–1942) are highlights of the international architectural engineering of that time period.[67]

Typical — in the sense of the international turning point around 1930 — are, in Italy, the Heliotherapeutic

90 *Pier Luigi Nervi: Design for the main railroad station in Rome (1943)*

Convalescent Home for Children in Legnano (1937–1938) by Enrico Peresutti (1908–1975), Gian Luigi Banfi (1910–1940), Lodovico di Belgioioso (* 1909), and Ernesto N. Rogers (1909–1969), the Asilo Sant'Elia in Como (1938) by Giuseppe Terragni, the convalescent home for children in S. Stefano d'Aveto (1939–1940) by Luigi Carlo Daneri (* 1900), and the Tuberculosis Hospital in Alessandria (1938) by Ignazio Gardella (* 1905).[68] Subsequent significant architects of the time are Franco Albini (1905–1977), Mario Ridolfi (1904–1984), Giuseppe Samona (1898–1983), Luigi Piccinato (* 1899), and Adalberto Libera (1903–1963). Libera especially excelled in buildings that incorporated the harmonious interpretation of nature and technology

(the house of the writer, Curzio Malaparte, on Capri).

The architectural and urban demonstration of power of the Fascist state is also expressed through major planning projects and in cooperation with diverse architects often of varied political origin, as in the complex of the Stadio de Marmi and the Fascist Party headquarters, which was begun in 1941 by Enrico Del Debbio (1891–1972),[69] the master plan for the University City of Rome (Fig. 91), which was developed under the direction of Marcello Piacentini, in cooperation with Giuseppe Pagano (1896–1945), Gio Ponti (1891–1979), and Giovanni Michelucci, as well as in the planning and fragmentary realization of EUR 42, which was planned for the world exhibition of 1942 in Rome (Figs. 92,

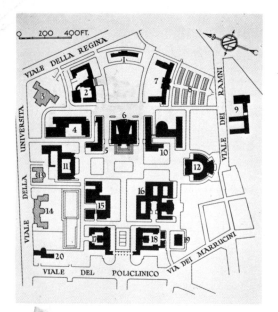

91 Marcello Piacentini: University City of Rome (1933–1935) master plan

93), today a satellite town of Rome. In particular, the various monumental structures for this exhibition and their symbolic urban intertwining with the structuring geared to the dimensions of ancient Rome are to be viewed as most important developments, like Fascist housing, and were hardly surpassed during the postwar times.[70]

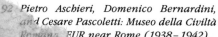

92 Pietro Aschieri, Domenico Bernardini, and Cesare Pascoletti: Museo della Civiltà Romana, EUR near Rome (1938–1942)

93 G. Guerrini, A. La Padula, M. Romano: Palazzo delle Civiltà, EUR near Rome (1938–1942)

National Socialist Architecture in Germany

German architecture after 1930 was in the process of general transformation, when its direction was decisively changed due to the political events of 1933. Buildings by Hugo Häring, Hans and Wassily Luckhardt, Hans Scharoun (Fig. 94), and Richard Doecker corresponded to the new tendencies geared to basic organic principles.[71] In opposition to their work, architecture in Germany after 1933 was regimented in the sense of a neoclassical tradition due to the National Socialist ideology, which was founded by Alfred Rosenberg (1893–1946) and radically realized by Adolf Hitler (1889–1945). The architect Julius Schulte-Frohlinde expressed it clearly in 1936: "Our form of government does not coincide with the expression "modern" which the Führer has once very precisely characterized . . ."[72]

The two most important representatives of National Socialist architecture are Paul L. Troost (1878–1934), whose style was considered by Hitler as a model for many subsequent buildings, and Albert Speer (1905–1981),

94 Hans Scharoun: Home for singles, Breslau (1929) view from the courtyard

95 *Paul L. Troost: Party buildings at the Königsplatz in Munich (1934)*

96 *Werner March: Olympic Stadium in Berlin (1936)*

97 Albert Speer: State Chancery in Berlin (1938–1939)

98 Albert Speer: Zeppelin field in Nürnberg (1936)

whose extensive planning authority and personal contact with Hitler let his architectonic realization grow into gigantic proportions and led to results which had seldom before been possible.[73] Troost's buildings for the party at the Königsplatz in Munich (Fig. 95), as well as the Haus der Kunst, which was completed in 1937, are signs of the new era and are starting points of a National Socialist concept of architecture. A sacral architecture of temples, memorials, and shrines as defined by the party, were the focal point.[74] Even such old structures as Strasbourg Cathedral were to be converted to a memorial to the unknown soldier.[75]

On the other hand, construction of industrial complexes, as for example by Martin Schupp, Fritz Kemmer, Herbert Rimpl, Hans Vaeth, and Albert Speer (rocket center in Peenemünde), as well as transportation buildings (for example, bridges by Paul Bonatz [1877–1956], Ulrich Finsterwalder, and Friedrich Voss) were adapted to functional needs.[76] However, housing construction was especially subject to preconceived planning ideas, forced into the service of National Socialist ideology, since Adolf Hitler was especially interested in housing, according to Alfred Rosenberg.[77] Single-family housing, housing estates, as well as the party schools for the National Socialist youth were planned according to preindustrial ideals and sought a rustic crudeness as in numerous architectural monuments.[78]

Sports also served National Socialist ideology as was shown in the powerful expression of Werner March's Berlin Stadium of 1936 (Fig. 96). It served the Olympic Games of 1936 along with the Maifeld, the Sport Academy, and the House of German Sports. March also sought a historical connection to the Olympia of antiquity, with the games to be transferred to Berlin entirely and permanently after the victory of Hitler's war.[79]

The work of Albert Speer, along with Hitler's own far-reaching architectural plans, became the symbol of the official architecture of the state. Speer visually expressed the ambitions of the manipulated mass-society by means of the Zeppelinfeld, the arena for mass rallies in Nürnberg, with a capacity for about 240,000 people (Fig. 98) and the unfinished Congress Building with 400,000 seats. Barbara Miller Lane rightfully indicated surprising analogies to Egyptian death temples.[80] In 1934, Speer also realized for the first time the light-dome in Nürnberg, with 130 spotlights and 13¼ yd. (12 m) spacing, which was visible at a distance of 3½–9 miles (6–8 km).[81] In 1937, at the world's fair in Paris, he made political points at the German pavilion by architectural means:

At the exhibition area, the building sites of Germany and the Soviet Union were directly across from each other, an intended point of the French directorate of the exhibit. By accident, I lost my way when visiting Paris and ended up in the room where the secret design of the Soviet Pavilion was exhibited: a group of figures on a platform, 10 meters high, strode triumphantly toward the German pavilion. Subsequently I designed a cubic mass, divided into heavy columns, which seemed to stop the assault, while an eagle with a swastika in its claws looked down upon the Russian pair from

99 Albert Speer: "Great hall with cupola," Berlin (1940) project

the ledge of my tower. I received a gold medal for the structure, as did my Soviet colleague.[82]

Speer created the key work of the National Socialist party with the construction of the State Chancery (Fig. 97) in Berlin (1938–1939): "It became a symbol of the revival of Germany, of the triumph of Nazism, and of the future glories of the German people."[83] The building consisted of a powerful neoclassic facade and long halls and passages, which led to the central office of Hitler. One of the leading German art historians, Wolfgang Lotz, compared the completed building in 1940 with the best works of the Italian Renaissance.[84]

In the plans for redesigning Berlin, which were not realized, Speer expressed in a grandiose manner the power and subordination of Hitler's plans. This new urban design with a central north-south axis, which culminated in a huge hall (Fig. 99), was planned as center for the world capital. The diameter of the cupola was projected to be 275 yd. (250 m), the meeting hall was to hold 150,000 to 180,000 people: "The model had been, in a certain sense, the Pantheon in Rome. The cupola in Berlin was also to receive a round opening for light; yet this opening had a diameter of 50 yd. (46 m) and thus surpassed the entire diameter of the cupola of the Pantheon (47 yd.; 43 m) and of the Basilica of St. Peter (48 yd.; 44 m). The interior space covered seventeen times the inner area of St. Peter's Basilica."[85]

The culmination of the tendencies however, which were geared toward war and expansion of power, were the military structures, especially the Atlantic Wall, a fortification system from Norway to France. In its functional design in reinforced concrete and accordingly modernist formal language, the numerous bunkers, submarine depots, and other military tasks the majority of the national resources were invested and they thus served, as in the other warfaring countries of the period, the destructive general strategies. It is significant that it was the language of modern architecture which made these gigantic anti-human structures possible.[86]

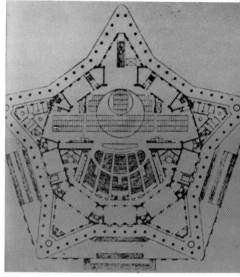

100   K. S. Alabyan and W. Simbirzev: Theater of the Red Army in Moscow (1934–1939) plan

Stalinistic Architecture in Russia

Numerous Russian and foreign architects had participated in the contest for the Palace of the Soviets in Moscow in 1931. The first prize was bestowed upon the team of Jofan, Helfreich, and Shukov and indicated clearly the direction of the development that Russian architecture was to take for more than two decades and that conformed to Stalin's (1879–1953) view of state and culture. The Russian Pavilion at the world's fair in Paris of 1937 by B. F. Jofan can be understood as Stalin's programmatic representation of art, just as the German Pavilion across the way was the expression of Hitler's ideas.

Among the influential architects of the new style of socialist realism, as proclaimed by Stalin, were W. G. Helfreich and V. A. Shchuko (1878–1949), who also built the Gorky Theater in Rostow (1930–1935) and the Lenin Library in Moscow (1937–1939).[87] Karo S. Alabyan (1897–1959) and Wassily Simbirzev built the Theater of the Red Army in Moscow (1934–1939) and searched for a formal symbolism in accordance with the political building task, by developing the structure from the plan of a five-pointed star (Fig. 100). Here, the prominence of the form seems to be rather hindering the functional process of the interior, more so than was the case with the comparable building of the Pentagon in Washington, D.C., of about the same time period (1934), by Bergstrom and Wittmer (Fig. 101), about which Lewis Mumford wrote: "An effete and worthless baroque concept, resurrected in the nineteenthirties by the United States military engineers, and magnified into an architectural catastrophe." The building of the Supreme Soviet in Kiev by V. I. Zabolotni of 1939 has strong baroque elements added to the basic neoclassicism.[88]

A further component of Russian architecture of the 1930s is shown by the architects L. R. Rudnev and W. O. Minz. The blocklike monumental uniformity creates an analogy to Stalin's militaristic ambition regarding the Frunse Academy in Moscow of 1932–1937. Rudnev is further responsible for the equally representative building of Lomonossov University in Moscow (Fig. 102) of 1948–1952 (in cooperation with S. J. Tschernischov, P. W. Abrossimov, and A. F. Chrjakov), whose powerful, symmetrically conceptionalized silhouette is a distinctive symbol of the city, but conforms to American skyscrapers of an earlier period, about which Malevich had warned many years before. Here, as well as there, the focus is on dimension and outer values: the building is 262½ yd. (240 m) high, the depth of the shaft measures 207¾ yd. (190 m) with a width of 492 yd. (450 m). Yet this monumental effect from a distance was obtained by means of functional handicaps in the interior: "The initially regimented horizontal and vertical forms are making a good functional solution rather difficult with regard to clarity and the use of the building."[89]

101 G. E. von Bergstrom and Wittmer: Pentagon in Washington, D.C. (1934)

France Between 1930 and 1950

As usual in regard to international architecture, the work of Le Corbusier of around 1930 shows a turning point, which leads him away from rather abstract solutions to more and more empirically founded plans and buildings (Fig. 103). His Swiss Pavilion in the Paris Cité Universitaire (1930–1931), his building for the Salvation Army in Paris (1931), and city planning for Algiers (1930, Fig. 104), Antwerp, and Rio de Janeiro (1936), as well as the plan for the reconstruction of the city of St. Dié (1945), which was destroyed during the war, were anticipated to be realized in adjustment to the circumstances. The planning and initial realization of the Unité d'Habitation in Marseilles (1947–1952) was the long-awaited crowning achievement of Le Corbusier's work.[90] Free of restrictions from the building authorities and thus above the building laws at that time, Le Corbusier realized his prototype of a vertical city unit with 337 single-family houses with 23 variable types, similar to two-story apartments, arranged in 14 stories, with a shopping and service tier inserted in the middle of the floors, and topped off with roof gardens and sports facilities. The block, which is 61¼ yd. (56 m) high and 171¾ yd. (157 m) long, is an important organizational element in the urban context (Fig. 105).[91]

Besides Le Corbusier, whose work and example reached numerous countries on earth, mainly through the

103 Le Corbusier: Villa Savoye, Poissy (1929–1931)

association of the CIAM (International Congresses for Modern Architecture), the buildings by Pierre Chareau (1883–1950) in France after 1930 must be pointed out, especially his Maison de Verres in Paris of 1931–1932, as well as the structures of André Lurçat (1892–1970), namely his school in Villejuif of 1931–1933, and the works by Eugène Beaudouin (* 1898) and Marcel Lods (1891–1978), which strongly conform to the sentiment of the time, pointing toward the organic and the integration of technology into nature.[92] Beaudouin and Lods created — with the Cité de la Muette in Drancy in 1933–1935 — a housing unit of 1,200 apart-

104 Le Corbusier: Design for a city street, Algiers (1930)

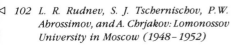

◁ *102 L. R. Rudnev, S. J. Tschernischov, P. W. Abrossimov, and A. Chrjakov: Lomonossov University in Moscow (1948–1952)*

105 Le Corbusier: Unité d'Habitation in Marseille (1947–1952)

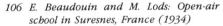

106 E. Beaudouin and M. Lods: Open-air school in Suresnes, France (1934)

ments of high rises and row houses in a mixed layout, as well as the open-air school in Suresnes of 1934, a building complex structured by means of pavilions, ramps, and covered walkways, and an organic total connection between nature and buildings was achieved (Fig. 106).[93] Their design for the competition of an exhibition hall with a hanging roof in 1934 finally created an epoch-making principle of the synthesis of architecture and architectural engineering. And the Maison du

107 J.-C. Dondel, A. Aubert, P. Viard, and M. Dastuge: Museum of Modern Art, Paris (1937)

Peuple in Clichy was created in 1938 in cooperation with Jean Prouvé (1901–1984) and W. Bodiansky. It was a multipurpose building, which could be used for a market, meetings, and as a cinema in various flexible ways.[94]

Beside these more or less modern and rational forms of architecture, in France a strong tendency towards neoclassicism can also be recognized, one which meets the official task of the state as an expression of power.

Auguste Perret's Museum for Public Work in Paris of 1937, as well as the Museum of Modern Art in Paris by the architects Jean-Claude Dondel (* 1904), André Aubert (* 1905), Paul Viard (1880–1943), and Marcel Dastuge (1881–1970) of 1937 (Fig. 107), correspond to comparable buildings in Germany, Russia, and Italy and are thus variants of the different stages of a conservative international architecture after 1930.

III

Syncretic Tendencies: Urbanistic Architecture and Building Within a Context

The International Situation After 1950

Architectural development around 1950 brought a new transformation, comparable to those around 1910 and 1930, which now expressed not only the worldwide expansion of regional activities, but also the newly created building tasks and changed methods and their solution. A great number of problems derived from the massive destruction of World War II and resulted in debates in regard to the character and goals of their reconstruction.[1] For example, new forms of building were developed that were no longer founded on the principles of support and the weight of wall and roof, but were constituted by the difference in air pressure. Materials in tension and the building of mobile elements were now possible.[2] The most

elementary as well as the highest development of technology, with regard to works in art and architecture, appeared in an immediate and authentic form, no longer translated metaphorically. The launch pads for rockets in the John F. Kennedy Space Center in Florida by Max Urbahn (1962–1966) are mobile casings consisting of vertical units, as high as skyscrapers, with the focus on functionality (Fig. 132).

Among the leading new architectural tasks, which replaced the factory as a type signifying the time around 1910 and that of the sanatorium signifying the time around 1930, a great number could be mentioned: nuclear power plants, airports, temporary exhibition halls, and vacation homes.[3] Yet, this dominance of diversity was added to the complexity of coordinated hybrid forms—multipurpose halls and buildings, structures which can serve changing demands are symptomatic.[4] Dynamic construction and lightweight buildings opened up opportunities, which did not exist until then. Re-use, speedy construction, even buildings that erect themselves were conceived, with an added totally new relation to the existing environment and tradition.[5]

Remarkable also was the renewed attention directed to basic questions, seeking to develop new forms of a new architectural theory.[6] The relation to other art forms such as sculpture, painting, music, dance, film, and literature changed decisively; buildings could even be viewed as themes for artists.[7] The cliché of earlier, generally accepted approaches was questioned, and the axiom of "modern architecture" of times past was pointed out with retrospective irony: "Serious architects became obsessed with the idea that structure should be 'expressed honestly.' Honestly usually meant straight lines and right angles."[8]

The theoretical vocabulary after 1950 produced expressions such as "group form" or "collective form" that tried to transcribe a concept new to this time period.[9] The single, isolated building was no longer the focal point, rather the connection of a group of buildings with a similar or integrated function. Adaptability, openness, and flexibility were especially demanded for urbanism, and comprehensive systems have superseded the perfect isolated object that had been viewed as a totality with regard to the architectural work.[10] It was rightfully spoken of "urbanistic architecture" as

well as of the necessity to avoid "planned mistakes": "Many illnesses and inadequacies of our present cities, indeed of our total postwar reconstruction, were planned mistakes, were the grafting of false assumptions of any kind of conception and theories on a differing practice."[11] City planning and architecture with comprehensive goals had therefore increased significantly, and architects such as Aldo van Eyck, Arata Isozaki, Aldo Rossi, and Rob Krier have consequently suggested ways to achieve their fusion.[12]

Architecture in the United States After 1950

American architecture between 1950 and 1970 was a mirror image of the international development, due to the complexity and the co-existing numerous tendencies.[13] The wealth of significant clients, the co-existence of various social groups, and the large number of immigrants from all parts of the world made the United States the center of innovation, but at the same time, it also became the arena for a tense power play. Several generations had worked side by side, and a hybrid situation of immense richness resulted.

Frank Lloyd Wright, an architect of the older generation, continued to be active, yet not only with regard to works of less radiance, but with provocative contributions of lasting significance.[14] The Price Tower in Bartlesville, Oklahoma (1953–1956), shows an imaginative imprint on the high-rise housing structure, representing an important alternative to the Unité d'Habitation by Le Corbusier and the high-rise buildings by Mies van der Rohe. He inserted a spatially free form into the urban context with the Solomon R. Guggenheim Museum in New York (1956–1959) (Fig. 108), and created a unity of building and landscape in the Community and Administration center of Marin County in San Rafael, California (1959–1961). Wright also built a number of fascinating religious buildings during the last years of his life, which were partly completed only after his death: the Beth Sholem Synagogue in Elkins Park, Pennsylvania (1959), the Unitarian Church in Madison, Wisconsin (1965), and the Orthodox Church in Wauwatosa, near Milwaukee (1961). There are also buildings for education, public and private administration, and a great number of unexecuted projects about which Henry Russell Hitchcock commented: "Future generations have more material from Wright than they are able to process in the near future: a tremendous oeuvre, a huge amount of truly fascinating drawings, and a whole legacy of publications, which accompany his works."[15]

But the old masters of international architecture, besides Wright, have also left their lasting visible traces in American architecture: Gropius, Mies van der Rohe, Le Corbusier, Mendelsohn, Nervi, Aalto, and Eliel Saarinen.[16] None of them, however, had been able to create a tradition that joined the present and the past in such an inseparable way as Wright has done through his work. Walter Gropius in-

108 Frank Lloyd Wright: Design of the Guggenheim Museum, New York (1956–1959)

*109 L. Mies van der Robe: Farnsworth house,
Plano, Illinois (1945–1950)*

fluenced the younger generation predominantly through his teachings at
Harvard. His Graduate Center at Harvard University (1949–1950, Fig. 74)
was the beginning of a number of education buildings, which he could realize in cooperation with the team of
former pupils called "The Architect's
Collaborative" (TAC), founded in
1945.[17] Many subsequent buildings by
Gropius, mainly single-family houses,
were developed in cooperation with
Marcel Breuer.[18] Numerous assign-
ments in foreign countries could be
carried out by Gropius with TAC: the
American Embassy in Athens (1961),
the University City in Baghdad
(1962), as well as an apartment block
in Berlin and factories in Berlin and
Hamburg. The urban work of the unexecuted Boston Bay Back Center
(1953) and the Pan-Am Building in
New York (1961) show his arrival at
gigantic dimensions and simplified
forms. A great number of younger architects such as Paul Rudolph
(* 1918), Hugh Stubbins (* 1912),
John Johansen (* 1916), and John Andrews (* 1933) were decisively influenced by Gropius, even though
subsequently going their own way.

The greatest lasting influence on architecture in the 1950s and 1960s, besides Wright, was that of Ludwig Mies
van der Rohe, through his teaching
position at the Illinois Institute of
Technology in Chicago and the exemplary buildings executed by him in
America, among them the entire
campus complex of the Illinois Institute of Technology in Chicago (1938–
1955).[19] The concept of Mies van der
Rohe, which was directed toward industrialization and harmonious proportions, corresponded with the
American tendency toward standardization. During his productive years in
Chicago, Mies van der Rohe built the
house for Dr. Edith Farnsworth in
Plano, Illinois (1945–1950, Fig. 109),
the high-rise apartment block on Lake
Shore Drive in Chicago (1951), the
Seagram Building in New York
(1955–1958, in cooperation with Philip Johnson, Fig. 110), as well as numerous other buildings, which are
variants of these given prototypes.[20]
Mies van der Rohe was also active
beyond the borders of the United
States by building in Mexico, Germany (the National Gallery in Berlin
of 1963–1968), and Canada, while his
influence expanded into nearly all
countries on earth.[21] Large-scale

works by Skidmore, Owings, and Merrill, as well as the early phases of the work of Minoru Yamasaki, Philip Johnson, I. M. Pei (Fig. 111), C. F. Murphy, and Schipporeit and Heinrich are clearly influenced by the concepts of Mies van der Rohe. Especially the work of Louis Skidmore (1897–1962), Nathaniel Owings (1903–1984), and John D. Merrill (1896–1975), with their chief designers Walter Netsch (* 1920) and Gordon Bunshaft (1909–1990), have formed significant parts of the American environment. A development, swaying between innovation and consolidation which began with Mies van der Rohe, covers a wide span from the Lever House in New York, designed by Gordon Bunshaft and completed in 1952, to the buildings of the Inland Steel Company in Chicago (1955–1957), designed by Walter Netsch, the Pepsi-Cola Company in New York (1961), and the Fourth Financial Center in Wichita (1972–1974, Fig. 112) to the John Hancock Center (1969) and Sears Tower in Chicago (1970–1974), as well as the First Wisconsin Plaza in Madison (1975, Fig. 113).[22] Nor can these traditions be denied, in reference to C. F. Murphy's Administration Center in Chicago (1966), Minoru Yamasaki's (* 1912) World Trade Center in New York (1960–1976, Fig. 114), as well as the Lake Point Tower in Chicago (1968) by Schipporeit and Heinrich, the latter based on an earlier design by Mies van der Rohe.

Even Le Corbusier influenced American architecture, first through the project of the building of the United Nations in New York (1947), which was later (1948–1950) realized with significant alterations by the firm of Wallace Harrison (1895–1981) and Max Abramovitz (* 1908), and through the Center for Visual Arts at Harvard University in Cambridge (1961–1964, Fig. 115), seeking to envision a new educational concept.[23] The Building for Environmental Design in Berkeley by Vernon de Mars and John Esherick (1964, Fig. 116) and the Town Hall in Boston by Kallmann, McKinnel, and Knowles (1962–1968) can be considered as fashioned after the Center for Visual Arts of Harvard. José Luis Sert (1902–1983) also follows in the tradition of Le Corbusier with his buildings (Law and Education Building, Boston University, 1963; Married Students Dormitories, Harvard University, 1964).[24]

Richard Neutra (1892–1970) had greater regional influence, namely in California, and through individual tasks, as compared to the old masters and their effect on American architecture.[25] His goal was the integration of the house and the given landscape and vegetation, without neglecting the technological components. Thus, single-family houses, for example, the house for Warren D. Tremaine in Santa Barbara, California (1947–1948) must be especially pointed out, as well as the community facilities (Eagle Rock Community Center, 1954) and holiday hotels where Neutra's achievements are most apparent.[26]

Erich Mendelsohn, Pier Luigi Nervi, and Alvar Aalto, like numerous other Europeans, have enlivened the American architectural scene only with single buildings, first Mendelsohn with

110 L. Mies van der Robe and Philip Johnson: Seagram Building, New York (1955– 1958)

111 I. M. Pei: John Hancock Building, Boston (1975)

112 L. Skidmore, N. Owings, and J. D. Merrill: Fourth Financial Center, Wichita, Kansas (1972–197

113 L. Skidmore, N. Owings, and J. D. Merrill: First Wisconsin Plaza, Madison, Wisconsin (1975)

114 *Minoru Yamasaki: World Trade Center, New York (1960–1976)*

115 Le Corbusier: Center for Visual Arts at Harvard University, Cambridge, Massachusetts (1961–1964)

the Maimonides Health Center in San Francisco (1946–1950) and the B'Nai Amoona Synagogue in St. Louis (1950, Fig. 117)[27]; Aalto with the student housing project of M.I.T. in Cambridge, Massachusetts (1947–1949); and Nervi with the George Washington Bridge Bus Terminal in New York (1962, Fig. 118).

However, the number of architects from foreign countries working in the United States is much larger: Matthew Nowicki (1910–1950) from Poland was a pioneer in lightweight construction with his hall in Raleigh, North Carolina (1950–1953), also opening up new possibilities for the construction of multipurpose halls.[28] Serge Chermayeff (* 1900) from Russia, Konrad Wachsmann (1901–1980) and Oswald M. Ungers (* 1926) from Germany, Friedrich St. Florian and Raimund Abraham from Austria, and Jerzy Soltan (* 1913) from Poland stood out chiefly as teachers; Eduardo Catalano, Cesar Pelli, Rodolfo Ma-

116 V. de Mars and J. Esherick: Environmental Design Building, Berkeley (1964)

chado, Jorge Silvetti (* 1942), Diana Agrest and Mario Gandelsonas, and Rafael Vinoly from Argentina; John Andrews from Australia; Paolo Soleri from Italy; Moshe Safdie from Israel; and James Stirling from England influenced the American scene with works and concepts that will be discussed later.

Besides the large architectural firms such as Skidmore, Owings, and Merrill, or Harrison and Abramovitz, as well as Hellmuth, Obata, and Kassabaum, the achievement of the individual architect became nevertheless significant. During his few years of independent work, Eero Saarinen (1910–1961) made a particular contribution to American architecture.[29] Saarinen's work shows tremendous change, seen as typical during this

117 Erich Mendelsohn: B'Nai Amoona Synagogue in St. Louis (1950)

118 Pier Luigi Nervi: Bus terminal at the George Washington Bridge in New York (1962)

transitional period of American architecture: the Technical Center of General Motors in Warren, near Detroit (1949–1956), which had been started together with his father, Eliel Saarinen, still shows a clearly noticeable influence of Mies van der Rohe. The Chapel and the Kresge Auditorium of the Massachusetts Institute of Technology in Cambridge (1954–1955) and the Hockey Stadium of Yale University in New Haven (1956–1958) show a detachment from the classical model in the sense of a stronger inclusion of engineering elements, in order to finally find a figurative, dynamic conception within the two airport buildings in New York (1958–1962) and Chantilly (1958–1962, Fig. 119), which showed the mastery of the new perception of space with a sufficient balance of architecture and architectural engineering.[30]

Saarinen's more personal tradition is brought to a more systematic level and to internationally relevant results, which significantly influence our time, through the work of the architects Kevin Roche (* 1922) and John Dinkeloo (1918–1981), who were both former collaborators of Saarinen and continued his firm.[31] The twelve-story Ford Foundation building in New York (1966–1967) shows the successful concept of an office high rise that includes city space. The complex of the Knights of Columbus and the Veterans Museum in New Haven

119 Eero Saarinen: Dulles International Airport, Chantilly, Virginia (1958–1962)

120 K. Roche and J. Dinkeloo: Oakland Museum, California (1973)

(1969–1970) combine urban flow and architecture. A park landscape is integrated in a museum complex of terraces (Fig. 120) made up of grouped building elements to form the Oakland Museum, and signlike design forms were created for the office high rise, leading to a new phase of development through such commissions as the administration building of the College Life Insurance Company in Indianapolis (1967–1973, Fig. 122), as well as the building of the United Nations Development Corporation in New York (1976).

Among the American architects of the middle generation, Paul Rudolph (* 1918) started out being influenced by his teacher Walter Gropius in his early work, but soon arrived at independent solutions.[32] The stages of his development are marked by the School of Art and Architecture at Yale University in New Haven (1958–1964), the Laboratory Building of the Endo firm in Garden City, New York (1966), and the project of the New York Graphic Arts Center, which was developed in 1967 combining prefab-

121 Philip Johnson: Kline Science Center Tower, Yale University, New Haven, Connecticut (1964–1966)

122 K. Roche and J. Dinkeloo: Administration building of the College Life Insurance Company, Indianapolis (1967–1973)

123 Gunnar Birkerts: Federal Reserve Bank, Minneapolis (1968–1973)

124 Bertrand Goldberg: High-rise housing, Marina City, Chicago (1964)

rication and terrace construction within a coherent plan.

Philip Johnson is in a line of descent from Mies van der Rohe.[33] His own house in New Canaan, Connecticut (1949), already translates his teacher's expression of form into a more realistic and clear, down-to-earth building method, pursued with consistency in the examples of subsequent single-family houses, museums, and education buildings (for example, the Kline Science Tower, Yale University in New Haven (1964–1966, Fig. 121), so that a historic-eclectic conception of architecture developed, which is hardly any longer related to that of Mies van der Rohe.[34] Additionally, there is an element of Pop architecture constituted by means of colored plastic material and flexible, open spatial forms, as was the case in the exhibition buildings of the New York State Pavilion at the World's Fair in New York in 1964.

Individual achievements with personal characteristics are seen in the buildings of a large group of architects, unmistakably imprinted by the personality of their creator: Harry Weese (* 1915), Edward Larraby Barnes (* 1915), Gunnar Birkerts (* 1925) with the building of the Federal Reserve Bank in Minneapolis (1968–1973, Fig. 123), Cesar Pelli (* 1926) with the San Bernardino City Hall in California (1974–1975, Fig. 135), John Johansen (* 1916) with the Mummer's Theater in Oklahoma (1968),[35] Ehrman B. Mitchell (* 1924) and Romaldo Giurgola (* 1920) and Bertrand Goldberg (* 1913) with the high-rise housing group,[36] Marina City in Chicago (1964, Fig. 124).[37] This subjectivism is exaggerated and loses

the relevancy of Frank Lloyd Wright's original empathy for the task, in the works of Bruce Goff (1904–1982), such as the Bavinger House in Norman, Oklahoma (1957), and of Herb Greene (* 1929), such as the Prairie House in Norman, Oklahoma, of 1961.

Louis I. Kahn and the Young Generation

The comparison of the multitude of buildings by American architects, founded on subjective and highly expressive efforts, marks the exceptional significance of the work of Louis I. Kahn (1901–1974), who can be placed among the old masters from this perspective, and who leads to a new synthesis independent of the conceptions of Wright, Le Corbusier, and Mies van der Rohe (see Fig. 125). Kahn's work and teachings fuse past and present into a new unity.[38] His far-reaching philosophy of architecture and the integration of traditional values into contemporary practice has influenced international architecture in a provocative manner, as no other architect of our time has achieved. His five primary concerns can be reduced to 1) concern for composition and the integrity of the structure, 2) respect for the material, 3) concern for space as the essence of architecture, 4) light as the shape of the structure, and 5) the architecture of connections. Kahn was concerned with founding a new architectural articulation in a sense similar to what Gertrude Stein (1874–1946) had done in literature, when she formulated: "I like the feeling of words doing what they want to do and not what they have to do."[39] Kahn

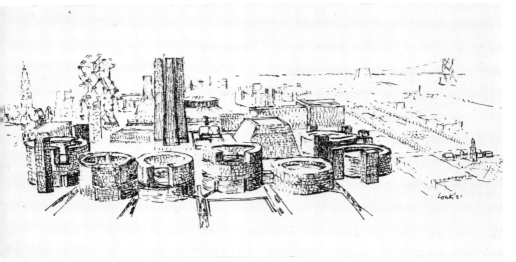

125 Louis I. Kahn: Design for the center of a city (1957)

imagined what a building wanted to be and thus arrived at the imminent laws of the singular values of the total reality of space.

Louis I. Kahn had developed his own independent solutions relatively late and only after many years of work in other architectural firms. His Art Gallery at Yale University in New Haven (1951–1953, Fig. 126), his Bath House of the Jewish Community Center in Trenton, New Jersey (1955–1956), and the Research Laboratories of the University of Pennsylvania in Philadelphia (1958–1960, Fig. 127) had, however, an immediate worldwide influence on architectural concepts.[40] These tasks are further expanded and the soundness of the underlying idea is proven through the projects such as the Unitarian Church in Rochester, New York (1959–1962), the Salk Institute in La Jolla, California (1964–1968), as well as the Philips-Exeter Academy Library in Exeter, New Hampshire (1967–1972), and the Kimball Art Museum in Fort Worth (1967–1972). However, highlights of

126 Louis I. Kahn: Art Gallery of Yale University in New Haven, Connecticut (1951–1953)

127 Louis I. Kahn: Research Institute of the University of Philadelphia (1958–1960) plan of the first floor

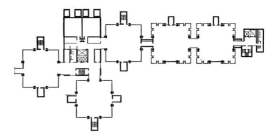

Kahn's work are in India (Indian Institute of Management in Ahmedabad, 1966–1967) and Bangladesh (plans for the capital of Dacca and construction of the central government buildings started in 1968 and completed in 1982).[41]

The influence and liberating effect of Louis Kahn on the architects of the younger generation should not be underestimated, although an immediate causal relationship or direct connection cannot always be proven. Nevertheless, these effects are clearly expressed in the works of numerous architects, for example, in the buildings and publications of Charles Moore (* 1925) and Roberto Venturi (* 1925). Both are successful — in quite different ways — in opening up the formalistically restrictive character of the new architecture, in order to be able to take the given facts more into account and to bring man and his environment into a realistic harmony.[42]

This is demonstrated by Charles Moore and the housing in New Haven, Connecticut (1966–1972), the Faculty Club of the University of California in Santa Barbara (1968), the ten Sea Ranch vacation houses in Big Sur, California (1966, in collaboration with Donlyn Lyndon, Turnbull and Whitacker, Fig. 128),[43] and housing and office buildings. Venturi's Guild House in Philadelphia (1960–1963,

128 Moore, Lyndon, Turnbull, Whitaker: Sea Ranch, Big Sur, California (1966)

129 Roberto Venturi: Guild House, Philadelphia (1960–1963)

130 John Esberick: "The Cannery" shopping center, San Francisco (1968)

Fig. 129), the building of the faculty of Mathematics at Yale University in New Haven (1970–1976) and the Art Museum at Oberlin College at Oberlin, Ohio (1973–1976), as well as numerous other single-family houses reveal an previously unknown freedom from formal clichés and an original freshness in problem solving. A new relation to tradition was thus made possible, as was also shown in the ever-increasing efforts for reusing older buildings for new purposes (recycling). John Esherick's shopping center "The Cannery" in San Francisco of 1968 (Fig. 130) is one of the most prominent examples.[44]

The best possible application of technical and scientific results of research is manifested in Richard Buckminster-Fuller's radar stations, exhibition buildings (Fig. 131) and projects for buildings on the moon, as well as in Max Urbahn's mobile structures for the Kennedy Space Center in Florida (1962–1966, Fig. 132). Private experiments also sought to bring together architecture for mass use and technology on a new level. Examples are the plans of Disneyland in Los Angeles[45] and Disney World in Florida (1972) by Welton Beckett.[46] Yet, in general, a specific characteristic applies especially to architecture in southern California: "In Los Angeles, a billboard often takes the place of a building — or a building replaces a billboard."[47]

131 Richard Buckminster-Fuller: American pavilion of the Montreal world's fair (1967)

132 Max Urbahn: Launching ramps at Cape Kennedy, Florida (1962–1966)

136 *Viljo Revell: Town Hall in Toronto, Canada (1965)*

137 *John Andrews: Scarborough College in Toronto (1964–1966)*

135 *Cesar Pelli: City Hall in San Bernardino, California (1974–1975)*

138 *Moshe Safdie: Habitat '67, Montreal (1967)*

The most spectacular Canadian buildings stem from foreign architects: the Finnish architect Viljo Revel built the town hall in Toronto (1958– 1965, Fig. 136) in cooperation with John B. Parkin. The Italian Luigi Moretti (1907–1973) built the Torre della Borsa in Montreal (1964–1965) and the Australian John Andrews (* 1933) created at Scarborough College in Toronto (1964–1966, Fig. 137) an educational complex based on a new linear conception and internalized circulation.[52] Andrews continued with a second educational building, the Student Housing project of the University of Guelph, which was completed in 1969, while maintaining his architectural conception, geared towards a comprehensive linear structure. Significant buildings in the United States by Andrews are the Gund Hall at Harvard (1969–1972) and the passenger terminal at the Miami Beach, Florida, pier (1967).[53]

In 1967, Moshe Safdie (* 1938) built experimental housing units, Habitat '67, for the Montreal world's fair. These units were developed from the terrace principle, seeking new possibilities for mass housing (Fig. 138), by means of industrial production of the units (14 × 6.5 × 4 yd.; 13 × 6 × 3.5 m). Initially, 900 apartments for approximately 5,000 inhabitants were planned. However, only 158 apartments for approximately 700 inhabitants were completed in 1967, which explains the considerable rise in cost.[54] Safdie was able to develop his principle further with regard to new projects for New York (1968), Puerto Rico (1968–1971), and Jerusalem (1969).[55]

European Architecture After World War II

In comparison with the situation of architecture in the United States and Canada, architecture in most European countries was determined by the catastrophic results of World War II. Besides the great destruction and the nearly complete cessation of private building during the war years, and the concentration on construction in the interest of war, resulted in a significantly modified architectural view.[56] Reconstruction problems also significantly determined the building volume in Russia, Poland, Germany, France, and England, yet the opportunity for a changed concept in planning was, in most cases, not utilized.[57] The great financial difficulties and the necessary rapidity of reconstruction also lowered quality. Most countries accepted without criticism the often obsolete models of prewar urbanism and produced thus a false continuity, which did not correspond to the new situation.

City Planning and Educational Buildings in England

Plans that were already prepared by Sir Patrick Abercrombie (1879–1957) during the last years of the war elevated urban planning and restoration to a new level, and errors as in many other countries were thus avoided. Satellite cities such as Stevenage (1966) and Harlow (1966), planned by Frederick Gibberd (* 1908) and Hemel Hampstead, developed during the first years after the war.[58] A new

139 James Stirling: Housing quarters in Runcorn New Town (1967–1974)

phase appeared, "the second generation of new towns" and turned into a changed conception, due to higher housing density of cities like Cumbernauld (planner Hugh Wilson), Thamesmead, Runcorn, Irvine, and Milton Keynes, arriving at intensively discussed solutions, especially regarding Cumbernauld and Milton Keynes, the latter planned by Llewelyn and Davis in 1970.[59]

Housing developments in London, often erected under the patronage of the London County Council, offered rich alternatives. Churchill Gardens (1948–1962) by Philip Powell (* 1921) and Hidalgo Moya (* 1920), as well as Golden Lane (1952) by Chamberlain, Powell, and Bon are examples of an urban concept, as had not existed before the war. The social housing of James Stirling (1926–

1992) in Runcorn New Town (1967–1974, Fig. 139), attempted to integrate various social groups as well as open semi-public spaces into a new neighborhood, but failed to survive social tensions. It was demolished in 1990.

The "Festival of Britain" in 1951 brought an initial coordination of strengths targeted towards a new beginning and culminated in the great Festival Hall by Robert Matthew (1906–1975) and the "Dome of Discovery" by Ralph Tubbs (* 1912). The Concert Building at the southern bank of the Thames (1960–1967), erected by Hubert Bennett and the London City Council, placed a further accent, finally reaching a conclusion with the National Theater (Figs. 140, 141), which was designed by Denys Lasdun and was a crowning point at its completion in 1976.[60]

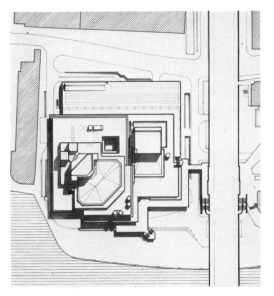

140 *Denys Lasdun: National Theatre, London (1976) site plan*

English school buildings are conceptualized with standardization in mind and as a public enterprise. The architects chiefly occupied with this task are the firm Architects' Company Partnership, James Cubitt, Drake and Lasdun, Rosenberg, Yorke and Mardall, as well as Ove Arup (* 1895).

141 *Denys Lasdun: National Theatre, London (1976)*

142 Patrick Hodgkinson: Terrace complex, Foundling Court, Bloomsbury, London (1970–1972)

143 J. Stirling and J. Gowan: Faculty of Engineering building of the University of Leicester (1960–1963)

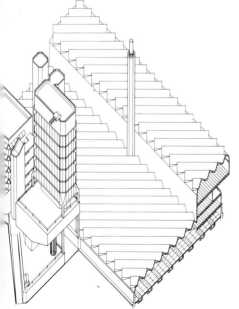

144 Cedric Price: "Thinkbelt" project (1963)

145 Ron Herron: Walking City (1964) project

English university architecture has developed, to an even greater degree, forms of an exemplary maturity, which can be detected in buildings by Sir Leslie Martin (* 1908), Denys Lasdun, and James Stirling (1926–1992). Sir Leslie Martin found exemplary solutions with regard to the Gonville and Caius College in Cambridge (1960–1962), as well as the Departments of Zoology and Psychology in Oxford (1966–1971).[61] Denys Lasdun was able to unite linear structures and terraced buildings to form a megastructure at the University of East Anglia (1962–1964). Regarding outstanding individual buildings, James Stirling's and James Gowan's (* 1924) Faculty of Engineering project at the University of Leicester (1960–1963, Fig. 143) stand out, as well as James Stirling's Institute of History in Cambridge (1965–1966).[62]

Since the 1950s, the architects Peter Smithson (* 1923) and Alison Smithson (* 1928) have had a stimulating effect on English architecture.[63] Their school in Hunstanton (1954) and the building for the newspaper *The Economist* in London (1960–1964) are only parts of a far-reaching activity, which was to a great degree discussion and polemics, creating in this way a fruitful effect.[64] The housing developments Golden Lane (1951–1952, projected) and Robin Hood Gardens (1972) created programmatic types of urban mass housing, as did Patrick Hodgkinson's Foundling Court of 1970–1972 (Fig. 142). Cedric Price (* 1934) and the group Archigram with Peter Cook (* 1936), David Greene (* 1937), Michael Webb (* 1937), Ron Herron (* 1930), and

Warren Chalk (* 1927),[65] participated in a stimulating architectural discussion in England to the same extent through visions of urban life in the future (Fig. 145); Cedric Price with provocative projects such as Fun Palace (1961) and Thinkbelt (1963, Fig. 144) and in cooperation with Lord Snowdon, the bird house in the London Zoo (1962–1965).[66]

Model Case—Finland and Scandinavia

Finland and the Scandinavian countries, which were less involved in World War II in Europe, created planning concepts early on, and especially pushed ahead with the construction of satellite cities to ease the burden of the old towns. Farsta, Vällingby (Fig. 146), and Lidingö near Stockholm, Täby Kortedala near Göteborg, and Tapiola near Helsinki (Fig. 147) are excellent examples of newly planned cities, where the most modern results in city planning could be taken into account.[67]

The work of the leading Finnish architect Alvar Aalto (1898–1976) reached complete maturity during the years after 1950. His administration center for Säynätsalo (1950–1952) became the symbol of international efforts, which were geared to regional tradition, the transformation of an object-oriented monumental form into an ensemble of single units, and the integration of function (Fig. 81). Subsequent buildings by Aalto, such as the Finnish Social Insurance project (1952–1957), the church in Imatra (1958), the central Auditorium of the

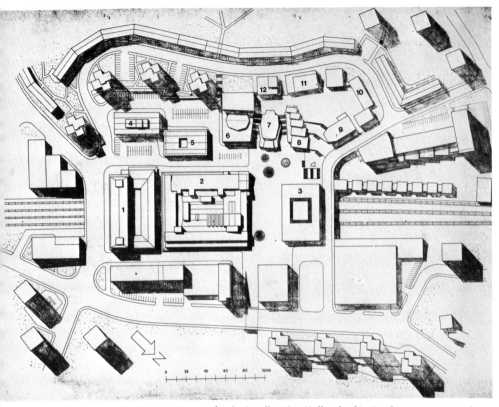

146 S. Backström and L. Reinius: Project for the Satellite City Vällingby (1–3: administration and shopping centers; 4–5: street of shops; 6–12: cultural centers)

Technical University of Otaniemi (1962–1964),[68] the University Center of Helsinki with the Finlandia Hall (1974), as well as numerous buildings in Germany (Fig. 155), Switzerland, France, and America (Library of the Benedictine University, Mont Anyel, in Oregon, 1967–1970), all represent stages in a consistent path of development, with the organic and psychic reality of man always as focal point.[69]

Besides Aalto's buildings in Finland, the structures of the following architects must be pointed out: Viljo Revell (1910–1964), Aulis Blomstedt (1906–1979), Arne Ervi (1910–1977), as well as Kaija Siren (* 1920) and Heikki Siren (* 1918).[70]

The most clearly defined personality is Reima Pietilae (* 1923). His major early work, in collaboration with Raili Paateleinen, the student house "Dipoli" at Otaniemi University (1964–1966), is a powerful synthesis of rational and irrational energy.[71] The Suvikumpu housing development in Tapiola (1968) and the church in Kaleva also supersede Aalto's conception and create free imaginative spatial forms based on reality (Fig. 147).

Within the framework of Swedish architecture, which was greatly supported by the labor unions, the satellite cities (Vällingby, with plans by Backström and Reinius, 1957, Fig. 146) and other housing developments

147 Reima Pietilae: Suvikumpu housing development, Tapiola, Finland (1968)

must be pointed out, along with exceptional individual buildings by Sven Markelius (1889–1972), Fritz Jaenecke (1903–1978), and Stan Samuelson, as well as Ralph Erskine (* 1914).[72]

Norwegian architecture between 1950 and 1970 can be seen as a continuation of the development of the 1930s, and is expressed in late works by Arne Korsmo (1900–1968), as well as by the younger architects who developed under his influence, such as Christian Norberg Schulz, Haakon Mjelva, Sverre Fehn, together with Kjell Lund (* 1927) and Nils Slaato (* 1923).[73]

Like Finland, Denmark has also produced a number of significant architects whose buildings influenced many parts of the world. Arne Jacobson (1902–1971) in his later years erected schools like the one in Gentofte (1952–1956), the town hall in Rödovre (1955–1956), and the SAS building in Copenhagen (1959), all according to a synthesis of form elements of Mies van der Rohe and Scandinavian empiricism.[74] But Jacobson was also active in England, Germany, Sweden, and Pakistan, and furthermore contributed through the buildings of the firm of his former colleagues, Hans Dissing (* 1926) and Otto Weitling (* 1930), to spread the concept of Danish architecture internationally. Eva and Nils Koppel, Erik Christian Sörensen (* 1922),[75] Jörgen Bo (* 1919), Vilhelm Wohlert (* 1920),[76] Halldor Gunlogsson, and Jörn Nilson (* 1919) are among the prominent architects who stand out chiefly for their single-family houses and multiple-housing projects.

Jörn Utzon (* 1918) also became known through his accomplished single-family houses, multiple housing, and spectacular buildings in foreign countries.[77] The Sydney opera house, designed in 1957, and completed by others due to differences of opinion between the architect and the client —Utzon resigned in 1966—can be viewed as one of the epoch-making buildings of a new dynamic architecture.[78] The less-recognized housing developments in Helsingborg (1958–1960) and Fredensborg (1962–1962) are exemplary solutions in the manner of grouping courtyard houses between a closed semi-private land-

148 Jörn Utzon: Housing development in Fredensborg, Denmark (1962–1963)

scape and the public parking area (Fig. 148). Privacy and communication are, in this case, harmoniously combined. Among the numerous unfinished projects of Utzon are the Theater in Zürich (1964), a museum in Aalborg, the Melli Bank in Tehran (1958), and the stadium in Jeddah (1969). Utzon's latest works in the Middle East, such as the Parliament in Kuwait (Fig. 242), are part of the developments since 1970.

Continuation of a Tradition in the Netherlands

The first postwar years in the Netherlands were occupied with large-scale reconstruction of the cities that were destroyed during the war, as well as the reclamation of land for the establishment of new cities.[79] The planning and buildings of the architects Jo-hannes Hendrik van den Broek (1898–1978) and Jacob Beren Bakema (1914–1981) had a great influence on the reconstruction of Rotterdam. The first European area for pedestrians was realized in the shopping center Lijnbaan in Rotterdam (1951). Subsequent individual buildings of the team, which was primarily active in urban planning, are the Montessori Gymnasium in Rotterdam, the auditorium of the Technical University in Delft, and the town hall in Marl, in Germany (1960–1967).[80] Besides van Broek and Bakema, architects such as Herman Haan,[81] Jan Trapman, and Herman Hertzberger (* 1932) must be pointed out, as well as Jan Habraken,[82] Rem Koolhaas (* 1944), and Herman Hertzberger (Fig. 221) who characterize the new developments after 1970.[83]

The most important personality in Holland is Aldo van Eyck (* 1918), whose orphanage in Amsterdam

149 Aldo van Eyck: Children's house in Amsterdam, (1958–1960)

150 Aldo van Eyck: Children's house in Amsterdam (1958–1960) plan of the upper floor

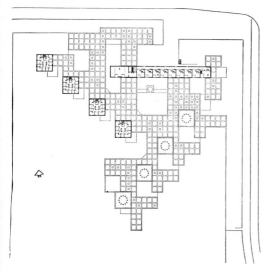

(1958–1960) became known all over the world, due to the exemplary concept of this building.[84] A home for 125 children of all ages was created here, articulating a revolutionary synthesis in the consideration of the individual and the group, inner and outer space, extended and small areas: "The building was conceived as a configuration of intermediary places clearly defined. This does not imply continual transition or endless postponement with respect to place and occasion. On the contrary, it implies a break away from the contemporary concept (call it sickness) of spatial continuity and the tendency to erase every articulation between spaces, i.e., between outside and inside, between one space and another. Instead, I tried to articulate the transition by means of defined in-between places which induce simultaneous awareness of what is signified on either side."[85] Aldo van Eyck re-adopted a previously formulated concept of L. B. Alberti, when realizing the house for children in Amsterdam (Fig. 149, 150), the analogy of city and house: "a small world within a large one, a large world within a small one, a house as a city, a city as a house, a home for the children—to create that was my goal."[86]

France After 1950

French postwar architecture is dominated by the work of Le Corbusier, although Auguste Peret also achieved lasting influence with his reconstruction of Le Havre and Amiens.[87] Le Corbusier's Unité d'habitation in Marseilles (1947–1952) served as an example, but did not have the expected impact on urban rejuvenation as had been anticipated by the architect. Nevertheless, subsequent units were built in Nantes (1952–1953), Berlin (1956–1958), Meaux (1959), Briey-La-Forêt (1957), and Firminy. The other work of Le Corbusier from the early 1950s show the change of his architectural conceptions from the 1920s: With the chapel in Ronchamp (1950–1954), he created a dynamic space (Fig. 151), with the characteristic and meaningfully hanging ceiling.[88] Le Corbusier continued with this dynamic concept of space with the pavilion for the Philips firm at the Brussels world's fair of 1957, here for a temporary exhibit, which integrated light, sound, and picture to form an "electronic poem."[89] He arrived at an integration of brickwork and the technique for vault construction, when using traditional building materials for the construction of the Jaoul houses in Neuilly (1954–1956).

The late works of Le Corbusier include the La Tourette monastery in Eveaux near Lyons (1957–1960), the church St. Pierre in Firminy (1963–1965), and the designs for a high-rise hotel in Paris and a hospital in Venice (1965). The major emphasis of Le Corbusier's work, however, was on his buildings in India, the planning of the city of Chandigarh (1951, Fig. 189) and the construction of the most important administration buildings in this city, the Supreme Court (1952–1956), the Office of the Secretary (1958), and the Parliament (1959–1962), as well as buildings in Ahmedabad (the museum of 1956, the mill

150a Ricardo Porro: Center for Art, Liechtenstein (1969–1975)

owners building of 1954–1956, as well as single-family houses).[90]

City planning and architecture in France are greatly influenced by Le Corbusier. The satellite city Le Mirail near Toulouse (1961) by Georges Candilis (* 1913), Shadrach Woods (1923–1973), and Alexis Josic (* 1921) carries the principles of the old master further, in providing for pedestrian zones on several levels.[91] Vladimir Bodiansky (1894–1966) and the Atbat firm, directed by him, were pioneers in the construction of mass housing in France and North Africa.[92]

151 Le Corbusier: Chapel in Ronchamp (1950–1954)

152 Yona Friedman: "Paris Spatial" (1960) project

153 R. Piano and R. Rogers: Georges Pompidou Cultural Center, Paris (1976)

Eugène Beaudouin built the Cité Rotterdam in Strasbourg in 1951–1953. Emile Aillaud was searching for forms of an ingenious structuring of a city organism when building the housing settlements in the vicinity of Paris and the housing of Forbach (1961–1963).

Outstanding individual buildings are credited to Oscar Niemeyer (Communist party headquarters in Paris, 1971), Guillaume Gillet (* 1912) (church in Royan, 1954–1959), Andrault (* 1926) and Parat (* 1928) (shopping center in Sceaux-les-Blagis, 1958–1961), José Louis Sert (Fondation Maeght in Saint-Paul-de-Vence, 1961–1964), and René Sarger (* 1917) (market hall in Royan, 1955–1956), as well as the experimental houses of Jean Prouvé (1901–1984), Ionel Schein (* 1927), and P. and C. Häussermann. To be recognized further are the vacation houses and hotels by M. Marot and A. Minangoy in Villeneuve Loubet (1970) and Jean Balladur (* 1924) in Languedoc-Roussillon (La Grande Motte). Renzo Piano (* 1937) and Richard Rogers (* 1933) won first prize at the international competition for the Centre Pompidou in Paris (Fig. 153) and, in building the cultural center, erected a multipurpose structure of extraordinary flexibility.[93] Visionary urban concepts were created by Yona Friedman (* 1923) with his plan for "Paris Spatial"[94] (Fig. 152), Alain Bourbonnais (* 1925), and Paul Maymont (* 1926).

German Architecture Between 1950 and 1970

German postwar architecture is marked by the destructions of World War II and determined by speedy reconstruction, as well as the attempt to link up with the time prior to 1933.[95] Architects of the older generation, who were hindered by the rule of National Socialism, now arrived at belated results: Hans Scharoun (1893–1972) with high-rise housing in Stuttgart and the Philharmonic Hall in Berlin (1960–1963, Fig. 154);[96] Wassily Luckhardt (1889–1975) and Hans Luckhardt (1890–1954) with housing and commercial buildings in Berlin and Munich, as well as the Parliament Building in Bremen (1962–1969),[97] and Ernst May (1886–1970) and Walter Schwagenscheidt (1886–1968) with urban design and large housing developments in Hamburg and Frankfurt.[98] The old masters of German architecture from the 1920s also came back to Germany from emigration, for prominent individual commissions: Walter Gropius for high-rise housing in Berlin and factory buildings in Hamburg and Selb (Rosenthal, manufacturing plant for porcelain, 1963–1967) and Mies van der Rohe for the national gallery in Berlin, completed in 1968 and considered to be the climax of his late work.[99]

Besides the German architects, there was a strong foreign influence from architects from other countries, most clearly visible at the International Building Exhibition (Interbau) of 1957 in Berlin in which, among others, Walter Gropius, Oscar Niemeyer, and Alvar Aalto participated.[100] Also active in Germany were Hugh Stubbins (Congress Hall in Berlin, 1957); Philip Johnson (Museum in Bielefeld); Alvar Aalto (cultural center in Wolfsburg and high-rise housing in Bremen-Vahr, Fig. 155);

154 Hans Scharoun: Philharmonic Hall in Berlin (1960–1963)

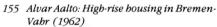

155 Alvar Aalto: High-rise housing in Bremen-Vahr (1962)

van den Broek and Bakema (town hall in Marl); Max Bill (Hochschule für gestaltung in Ulm, 1952–1955); Justus Dahinden (Schwabylon in Munich, 1970–1974); Arne Jacobson, Dissing and Weitling (town hall in Mainz, 1973); and Ernst Gisel (student center in Mainz, 1964–1969).[101]

Those building tasks that found an early and adequate expression in Germany are primarily factory and office buildings. The handkerchief factory in Blumberg (1951) by Egon Eiermann was one of the most prominent postwar buildings. Additional noteworthy architects include Friedrich Wilhelm Kraemer (* 1907), Ernst Neufert, Fritz Schupp,[102] Günter Wilhelm (* 1908), Paul Schneider-Esleben (* 1915), Gerhard Weber (Fig. 156), Helmut Hentrich (* 1905), and Hubert Petschnigg.[103] The type of office high

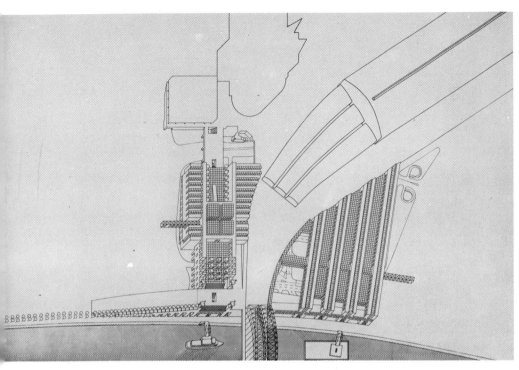

159 *Oswald Mathias Ungers: Design for the new Wallraf-Richardtz Museum and Ludwig Museum in Cologne (1975)*

and research of Frei Otto (* 1925), lightweight construction was advanced scientifically and a great number of buildings for exhibits were realized, which culminated in the German pavilion at the world's fair in Montreal in 1967.[109] In 1972, the architects Günther Behnisch (* 1922) and Partners (Fritz Auer, Winfried Büxel, Manfred Sabadke, Erhard Tränkner, Karl-Heinz Weber) planned Olympia Park on a grand scale, with the stadium and numerous subsequent sports facilities, for the Olympic games in Munich. Günter Grzimek was involved with the planning of the park landscape and Frei Otto and the engineers Fritz Leonhardt and Andreä with the roof.[110] The movable roof of the Abbey Church in Bad Hersfeld of 1968 (Fig. 158) was a fascinating solution by Frei Otto, of the specific task of a modern use for concerts, of a historical monument in which the old substance was unchanged.[111]

Swiss Architecture Between 1950 and 1970

Swiss architecture attained a high standard regarding the construction of schools and housing during these decades.[112] Terrace housing, in particular, was developed, corresponding to the topography of the country, arriving at convincing solutions with examples such as buildings of the group Atelier 5 (Halen housing, 1959–1961, Fig. 161), Stucky and Meuli (housing in

◁ *160 Rob Krier: Diekes house in Luxembourg (1974)*

Zug, 1957–1960) as well as Scherer, Strickler, and Weber (Mühlehalde housing, 1966).[113] The Pyramid at Lake Zürich was developed by Justus Dahinden as a combination of office and housing space.[114] Jacques Schader (Freudenberg Canton School in Zürich, 1958–1961), Dolf Schnebli (* 1928, Swiss school in Naples, Italy, of 1966), as well as Förderer, Otto, and Zwimpfer (University for Trade in St. Gall, 1960–1964), erected exemplary school buildings.[115] Office buildings, such as the Nestlé Building in Vevey of 1960, are by Jean Tschumi (1904–1962). Large housing developments using industrial manufacturing processes were developed in Geneva (Meyrin and Le Legnon), Wintherthurn (Grützefeld), and Bern (Tscharnergut).[116] The youngest generation, formed by Dolf Schnebli and Aldo Rossi, is represented by the buildings of Tita Carloni (* 1931), Bruno Reichlin (* 1941), Fabio Reinhart (* 1942), and especially Mario Botta (* 1943), who after 1970 will emerge as the most important architect of his country.

Building in Austria

Within the framework of Austrian architecture between 1950 and 1970, the following achievements have to

◁ *161 Atelier 5: Housing development Halen near Bern (1959–1961)*

be pointed out: buildings such as the Vienna civic hall (1955–1958) by Roland Rainer (* 1910); the pavilion of Austria at the Brussels world's fair in 1958 (used again in 1964 in the Museum of the Twentieth Century in Vienna) by Karl Schwanzer; the Concert Hall, Brucknerhaus in Linz (1974) by the Finnish architects Kaija and Heikki Siren; and the Retti candleshop (1964–1965) as well as the Schullin jewelry shop (1972–1974, Fig. 162a) by Hans Hollein, both in Vienna.[117] Rainer (civic halls in Bremen of 1961–1964 and Ludwigshafen of 1962–1965), Hollein (Feigen Gallery in New York and the Museum in Mönchen–Gladbach), and Ottokar Uhl (* 1931) with the church in Tägu, Korea, all received commissions from foreign countries as well.[118] The architect Rob Krier, from Luxembourg, is teaching in Vienna but his buildings are primarily in Luxembourg (Fig. 160) and Germany.

Postwar Architecture in Italy

The continuity of architectural development from the time of Mussolini till the postwar period is obvious, and many architects could continue with their activities hampered only partially.[119] The main railroad station in Rome Statione Termini, which was completed by Calini and Montuori in 1950, could be directly attached to the main wing, which had already existed in Mussolini's time. The two most prominent high rises, both in Milan, are the Pirelli Building (1957–1961), by Gio Ponti (1891–1979) and Pier Luigi Nervi, and the high-rise Torre Velasca, with floors of offices and

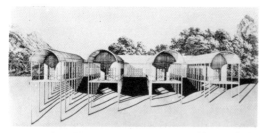

162 *Aldo Rossi: House in Borgo Ticino, Switzerland (1974) design*

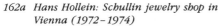

162a *Hans Hollein: Schullin jewelry shop in Vienna (1972–1974)*

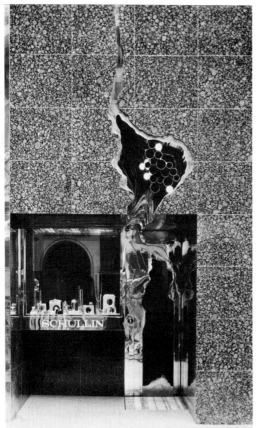

apartments, by Belgioioso, Peresutti, and Rogers (1956–1957). The remaining large office buildings were adapted to international development, while housing by Luigi Moretti (1907–1973), Leonardo Ricci, Marcello d'Olivo (* 1921), Mario Galvagni, Angelo Mangiarotti, and Bruno Morasutti developed a more specifically Italian style. Regarding industrial buildings, in particular Gino and Nani Valle (Zanussi factory in Pordenone, 1959–1961) should be mentioned. Educational buildings of a powerfully individual expression stem from Enrico Castiglioni (* 1914) in Busto Arsizio (Trade School of 1960–1965), Vittoriano Viganò (* 1919) in Milan (Institute Marchiondi of 1957–1958), and Paolo Portoghesi (* 1931) in Cesenatico (Colonia Marina of 1962–1965) and L'Aquila (Istituto Tecnico Industriale of 1969–1976).[120] One of the most important Italian architects was Carlo Scarpa (1906–1978), who in his restorations (Castel Vecchio in Verona of 1964), exhibitions, monuments, and cemeteries (Brion-Vega Tomb and Cemetery in San Vito, Treviso, of 1970–1972), established a new harmony between the craft of building and the expression of content.

Giancarlo de Carlo (* 1919) developed coherent plans on the basis of new social insights into student housing at the University of Urbino (1963–1965), which are also the focal point of his housing in Milan and Terni. The goal of de Carlo is the participation in the developmental process, by mass housing tenants, which has been on the decline in his opinion, during the past decades: "During the past fifty years, indeed more than during any other epoch, those who use and must live with the architecture have been excluded."[121]

The following projects refer to foreign architects occupied in Italy: the project for a hospital in Venice by Le Corbusier, and for an exhibition building in Venice by Louis I. Kahn, as well as the administration building by Oscar Niemeyer in Segrate for the firm of Mondadori.[122] In Florence, when attempting to renovate the Villa Strozzi, a group of architects (such as Alvar Aalto, Hans Hollein, Richard Meier, Giovanni Michelucci, Carlo Scarpa, and Ignazio Gardella) was invited to design parts of a larger cultural center.[123]

Experimental architecture in Italy is expressed in works by Leonardo Savioli,[124] Aldo Rossi (* 1931), Rinaldo Semino, Massimo Scolari, Franco Pur-

ini, Vittorio Gregotti (* 1927), and Carlo Aymonino (* 1926), as well as through the activity of the groups Archizoom 9999, Superstudio in Florence, and G.R.A.U. in Rome.[125] Their work as well as Rossi's important realization in Gallaratese near Milan (1970), Broni (1973), and Modena are solutions of highest significance with regard to the international situation of the 1960s and 1970s (Fig. 162).

Spanish and Portuguese Architecture Between 1950 and 1970

The architectural situation in Spain is similar to modern results in other countries in spite of the government of Generalissimo Franco (1892–1975), and can be considered equal to international efforts. Outstanding industrial buildings stem from J. M. Mar-

Julio Cano Lasso (* 1920) built in co-operation with Alberto Campo Baeza (* 1946) the University for Workers in Almeria. Emilio Donato and Uwe Geest built houses and settlements, several of the latter for socialist labor communes in Algeria.

In Portugal, works of the following architects should be pointed out: Franciso Keil Amaral, Eduardo Ana-hory, and Fernando de Tavora as well as Marcelo Luiz Correia de Lima Costa, who experimented with new forms of a figurative architecture. The work of Vieira Alvaro Siza (* 1933) points to developments after 1970.[128]

Architecture in the Soviet Union

For several decades, architectural development in Russia and in Eastern European countries, which were under Russian domination, took a different course from western Europe. Nikita Krushchev (1884–1971), who

2,000 inhabitants, in a microclimate, necessary for the region, were made public. These projects were continued through the plans of younger architects, such as the NER group (New Element Urban Development) and the members Alexej Gutnov, A. Baburov, G. Djumenton, S. Kharitonova, I. Lezava, and S. Sadovsky.[131] There are further projects by Georgi Borisovski of hanging cities and plans for large environments in which the results of the West were assimilated and continued in this area. Borisovski writes with regard to the interpretation of one of his projects: "The houses are retained by widespread supports, which are functioning due to pressure. Cables or nets are spread on top, from which ceilings and walls are suspended. Two houses which are placed diagonally make room possible on the upper front side for a protected inner area (winter garden, sports arena, hall). Even a network of streets on several levels can be constructed through the tecture in Czechoslovakia is marked by exemplary housing projects, which continue the 1930s tradition, as well as by buildings by Jan Srámek and Alena Srámková and those of the SIAL group in Liberec.

Polish postwar architecture arrived early on at experimental solutions, which are marked by open building systems and temporary structures by Sophia Hansen (* 1924) and Oskar Hansen (* 1922).[136] Jacek Nowicki and Halina Skibnievska were pioneering for the design of new housing quarters. Large-scale designs for a new center of Warsaw stem from Zbigniew Karpinski and Marek Leykam (1958). Leykam also built office buildings in Poznan (1952) and the youth hostel in Plock (1959). Jerzy Soltan (* 1913) built, in cooperation with Zbigniew Ihnatowicz, the central railroad station in Warsaw, and the sports center in Warsaw-Mokotów (Fig. 166),[137] with Ihnatowicz, Tomaszewski, and Wittek. Jan (* 1920) and Krystina Dobrowolski (* 1924) are the architects of the airport in Warsaw (1969), as well as of office buildings and commercial structures.

Yugoslavian architecture after 1950 developed in a slightly different way than in the rest of the East European countries and corresponded to its special political position.[138] Besides important buildings, such as for example by the architects Venceslav Richter (* 1917), Boris Magas (* 1930), Vladimir Turina, Milorad Pantovic, and Ivan Vitic (* 1917), who built housing in Sibenik (1952) and the exhibition halls in Zagreb (1975), there was the execution of large-scale plans, based on industrialization, as was demon-

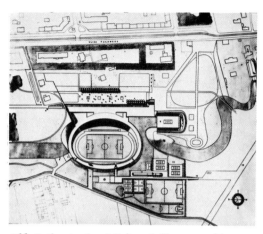

166 Z. Ihnatowicz, J. Soltan, L. Tomaszewski, and W. Wittek: Sports center in Warsaw-Mokotów (1960)

strated by the systems of aluminum houses in Zagreb by Zelko Solar and Bogdan Budimirov.[139] The city of Skopje in southern Yugoslavia, which had been destroyed by an earthquake, was rebuilt according to new plans by the Japanese architect Kenzo Tange of 1965, in cooperation with Yugoslavian architects and in a revolutionary style of city planning.[140] Janko Konstantinov designed the communication center in the city in a monumental shape (1968–1974).

Architecture of the Third World

The entry of the architecture of the southern hemisphere into international architectural development can be considered as an important event in itself, especially due to its specific component that building was again viewed in connection with a country's life-sustaining energy. The task far surpasses the limited area of operation in Europe and America and in-

167   Emilio Duhart: United Nations building in Santiago, Chile (1960–1966)

cludes the power to make decisions regarding irrigation problems, food problems, housing for the needy, and building with very limited financial resources — problems which can be fruitful regarding the total architectural development.[141] The social basis, formed regionally by various traditions, is the deciding factor in the different parts of the southern hemisphere and thus establishes the building effort.[142] Building, also in the sense of an elementary satisfaction of basic needs (slums) not designed by architects, became a deciding factor.

The most lasting effect upon the architecture in the Third World was attained by Le Corbusier's concepts, manifested on a major scale in South America, in India through his buildings and planning, and through his pupils in Japan. This is apparent in the buildings by Oscar Niemeyer in Brazil, Carlos Raul Villanueva in Venezuela, the United Nations building in Santiago, Chile (1960–1966, Fig. 167) by Emilio Duhart (* 1917), a former associate of Le Corbusier, and the plans by Lucio Costa (* 1902) for the new capital of Brazil in Brasilia of 1956 (Fig. 170) and the plans by J. L. Sert and P. L. Wiener for Chimbote in Columbia (1949). In India, a generation of architects was influenced by the construction of the city of Chandigarh and by Le Corbusier's commissions for Ahmedabad. In more recent times, the educational influences of

Kahn's concept and the example of his work in Ahmedabed and Dacca are more and more the focal point.

The Revolution in Latin America

The various countries in Latin America have had a significant increase in population, which is not to be underestimated and which gave the subcontinent an explosive vitality in its social structure as it was pressing towards new goals. The differences between the classes are still significant in most countries, and very often a military regime supported with capital from foreign countries is interested in the existing order. Nevertheless, there are significant differences within the various countries, which also manifest themselves in the different types of architecture.[143]

Mexican Architecture After 1950

The self-evaluation in Mexico was manifested by two great international events, seen in two powerful architectural expressions: the university city in Mexico City, which was founded in 1950, and the Olympic Games, which were held in 1968 in Mexico City.[144] A large number of Mexican architects were involved in the construction of the various departmental buildings and sports facilities of the university: José Villagran de Garcia (* 1901), the old master of Mexican architecture; Mario Pani (* 1911) and Enrique de la Mora (* 1907), who were mainly concerned with planning; as well as Salvador Ortegas Flores, Raul Cacho, Eu-

genio Piszar, Felix Sanchez, Francisco J. Serrano, Luis MacGregor, Fernando Pineda, Alfonso Liceaga, Sergio Garcia Lascurain, and Alberto T. Arai, who executed the various buildings. The whole complex was constructed and perceived as one of the great national community efforts. The central library (1951–1953), designed by Juan O'Gorman (1905–1982), as well as the Olympic Stadium by Augusto Palacios, Raul Salinas, and Jorge Bravo are especially noteworthy.[145] The entire planning of the buildings for the 1968 Olympic Games was in the hands of Pedro Ramirez Vazquez, who also built the Museo Antropologico and the Hotel Camino Real, which were completed at the same time.[146]

The task of housing construction was solved by Mario Pani by building the Centro Urbano Presidente in Mexico City (1950–1952) as well as by the project Tlaltelolco, which was created in an outstanding cultural-political way, by stacking from four- to twenty-two-story high rises for about 20,000 inhabitants. Buildings in the Aztec and Spanish tradition (Plaza of the Three Cultures) were included as central and thus the unique building style of the present was joined to the living tradition of the country.[147] Max Cetto (* 1903), and Francisco Artigas (* 1916) stood out in regard to single-family houses and Enrique de la Mora (* 1907) and Sordo Madalena (* 1916) with exemplary office buildings. The houses, gardens, and religious buildings by Luis Barragan (1902–1988) elevated the regional characteristics of Mexican architecture to a level of serene and emotional quality. Nature and architecture, color

168 E. de la Mora, F. L. Carmona, and F. Candela: St. Vincent's Chapel in Coyoacán, Mexico (1959–1960)

and form, physical sensibility and a mystical simplicity are merged into a unique environmental harmony.

The work of the engineer Felix Candela (* 1910), who immigrated from Spain, holds a special position.[148] By 1950, he had already created a shell construction with a span of 11 yd. (11.8 m) and a minimal shell thickness of only ½ in. (1.5 cm), when building the Pavilion for Nuclear Research within the framework of the University City. Subsequent buildings by Candela, such as his churches in Cuernavaca (1957), Coyoacán (1959–1960), and Monterrey (1959–1960), the market hall and the St. Vincent's Chapel (Fig. 168, 169) in Coyoacán, and a restaurant in Xochomilco mark him as an international expert in shell architecture. However, when building the sports palace for the Olympic Games in Mexico City (1966–1968), he decided upon a construction of steel with hyperbolic paraboloids and a roof of copper, arriving thus at a span of 182½ yd. (166 m).[149]

169 E. de la Mora, F. L. Carmona, and F. Candela: St. Vincent's Chapel in Coyoacán, Mexico (1959–1960) elevation

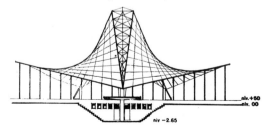

Building in Central America

Cuba and the Central American countries have a relatively long tradition in the construction of hotels, clubhouses, and buildings for sports and recreation, among which are the Tropicana Club and Nautica Club in Havana by Max Borges (* 1918) and the representative hotels El Panama in Panama City (1946) by Edward Durrel Stone (1902 – 1978) and Caribe Hilton in San Juan (1950) by the architects Osvaldo Toro (* 1914) and Miguel Ferrer (* 1915) in cooperation with Louis Torregrosa. After the Fidel Castro (* 1927) revolution, the main activity was directed to housing, schools, and community planning, which developed and blossomed into imaginative forms. With regard to the construction of schools, the following are especially noteworthy: the Art Academy (1962 – 1965) and the Academy of Modern Dance (1963 – 1965) by Ricardo Porro (* 1925, Fig. 150a), as well as the Academy of Music (1963 – 1965) by Vittorio and Roberto Garatti. The laboratories of the Institute for Engineering are by Manuel R. Gutierrez and Mario G. Suarez. Exemplary housing was developed in Havana by the architects Paolo Romero and Fernando Salinas (Fig. 169a).[150]

In Puerto Rico, the new building of the University in San Juan by Henry Klump (* 1905), as well as housing and hotels by Osvaldo Toro and Miguel Ferrer must be pointed out. In cooperation with the engineers Weidlinger and Salvadori, they developed the beach pavilion of the Caribe Hilton, which is one of the most convincing shell construction buildings of the country. A. Miranda created the grandstands at the stadium in San Juan, and Jorge del Rio built an exemplary housing development for the aged in Cidra (1967 – 1969).[151]

In El Salvador, Karl Katstaller and Ehrentraut Schott built the State Museum and Education buildings in San Salvador. In Panama, as well as in Mexico and Puerto Rico, the new construction of the university is the expression of national prestige. One of the most outstanding buildings in Guatemala is the synagogue in Guatemala City developed from the Star of David by the architects Jorge Montes and Carlos Haeussler in cooperation with Felix Candela (1959 – 1960).

Architecture in South America After 1950

In the context of South American countries, Venezuela, Brazil, and Argentina should be pointed out as centers of concentration of the new architecture. In Peru, however, luxurious residences in the capital of Lima and an internationally supported experimental housing development (Previ Housing) were the focal point,[152] while in Colombia, construction also had an influence beyond its borders, namely, the buildings by Juvenal Moya and the firm of Pablo Valenzuela and José M. Obregon (Olympic Stadium in Cartagena).[153] Rogelio Salmona, Herman Vieco, and E. Zarak build terrace houses in Bogotá for low-income residents (1967), which represented a valuable alternative to mass housing. Salmona also built the Museum of Modern Art in Bogotá.

*169a   Paolo Romero and Fernando Salinas: Housing development in Habana del Este, Cuba
(1962)*

Architecture in Venezuela was dominated by Carlos Raul Villanueva (1900–1975) and the favorable economic situation made the construction of a new national university possible.[154] Villanueva spoke about the significance of the university city during construction: "The architectural system of the group of buildings of the university city, finished or unfinished, with the library and the auditorium maximum as focal point contain the intellectual manifestation of the university as well as of the capital."[155] Other architects in Venezuela, like

Guido Bermudez (* 1925), Vegas and Galia, Millares, Hoffmann, and Branco, as well as Carlos Guinard, were building housing developments, educational buildings, and single-family houses. Under the government of Perez Jiminez alone, 85 super blocks were constructed in Caracas, in which 160,000 people were living, 12 percent of the inhabitants of the city.[156] Jorge Romero Gutierrez designed the Heliocoid Shopping Center and Alejandro Pietri, the Aquarium in Caracas (1961). The concrete bridge across Lake Maracaibo

(1959–1967) with a total length of 9656 yd. (8,778 m) and a span of up to 258½ yd. (235 m) with the roadway 50 m above the water table, was a construction of exemplary engineering by the Italian Riccardo Morandi.[157]

The oldest tradition for the modern development of South American architecture existed in Brazil and here it was developed most extensively.[158] The highlight of the development was the planning and construction of a new capital in the center of the country. Lucio Costa's (* 1902) plan for the capital, Brasilia (Fig. 170), which won first prize in the 1956 contest, is based on the crossing of two axes, with the central governmental buildings at the head of the central axis.[159] The buildings of the Parliament, the Palace of the President, and of the cathedral, designed by Oscar Niemeyer (* 1907), are symbolic systems but not solutions to the posed architectural as well as political problems.[160]

Oscar Niemeyer also influenced Brazilian architecture decisively with his other buildings and plans. His high-rise houses in São Paulo, single-family houses (his own residence in Rio de Janeiro, 1953–1954), and educational buildings are planned with dynamic freedom and very often with curved forms, which do not always conform to the functional necessities. Some housing developments, besides Niemeyer's work, must be pointed out, where adequate solutions were pursued regarding the social reality. The housing developments Pedregulho (1947–1954, Fig. 171) and Gavea (1952) in Rio de Janeiro stem from Affonso Eduardo Reidy (1909–1964). The Pedregulho development

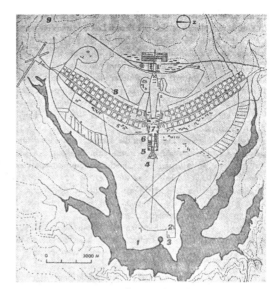

170 *Lucio Costa: Plan for Brasilia, the capital of Brazil (1956)*

is harmoniously integrated into the landscape[161] and was planned as social housing for 570 families — mostly city employees whose rent was deducted from their salary. A kindergarten, swimming pool, sports hall, medical center, laundry, and shopping facilities are part of the complex. Brazil's most famous master in the field of landscape architecture is Roberto Burle-Marx (* 1909).[162] Subsequent housing was erected by the architects Francisco Bolonha (* 1922), Rino Levi (* 1901), and the brothers Marcel (* 1908), Milton (1914–1953), and Mauricio (* 1921) Roberto. Other Brazilian architects are Lucjan Korngold (* 1897), Osvaldo Bratke (* 1907), Sergio Bernardes (* 1919), David Libeskind (* 1928), and Lina Bo Bardi, who built the museum in São Paulo in 1969 (Fig. 172).[163] Joaquim Guedes

171 *Affonso Eduardo Reidy: Housing development Pedregulho, Rio de Janeiro (1947–1954)*

172 *Lina Bo Bardi: Museum of Art in São Paulo (1969)*
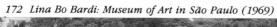

(* 1932) with the D. Toledo house in Piracicaba, São Paulo (1963), and Eduardo Longo (* 1942) are recognized among the younger architects, as well as Mario Perez de Arce in Chile with his housing, educational, and religious buildings in Santiago.[164]

The situation of modern architecture in Brazil, as was that in Argentina, is based on the development during the pre-1950 years and is marked by buildings and projects by Eduardo Catalano and Horatio Caminos. Both are responsible for planning the framework of the university city of Buenos Aires which has been only partially realized.[165] The international contest in 1962 brought fascinating designs for the Peugeot Building in Buenos Aires, for example, by Viljo Revell and Enrico Castiglioni. A new development began with the building of the Bank of London and South America in Buenos Aires (Fig. 173) by the architects S. Sanchez Elia, F. Peralta Ramos, Alfredo Agostino, and Clorindo Testa (1967), as well as subsequent buildings of the leading Argentine architect Clorindo Testa. Younger architects (Estudio Cinco in Buenos Aires) distinguished themselves by the free use and inclusion of plastic materials and by imaginative forms, which often include elements of the pop culture.[166] The architects Rafael Vinoly (* 1944), Flora Manteola (* 1936), Javier Sánchez Gómez (* 1936), Josefa Santos (* 1931), and Justo Solsona (* 1931) developed a new imaginative architecture, which was expressed in large-scale buildings, such as the Color Television Production Center in Buenos Aires of 1978–1979, which points to the new phase after 1970.

173 S. Sanchez Elia, Clorindo Testa, and others: Bank of London and South America in Buenos Aires (1967)

The Rebuilding of the State of Israel

The particular significance of the architecture of Israel is based upon the establishment of a new state, whose total population stemmed from 70 different countries and consisted of only 700,000 inhabitants at the time of the declaration of independence.[167] Development is therefore defined equally by urbanization, planning of housing developments, and the establishment of the kibbutz, as well as the creation of factories, nuclear power plants (Fig. 174), and office build-

174 Philip Johnson: Nuclear reactor, Rehovot, Israel (1961)

175 Z. Hecker, A. Neumann, and E. Sharon: City Hall in Bat Yam, Israel (1959–1963)

ings.[168] Urbanism, however, was most urgent and a great number of new cities were planned and realized.[169] The outstanding personality of planner Heinz Rau was only effective to a limited degree.

Architects who are articulating the new tasks in an exemplary manner include Arieh Sharon (1900–1984), Alfred Neumann (* 1968), and Dov Karmi (1905–1962). Significant single buildings are the Mayer House in Tel Aviv by Y. Perlstein (1966), the El-Al Tower in Tel Aviv by Dov Karmi and Ram Karmi, the Israel Museum by Al Mansfeld, the Synagogue of the Hebrew University in Jerusalem (1957) by Heinz Rau and D. Resnik, and the Engineering Department of the Technical University (Technion) in Haifa (1960–1964) by Alfred Neumann and Zvi Hecker. The work of the team of Neumann, Hecker (* 1931), and Sharon (* 1933) must be noted (city hall in Bat Yam, 1959–1963, Fig. 175; terrace housing development, Ramat Gan, 1960–1965), Arieh and Eldar Sharon (Bungalow Hotel in Sarem-El-Sheikh, 1968–1969), as well as buildings by Zvi Hecker (Ramot Housing Development in Jerusalem, 1972–1973) and Moshe Safdie (Israel Habitat, design of the area of the Wailing Wall in Jerusalem, and the Research Institute in the Negev Desert).

Contemporary Architecture in the Arab Countries

The equilibrium of world architecture had shifted due to the rapid intensive building activity in the Arab countries in connection with the new construction of the State of Israel and the urban architectural articulation of this immense project. Prominent architects from all parts of the world were, at least partly, involved with working for a few years for Arab clients. Thus, a complex of buildings evolved that corresponds to the immense affluence, developed in a short time, as well as to the change in international architecture.[170]

A large-scale program for the new design of Baghdad in Iraq began to develop as early as 1960 for which plans were obtained by Frank Lloyd Wright, Le Corbusier, Gropius, Aalto, and Werner March. However, only parts of the whole were executed, for example, the university city by Walter Gro-

176 Walter Gropius: University City of Baghdad (1962) plan

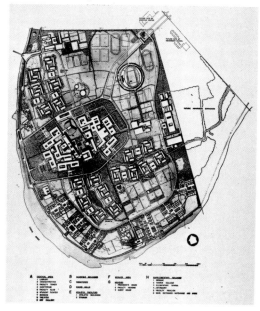

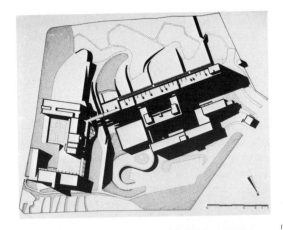

pius (1962, Fig. 176). José Louis Sert build the American Embassy in Baghdad. R. K. Chadirji is noteworthy among the Iraqi architects for his houses and office buildings. Educational buildings and hospitals by Michel Ecochard (* 1905) in Saïda, Baabda, and Beirut (Fig. 177) should be pointed out[171] in Lebanon; and in Jordan, the project for the royal palace in Amman by Paolo Portoghesi (1973–1975).

A manifestation of representative power, which only rarely relates to local traditions, was possible due to the special financial situation of oil-producing countries such as Saudi Arabia and neighboring sheikdoms (Kuwait, Qatar, United Arab Emirates). Architects from nearly all countries of the world were summoned for the achievement. Minoru Yamasaki built the Dharan Airport (Fig. 178) in cooperation with Ralph M. Parson.[172] Kenzo Tange designed the airport of Kuwait in 1967 (Fig. 179).[173] The hotel and conference building in Riyadh (Fig. 180) stems from Trevor Dannatt.[174] Frei Otto built the Mecca community center with Rolf Gutbrod.[175] Numerous subsequent firms were commissioned with the development of large-scale planning: Skidmore, Owings, and Merrill, and Hellmuth, Obata, and Kassabaum

177 *Michel Ecochard and Henri Eddé (A.T.B.A.T.): Hospital in Beirut (1961) site plan*

178 *Minoru Yamasaki: Dharan Airport, Saudi Arabia (1974)*

179 *Kenzo Tange: Kuwait Airport (1967) project (completed in 1981)*

180 Trevor Dannatt: Conference center and hotel in Riyadh, Saudi Arabia (1966–1975)

(university in Riyadh), William L. Pereira (hotel and conference center in Qatar), Minoru Yamasaki (office for the Saudi Arabian Monetary Agency, Riyadh), Michel Echochard (museum in Kuwait, 1960), Franco Albini (museum in Riyadh), Jörn Utzon (Parliament in Kuwait, Fig. 242), Reima Pietilae (Sief Palace in Kuwait), Hentrich and Petschnigg,[176] Peter and Alison Smithson, Karl Schwanzer, Sir Leslie Martin (government center in Taif, Saudi Arabia, 1972–1976),[177] Felix Candela (sport center in Kuwait),[178] Candilis and Woods, Perkins and Will, Caudill, Rowlett, and Scott (youth center in Qatar, housing in Dharan and Abquiq), as well as TAC (hospitals for Abu Dhabi, office buildings in Kuwait). The significance of this shift in

180a S. Lindstroem, V. Byran, Dyckerhoff, and Widmann: Water tower in Riyadh, Saudi Arabia (1969–1971)

accent in the international architectural scene can not yet be estimated. However, Arab architects, such as Rifat Chadirji (* 1920), Mohamed Saleh Makiya (*1917), Hisham A. Munir, Karim Jamal (* 1944), and Medhat Ali Madhloom are able to contribute only little to the preservation of traditional architectural possibilities. This will change significantly in the new developments after 1970.[179]

In Iran, a building activity of tremendous dimensions has taken place since 1950. Projects of magnitude are being taken on by Perkins and Will (educational buildings, hospitals, cultural centers), Skidmore, Owings, and Merrill (Iranian Air Force Academy), and by I. M. Pei, William L. Pereira, and Kenzo Tange, who worked temporarily on large scale projects. Iranian architects, on the other hand, search to continue with native tradition: Heydar Ghiai with the Senate Building in Teheran (1959), Pakniya and Moayed-Aahd with the Central Library of the University of Teheran and Abdolaziz Farmanfarmaiyan with the Mosque of the University in Teheran (1966).

New Architecture in Africa

The development of architecture in Africa is diverse and, since 1950, is expressed differently in the various climatic regions. In principle, a step-by-step recovery of their own tradition, which had been lost during the colonial regime, is taking place.[180]

French tradition influenced North Africa including Morocco, Tunisia, Algeria, Libya, and Egypt, as well as the

181 Elie Azagury: Residence of the architect, Casablanca (1966)

182 A. Faraoui and P. de Mazières: Hotel in Boumalne du Dades, Morocco (1976)

other Islamic states. In Morocco, a transitional architecture was found that was suitable to the social and climatic situation, which was expressed in buildings by Candilis and Woods as well as by André Studer (housing development in Casablanca).[181] Jean Francois Zevaco (* 1916) and Elie Azagury (* 1918, Fig. 181), Abdeslam Faraoui (* 1928), and Patrice de Maziéres (* 1930), Henri Tastemain (* 1922), and Eliane Castelnau

183 Roland Simounet: Djenan-El-Hasan housing development, Algeria (1958–1959)

(* 1923), as well as Mourad Ben Embarek were the native architects, who continued with tradition and the given situation and were able to arrive at their own independent solutions (Fig. 182) as manifested especially in the new Courthouse of Agadir (1967–1968) by Azagury and the new airport in Casablanca by Ben Embarek of 1977 (Fig. 240).[182] Roland Simounet built exemplary housing developments in Algeria (Djenan-El-Hasan, 1958–1959, Fig. 183, and Timgad, 1959–1962). The Danish architects Bo and Wohlert completed the Occupational Training Center in Monastir and Tunisia in 1973.[183] In Sudan, Paolo Portoghesi developed plans for the International Airport (Fig. 185) and the Officers Club in Khartoum. Projects by numerous foreign firms (Perkins and Will, and Justus Dahinden, Fig. 184) must be pointed out in Egypt, as well as a smaller group of native architects among them Hassan Fathy, (1900–1989), who attempted to solve the considerable problems with differing views and roles.[184] Fathy's village of Gourna near Luxor was a pioneering example in the development of new possibilities of participation.

Architecture in West Africa has a stronger commitment to the English tradition of building and is often expressed in an important manner in extensive building complexes.[185] Senegal and Guinea, however, are under the influence of French colonial architecture.[186] Universities were built by E. Maxwell Fry, Jane Drew, Drake and Lasdun (University of Ibadan), Renato Severini and COMTEC (University in Cape Coast), and Arieh and Eldar Sharon (University in Ife, 1968–1970, Fig. 186). The first expression of an architecture of Africans for Africans developed mainly in Nigeria through the architects Olewole Olumuyiwa, Ekwueme, and David Olatunde.[187]

Central and South Africa continues to be defined by a mixture of — not always distinguishable — traditional and contemporary forms of architecture. The high rises in Leopoldsville by Claude Laurens, as well as other buildings in the Congo by Belgian architects are in the tradition of Belgian colonialism. Only in rare cases are non-African architects successful in finding a synthesis of the international results and the specific given situation in Africa, as was the case of Julian Elliott and his housing developments in Elisabethville and the new University of Zambia in Lusaka (1965–1968, Fig. 187), and Montgomery, Oldfield, and Kirby in the Bank of Zambia staff maisonettes in Lusaka, Zambia, of 1971 (Fig. 241).[188] Roland Simounet has attained this synthesis, which was directed towards simple and clear forms

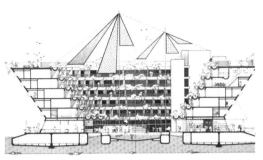

184 Justus Dahinden: Perle du Caire floating hotel in Cairo, (1976) project

(Fig. 188), in Tananarive, Madagascar, in the student dormitories of the university (1962–1972).[189] Native architects such as José Ravelomamantsoa, Jean Rafamatanantsoa, and Jean Rabemanantsoa have extended modern principles to housing developments and city complexes under his influence.[190] In Mozambique, the work of Amancio d'Alpoim Guedes should be pointed out. He is searching for a new African personality with his educational buildings, churches, and hous-

185 P. Portoghesi and V. Gigliotti: International Airport, Khartoum (1973)

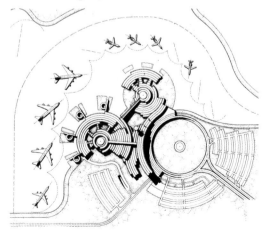

186 Arieh and Eldar Sharon: University in Ife, Nigeria (1968–1970)

187 Julian Elliott: University of Zambia, Lusaka (1965–1968)

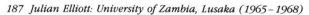

188 *Roland Simounet: Student housing development of the University in Tananarive, Madagascar (1962–1970)*

ing developments, even though they evolved from Portuguese tradition, as well as with his theories. In harmony with ancient African architecture, his definition of architecture is also influenced by Antonio Gaudi and surrealism: "We must become technicians of the emotions, tear-jerkers, exaggerators, analysts of dreams, performers of miracles, messengers; and invent raw, bold, vigorous and intense buildings without taste, absurd and chaotic —an architecture related to people, an architecture the size of life. . . . Building shall belong to the people, architecture shall once more become real and alive, and beauty shall be again warm and convulsive."[191]

East African architecture also shows the influence of England and architects such as Norman and Dawbarn, H. Richard Hughes, and Peatfield and Bodgener, who developed a feeling for native needs, due to working in the country for decades. Ernst May designed a number of exemplary buildings during the time of his East African emigration (Cultural Center in Moshi, about 1955). Justus Dahinden built church centers in Uganda, conceptualized after African works of art (church in Mityana, 1965–1972; church in Namugongo, 1968–1973).[192] The South African Republic remained, however, during the 1950s and 1960s an island with regard to contemporary architecture in Africa, which transfers foreign architectural forms to a society based on inequality.[193] The concept of Le Corbusier appeared early on, in the buildings by Rex Martienssen and the large-scale buildings by John Fussler and Norman Hanson. This continuation in the works of Munnik, Visser, and Black as well as Monty Sack and their English colonial tradition remains a foreign body within the total African context.

Architecture in India, Pakistan, and Bangladesh

The new architecture of the subcontinent of India in the 1950s and 1960s is defined by outside influence, as was manifested by English colonial rule and especially the creation of new cities.[194] Special problems of Indian city planning are the exceptionally high density of population, substantially higher than in comparable cities in Europe and America.[195] In more recent times, new cities were founded: Planning and construction of Islamabad was carried out by C. A. Doxiadis, and building and living space for 50,000 inhabitants was planned and realized by diverse architects by 1967.[196] The creation of a new capital, which Le Corbusier was commissioned to execute in 1950,[197] for the province of Punjab had been necessary in India, due to the separation of the country from Pakistan. The city of Chandigarh was begun in 1951 in cooperation with Pierre Jeanneret, E. Maxwell Fry, and Jane Drew, as well as a great number of Indian architects (Fig. 189) and culminated in the buildings designed by Le Corbusier for the capital (Parliament building, 1959–1962; Office of the Secretary, 1958; Supreme Court, 1952–1956). An area for 150,000 residents was the first part of a town conceptualized for 500,000 inhabitants.[198] The total cost for the construction of the city of

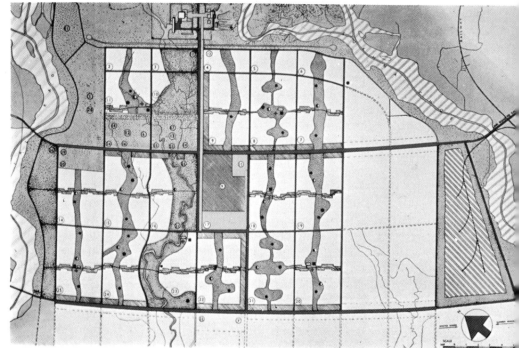

189 Le Corbusier, P. Jeanneret, E. Maxwell Fry, and J. Drew: City of Chandigarh (1951) site plan

190 B. V. Doshi: Research Center of Gurajat University, Ahmedabad (1962–1964)

191 Louis I. Kahn: Government Center, Dacca (1962–1974)

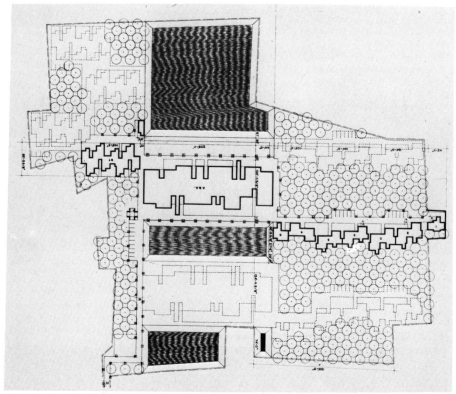

192 Stanley Tigerman: Bangladesh Polytechnic Institute, Dacca (1974)

Chandigarh was minimal in comparison to European and American city planning, the cost of the simplest type of house amounting to approximately one thousand U.S. dollars.[199] The city of Auroville, near Pondicherry, was planned and built according to the basic philosophy of Sri Aurobindo, an ideal city developed from a circle into a spiral, as designed by the French architects Anger and Heymann.[200] The new capital of the formerly eastern part of Pakistan — nowadays, Bangladesh — had been designed by Louis I. Kahn. The shape which grew from segments into a whole with the government center Sher-E-Banglanagar (1962–1974) is integrated into the tradition of the country (Fig. 191).[201] The Ayub hospital in Dacca (1962–1982) was also designed by Kahn.

The second center of the new architecture in India is located in Ahmedabad, with buildings by Le Corbusier (Clubhouse of Millowners, 1954; museum, 1956; single-family houses),[202] Louis I. Kahn (Indian Institute of Management, 1963–1967), C. M. Correa (* 1927, Gandhi Museum, 1963),[203] and B. V. Doshi (Gurajat University [Fig. 190], housing developments and single family houses). Kahn's complex for the Institute of Management contains residential buildings, student housing, a library, and a water nent of India: E. D. Stone built the American Embassy in New Delhi (1954–1958), a hotel in Karachi, and the Pakistan Institute of Science in Islamabad, which houses the first nuclear reactor in the country (1961).[204] Annibale Vitellozzi built the stadium in Calcutta; and, in Trombay, the Indian Atomic Research Center was developed in 1962 according to the plans of L. Calini and V. Patel. Stanley Tigerman designed the Bangladesh Polytechnic Institute in Dacca (Fig. 192).[205] The following buildings by Indian architects should be pointed out: the University of Bangalore (1965) by Kanvinde and Rai, the University of Jodhpur (1965) by Uttam C. Jain,[206] and of the Institute of Catering Technology and Applied Nutrition in Bombay by C. M. Correa,[207] and subse-

Architecture in Australia and New Zealand

The most significant architecture in Australia was influenced by America and Europe. Harry Seidler (* 1923) derives from Walter Gropius regarding his office high rises (Australia Square Tower in Sydney, 1967) and residential buildings, and arrives at a vocabulary of forms suitable to the nature of his country.[209] The Sydney Meyer Music Bowl in Melbourne (1959) was created by the architects Yuncken, Freeman Brothers, Griffith, and Simpson, with a dynamic membrane architecture and a roof of aluminum sheeting. The Academy of Science in Canberra by the architects Grounds, Romberg, and Boyd is in the shape of a large dome (Fig. 194). The most spectacular building in Australia is the Sydney Opera House designed in 1957 and begun in 1959 by Jörn Utzon and completed by Australian architects in 1966, after his resignation.[210] The powerful shell architecture (Fig. 193) became, nevertheless, a symbolic form for the cultural efforts of Australia. Numerous single-family houses by the architects Bruce Rickard and Harry Seidler in Australia, as well as by Warren and Mahoney, Tengrove and Marshall in New Zealand, document a remaining regional distinction, on the basis of the new empirism and is comparable to the architecture of a north European climate.[211]

Postwar Architecture in China

The century-old tradition of Chinese architecture was confronted with change during the last decades, due to political events that created a new dialectic reality. In particular, the views of Mao Tse-tung (1893–1976) and the cultural revolution he initiated also had a decisive influence on architectural change.[212] The architecture, initially under Russian influence, which corresponded to the early state of political consciousness, developed more and more into an architecture that came closer to the specific nature of the country.[213] Due to the transfer of the entire land to the government, a basis for extensive new planning was created. The differences between mass housing and Hong Kong luxury hotels, and the building task in China, conceptualized from a different basis, are therefore obvious.[214]

Housing quarters with community establishments, kindergartens, and public parks are no longer to be viewed as individualistic designs in China.[215] Planning and collective achievements take precedence over design problems, so that satellite cities, housing complexes, and areas of production are adapted to the new reality in the sense of communal thinking, introduced in 1958. The same view can be applied to sites for mass parades, sports, and assembly halls (Congress Hall in Beijing for approximately 100,000 people, 1958–1959).[216] One of the central buildings was the Mao Tse-tung Memorial Hall in Beijing of 1979 (Fig. 195).

A totally different architectural development, although also linked to Chinese tradition, is characteristic in Taiwan and Hong Kong, where the basic thoughts are concepts of western society. In Taiwan, they are expressed in educational buildings, such as Kenzo Tange's Junior College of the University of the Sacred Heart (1967–1968) and the chapel of Tunghai University in Taichung (1958–1959) by I. M. Pei.[217] The architecture in Hong Kong is under a strong British influence and is characterized by buildings by Palmer and Turner, Ove Arup, and the Chinese architect Tao Ho.

195 The Mao Tse-tung Memorial Hall in Beijing (1979)

Japanese Architecture Between 1950 and 1970

Postwar architecture in Japan had a worldwide influence as in no other country on earth and opened up possibilities which were considered utopic a few years earlier.[218] The 1930 tradition was continued by the architects Junzo Sakakura (1904–1969), Mamaru Yamada (* 1894), and especially Kunio Mayekawa (* 1905), who created buildings often influenced by Le Corbusier and demonstrated the conquest of the technical tasks of the time. The festival halls by Mayekawa in Tokyo (Fig. 196) and Kyoto (1960–1961), as well as the Harumi Apartments in Tokyo (1959) are the first signs of Japanese independence. Le Corbusier designed the Museum of Western Art in Tokyo, built in 1959 by Mayekawa, Sakakura, and Takamasa Yoshizaka, who all had been his former students in Paris.[219]

The most significant architect of Japan is Kenzo Tange (* 1913) whose development in the 1950s and 1960s mirrors most clearly the path of Japa-

196 Kunio Mayekawa: Festival hall in Tokyo (1960)

nese postwar architecture.[220] Since the construction of the Peace Center in Hiroshima (1949–1956), a symbol of the determination to survive after the catastrophe of the nuclear bomb, Tange erected a greater number of public buildings: town halls in Tokyo (1952–1957), Kurayoshi (1955–1956), Imabari (1957–1959), Takamatsu (1955–1958), and Kurashiki (1958–1960), but also the Olympic halls in Tokyo (1961–1964) and the cathedral in Tokyo (1962–1964).[221] The communication center in Kofu (1964 to 1966) opened up new possibilities for an unification of architecture and city planning (Fig. 197).[222]

Planning and execution of the Osaka world's fair in 1970 gave Tange the opportunity to build — in cooperation with Arata Isozaki, Kisho Kurokawa, and Kiyonori Kikutake — the central megastructure of the main pavilion, from which point the other elements of the exhibit were placed.

Yet even more decisive than his buildings are his urban works, in which he shows a possibility of a synthesis of technology and the conception of human values (Tokyo plan of 1960, Tokyo plan 1960–2000, of 1970).[223] Still another urban plan for the city of Skopje (1965), which had been destroyed by an earthquake, was awarded first prize in the international competition and implemented mostly in cooperation with Yugoslavian architects. New categories to city plan-

197 Kenzo Tange: Communication center in Kofu (1964–1966)

198 Kisho Kurokawa: Nagakin capsule tower Tokyo (1970–1972)

199 *Kiyonori Kikutake: Aquapolis for Expo '75 in Okinawa (1975)*

ning such as the concepts of "City Gate" and "City Wall" were introduced in Yugoslavia. Tange's activities spread to many countries during subsequent years: city planning at Bologna (1970), Yerba Buena Center in San Francisco (1968–1969), universities (Constantine, 1975; Oran, 1972) and vacation villages (Andalouses and Madraque, 1973) in Algiers, as well as buildings and plans in Iran, Kuwait, Nepal, Saudi Arabia, and the United States.[224] In Tokyo, furthermore, during that time, buildings of the embassies of Kuwait (1966–1974) and Bulgaria (1972–1974) were developed, as well as hotels and cultural structures.

A group of younger Japanese architects carries this development—initiated by Tange—further, searching for new forms of extensive urbanization and industrialization. In 1960, the following architects came before the public with the metabolic manifesto: Kiyonori Kikutake (* 1928, Fig. 199), Fumihiko Maki (* 1928), Masato Otaka, and Noriaki Kurokawa (* 1934, Figs. 198 and 202). In particular, Noriaki (Kisho) Kurokawa has attained exceptionally broad possibilities of architectonic expression through his far-reaching international work (Nakagin high rise in Tokyo of 1970–1972, Fig. 198; Fukuoka Bank in Fukuoka City of 1975, Fig. 202) and projects for Africa, Paris, and Germany.[225] Maki built the complex of the Rissho University in Tokyo (1967–1968).[226] Kikutake built not only town

200 *Y. Murata and M. Kawaguchi: Fuji pavilion at the Osaka world's fair (1970)*

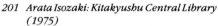

201 *Arata Isozaki: Kitakyushu Central Library (1975)*

halls, apartments, and religious structures, but also technological buildings such as "Aquapolis" for Expo '75 in Okinawa (Fig. 199).[227] Besides the visionary plans for megastructures, the members of the Metabolist Group also executed educational complexes and vacation villages, where the imaginary strength of their technology can be proven in reality. Kurokawa, in particular, attained fascinating results with his prefabricated-cell structures.[228]

The youngest generation of Japanese architects such as Akira Shibuya (* 1939), T. Akiyama, I. Kawakami, A. Isozaki (Fig. 201), and U. Shirashi is experimenting with the basic new metabolic ideas, and Yutako Murata and Mamoru Kawaguchi with different types of buildings (Pavilion at the Osaka world's fair, 1970, Fig. 200).[229]

202 *Kisho Kurokawa: Fukuoka Bank in Fukuoka City (1975)*

203 *SITE (James Wines): Department store in Houston, Texas (1975)*

IV

Autonomous Architecture Since 1970: Regional Identity and the Regaining of Tradition

Transformations Around 1970

Following the transformations around 1910, 1930, and 1950, based on the innovative impact of previous generations, the years around 1970 produced a new concept of architecture by a generation of architects born in the 1930s and 1940s.[1] Their work on various levels, to a degree, continued earlier trends from the 1960s, but they otherwise distanced themselves from the earlier achievements and established a new set of goals.

Among the characteristics defining the innovative results of this generation is a fundamental acceptance of the stylistic diversity of new multicultural approaches, which had previously not existed or were not recognized as such. The fact is that not every building type is acceptable or applicable in every part of the world. There are many different types of clients, a truth that is now being expressed in many facets of architecture.[2]

In opposition to earlier achievements, a new pragmatic and realistic attitude is the basis for design decisions that are no longer, as often was the case in the 1960s, dominated by illusions and patterns of wishful thinking that—in many cases—did not correspond to reality. A new down-to-earth attitude is demonstrated, and the requirements of a changed situation are now being faced, although not necessarily always solved. A realistic desire has replaced a hostile attitude toward misdirected humanitarian goals of the past. Reality is approached methodically and programmatically, and architects are beginning to understand that they have to take responsibility for the environment they create, that they can no longer blame other professions (sociology, politics, linguistics) for past mistakes.[3]

The realism of such an approach is also being developed in various selective applications of available technologies, using those of either high or low technological means according to the specific regional and social situations. It is an appropriate approach, one that is no longer dogmatic regarding the use of technological trends, commercially promoted materials, or the display of building forms and shapes regardless of socioclimatic or political determinants. Developing methods and strategies in accordance with each unique regional and social situation is now seen as desirable.

Some of the consequences of this realistic focus are previously neglected tasks of a new social responsibility now demanded by society, for example, libraries for the blind, centers for physically and mentally handicapped people, clinics for drug addicts, homes for unmarried parents, daycare centers, and the least solved— housing for the masses. Each of these special tasks can surprisingly benefit architectural design in general: for example, the design for a library for the blind can apply to, and improve, other building tasks as well. The fact that women and children and the homeless have to be served by architecture is a basic challenge to the qualification of the architect, and only those who tackle and solve these and other new problems are worthy to be the representatives of architecture in our time.

American Architecture Since 1970

The complexity of current international architecture is reflected in American architecture, which in the last two decades has become a mirror of several architectural tendencies from all parts of the world. In no other country has the multilayered and hybrid situation found such sophisticated architectural articulation as in America. Architects from all other countries bring regional characteristics of their respective countries of origin. It is in this sense that—in contemporary American architecture—European, Latin American, Asian, and African architecture become a totality of multicultural complexity, an architecture in which the first, second, and third world co-exist side by side.[4]

In addition, newly evaluated architectural traditions that were previously neglected are becoming integrated into the mainstream. In this regard, new buildings for American Indian and African-American communities have to be seen side by side with the high-rise headquarters of large corporations and others that have mistakenly and for much too long alone represented American architecture. The fragmented image of an American architecture exclusively represented by mainstream official architecture or certain temporarily fashionable styles has to be deconstructed.[5]

It is therefore necessary to compare Thomas A. Hodne's buildings for the Sioux Community College in Kyle, South Dakota, of 1980 with Philip Johnson's Headquarters for I. T. and T. in New York of 1984 and evaluate their relevance to their clients and to society in general. Regardless of the fame of the one building and the obscurity of the other, it is imperative to see them on the same level, to see both as legitimate articulations of the present multicultural reality in architecture. Antoine Predock's Fine Arts Center of Arizona State University in Tempe, Arizona, of 1987–1989, is another approach that regains qualities of a tradition that American Indian architects of past centuries had inaugurated. And this work can again be compared with the houses of Judith Chafee in Arizona, an American Indian architect who sees herself in the tradition of the international architecture of Walter Gropius and Le Corbusier.

The same complex approach is necessary in the reintegration of the African American tradition into the mainstream of American architecture, as these forms are also an expression of a newly achieved African-American identity. Donald Stull's Harriet Tubman Center in Boston of 1973–1974 is an example in which the forgotten and undervalued African tradition is rediscovered. Again, a comparison with existing traditions of architecture of European origins is necessary.[6] African-American tradition in architecture, like the American-Indian tradition, was not only undervalued for a long time, but both traditions were programmatically oppressed and in several regions nearly destroyed. The reconstitution of these and other multiple elements within a nonfragmented and complex American contemporary architecture is one of the most challenging goals to be faced if a truthful image of contemporary American architecture is to be achieved.[7]

The Continuation of a Tradition

To a large extent, contemporary American architecture, according to most publications, is seen in a fragmented way, and is in principle based on specific earlier European models, with slight timely modifications. The large architectural firms such as Philip Johnson; Skidmore, Owings, and Merrill; Hellmuth, Obata, and Kassabaum; Hugh Stubbins; Roche and Dinkeloo; I. M. Pei; Cesar Pelli; Kohn, Pederson, and Fox Associates; The Architects Collaborative; Paul Rudolph; and Kallmann, McKinnell, and Knowles concentrate on types of buildings established by the so-called masters of modern architecture.

In his early works, Philip Johnson was heavily influenced by Mies van der Rohe, but eventually emancipated himself from his master and by the 1970s was successfully articulating his own ideas, for example, in buildings such as the Pennzoil Plaza in Houston of 1976, the Transco Towers in Houston of 1970–1973, and culminating in the headquarters of the I. T. and T. Corporation in New York of 1984.[8] In several of his other works, such as the Rothko Chapel in Houston of 1971, Johnson achieved, in collaboration with Mark Rothko and Barnett Newman, a convincing new integration of the arts.

The immense architectural production of Skidmore, Owings, and Merrill, also based on the early example of Mies van der Rohe, has had numerous variations and adaptations in many parts of the world. The John Hancock Tower in Chicago of 1968 and the Sears Tower in Chicago of 1970–1974 are predominantly technological achievements that bring the principle of skeleton construction to the latest state of the art. In many other works by the firm, such the sun telescope at Kitt Peak National Observatory in Arizona of 1962, designed by Myron Goldsmith, and the Haj Terminal in Jeddah of 1975–1980, designed by Fazlur Khan, technologies were mastered and the results brought superlative dimensions to the height of a skyscraper and the span of a roof.

As with Skidmore, Owings, and Merrill, the firm of Roche and Dinkeloo continues a tradition originally rooted in the principles of Mies van der Rohe, but with additional adaptations from works by Eero Saarinen, who also began his career in the tradition of Mies van der Rohe. Roche and Dinkeloo had worked in Saarinen's office and they continued his concepts after Saarinen's death. In the 1970s and 1980s, they received major commissions, such as the College Life Insurance Company Building in Indianapolis (1973, Fig. 122), One U.N. Plaza in New York (1975), and the General Foods Company Headquarters in Rye, New York (1984). Following a great tradition, all these buildings were constructed with an advanced standard of architectural design and technology.

The extensive buildings by Hellmuth, Obata, and Kassabaum, including their Smithsonian Institution in Washington, D.C., of 1976, and the Ridgeway Center in St. Louis of 1981, also include the large-scale applications of earlier results. In other commissions, designed by the chief designer Gyo Obata (University and Airport Riyadh of 1985), new dimensions were explored, not only in scale but also in the climatic and cultural conditions of the area.[9]

Similarly, the successful career of I. M. Pei (* 1917) is to be seen in the same traditional context, even though Pei departs from the earlier accepted vocabulary. He is famous for his East Wing addition to the National Gallery in Washington, D.C., in 1979, which created a monumental framework in a language different from the neoclassical main building. Pei's addition to the Fine Arts Museum in Boston fulfills similar functions. Even his Grand Louvre entrance in Paris of 1983–1989 has in principle the same general idea, to create an extension by programmatically juxtaposing a new pyramidal form to the old structure. Pei has been very active outside the United States in recent years, with important commissions in China (Fragrant Hill Hotel outside of Beijing, 1983), Hong Kong (Bank of China, 1991), and Singapore (Overseas Chinese Banking Corporation, 1973–1984). More than in his American buildings, with the exception of his new Symphony Hall in Dallas of 1981–1989, Pei has here united technological and architectural principles.[10]

As do I. M. Pei and Roche and Dinkeloo, Cesar Pelli (* 1926) continues a tradition originally established by Mies van der Rohe, but with his own variations. After his earlier buildings (the Pacific Design Center in Los Angeles of 1976, the Rainbow Center Mall and Wintergarten in Niagara Falls of 1976–1978), his Museum of Modern Art residential tower in New York of 1977–1982, and his more recent buildings (Twin Towers in Houston in 1982) reflect his separation from the Miesian standards. This is especially transparent in Herring Hall of Rice University in Houston of 1985 where he found new ways to integrate a vocabulary into a given context. Pelli's latest achievements culminate in large-scale ensembles, such as his World Financial Center in New York, which attempts urban structuring of a new kind.[11]

Another firm directly influenced by Miesian tendencies is Murphy and Jahn, who continue the tradition of their earlier solutions, for example, in the Xerox Center of 1977 and One West Wacker of 1980–1982—both in Chicago. In the State of Illinois Center of 1980–1985, they break away from the earlier box form and create a contrast to the grid of the Chicago urban plan. Helmut Jahn (* 1940) and C. F. Murphy are involved in several international projects—the Arbitrage Offices in Johannesburg, South Africa, and the Fair Tower in Frankfurt (1991)—in which earlier tendencies are exaggerated to a point that makes the solution questionable.

Still another official variation can be seen in the work of the firm Kohn, Pederson, Fox Associates who in their Procter and Gamble World Headquarters in Cincinnati of 1982–1985 produced a prototype of corporate architectural symbolism. Many of their

other buildings, such as 333 Wacker Drive in Chicago and Hercules Inc. in Wilmington, Delaware, both of 1983, follow the now-established commercial principles that have been proven successful in the American context.

Whereas most of these firms follow the model of Mies van der Rohe, there is a group of other firms based on the work and teachings of Walter Gropius. Among these are the Architects Collaborative, founded by Gropius and his young collaborators, who continue to be successful in many countries of the world. A few of the more spectacular solutions are the Kuwait Fund Headquarters Building in Kuwait of 1978, the Kuwait Sheraton Hotel of 1978, and the Bernardin Hotel Resort in Piran, in the former Yugoslavia, of 1977–1978, and all, more or less, follow the earlier models of the firm when Gropius was still working.

Other buildings exhibiting Gropius' influence can be seen in works by Hugh Stubbins (* 1912), Paul Rudolph (* 1918), and John Johansen (* 1916), who were all pupils of Walter Gropius. In his Citicorp Building in New York of 1976, Stubbins developed his own high-rise architectural style in an urban context, though to some degree, it reflects the established tradition. Like Hugh Stubbins, Paul Rudolph began as a pupil of Walter Gropius, and soon departed from the old architectural language to find his own way. Much of his work took place outside the United States, where prominent examples, such as the Bond Center in Hong Kong of 1988, condominiums in Singapore of 1979 and 1981, and the Dharmala Corporation Headquarters in Jakarta, Indonesia of 1984, all exaggerate the dramatic tendencies of his personal architectural language. While Johansen was — in his early development —influenced by Gropius, he was the most radical in his departure from the concept of his teacher, for example, in houses (his own house in Stanfordville, New York, of 1973) and architectural experiments in an urban context.

The firm of Kallmann, Mckinnell, and Knowles in Boston began under the influence of Walter Gropius and Le Corbusier. They received prominence with their Boston City Hall, completed in 1967, and continued the same tendencies in reinforced concrete which they further expanded in their Washington-University School of Business in St. Louis of 1982–1986. In collaboration with McKinnell and Word, Kallmann also completed the Athletic Center of Harvard University (1990).[12]

Further Lessons from Louis I. Kahn

The work of Louis I. Kahn (1901–1974) had tremendous implications in the decades between 1950 and 1970, which became further accentuated during the last years of his life. Although Kahn died in 1974, the reverberations of his work and teachings made an enormous impact on the architects of the younger generation, not only in the United States but also in other parts of the world. The reintegration of lessons learned from Kahn has to be considered as important as the reintegration of the American-Indian and African-American traditions in the establishment of an appropriate image for the American architecture

in our time.[13] Kahn's late works in the United States (the Kimball Art Museum in Fort Worth, Texas, of 1967–1972, the Library of the Philips Exeter Academy in Exeter, New Hampshire, of 1967–1972, the Yale Center for British Art in New Haven of 1972–1977) are refined masterpieces of a new architectural concept unique in its clarity and powerful poetic vision. By far Kahn's greatest work is the National Assembly in Dacca, Bangladesh, completed in 1982 after the death of the architect. The complex, which is integrated into the master plan of the capital city of Dacca, is the culmination of twentieth-century architecture.

Kahn's influence is shown in several, often contrasting, directions. It is a liberating energy from which the basic convictions of his fundamental architectural philosophy grew into diverse creative results. The proof of this statement can be seen in the diversity of those architects upon whom he made an impact, among them, Robert Venturi, Denise Scott-Brown, Charles Moore, Moshe Safdie, Romaldo Giurgola, Thomas R. Vreeland, Serge Santelli, Miguel Angel Roca, Manuel Vincente, Balkrishna Doshi, Charles Correa, and many others. The worldwide expansion of Kahn's basic philosophy has decisively changed the architectural scene on an international level, in direct contrast to the superficial vocabulary applied by stylistic nomenclature of short-lived fashionable terms such as Postmodernism, Late Modernism, and Deconstructivism.[14]

In this regard, the works by Robert Venturi (* 1925) and Denise Scott Brown are of greatest significance, as they early transcended the superficial that of rethinking architecture in general and at the same time regaining continuity with the Modern Movement. While the apparent stylistic similarity of the works by Richard Meier (Fig. 133), Peter Eisenman, John Hejduk, Charles Gwathmey, and Michael Graves at that time appears understandable, their subsequent development has proven beyond any doubt that their works are basically different from each other. Nevertheless, all of the New York Five, as they were often called in the early years of their career, made a specific imprint on the general panorama of contemporary American architecture.

The most successful architect of the group, Richard Meier (* 1934), encompassed the widest possible tasks in solving problems in his works of the time: social housing, residences, and cultural centers. Unlike his contemporaries, he neither rejected nor merely continued the modernist language. Instead, he reversed it in an historistic approach. In his Twin Park Housing in the Bronx of 1972, Meier reconstituted the existing urban fabric of the site and offered a solution for low-income housing, which was, and has remained, one of the most neglected building types in American architecture. Meier also built private residences, such as the house in Old Westbury, Rhode Island, of 1971 in which he applies, but transforms, the general idea of Le Corbusier's early houses. In 1976, he designed the Bronx Development Center, creating an architectural form for a social task that did not exist before. His Visitor's Center in New Harmony, Indiana, of 1975–1978 is another innovative building type.

In several of his more recent commissions, such as the Seminary in Hartford of 1981, the High Museum in Atlanta of 1980–1983, and the Museum for Arts and Crafts in Frankfurt, Germany, of 1984, Meier follows his own established rules and gives sophisticated examples of an architectural solution innovatively serving the given task. In his most recent works, such as the City Hall and Library in The Hague (1987), the Madison Square Towers in New York, the Bridgeport Center in Bridgeport, Connecticut (1989), and especially the Getty Center in Los Angeles, Meier departs into a new territory of architectural expressiveness, which has brought a new dimension to American architecture.[18]

A contrast to the work of Richard Meier is that of Michael Graves (* 1934), who in his early houses, such as the Hanselmann House in Fort Wayne, Indiana, of 1967, the Benacerraf House in Princeton of 1969, and the Snyderman House in Fort Wayne, Indiana, of 1972, appeared on the surface to be within the language of the New York Five. But a dramatic change in his development took place in Graves's Cultural Center Bridge between Fargo, North Dakota, and Moorhead, Minnesota of 1977, and particularly his Regional Library in San Juan Capistrano of 1983, his Portland Building of 1983–1984, and his Humana Headquarters in Louisville, Kentucky, of 1983, in which he reincorporated color with classical and metaphorical elements. In Graves' Walt Disney World Swan Hotel in Lake Buena, Florida, of 1989–1990, these tendencies culminate in the overexaggeration of a figurative and narrative architectural language. They are "metaphorical landscapes" which, in the concept of the architect, consolidate the built form with a complexity and figurative art character prevalent in former centuries as well as in earlier phases of the twentieth century.[19]

Still another step in the transformation of early surface conformity of the New York Five into a different articulation of individual architecture can be seen in the buildings by Charles Gwathmey (* 1938) and Robert Siegel (* 1939) who, in their Perinton Housing in Perinton, New York, adapted a new image in the grouping of individual houses. In their various residences for the de Mesnil family in East Hampton, New York (1979), Santa Monica, California, (1981) and Houston, Texas (1979), as well as in numerous office buildings and such housing as Island Walk Cooperative Housing in Reston, Virginia (1975), and Pence Street Family Housing in Columbus, Ohio (1978, Fig. 205), and especially in the Sycamore Place Housing for the elderly in Columbus, Indiana (1978), the architects re-established a continuity between their work and the heroic phase of early modern architecture in Europe, seen most significantly in the work of Le Corbusier.[20]

The most poetic member of the original New York Five is John Hejduk (* 1929), who as an architect, writer, and teacher had an important impact on the development of American architecture. After his restoration of the Cooper Union Building in New York in 1975, his visionary projects created powerful manifestations that enrich architectural form and space by using a vocabulary that expands into meaningful applications, as in his "Thirteen Watchtowers for Cannareggio" of 1978 and his "House of the Inhabitant Who Refuses to Participate" of 1978. In his recent work in Europe, his apartment blocks in Berlin (Tegel, Kreutzberg, and Friedrichstrasse) and in Oslo (Oslo Security Building), he attempts to integrate the underlining poetic vision into the urban reality of the built form without losing the inner fascination of the meaning (Fig. 220).[21]

Peter Eisenman (* 1932) changed his architectural vocabulary sharply since his early work as a member of the New York Five, which had been primarily devoted to a systematic investigation into the internal essence of architecture. His houses from the 1960s and 1970s were prototypes of how architecture can be practised without any nonarchitectural interferences, and as a result, arrived at a self-referential language which had more educational than pragmatic character.

However, an important transformation has taken place in Eisenman's

205   Gwathmey and Siegel: Pence Street Family Housing, Columbus, Ohio (1978)

195

work since the mid-1980s, first seen in the Wexner Center for the Visual Arts in Columbus, Ohio, of 1987–1990 (Fig. 206) in which the memory of the site, its juxaposition with existing structures, and a new concept of meaning were introduced. This development is continued in projects such as the Bio-Center of the University of Frankfurt in Germany, in which complex principles on several levels determine the architectural form, and in the project for a college of Design, Architecture, and Planning in Cincinnati of 1991–1993 in collaboration with Lorenz and Williams.[22]

Other than the New York Five, there were further attempts to regain a continuation with tradition as manifested in works by such architects as Stanley Tigerman (Fig. 134) and Harry Weese (Fig. 207) in Chicago, Frank O. Gehry in Los Angeles, and Gunnar Birkerts in Michigan (Fig. 123). In his early buildings, especially his Illinois Regional Library for the Blind and Physically Handicapped in Chicago of 1977, Stanley Tigerman (* 1930) created a prototype for a new building problem and set a standard for its solution. Other smaller buildings, such as the Daisy House in Porter, Illinois, of 1978 and his project for a house "in the Intention of the Madama Plan" of 1981 programmatically refer to historic models given valid contemporary articulation. Tigerman's work has expanded to Bangladesh (Fig. 192) and recently also to Japan (mixed-use apartments in Fukuoka of 1988–1989).

The Village Hall in Oak Park, Illinois, of 1973–1974 by Harry Weese (Fig. 207) is a direct adaption of Alvar

206 Peter Eisenman: Wexner Center for the Visual Arts, Columbus, Ohio (1987–1990)

Aalto's Village Hall in Sänätsalo in Finland of 1950–1952 but with a new solution by means of creative appropriation.

The work of Frank O. Gehry (* 1929) takes on a new methodology beginning with his own house in Santa Monica, California, of 1978–1979 which he continuously altered spatially by restructuring its interior organization as well as his Edgemar Development in Santa Monica, California, of 1988 (Fig. 209). In the Loyola Law School in Los Angeles of 1984–1985, a

207 Harry Weese: Oak Park Village Hall, Oak Park, Illinois (1973–1974)

208 Thomas Hodne: Pine Point Experimental School, White Earth Chippewa Reservation (1980)

209 Frank O. Gehry: Edgemar Development, Santa Monica, California (1988)

210 Antoine Predock: Arizona State University Fine Arts Center, Tempe, Arizona (1987–1989)

comprehensive environment was created with independent units which in their juxtaposition and spatial harmony create a new meaningful ensemble. Gehry also built several houses and restaurants, for example, the Fishdance Restaurant in Kobe, Japan, of 1987, but his work culminated in two major commissions, the Aerospace Museum of 1985–1987 and the Disney Concert Hall of 1988–1989, both in Los Angeles.

Gunnar Birkerts (* 1925) began with innovative technological structures (Tougaloo College Library of 1965 and Federal Reserve Bank in Minneapolis of 1967–1973, Fig. 123) in order to arrive at new explorations of subterranean buildings (Law School of the University of Michigan in Ann Arbor, 1988–1989).

Redefining American Architecture

In addition to the tendencies that relate to past traditions, either in the concept of Louis I. Kahn or in the historicist approach to Modernism, other regional tendencies can be recognized that focus on a redefinition of the essense of American architecture. They vary according to geographical regions, such as the Southwest, the New England States, Florida, and the West Coast, and also in regard to ethnic origins, such as the revival of the American Indian and African-American traditions in contemporary versions.

American-Indian architecture in our time has found new expressions in works by several firms, some with relation to American-Indian architects, some with American-Indian communities as clients. One of the practicing American-Indian architects is Judith Chafee in Arizona, who absorbs the tradition of Walter Gropius, Le Corbusier, and other architects of the Modern Movement, transforming their concepts into the very different regional conditions of the American West. Her houses in Tucson, Arizona, of 1980–1990 are masterful adaptations to the specific climatic and cultural conditions of the region (Fig. 211).

Buildings clearly shaped by a reevaluation of traditions of the American Indian are visible in works by the Hodne Partnership, for example, in the Oglala Sioux Community College in Kyle, South Dakota, of 1980; the Red Cloud Tribal Government Center in Pine Ridge, South Dakota, of 1980; the Pine Point Experimental School of the White Earth Reservation of 1980 (Fig. 208); and the Native American Center for the Living Arts in Niagara Falls, New York, of 1981. These are revitalizations of the inherent spirit of old Indian buildings such as those in Mesa Verde, Colorado, and are very different from the other American vernacular languages in architecture. Bound to the earth and full of imaginative signs and symbols, these buildings represent a powerful reincarnation of a nearly lost tradition.[23]

Other architectural manifestations, such as the houses in Florida by William Morgan, the various solutions of Antoine Predock (* 1936) in New Mexico, Arizona, and Nevada (The Fine Arts Center of Arizona State University in Tempe, Arizona, of 1987–1989, Fig. 210, and the Las Vegas Library and Discovery Museum of

211 *Judith Chafee: Shade house, Tucson, Arizona (1980)*

1990), and houses by Bart Prince (* 1947) in Albuquerque, all follow existing traces of a traditional continuity kept alive in major works by Frank Lloyd Wright, Bruce Goff, and Herb Greene. This type of architecture, which begins to resurface on a larger scale, has references to the growing necessity to live in harmony with the natural environment.[24]

African-American elements in American architecture are also beginning to emerge, with major buildings in which a combination of American and African elements are combined into a new whole. Among the leading African-American architects practicing today are Donald Stull in Boston (Harriet Tubman Center in Boston of 1973–1974, Fig. 212), Bryant and Bryant in Washington, D.C., J. Max Bond in New York, Wendell J. and Susan B. Campbell in Chicago, Harvey B. Gantt in Charlotte, North Carolina, Robert P. Madison in Cleveland, Ohio, and Charles F. and Cheryl L. Mcafee in Wichita, Kansas.[25]

212 *Donald Stull: Harriet Tubman Center, Boston (1976)*

The Young Generation

The young generation of American architects reflects a new experimental phase of architectural practice with clearly articulated regional differentiations. The buildings by Arquitectonica (Bernardo Fort-Brescia, * 1954, Hervin Romney, * 1941, and Laurinda Spear) in Florida (The Atlantic in Miami of 1979) are of a very different nature than those by Erick Owen Moss (* 1943, Central Housing Office Building, University of California in Irvine of 1988–1990) and the firm Morphosis (Tom Mayne, * 1944, and Michael Rotondi, * 1949) in California ("Kate Mantalini's" Restaurant in West Hollywood of 1987 and the Salik Health Fare Center in Los Angeles of 1991), and they can be clearly distinguished from those of the Texas firms Taft Architects (John C. Casbarian (* 1946), Danny Samuels (* 1947), and Robert H. Timme) (River Crest Country Club in Fort Worth of 1984), Andrew Batey (* 1944) and Mark Mack (* 1949), and Clovis Heimsath.

Such young architects on the East Coast as Robert M. Kliment and Frances Habsband (Computer Science Building at Columbia University, New York, 1981–1983), George Ranalli (First of August Shop in New York of 1975–1977, Fig. 214), Steven Holl (* 1947, Martha's Vineyard house, Fig. 213), Susana Torre (* 1944, Fire Station No. 5, Columbus, Ohio, of 1985–1987), Peter Pran and Carlos Zapata, Todd Williams (* 1943) and Billie Tsien (* 1949), and Simon Ungers (* 1957), excel in disciplinary structural buildings in which the language of contemporary architecture is in the process of being clarified and enriched. The projects and buildings of Bernard Tsckumi (* 1944) introduce new layers of meaning and the environment. His first realization is the Parc de la Villette in Paris (1982–1985). The Cambridge Seven Associates, Inc., (Louis I. Bakanowsky, Peter Chermayeff, Alden B. Christie, Paul E. Dieterich, and Terry Rankine) specialize in the design and construction of aquarium complexes (New England Aquarium in Boston of 1969, the National Aquarium in Baltimore of 1981, and the Tennessee Aquarium in Chattanooga of 1992). Since his works in the field of "de-architecture" in the 1970s (Fig. 203), James Wines (* 1932) has expanded into visionary combinations of manmade forms and nature that overcome the limitations of the urban environment as solely manmade reality (West Hollywood Civic Center, project of 1987).[26]

American architecture in the 1970s and 1980s has reached a complex and exciting state of development. Enriched by the work of several generations and, at the same time, expanding formerly respected limits, a new freedom has been achieved, one that crosses borders, invites contributions from other parts of the world, and exports works of American architects into other countries — expressing the universal interrelatedness of the architectural scene today.

Contemporary Architecture in Canada

American and Canadian architecture since 1970 have developed along parallel lines with many interchanges taking place, for example, Mies van der Rohe and I. M. Pei building in Canada and Canadian architects such as Arthur Erickson building in the United States. More specific achievements in the Canadian environment are complexes such as the Toronto Eaton Centre by Bregman and Haman and Zeidler Partnership of 1973–1977, the Winnipeg Art Gallery by Gustavo da Roza (* 1932) of 1971, the House for the Aged in Picton, Ontario, of 1973 and the St. Lawrence Center for the Performing Arts in Toronto of 1983 by Ronald James Thom (* 1923), Moshe Safdie's National Gallery in Ottawa of 1986–1988, Raymond Morimura's Scarborough Civic Center of 1973 and Metropolitan Library in Toronto of 1977, and the Sedgewick Library of the University of British Columbia in Vancouver of 1969–1972 by Rhone and Iredale. The Missasauga City Hall by Edward Jones and M. Kirkland of 1982–1986 inaugurated a new phase in Canadian architecture, as did houses and ski resorts in the northern climate by Peter Rose

213 Steven Holl: Martha's Vineyard house (1984)

(* 1943) and his Pavillion 70 in St. Sauveur, Quebec, in collaboration with Peter Lankrs and J. V. Righter of 1977–1978.

214 George Ranalli: First of August Shop, New York (1977)

The work of Arthur Erickson (* 1924) is of special importance for the situation in Canada as it is for the Middle East and Southeast Asia where he received several commissions. His major works in Canada are the Museum for Anthropology at the University of British Columbia in Vancouver of 1971–1977, the Performing Arts Center in Calgary, Alberta, of 1978, the Robson Square Complex in Vancouver of 1979, and the Space Sciences Center in Edmonton, Alberta, of 1981–1983.

A uniquely Canadian building by Douglas Cardinal (born 1934) is the St. Mary's Church in Red Deer of 1965–1967, actively reconstituting elements of his Indian tradition. For Cardinal, it is important to build in harmony with the earth and the human body: "Learn from your body. Solve the problem organically, you have a brain, a stomach, a mouth, a heart, a pair of lungs. You think, eat, talk, feel, breathe. Build around what you are and want to be." His Museum of Man in Hull of 1986–1989 is the culmination of his endeavors to create a new synthesis in which several of the lines of development of Canadian architecture are united.[27]

European Architecture Since 1970

Contemporary architecture in Europe evolved differently than it did in America. Instead of the complexity and hybrid situation in America, where nearly all international tendencies are manifested side by side and often in a creative contrast, a stronger regional and national differentiation is visible in Europe, one which increasingly brings out the unique traditions of the architectural past. According to the more intense urban reality and the historic presence of significant places and memories, the present situation is also much more determined by architectural concepts integrated into the existing urban fabric. Even the individual buildings by architects such as James Stirling, Aldo Rossi, Gottfried Böhm, and Oswald Mathias Ungers relate to the context of earlier, historically defined, built environments and thus constitute a more homogeneous and continuous interrelationship between architecture and urbanism than in other parts of the world. The interrelation between different European countries is manifested in buildings by Stirling, Rossi, Hollein, and Aalto in Germany, Ricardo Bofill in France, Erskine in England, and Botta in France even before the new political unity became reality.

English Architecture Since 1970

In the last two decades, architecture in England has taken an important step in consolidating its earlier experimental phases, and architects such as James Stirling (1920–1992), Denys Lasdun, Colin St. John Wilson, and Norman Foster have given new articulations to the specific situation. Stirling's last buildings and projects have matured in a way that defined his previous powerful presence in international architecture. Many of his works were built in the United States as well as in Germany, such as the Staatsgalerie in Stuttgart of 1975–1984 and the

Science Center in Berlin of 1979–1988. Among the buildings in England, the addition to the Tate Gallery in London (1980–1985) and the recycling of the Tate Gallery in Liverpool are successful adjustments to the existing urban fabric. Stirling's major concern was the basic humanization of the environment according to the specific site and cultural tradition of each of his commissions.

On the other hand, Denys Lasdun (* 1914) continued his monumental approach toward urban accentuation culminating in the National Theatre of 1971–1975 on the South Bank in London (Figs. 140 and 141), while Patrick Hodgkinson set an urban accent with his Foundlings Courts housing of 1970–1972 in London (Fig. 142), and Colin St. John Wilson (* 1922) extended his earlier work of housing (in Haringey, London, of 1974–1977) and educational buildings with the British Library Building at St. Pancras in London, designed in 1975. In buildings by Norman Foster (* 1935), Richard George Rogers (* 1933), and Nicholas Grimshaw (* 1939) the approach of high technology in contemporary architecture has been given a sophisticated articulation. Rogers' Lloyd's Headquarters in London of 1978–1986, Foster's Sainsbury Center of the University of East Anglia of 1977 in Norwich, and Grimshaw's Sainsbury's housing and superstore at Camden Lock, London, of 1987–1989 stand out as convincing examples in their category.[28]

Tendencies of the younger generation can be seen in works by Jeremy Dixon (* 1939), Terence Farrell (* 1938) (TV Center, Camden Lock,

215 Venturi, Scott Brown, and Associates: Extension to the National Gallery, London (1991)

of 1981–1983), Quinlan Terry (* 1937), and John Outram (* 1934). The housing complexes on Alexandra Road of 1961–1979 by Neave Brown in collaboration with the Camden Architects Department, and the St. Mark's Housing in Maida Vale, London, by Jeremy and Fenella Dixon of 1976–1978 are examples of social housing. One of the major works influencing the situation of English architecture was the extension to the National Gallery in London by Venturi, Scott Brown, and Associates of 1991 (Fig. 215). The work of the Iraqi architect Zaha Hadid, who works and teaches in London, points in a direction of new architectural possibilities. Her first realizations in Germany (a fire station in Weil of 1991), in Japan (Moon Soon Restaurant in Sapporo of 1990), and in Holland (pavilion in Groningen) define the dynamics of an architectural space no longer limited by the rules of modern architecture.

216 *Reima Pietilae: Kaleva Church, Tampere*
(1976–1978)

Architecture in Finland and Scandinavia Since 1970

The contemporary situation of architecture in Finland is characterized by the continuation of a long tradition manifested in, among other works, the late buildings by Alvar Aalto, especially his Finlandia Hall of 1974 in Helsinki. In addition to his activities in several other countries (Germany, the United States, Switzerland, and France), Aalto's late works have had a great impact on Finnish architecture.

Making their contribution to the built environment, the new generation of Finnish architects after Aalto is led by Reima Pietilae (* 1923), who in collaboration with Raili Paatelainen articulated a powerful version of Finnish identity. Among his major early works were the student center Dipoli

217 *Kari Virta: Sinikello day-care center (1988)*

of the University of Otaniemi of 1966. Later works of his office are the Kaleva Church and the Church and Market Halls, both in Tampere of 1976–1978 (Fig. 216). Like Aalto before, Pietilae built major works outside of Finland, among them his Sief Palace in Kuwait of 1983, and the Finnish Embassy in New Delhi (1983–1985).

Besides Pietilae, other architects in Finland are Kari Virta, whose campus of Oulu University in the north of the country was completed in 1973, as well as his day-care center in Sinikello in 1988 (Fig. 217); Kari Jaervinen and Timo Airas (Kindergarten in Laensi-Sakylae of 1980), and Timo Penttilae and Heikki Saarela built residential buildings, among them the Helsinki apartment house of 1981.

Swedish architecture in the last decades is dominated by the work of Ralph Erskine (* 1914) who was also actively engaged in large-scale building in England, where his Byker Development in Newcastle-upon-Tyne of 1968–1978 had a stimulating influence on the situation. One of his recent works in Sweden is the hospital restaurant in Stockholm of 1987. An organic revival was introduced in Sweden in Erik Asmussen's Almandinen Rudolf Steiner Seminary in Jaerna of 1974.

Among the Norwegian architects since 1970, the work of architects such as Sverre Fehn (* 1924), Geir Grung (* 1926), and Hakon Mjelva (* 1924) continue the earlier developments from the 1960s. Of the younger generation, Kjel Lund (* 1927) and Nils Slaato (* 1923), J. Digerud and J. Lundberg (Project for the Norwegian University Press in Oslo of 1978–

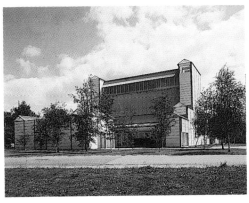

218 Jörn Utzon: Bagsvaerd Church, Copenhagen (1974–1976)

1980), and Arne Henricksen (* 1944) stand out. The major buildings of Lund and Slaato are the Bank of Norway in Oslo of 1979–1985 and the Cultural Center in Stavanger of 1983–1985. John Kristofferson built the Planetarium in Tromso in 1987–1989.

Denmark has a brilliant architectural tradition and a great number of Danish architects have contributed to the high quality of residential architecture. The late works by Jörn Utzon (* 1918) set a standard upon which the work of the younger generation can be measured. The Lutheran church in Bagsvaerd near Copenhagen of 1974–1976 is a powerful articulation of a religious space (Fig. 218). Romaldo Giurgola described the building: "This building expresses an aspiration for spirituality which is complex, intimate, and yet common to people, it does so with simple protective signs, leaving the actual making of symbols to the user." Arne Jacobsen's work was continued by his former collaborators Hans Dissing (* 1926) and Otto Weitling (* 1930), who were also engaged in buildings in Germany, among them the city halls in Mainz of 1973 and

Castrop-Rauxel of 1977. Other Danish architects active since 1970 are Jörgen Bo (* 1919), Vilhelm Wohlert (* 1920), Halldor Gunlogsson and Jörn Nilsen, Hans Munk Hansen (who also worked in North and Central Africa), and Henning Larsen, whose masterpiece outside of Denmark is the Ministry of Foreign Affairs in Riyadh, Saudi Arabia, of 1981 – 1984.[29]

Dutch Architecture Since 1970

As Scandinavian architecture follows the lead of Aalto and Utzon, in the Netherlands, Dutch architects are strongly under the influence of Aldo van Eyck (* 1918) who pioneered a new concept of architecture in harmony with human scale and emotional involvement. Already in some of the late works by Johannes Hendrik van den Broek (* 1898) and Jacob Berend Bakema, there was a special emphasis on buildings for social purposes (old people's housing in Delft of 1968 – 1976 and Drachten elementary school for handicapped children of 1965 – 1971). In van Eyck's work, this trend will come to dominating relevance. Van Eyck's buildings after 1970 include housing in Zwolle in collaboration with Theo Bosch (1975 – 1977), a clinic for drug addicts in Helmond in collaboration with Hannie van Eyck (1982 – 1983), and his most important work, the home for single parents and their children in Amsterdam (1976 – 1980). Until then, the focus put on these particular types of building tasks was virtually unknown and the emphasis placed on them by Van Eyck is significant for the present situation of architecture in

general. Beyond this, the detailed care given to each specific solution by the architect makes these works important in the larger context. They are as representative of Aldo van Eyck's concept as his early work, the Children's House in Amsterdam of 1958 – 1960 (Figs. 149 and 150).

Under the influence of Aldo van Eyck, Dutch architects have achieved important solutions for social and cultural buildings as well as for housing. His pupils Theo Bosch and Piet Blom (* 1934) have continued his concept with new applications, and the outstanding work of Herman Hertzberger (* 1932) is yet another example. Hertzberger's Central Beheer in Apeldorn of 1968 – 1972 is a revolutionary realization of an office complex in a new structural order, and his "De drie Hoven" in Amsterdam of 1972 – 1974 is an important example of an old people's home (Fig. 221).

By far, one of the most important architects of the younger generation is Rem Koolhaas (* 1944) who has excelled in housing complexes, cultural centers, and — most recently — a design for the new media center in Karlsruhe (1991). Still other architects who have made significant contributions to the renewal of Dutch architecture are Tom Alberts (the NM Bank in Amsterdam of 1983 – 1988), and the firm Architektengroep (housing in Kalf of 1981 – 1982, the city hall in Ouderkerk aan de Amstel of 1979 – 1980).[30]

Architecture in Belgium Since 1970

Belgian architecture in recent years is most convincingly displayed in the work of Lucien Kroll (* 1927), especially in his various buildings for the Catholic University of Louvain in Woluwe, such as the Medical Faculty Housing. Kroll has also received commissions in France (housing in Alençon, Normandy, of 1971) and Africa (master plan for the new capital city of Kimihurura, Rwandi, of 1970–1975). His ambition to create an alternative architecture in which the user plays a role is most clearly articulated in his often indeterminate structures in Woluwe. In regard to this work, Kroll advocated an architectural "landscape" in favor of user interaction, which he explains: "We are betting on differences, on organic textures. The participation of its future occupants is one of the means likely to lead to that landscape which is composed of present differences and which welcomes future differences."[31]

The architecture in neighboring Luxembourg is characterized by buildings and projects by Rob and Leon Krier (Fig. 160), Roger Taillebert (European Parliament of 1978), and the recently completed complex for the Deutsche Bank by Gottfried Böhm (1991).

Contemporary Architecture in Germany

German architecture since 1970 is, as in the two decades before 1970, determined by a complex situation to which foreign and local architects have contributed. Among the works by foreign architects are James Stirling's Staatsgalerie in Stuttgart of 1975–1984 and the Science Center in Berlin of 1988. They had, as Stirling's teaching in Düesseldorf, enormous impact on the German situation. But also influential were Austrian architects such as Hans Hollein and Ottokar Uhl; Scandinavian architects such as Aalto, Jacobsen, Dissing, and Weitling; and American architects such as Richard Meier (Museum of Arts and Crafts in Frankfurt of 1984), John Hejduk (house in Berlin-Krentzberg, Fig. 220), and Frank O. Gehry (Vitra Design Museum in Weil of 1987, Fig. 222). The IBA (Internationale Bauausstellung) in Berlin, with buildings by, among others, Aldo Rossi, John Hejduk, Peter Eisenman, Charles Moore, Paolo Portoghesi, Alvaro Siza, Kisho Kurokawa, and Arata Isozaki has not only stimulated the housing situation, it has also proven to be of great significance for the development of contemporary architecture in general.

Works by German architects are also of exemplary significance, with the greatest impact made by leading personalities such as Gottfried Böhm and Oswald Mathias Ungers, who have replaced the impact by the old masters from the prewar period. The work of Gottfried Böhm (* 1920) has especially become important for the new situation. His community centers in Bocholt (1973), Kettwig (1977), Bergisch-Gladbach (1977–1980), and his housing schemes in Chorweiler (Fig. 219) and Porz-Zürndorf of 1981 — as his major buildings for cultural and civic purposes — are outstanding articulations of the new situation. For Böhm, it is the context of the environment that determines the shape and form of the building and only in this context can a realistic and pragmatic

219   Gottfried Böhm: Housing in Chorweiler (1969–1975)

220 John Hejduk: House in Berlin-Krentzberg (1989)

221 Herman Herzberger: De drie Hoven, Amsterdam (1972–1974)

222 Frank O. Gehry: Vitra Design Museum, Weil (1987)

architecture develop. Böhm's buildings, which in recent years extended beyond the borders of Germany, are complex manifestations in which the elements and visual stimulations of sculpture and painting are organically integrated.

The architecture of Oswald Mathias Ungers (* 1926) grew out of a different background but has achieved similarly unique solutions. Unger's recent work, including his Institute for Polar Research in Bremerhaven of 1979–1980, the German Architecture Museum in Frankfurt of 1979–1984, the gallery and exhibition hall of the Fair Complex in Frankfurt of 1980–1983, and especially his Badische Regional Library in Karlsruhe of 1980–1991, are all masterpieces of a classical spirit in contemporary architecture integrated into the urban and historic context and enriched with works by painters and sculptors (Fig. 223).

Although he is Austrian, Hans Hollein (* 1934), who teaches at the Kunstakademie in Düsseldorf, has contributed to the German architectural scene with two major buildings, his museum in Mönchengladbach of 1972–1982 and his Museum of Modern Art in Frankfurt of 1982–1990. Both museums, which are tailormade for specific works by contemporary artists, adjust also to the specific urban fabric of the respective cities.

The wide range of architecture in Germany is furthermore characterized with buildings by Harald Deilmann (* 1920), von Gerkan and Marg (Airport in Berlin-Tegel of 1974), Werner Düttmann (Housing Mehringplatz, Berlin of 1970–1975), Helge Bofinger (* 1940), Josef Paul Klei-

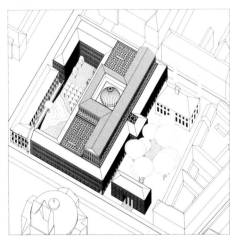

223   O. M. Ungers: Badische Landesbibliothek, Karlsruhe (1991)

hues with housing in Berlin (Block 270 of 1979), and by the Luxembourgian Rob Krier with housing in Berlin (Fig. 160). The architecture in former provinces of Eastern Germany is represented (by the Neues Gewandhaus in Leipzig of 1975–1981) by Rudolf Skoda.[32]

Other architectural representation can be seen in works by Frei Otto (* 1925) who, in collaboration with Günter Behnisch (* 1922), was instrumental in the Olympic Buildings in Munich of 1972. In collaboration with Carlfried Mutschler, Otto built the Multihalle in Mannheim (1975) and a large number of buildings in the Middle East in collaboration with Rolf Gutbrod (Conference Center in Mecca of 1974).

Architecture in Austria Since 1970

Austria, like Germany, has been influenced by architects from other countries, for example, the Finnish architects Kaija and Heikki Siren (Konzerthalle Brucknerhaus in Linz of

1974), but for the most part, Austrian architecture is determined by architects such as Hans Hollein, Ottokar Uhl (* 1931), Gustav Peichl (* 1928), Wilhelm Holzbauer (* 1930), and Guenter Domenig (* 1934), who — on various levels — express the Austrian identity. Hollein's major work in Austria is the Austrian Travel Agency in Vienna of 1976 – 1978, a historistic showpiece in line with the functions of the client. His Haas House in the center of Vienna of 1985 – 1991 creates an urban accent in the context of a historical environment. Both Holzbauer and Uhl are mainly concerned with housing, for example Holzbauer's Vienna housing of 1976 – 1978, and Uhl's Housing in Hollabrunn of 1972 – 1976 in which, to a large extent, the user was part of the process of decision making. Peichl built several centers for Austrian Radio and TV (Eisenstadt of 1971 – 1972 and Vienna of 1979 – 1980). In his savings bank in Vienna of 1975 – 1980, Günther Domenig created an expressive figurative form of architecture, while the center for the blind in Unterdambach by Johann Staber of 1972 – 1976 stands out as a prototype for buildings for the handicapped. New forms of experimental architecture continue to be developed by firms such as Coop-Himmelblau (Funder Werk in St. Veit-Glan of 1988) and Missing Link.[33]

Swiss Architecture Since 1970

Swiss architecture has in the last two decades developed along the lines of earlier achievements, based on the work of such architects as Atelier 5, Dolf Schnebli (* 1928), and Justus Dahinden (* 1925), who in their recent buildings continue their typical Swiss solidity and thoroughness. The southern part of Switzerland, with its School of Ticino, has continued to grow equally with works by Bruno Reichlin (* 1941) and Fabio Reinhart (* 1943) and Luigi Snozzi (Casa Biancetti, Ticino, 1975). A culmination of European architecture can be seen in the work of Mario Botta (* 1943), who reached architectural maturity in his School in Morbio Inferiore of 1972 – 1976 as well in other realizations, for example, several residences in the Ticino. In his large-scale works, Botta transcended Swiss borderlines, setting major examples in France (the André Malraux Cultural Center in Chambery, Le Bas, of 1982 – 1987, and House of the Books in Villeurbanne, near Lyons of 1988). The discipline of architectural engineering found new imagination in realizations by Santiago Calatrava (* 1951), specifically as manifested in his railway station in Zürich-Stadelhofen of 1983 – 1984.[34]

In neighboring Liechtenstein the Center for Art of 1969 – 1975 by the Cuban architect Ricardo Porro (* 1925) is one of the outstanding buildings (Fig. 150a).

Architecture in France Since 1970

Following the impact made by Le Corbusier, Georges Candilis, and Vladimir Bodiansky, who, as the old masters, dominated architecture in France over several decades, a new generation came forth that continued the earlier development but with stronger emphasis on integrating individual buildings into the urban fabric. The work of Roland Simounet is typical of this concept, as seen in his pioneering buildings in Algeria and Madagascar as well as in his buildings in France, such as the Museum Picasso in Paris of 1976–1985, the Museum for Prehistory in Nemours of 1976–1980, and the Museum of Modern Art in Northern France in Villeneuve-d'Ascg of 1978–1983. Simounet's earlier experience in Africa was continued in his residential quarter in Courcourconnes in d'Evry of 1972–1975, in which he created a continuing architecture in a newly founded city (Fig. 224). Roger Taillibert (* 1926) had a major impact on the development of sport buildings in France and beyond, culminating in the Olympic Complex in Montreal of 1974–1976. He is also recognized for large-scale administration complexes such as the European Parliament in Luxembourg (1978).

The official government policy of President Mitterand led to several large-scale realizations for Paris, among them Le Grande Arche of the Place de la Défense of 1982–1990 by Johann Otto von Spreckelsen, the Parc de la Villette by Bernard Tschumi of 1982–1985, the renovation of the Musée d' Orsay by Gae Aulenti of 1986, the new Opera House at the Place de la Bastille of 1982–1990 by Carlos Ott, the Institute du Monde Arabe of 1987–1988 by Jean Nouvel, the Ministry of Economics and Finances by Paul Chemetov, Borja Huidobro and Christian Devilliers of 1982–1988, and the 1983–1984 addition to the Louvre by I. M. Pei. The

224 Roland Simounet: Housing d'Evry, Cour cour connes (1972–1975)

Mitterand government housing policy is best expressed in large-scale residential complexes, such as Ricardo Bofill Levi's (* 1939) Palais d' Abraxas in Marne-la-Vallée of 1978–1983, his Les Arcades Du Lac and Le Viaduc in Saint-Quentin-en-Yvelines of 1981 (Fig. 224a), and Nuñez Yanowsky's (* 1942) Arena Picasso, also in Marne-la-Vallée, of 1980–1985.

Other conceptions in France with new and often spectacular shapes are Christian de Portzamparc's (* 1944) housing in Paris, Marie-Christine Gangneux's (* 1947) College Paul Eluard in Nanterre of 1983, and Fran-

224a Ricardo Bofill Levi: Le Viaduc, Saint-Quentin-en-Yvelines (1981)

çois-Hélène Jourda's (* 1955) and Gilles Perraudin's (* 1949) Ecole Européenne Hotelière in Nimes of 1990.[35]

Contemporary Architecture in Italy

In contrast to the situation in France which, to a great extent, is dominated by large-scale government projects and monumental formalistic aspirations, architecture in Italy has flourished on various levels, producing outstanding architects of international importance: Carlo Aymonino, (* 1926), Aldo Rossi (* 1931), Vittorio Gregotti (* 1927), Renzo Piano (* 1937), Giancarlo de Carlo (* 1919), Gae Aulenti (* 1927), and Paolo Portoghesi (* 1931). Aymonino's and Rossi's residential quarter of Gallaratese in Milan of 1970 is still of exemplary significance for the reintegration of architecture in the context of the city, which Rossi so brilliantly wrote about in his book *The Architecture of the City* in 1966. In the secondary school at Broni of 1979, the city hall in Borgoricco of 1983–1988, and in numerous other projects Rossi has made the case for a contemporary architecture based on the memory of place and the integration of urbanism and architecture.

Giancarlo de Carlo's housing schemes in Terni and Mazzorbo are exemplary solutions for user participation and have since been recognized, as have works by Rossi and Aymonino, prototypes for humane social housing in all parts of the world. De Carlo's Faculty of Education in Urbino of 1973–1975 is a masterpiece of recycling an old structure for a contemporary use. Vittorio Gregotti designed the Maserri Stadium in Genova and Renzo Piano the World Cup Stadium in Bari; both were completed in 1992. Gae Aulenti designed the Art Museum of Catalonia in Barcelona (1985–1992) and the Italian Pavilion at the World's Fair in Seville (1990–1992).

Paolo Portoghesi has contributed new typologies to social housing, in his Enel Housing in Tarquinia of 1981–1987, and his Great Mosque in Rome of 1976–1988, is one of the most significant religious buildings in Italy.

The young generation of Italian architects experiments with solutions for social architecture, among them Giorgio Grassi (* 1935), Franco Purini (* 1941), and Laura Thermes (* 1943), and the groups Archizoom and Superstudio in Florence and G.R.A.U. (Alessandro Anselmi, Paola Chiantante, Gabriella Colucci, Anna Di Noto, Pier Luigi Erole, Federico Genovese, Roberto Mariotti, Massimo Martini, Pino Milani, Francesco Montuori, Patrizia Nicolosi, Giampietro Patrizi, Franco Pier Luisi, and Corrado Placidi) in Rome.[36]

Contemporary Architecture in Spain

In recent years, Spanish architecture has taken a significant turn. Since Franco's regime, it has reached a status of importance shown in a large number of outstanding buildings of high quality. While old masters such as José Antonio Coderch de Sentmenat (1913–1984), J. M. Martorell (* 1925), Oriol Bohigas Guardiola (* 1925), David Mackey (* 1933),

225 Rafael Moneo Valles: Museum in Mérida (1980-1984)

Francisco Javier Saenz de Oiza (* 1918), José Antonio Corrales (* 1921), and Ramon Vazquez Molezun (* 1922) continue to excel with important works, the next generation of architects, such as Ricardo Bofill (* 1939), Rafael Moneo Valles (* 1937), and Studio PER in Barcelona (Lluis Clotet Dallas, Christian Cirici Alomar, Pep Bonet Bartran, and Oscar Tusquets Guillen, all born 1941) is in the process of establishing a more disciplined architectural language. Among some outstanding achievements are the Labor University of Almeria by Julio Cano Lasso (* 1920) and Alberto Campo Baeza (* 1946) of 1976, the housing schemes by Martorell, Bohigas, and Mackey in Barcelona of 1974, the museum of Roman Antiquities in Mérida (Fig. 225), the town hall, offices and city center in Logrono of 1976-1981, and the new Seville airport of 1992 by Rafael Moneo Valles. New results are achieved by the architects José Ignazio Linazaro (* 1947) and Miguel Garay (* 1936),

and Enric Miralles (* 1955) and Carme Pinós (* 1954).

Several Spanish architects have also built in other countries, for example, Ricardo Bofill in France and Algeria, Rafael Moneo in America, and Enrico Donato in Algeria. More recent developments were increasingly enriched by a large number of buildings for the Olympic games by architects from other countries (Sant Jordi Sports Hall by Arata Isozaki of 1990) in Barcelona and the World's Fair in Seville of 1992 (Japanese Pavilion by Tadao Ando and English Pavilion by Nicholas Grimshaw).[37]

Architecture in Portugal Since 1970

Recent developments in Portugal are exemplified in works by Tomas Taveira (* 1938), Fernando Tavora, Francisco Keil Amaral Eduardo Anahory, Marcelo Luiz Correia de Lima Costa and, most importantly, Alvaro Siza Vieira (* 1933). Taveira's Shopping

Center and office complex in Amoreiras Lisbon of 1981–1987 is a spectacular urban concentration paralleling the work of such architects as Bofill and Nuñez-Yanowsky in France. Siza's housing schemes São Victor in Porto of 1974–1977 and Malagueira in Evora of 1977, his school of architecture in Porto (1984–1987), and his kindergarten in Penafiel of 1990 are exemplary solutions for these building types. In recent years, Siza, who studied between 1949 and 1955 with Tavora, expanded beyond the borders of his country and completed buildings in Germany (Housing Schlesisches Tor in Berlin of 1980) and France (Cité de la Jeunesse, in Paris, of 1990).[38]

Eastern European Architecture Since 1970

Dramatic changes have taken place in most of the countries of Eastern Europe in recent years that more than in most other parts of the world have transformed the architectural situation. The political changes caused by the reform movement of Mikhail Gorbachev (* 1931) and more recently by Boris Yeltsin (* 1931) and the parallel reevaluations of regional identities have had an important impact on building activities in the republics of the former Soviet Union as well on the states of Eastern Europe, which in the 1970s and 1980s, were under the influence of the Soviet Union. Also, in regard to building priorities, Eastern European development can be compared to changes in other parts of the world that lean toward a more

conscious and often systematic emphasis on social issues, with buildings for children and for the handicapped.

Outstanding examples are theaters for children in Moscow and Tashkent, youth hostels and sanatoria for workers in Poland and Russia, vacation architecture in the Crimea and in the Baltic states — all reflecting a changed situation that serves a part of the population neglected in the past decades of modern architecture. These parallel developments in East and West have been recognized by architectural historians and have led to a mutual understanding of basic issues that face architects in our time.[39]

Transformations in Soviet architecture took place in multiple waves after the death of Stalin in 1953. The first wave was initiated by Nikita Khrushchev (1884–1971) when he criticized the monumental symbolism of architecture and its promotion as an international Communist style. After rational building methods were introduced and prefabrication and standardization became the main goal in rebuilding of the country after the devastation of World War II, a second wave led to a more imaginative form of buildings that in the 1980s culminated in the reform movement promoted by Mikhail Gorbachev, called "Perestroika."

The contrasting manifestations of this second and important change can be seen in those buildings that still reflect the essence of Socialist Realism in architecture, such as the various works by L. V. Rudnev (1885–1956) and the buildings by Mikhail V. Posokhin (* 1919). Rudnev's Lomonossov University on the Lenin Hills in

Moscow of 1948–1952—a monumental representation of the survival of the Russian people—is symbolic architecture that does not harmoniously fulfill specific functions of circulation and efficiency (Fig. 102). On the other hand, Posokhin's Palace of Congresses in Moscow of 1960–1961 is basically a functionalist structure in which the multiple internal requirements are solved despite the historic context of the Kremlin into which it is set.

Posokhin's subsequent development represents the changes that occurred in the 1970s and 1980s, both in terms of the formal significance of the buildings and the changed emphasis given to previously unsolved building tasks. In his reorganization of the Kalinin-Prospect in Moscow and the headquarters of the Council for Mutual Economic Assistance (CMEA) of 1964–1969, Posokhin created an urbanistic form that clearly resembles modernist aspirations and at the same time sets an urban accent in this part of the city. In the Pitsunda Resort Complex of 1968 in Georgia, Posokhin created a harmony between buildings and landscape in a comprehensive environment containing seven hotels, a restaurant, cafeteria, swimming pool, summer cinema, and a dance hall, as well as facilities for sports and recreation. And still another dimension was inaugurated by Posokhin in his buildings for the Moscow Olympic Games of 1980. Here, he developed dynamic roof structures and fantastic building forms that were until then unknown in his country. The hanging roof in the sports hall is an example of an architectural expressiveness that was earlier articulated in other countries, such as the United States and Japan.

Posokhin also represented his country in two world's fairs, with his USSR Pavilion in Montreal in 1967 and Osaka in 1970, both buildings again reflecting the transformations that had taken place in those years. From a more technocratic building in Montreal, in which space explorations and Sputnik were exhibited, to the spiral shape and colorful dynamism of the building in Osaka, the development of Russian architecture was clearly represented.

The transformations are also visible in other buildings of the time, especially in works by Anatoli T. Poljanski, who became one of the leading architects in the design of vacation complexes in different parts of the former Soviet Union. Among his earliest realizations are the camps for the Young Pioneers in Artek and Massandra in the Crimea of 1961 and 1963 (Fig. 164). Light pavilions with open balconies are grouped together and integrated into the coastal landscape so that, as in Posokhin's complex in Pifsunda, a harmonious balance between manmade structure and nature is achieved. Another important complex by Polianski is in Issyk-Kul, Siberia, of 1975. Here, in a dramatically shaped building, most facilities are internally organized in sculptural forms that relate to the surrounding landscape of the mountains, to which large-scale works by sculptors and painters were added. In his Soviet Embassy in Athens of 1980, Poljanski assimilated another cultural tradition by his choice of materials and the classical language of form.

226 *Kubassov, Uliashov: Moscow Art Theater
(1973)*

Specialization among Russian architects has led to an emphasis on particular building types, among them buildings for children and leisure centers for workers. One of the leading teams in building leisure centers are the architects Cherniavski, Popov,

and Vasilevski, who created a prototype of this category in Voronov in 1976. Located 36 miles (60 km) east of Moscow in a beautiful landscape, the complex contains a sanatorium, theater, sports hall, swimming pool, and restaurant, all integrated into the surrounding landscape—an important element for the recreation of the users. In contrast to earlier phases of Soviet architecture where materials such as concrete and steel were preferred, here wood, travertine, and natural stone enhance the natural atmosphere of the total environment. The passenger terminal by Vitaly Sokhin in the harbor of St. Petersburg (1981–1983) is exemplary of a new architecture in the area of transportation (Fig. 227).

Other teams of architects have concentrated on buildings for children, which were pioneered in the Soviet Union. Two of these buildings are the Children's Musical Theater in Mos-

227 *Vitaly Sokhin: Passenger terminal, St. Petersburg (1981–1982)*

cow of 1980 by Krassilnikov and Velikanov and the Children's Animal Theater in Moscow of 1980 by Saevich, Gorbunova, and Lazarenko. Here, as in comparable realizations in other parts of the country, as in Tashkent in the Puppet Theatre by V. Kuzlianov of 1979, the architects focused on children's imagination, and every detail of the structure was conceived with their expectations in mind.

Among the important new theaters in Moscow are the Moscow Art Theater by Kubassov, Uliashov, Tsirkounov, and Manevich of 1973 (Fig. 226) and the revolutionary structure of the Theater at the Taganka of 1983 by A. Anissimov, J. Gniedovski, and V. Kulikova. The legendary tradition of the Taganka Theater was innovatively continued in a new structure by combining the city, architecture, and theater into a new unity.

The regional differentiations of the country, which in 1991 led to the actual reorganization of the new republics, was clearly visible before these changes, so that buildings in the Russian republic in the 1970s and 1980s were obviously different from those in Georgia (Fig. 229), Armenia, and in the Baltic (Fig. 228) and Asian republics. Against the previously promoted uniformity of Socialist Realism, a new emphasis was given to regional traditions and ethnic identity.

In the Baltic republics, this striving for cultural independence was especially manifested in a large number of outstanding buildings that no longer adhered to the standards of an ideology forced upon them by Russia. In Lithuania, the architect Vitautas Cekanauskas designed housing and office structures resembling the Swedish architectural tradition. The Sports Palace in Vilnius by Hlomauskas, Kriukelis, and Landsbergis of 1971 is a powerful architectural manifestation of the Lithuanian identity, and the Spa Complex in Druskininkai by R. and A. Shilinskas of 1981 developed fantastic circular spaces, which in earlier phases of Eastern European architecture were unknown.

The most astonishing regional architecture has been established in Estonia, where since the 1960s, local traditions have been reinstated. One example is the monumental choral auditorium in Tallinn of 1960 by the architects Kotli, Sepman, and Toelpus (Fig. 165), which was followed by several buildings of the same type in other Estonian and Lithuanian cities. The large roof structure in Tallinn creates space for 31,500 singers, with a seating capacity for an audience of about 150,000 people.

Other recent developments have produced a school of architects in Tallinn concerned with buildings in the rural environment. Architects such as Toomas Rein, Vilen Künnapu, Leonard Lapin, Avo-Himm Loover, and Tiit Kaljundi have created one-family houses, apartment blocks, sports facilities, and social buildings, all of which demonstrate a regional Estonian language, completely distinct and programmatically different from the architecture in the neighboring Russian republic. Among the outstanding examples of this architecture are the kindergarten in Pärnu of 1975–1978, the public sauna for farm workers in Kobela of 1973–1983, the recreation center in Paatsalu of 1976–1979 and

228 *Toomas Rein: Public sauna, Kobela* *(1973–1983)*

229 *Giorgi Chakhava: Offices for Road Engineering, Tblissi (1977)*

the sport and recreation center in Aegruder-Nelijärve of 1977 by Toomas Rein. The high quality of design is seen in a number of fascinating projects developed for an arctic cultural center, central among them the work by Vilen Künnapu, L. Lapin, and A. Alver in 1983–1984, shows the international significance of Estonian architecture in our time.[40]

Like Estonia, today an independent state, also in the Ukraine, Georgia, Armenia, and the Asian Republics of the former Soviet Union, the reinstatement of regional building traditions has led to outstanding results. Ukrainian architects built several summer camps for youth organizations in a terraced shape that incorporates the landscape environment into the ensemble (Pioneer Camp "Chaica" by T. Beliaieva, A. Lonkov, and L. Mouliar of 1978 and Camp "Ocean" by Igor B. Makkor of 1970). In his school of architecture at Kiev University of 1980, L. Filenko created a functional linear environment of great efficiency. And the Library for Children in Kiev of 1980 by Budilovski, Tseitlina, and Dorizo is one of the major examples for the change of priorities to serve children in a most appropriate and carefully detailed architectural form (Fig. 230).

Among the contemporary architects in Georgia, Giorgi Chakhava has a special position with several experimental buildings in the resort area of Batumi (1970–1979) and his office building for Road Engineering in Tblissi of 1977 (Fig. 229). This building, designed in bridgelike elements elevated from the ground, makes use of the hilly site and at the same time

230 *Budilovski, Tseitlina, and Dorizo: Children's Library, Kiev (1980)*

continues a tradition initiated by the architects Serafinov and Krawetz in 1931 with their similarly conceived complex for the State Industry in Kharkov.[41]

Architecture in the Republic of Armenia is in the process of continuing the old tradition of independent articulation of the Armenian people and their architecture. Buildings by Raphael Israelian (Museum of Ethnology in Erevan of 1974–1980), D. Torosian (Holiday Rest Center in Erevan of 1965), and G. Kochar (Writer's Rest Home near Erevan of 1980) are expressions of these ambitions. Israelian's museum especially caught the spirit of the old Armenian tradition in round-arched details, and the new "Swartnost" airport in Erevan, by the architects Tarchanian, Chatchikian, Tcherkesian, and Shechlian, completed in 1984, is both a functional and expressive realization of this building task.

The recent developments in the Asian republics of the former Soviet Union, Kasakstan, Turkmenistan, and Uzbekistan as well as the large territories of Siberia, part of the Russian republic, are still in their first phases of identifying the wishes of their heterogenous population. The southern republics, especially Uzbekistan, have moved toward a strong revival of Islamic traditions in several major buildings that clearly demonstrate their goal of architectural independence from Moscow, which over the past decades was often conceived as a colonial power. In Tashkent, for example, buildings by Rosanov (Lenin Museum of 1970) are side by side with buildings by A. Kossinsky, V. Kuzlianov, and V. Muratov, the former still in the tradition of earlier phases of Soviet architecture, the latter striving with individual differentiation toward the new identity of the Islamic population of their country. The National

Bath House by Kossinsky and Grigoriants in Tashkent of 1980 is a powerful example of tendencies towards an Uzbek identity, as are housing complexes by Kossinsky in Tashkent of 1980. A unique small structure pointing in the same direction is the Blue Dome Cafe in Tashkent of 1970 by V. Muratov, in which the old habit of sitting on carpets is reinstated as are elements from the old local Islamic past. It is significant that these architectural statements of independence from Russia were achieved before the political independence of the country.[42]

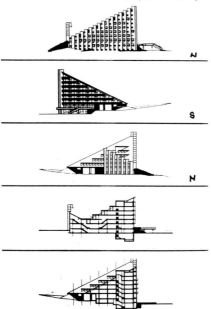

231 Buszko and Franta: Ustron Zawodzie Mountain Health Resort (1968–1978)

Contemporary Polish Architecture

Polish architecture also has, in the last two decades, regained independence from Soviet domination. The works of architects such as Buszko and Franta, Jan and Krystina Dobrowolski, Anna and Jerzy Tarnawscy, Jadwiga Grabowska-Hawrylak, and Wojciech Zablocki have, in various degrees, taken up the regional and local building tradition and achieved convincing results. This can most readily be seen in the comprehensive program of the Ustron Zawodzie Mountain Health Resort in Ustron by Henryk Buszko and Aleksander Franta of 1968–1978 which, conceived with the specific regional mountain formation in mind, creates a harmonious integration of building and landscape (Fig. 231). Various buildings by Anna and Jerzy Tarnawscy, for example, their Diagnostic Center in Wroclaw of 1974–1977, stand out as being in line with parallel tendencies in international architecture, as do a number of buildings by other Polish architects working outside of Poland. Large-scale housing schemes as well as buildings for students were designed by Jadwiga Grabowska-Hawrylak. Especially revolutionary was the Grunwald Housing Estate in Wroclaw of 1970–1975, built in collaboration with Z. Kowalski and W. Wasilewski. Here, high-rise apartments of various sizes for 2,150 inhabitants were established in a mixed-use combination.

The most recent manifestations of younger Polish architects are concentrated around the work and teachings of Romuald Loegler, who designed apartments, houses, and churches, mostly in the region of Krakow.[43]

Contemporary Architecture in the Czech and Slovak Republics

In the earlier phases of the twentieth century, architecture in Czechoslovakia reached a maturity that resulted in industrialized building methods and outstanding buildings for social and communal purposes, as seen in works by Ivan Matusik (Sanatorium for Miners in Bojnice of 1970–1975) and Ferdinand Milucky (Cultural Center in Piestany of 1980). Younger architects such as Karel Koutský (* 1940) and Jan Kozel (* 1940) continued this development with their Telecommunication Center in Cesce Budejovice of 1975, as did Jan Linek (* 1943) and Vlado Miluniy (* 1941) with their Old People's Home in Prague-Chodov of 1983–1989.

Of particular significance among new developments in the country are works by Alena Šrámková (* 1929) and the Team SIAL in Liberec. While Alena Šrámková, who collaborated with Jan Šrámek (1924–1978) until the death of her husband, concentrated on works within an urban and technological context, such as the building for the Prague train station of 1970–1979 and the office complex at Wenzel's Square in Prague of 1974–1983, the large production of the group SIAL under the director Karel Hubáček (* 1924) concentrated on changing the environment. From the early TV tower in Jested of 1964–1973, to their water tower in Prague-Želivka, and department store in

Prague of 1977, the firm created a fascinating body of works that recently expanded into urban planning and commissions outside of the country (recreation and housing in Berlin-Tegel of 1980).[44]

Hungarian Architecture Since 1970

The rich tradition of Hungarian architecture in the twentieth century has continued on several levels. In recent years, urban planning has resulted in new cities and city centers (the city center of Zalaegersteg by György Vadasz of 1977–1980, Fig. 232), housing has developed on a high level with buildings by György Vadasz, György Keves (* 1935), and Karoly Jurcsik and industrial complexes have found new comprehensive realizations. Also, there is outstanding architecture in rural areas specifically related to the folk tradition of the Hungarian countryside with a quality rarely found in any other country.

Of special importance for the international ranking of Hungarian architecture is the work of Imre Makovesz (* 1933). Makovesz has built farmhouses, leisure centers, and religious buildings, but his finest work is the House of Culture in Sárospatak of 1974–1977, a masterpiece of organic architecture built with materials popular in the past and in harmony with the conditions of the local tradition (Fig. 233). Paralleling the work of Makovesz is that of two groups, one centered around Andras Erdei, an architect who discovered a revival of wood carving in the rural environment (Workshop for Wood-carvers in

232 György Vadasz: City Center, Zalaegersteg (1977–1980)

233 Imre Makovesz: Culture House, Sárospatak (1974–1977)

Velem of 1979–1981); the other, in Pecs, includes works by György Csete (House of the Fountains in Pecs-Orfue of 1971) and Peter Oltai (clubhouse in Pécs of 1974).[45]

Contemporary Architecture in Rumania

Recent architecture in Rumania has, as a priority, technological achievements relating to shell construction, culminating in the State Circus in Bucharest by the architects N. Porumbescu, C. Rulea, S. Berkovici, and N. Pruncu of 1960 (Fig. 165a). Works by the leading Rumanian architect, Cezar Lazarescu (* 1923), include the summer theater in Mamaia of 1960, the Otopeni International Airport of 1978–1980, as well as parts of vast vacation complexes on the Black Sea coast (Belvedere vacation center in Olimp). The unfinished palace for the dictator Ceausescu in Bucharest became the symbol of architectural ambition building against the aspirations of the people, as seen in several other countries in Eastern Europe before the revolutionary movements of 1989 and 1990.[46]

Contemporary Architecture in Bulgaria

As in neighboring Rumania, a large part of the new architecture since 1970 in Bulgaria was devoted to the creation of vacation centers and tourist facilities on the Black Sea coast, which for many years attracted visitors from other Eastern European countries. Among them are the buildings by Nenkov and Hdshistojanov in Sadanska of 1983, and by Georgi Stoilov (* 1929). Other works of Stoilov are the Rila hotel and the radio center, both in Sofia. Several Bulgarian architects have been active in foreign countries, for example, Stefan Kolchev, the architect of the sports arena in Varna of 1970, and the National Theater in Lagos, Nigeria.[47] The Hotel Vitosha in Sofia of 1979 is a masterpiece by the Japanese architect Kisho Kurokawa (Fig. 234).

234 *Kisho Kurokawa: Hotel Vitosha, Sofia (1979)*

235 *Velimir Neidhardt: INA Trgovina office building, Zagreb (1975)*

Architecture in the Former Yugoslavia

Long before the former country of Yugoslavia's political deterioration, new architecture within its borders was determined by the regional differences between the northern and southern parts, the Christian and Islamic members of the population and their different historical views on how they defined architecture.

The most northern part of the country, today the independent republic of Slovenia, continues to have close ties to Austrian architecture, but also — especially in buildings by its leading architect, Edvard Ravnika (* 1908) — ties to Le Corbusier. Among the dominant contemporary Slovenian architects are Milan Mihelič (* 1925), with the department store in Novi Sad of 1972 and telephone building in Ljubljana of 1972–1978; Ciril Oblak (* 1934), with the Ljubljana Airport of 1973, a factory in Kranj of 1979; and Stanco Kristl (* 1922), the hospital of the University in Ljubljana of 1969–1974, the Children's Education Center "Mladi rod" in Ljubljana of 1972, and the Izoln Hospital of 1979. The works of Barbara (* 1944) and Bozo Rot (* 1935) include an elementary school in Idrija in 1981 and a home for the aged in Celje of 1982. Two groups of younger architects have extended their work from Slovenia to other parts of the former Yugoslavia: Studio 7 became famous for their opera house in Skopje of 1979, and the group Marko Deklava, Matiaz Gazzarolli, Vojteh Ravnikar, and Egon Vatovec for their administration center in Sežana in 1977–1979.

Among the major architects in Croatia are Velimir Neidhardt (* 1943, Fig. 235), Milan Šosterič (* 1942), Julije De Luca (* 1929), Branco Siladin (* 1936), Radovan Tajder (* 1945), Tomislav Odak (* 1941), and Marijan Hrzic (* 1944). Odak's residential area in Zagreb of 1980 and Hržić's crematorium at the Mirogoy cemetery in Zagreb of 1985 are outstanding examples of the recent developments. A highly sophisticated and often excellent formal maturity is characteristic of many of the houses, housing schemes, vacation centers, and factories by Croation architects.

The leading Croatian architect is Boris Magas (* 1930), who with his Zagreb kindergarten of 1975 found an excellent and unique solution for this task of social architecture (Fig. 236). The stadium in Split-Poljud of 1979 is Magas's masterpiece, as it harmoniously combines the requirements of architectural engineering with architectural principles of environment and context.

The long tradition of Serbian architecture appears in works by architects such as Stojan Maksimović (* 1934, Congress Center SAVA in Belgrade of 1976–1979), Mihajlo Mitrović (* 1922), and Aleksandar Dokic ("Labudovobrdo" housing of 1977 in Belgrade). All are intensely concerned with large housing complexes and have created a tradition of their own, which many younger Serbian architects follow. Two outstanding buildings in Belgrade are the "25th of May" Sports and Recreation Center of 1961–1973 by Ivan Antić (* 1923) and the National Library of the Province of Serbia of 1973 by Ivo Kurtovic (1910–1972).

236 Boris Magas: Kindergarten, Zagreb (1983)

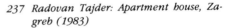

237 Radovan Tajder: Apartment house, Zagreb (1983)

The southern parts of the former Yugoslavia have a distinctly different architectural language. In the two past decades, long-neglected Islamic traditions have been revitalized. Bosnia and Herzegovina have produced such architects as Ivan Štraus (* 1928), who built the Museum for Aviation in Belgrade in 1975–1989; Zlatko Ugljen, who built hotel buildings (Ruza Hotel in Mostar of 1978) and the White Mosque in Visiko in 1980; Radosav Zeković (* 1936), who built the administration complex in Titograd in 1965–1978; and Andrija Mutnjaković (* 1929), who is engaged in new concepts of urban planning and has as his major work the National and University Library in Priština of 1980, which programmatically demonstrates the revival of a contemporary Islamic architecture (Fig. 238).

Yet another example is contemporary architecture in Macedonia, where regional forms are searched out by such local architects as Janko Konstantinov, who built the Telecommunication Center in Skopje in 1981, a work of powerful sculptural intensity. The capital of Macedonia, Skopje, was partly destroyed by an earthquake in the 1960s, and — by following the revolutionary plan by the Japanese architect Kenzo Tange of 1965 — its rebuilding process continues. The Cuban architect Ricardo Porro designed the vacation village in Vela Luca (1972) in a figurative provocative shape.[48]

Architecture in the Southern Hemisphere

In the decades after 1970, new architecture in the countries of the Southern Hemisphere continues to be a

238 Andrija Mutnjaković: National and University Library of Kosovo Priština (1980)

challenge to the very concept of architecture, because basic problems of survival are much more intense than in the countries of the Northern Hemisphere. The problems of housing the masses are — to a certain degree — unsolved in the Third World, and the great disparity between luxurious living styles and the slums could easily lead to violence and revolution.

The growing phenomenon of self-built structures in the cities, often uncontrolled and illegal, in itself is a previously unknown factor for the evaluation of architecture and poses a vital threat to otherwise accepted notions. It becomes more and more evident that the interdependence of rich and poor areas is relevant, not only in cities, but in the international context as well. Everything today is related to everything else, and a crisis in one area by necessity impacts all other parts of the global human environment.[49]

239 Antonio Attolini Lack: Monastery San Luis, Potosi (1980)

Architecture in Mexico After 1970

After the great breakthrough in Mexican architecture in the years following 1950, which culminated in the planning and building of the University City in Mexico City and the exemplary work of architects such as Mario Pani, Juan O'Gorman, and especially Luis Barragan, Mexican architecture went through a new phase of accommodation and expansion. Among the architects who contributed to these new developments were Ricardo Legorreta Vilchis (* 1931) with his Camino Real hotel in Mexico City, Teodoro Gonzales de Leon (* 1926) and Abraham Zabludovsky (* 1924) with their housing schemes and the El Colegio di Mexico complex of 1974–1975, Augustin Hernandez with his residence and office in Mexico City of 1975–1976, Antonio Attolini Lack (* 1931) with his San Luis Potosi monastery of 1980 (Fig. 239), and Fernando Gonzales Gortazar (* 1942) with his American Community Center in Guadalajara of 1972.[50]

Contemporary Architecture in Central America

In Cuba and other countries of Central America, architecture in the years after 1970 followed established patterns, articulating each country's desire for representation and national identity. After the revolutionary work of Paolo Romero and Fernando Salinas (Fig. 169a) and Ricardo Porro and Vittorio and Roberto Garatti in the 1960s, a new phase of conservatism took place, partly a result of the growing economic crisis. Nevertheless, school buildings by Josefina Rebellon as well as buildings for social purposes are still within the priorities of government policies on architecture.[51]

South American Architecture Since 1970

The differing developments in countries of South America reflect the diversity of political transformations that, in each country, had a different pace. Venezuela continues the urbanistic and architectural achievements of Carlos Raul Villanueva, laid out in his large housing estates in Caracas and in his design and execution of the major buildings of the University City of Caracas.

An exemplary model for dealing with the problem of low-income housing can be seen in Peru in the 1972 Previ-Housing competition, to which architects from several countries were invited to build a number of alternatives, focused on social issues and regional identity. Among the architects who built prototypes in Lima were the Japanese architects Maki, Kurokawa, and Kikutake, the British architect James Stirling, the Dutch architect Aldo van Eyck, the Swiss architects Atelier 5, the Indian architect Charles Correa, and the American architect Christopher Alexander.

In Colombia, architecture has reached convincing results with works in Bogota by Rogelio Salmona (* 1929) including his high-rise apartment buildings of 1965 – 1970 and his Museum of Modern Art of 1975.

In the last two decades, Brazilian ar-

chitecture continues to implement construction of the new capital of Brasilia, which created a new administrative and cultural center in the heart of the country. The work of younger architects has been strongly concentrated in São Paulo with Lina Bo Bardi's museum of 1969 (Fig. 172) and housing of 1974 by Joaquim Guedes (* 1932), an architect who recently expressed the opinion that the most important contemporary structures in Brazil are the favelas (slums) of Rio de Janeiro, which were built by their users.

The representative architects in Uruguay are Mario Paysse Reyes (* 1913), concentrating on residences and housing complexes (La Brava Housing in Punta del Este of 1970) and Eladio Dieste (* 1917), who — in his industrial and religious buildings — achieved a harmonious unity of architectural engineering and architecture.

Argentinan architecture in the last decades has had a spectacular flowering. Following the earlier works by the office of Sanchez Elia, Peralta Ramos, Alfredo Agostino, and Clorindo Testa, Testa's National Library of 1978 – 1980 became one of the major landmarks in the country. Other firms such as Baudizzone, Erbini, Lestard and Varas, and the firm STAFF (Villa Soldati Housing in Buenes Aires of 1972 – 1976) were engaged in public buildings in La Plata and Buenos Aires. Works by Manteola, Sanchez Gomes, J. Solsona, and Rafael Vinoly excelled in new concepts in mass housing (housing for the Mutual Bank in Buenos Aires of 1975) and their spectacular new TV Center in Buenos

Aires of 1976. A large number of Argentinian architects immigrated to the United States and, to some extent, shaped its complex situation in the 1970s and 1980s, among them Cesar Pelli, Eduardo Catalano, Rodolfo Machado, Jorge Silvetti, Mario Gandelsonas, Diana Agrest, and Rafael Vinoly.

The work of Miguel Angel Roca is concentrated in the city of Cordoba and encompasses high-rise apartment complexes, pedestrian malls, and public squares, by means of which the urban image of the city received a new articulation.

Architecture in Chile has continued the attempts of Mario Perez de Arce regarding low-income housing schemes. But a new experimental architecture has also been introduced in projects and buildings by Mario Montes.[52]

New Architecture in South Saharan Africa

Developments in Africa do not live up to the hopes of the early years following the independence of several of its countries around 1960. Although there were severe large-scale setbacks, individual building complexes and new cities continued to be built, for example, the Staff Maisonettes for the Bank of Zambia in Lusaka by Montgomery, Oldfield, and Kirby in 1971 (Fig. 241), and the new capital of Nigeria in Abuja designed by the Japanese architect Kenzo Tange in 1979, since implemented by African architects, among them Olewole Olumuyiwa. In collaboration with Roy Maclachlan, Kirby also built the clinic for the University of Zambia (1977). In Kenya, works by H. Richard Hughes and Reuben Musyoka Mutiso stand out. Concerted efforts are being made by groups of architects to build in harmony with the African tradition. Among these efforts are buildings in the Sahara region by Adaua, who used the old mud-brick technology, and a group working in Nianing, Senegal, who focused on building an agricultural training center. Seen in the context of the enormous challenges on this continent, these efforts are no more than insignificant glimpses into a mass strategy necessary for survival. Julian Elliott, who formerly lived in Zambia, designed the new campus of the University of Lusaka (Fig. 187). In the 1970s and 1980s, he worked in the republic of South Africa where he defined, as did Amancio Guedes—who formerly worked in Mozambique—an integration of old African traditions in a contemporary way. One of Elliott's major works is the New Middle Campus of the University of Capetown (1984–1986). Another important architect practicing in South Africa is Roelof Sorel Uytenbogaardt (* 1933), who designed the sports center of the University of Capetown (1977).[53]

Architecture in the North African Arab States Since 1970

In strong contrast to the developments in Africa south of the Sahara, architecture in the Arab states, including North Africa, the Middle East, and the Arabian peninsula, flourished, to a large part due to the immense riches

240 *Mourad Ben Embarek: Airport in Casablanca (1980)*

stemming from oil resources in several of these countries. Clients were able to invite leading architects from all parts of the world to build large campuses, international airports, and

241 *Montgomery, Oldfield, and Kirby: Staff maisonettes for the Bank of Zambia, Lusaka (1971)*

palaces for the rulers on a scale unrivalled in other parts of the world. Significantly, education played a major part in the new architecture, which will create a basis for the future development of the Arab states.

During the decades before 1970, Morocco had extensive impact from foreign architects, predominantly French and Swiss, who mostly concentrated on mass housing in the cities. The leading architects since 1970 are Abdeslam Faraoui (* 1928) and Patrice de Mazières (* 1930), who built hotels in the south of the country as well as the family planning center in Rabat (1976) and the Faculty of Medicine at the University of Rabat; Elie Azagury (* 1918), who built housing schemes and one-family houses in Rabat and Casablanca (Fig. 181) as well as the Tourist Village in Cabo Negro (1968); Charles Boccara, who built housing in Marrakech (1983); and Mourad Ben Embarek, who built the Casablanca airport (1980, Fig. 240).

The new situation in Algeria is more strongly directed toward large-scale planning and socialist programs. A number of foreign architects were invited to build the large universities: Oscar Niemeyer was commissioned for the University of Constantine (1977), Kenzo Tange for the University of Oran (1971), and the Finnish firm Devecon Oy for the University of Setif. The results were comprehensive, planned environments for education. The Danish architects Hans Munk Hansen and Vilhelm Wohlert built a technical training institute in Algeria. Tange also designed the new tourist center at Andalous on the Mediterranean coast and the new international airport for Algiers (1977). In the context of socialist village planning, architects from Spain were instrumental: Ricardo Bofill's Ablada Village, Enrico Donato's Qued Damous plan (1975–1976), and Eduardo Lagaro Ortiz's Guemar Housing scheme.

In Tunisia, only a few examples of a new architectural concept go beyond the earlier buildings by Olivier-Clement Cacoub, among them houses by the architect Tarek Ben Miled in Tunis of 1982.

In Libya, as in Algeria, a comprehensive program for rebuilding educational institutions and urban centers took place, for which several foreign architects were invited. James Cubitt built major parts of the University of Benghazi (1973) and Kisho Kurokawa designed the El-Fatah University in Tripoli (1981–1985). He also made plans for the Higher Institute for Management and Banking in Tripoli (1985). In addition, Kurokawa was involved in the planning of As-Sarir, a new town in the desert, in complete harmony with the traditional desert buildings from the past. The Finnish firm Devecon Oy, with Jauhiainen and Nuuttila, designed and built a new town, Ras Lanuf, in 1980–1984 according to the traditional settlement forms of the region.

Since 1970, Egyptian architecture has been dominated by the example of Hassan Fathy (1900–1989), who laid the basis for a rethinking of building in the Third World. His 1973 book, *Architecture for the Poor*, has become the handbook for architects in many other countries striving equally to achieve a regional identity. In his later

years, Fathy designed and built a few houses in the outskirts of Cairo to which his principles were applied (the Kazerouni house of 1978 and Dr. Mourad Greiss's house of 1984). In Hourani near Saqqara, Ramses Weissa Wassef created a crafts center under comparable aspirations, also using, as Fathy proposed, mud brick and simple technologies in order to create a harmonious relationship with tradition and the present environment.

Other architects in Egypt, such as Mahmoud El Hakim with his museum in Luxor of 1975, and Abdelbaki Ibrahim whose apartments in Cairo and buildings for the Cairo trade fair, incorporated modern means of construction and building technology to solve contemporary requirements. Several Egyptian architects had commissions outside of their country and were especially active in Saudi Arabia and the Gulf States, but the most spectacular realization is the new national university of Qatar in Doha by the Egyptian architect Kamal El Kafrawi of 1978–1980.[54]

Architecture in Iraq, Syria, Jordan, and Lebanon

Architecture in Iraq before 1970 was strongly based on planning schemes by architects such as — among others —Walter Gropius (University City, Fig. 176), Le Corbusier, Alvar Aalto, and Frank Lloyd Wright. Several buildings at the University City by Walter Gropius and his firm TAC were influential for Iraqi architects, who, like Hisham A. Munir, followed his model.

The two most important architects in Iraq, Mohamed Saleh Makiya (* 1917) and Rifat Chadirji (* 1926), both left the country but not before they were instrumental in major buildings, Makiya for several religious buildings (Khulafa Mosque in Baghdad of 1963), educational buildings (Kufa University of 1967), as well as bank buildings in Kufa and Kerbela of 1968, and Chadirji for houses such as the Villa Hamood in Baghdad of 1972.

A large number of foreign architects were invited to build major structures in Iraq, among them the Danish architects Skaarup and Jespersen with a housing program in Baghdad of 1983, Kaija and Heikki Siren of Finland with the Conference Palace in Baghdad of 1982, and Richard England from Malta with a housing complex in Baghdad of 1981–1982. The competition for the Baghdad State Mosque, announced in 1984, brought several fascinating entries from many countries. First prize was given to the American firm Venturi, Scott Brown, and Associates, and an outstanding entry came from the Jordanian architect Rasem Badran.

In Jordan, also, a large number of foreign architects built major works. Among them a group of architects from England, the Halcrow Group, built the Mausoleum Mosque in Amman (1980), Kenzo Tange built the campus of the new Yarmouk University (1976), and Roger Taillibert from France built the Jordan National Geographic Center in Amman (1980). The fascinating design for the Royal Palace in Amman (1977) by Paolo Portoghesi was not realized. The two leading Jordanian architects, Rasem Badran (* 1945) and Bilal Hammad, have been engaged in building individual houses and housing estates, among them the exemplary Ghueillen housing in Amman by Badran of 1984. Badran also excelled with projects for religious buildings, including the King Abdullah Mosque in Amman of 1979 and his competition entry for the Baghdad State Mosque of 1984.

Contemporary architecture in Lebanon, once a country with a flourishing modern expression, has suffered from the destructions of ongoing war. Among Lebanese architects, the work of Jafar Tukan stands out with houses and religious buildings (Aysha Sakkar Mosque in Beirut of 1971). In recent years, most of Tukan's activities, as those of other Lebanese architects, have moved to other Arab states, especially on the Arabian peninsula.

Architecture in the 1970s and 1980s in Syria is characterized by such projects as the Damascus public gardens of 1974 by Kenzo Tange, and housing, hotel buildings, and religious buildings by Syrian architects, among them Bourhan Tayara, who designed an orphanage in Damascus in 1978.[55]

Recent Architecture in Saudi Arabia and the Gulf States

Contemporary architecture in Saudi Arabia and the Gulf States (Kuwait, Bahrein, Qatar, and the United Arab Emirates) has seen a gigantic expansion. Due to the enormous oil resources, many foreign architects were invited to establish a framework for most of the public institutions for administration and communication as well as for state representation. An appropriate adaptation of local criteria and a sense for regional identity is slowly developing. As in other parts of the Middle East and in Africa, emphasis was given to buildings for education, and large campuses have been built to fulfill these requirements, for example, the University of Petroleum and Minerals in Dharan by Caudill, Rowlett, and Scott of 1972. It was one of the earliest examples of American architecture exported to the Middle East, as is King Faisal University in Dammam of 1980, by the Egyptian architect Ahmed Farid Moustafa of 1980.

More recent projects are Kenzo Tange's large plans for the King Saud University in Al-Gassim (1984) and the Arabian Gulf University in Bahrein (1982). Hellmuth, Obata, and Kassabaum built the King Saud University Campus in Riyadh (1984) and Skidmore, Owings, and Merrill built the campus of the University at Mecca (1988).

An innovative new concept was achieved in Kamal El Kafrawi's plan for the new Gulf University of Qatar in Doha (1978–1980). Here old traditions of the region, including natural cross ventilation by modern means of the old wind-tower system, were reinstated in a contemporary manner. Kisho Kurokawa's plan for the new National University of the United Arab Emirates in Al Ain was the winner in a 1988 competition, in which the Japanese architect adapted regional patterns of design including the strong interrelation of Arab art and architecture.

Hotels and conference centers are other examples of finding ways to adapt to the climatic and cultural tra-

ditions of the country. Frei Otto and Rolf Gutbrod translated the tent tradition of the region into a contemporary complex in their Hotel and Conference Center in Mecca of 1969–1974, in their Pilgrimage Tent complex in Muna, their project (in collaboration with Kenzo Tange) "Shadow in the Desert" of 1972, and finally in the sports hall in Jeddah of 1981. Trevor Dannatt gave a different solution to his Riyadh Conference Center and Hotel of 1975 (Fig. 180). The large number of hotel buildings in many other cities basically follow the general trends of international architecture of commercial chains but attempt to create individual shapes and spectacular forms, for example, William Pereira's pyramid-shaped Sheraton Hotel in Doha of 1984–1985.

Buildings of special significance in Riyadh, the capital of Saudi Arabia, are the Eye Clinic by Caudill, Rowlett, and Scott (1982–1983), the Television Center by M. and P. Novarina of 1982, the King Faisal Foundation by Kenzo Tange of 1976–1982, the Diplomatic Club by Omrania of 1984, the Ministry of Foreign Affairs by Henning Larsen of 1980–1986, the French Embassy by Guy Naizot of 1987, and the Japanese Embassy by Kenzo Tange of 1981–1985. A new urban accent for the city of Jeddah was created by the National Commercial Bank Headquarters of 1981–1986 by Skidmore, Owings, and Merrill.

State representation found architectural shape in Jörn Utzon's Parliament in Kuwait of 1979–1984 (Fig. 242), Franco Albini's Kasr El Hokm in Riyadh of 1984, Leslie Martin's palace in Taif of 1972–1976, Kenzo Tange's

242 Jörn Utzon: Parliament, Kuwait (1979–1984)

palaces for the king and the crown prince in Jeddah of 1977–1982, and Reima Pietilae's Sief Palace in Kuwait of 1983. The discrepancy between the feudalistic character of buildings for the government and housing for the general population comes out when comparisons were made between the architecture of the palaces and public housing — which, as in the case of the large-scale housing complex in Dammam by the Eggers Group, is catastrophic.

Modern means of transportation, especially airports, have found interesting solutions in the region. One of the earliest was Minoru Yamasaki's Airport in Dharan of 1965 (Fig. 178), followed by those of Page and Broughton in Dubai (1971), Kenzo Tange in Kuwait (1981, Fig. 179), Skidmore, Owings, and Merrill in Jeddah (1978–1985), and Hellmuth, Obata, and Kassabaum's in Riyadh (1983).

243 Malene Björn: Kuwait Towers (1977)

Water-supply systems, which require a large number of dams, water towers, and desalination plants, were given, especially in the area of water towers, significant forms. Sune Lindstroem's water towers in Jeddah (1978), Kuwait, and Riyadh (1975) are most convincing, and Malene Björns's Kuwait Towers of 1977 created a multipurpose complex in which the requirements for water supply are combined with social functions (Fig. 243).

Work by young Arab architects in the context of the overwhelming foreign domination only rarely gains acceptance or recognition. Among the firms with a number of realizations are Zuhair Fayez (Sammam Headquarters in Jeddah of 1981 and Ministry of Labor and Social Affairs in Riyadh of 1984), Abdel Wahed El-Wakil (Sulaiman Palace in Jeddah of 1981), Halim Abdelhalim (Osman Ibn Affan Mosque in Doha of 1984), Basil Al-Bayati (project for Telecom Tower in Riyadh), Abdullah Bokhari (project for Saudi Arabian National Center for Science and Technology in Riyadh), Samir Khairallah (VIP guest palaces in Doha of 1975), Jafar Tukan (kindergarten in Sharjah of 1975), and Beeah Group Consultant (project for a complex for the blind in Oman of 1979).[56]

Architecture in Israel Since 1970

Architects in Israel are creating a new environment in terms of planning and building new cities, workplaces, and recreation areas. In the 1950s and 1960s, the urbanist Heinz Rau laid the groundwork for the development of the country. His synagogue of the Hebrew University in Jerusalem of 1957 created a symbol for the new state. Al Mansfeld (* 1912) and Frederick Kiesler (1890–1965) in their buildings for the Israel Museum in Jerusalem continued this tendency, as did architects such as Karmi, Rechter, and A. and E. Sharon with their educational buildings, some of them in West Africa (Fig. 186), housing, and public structures. Jakov Rechter's housing in Talpiot-Jerusalem of 1980 and his Faculty of Administration of the Technion in Haifa of 1989 are excellent examples of the polarity of contemporary architecture in Israel. Other architects with outstanding examples of housing are Neumann, Hecker, and Sharon and Zvi Hecker (* 1931) (Remot Housing in Jerusalem of 1979 and The Spiral in Ramat Gan of 1984–1988).[57]

Recent Developments of Architecture in Iran

Before the Iranian revolution, Iran had made a strong international impact with architects such as Kenzo Tange and Louis I. Kahn engaged in major planning schemes of great importance. The American architect Hugh Stubbins built the Technical School of the Technical Institute in Shiraz (1972) and Hans Hollein the Museum of Glass and Ceramics in Tehran (1977–1978). One of the leading Iranian architects, Kamran Diba, who emigrated to the United States, also completed a large number of buildings signifying the high level of architectural maturity in the country. Among his executed buildings are the Children's Village in Shahsawer of 1966–1969, the student union and the mosque of the Jordi-Shapur University in Ahwaz of 1968–1973, the Museum of Contemporary Art in Teheran of 1977 (Fig. 244), and Shushtar New Town of 1978–1980, a completely new urban settlement designed according to the principles of the Islamic way of life.

One of the most recent realizations is the new University of Kernan by the firm Pirraz (Y. Shariatzadeh, M. Mirheydar, Y. Razzaghi, and B. Faravashi), which was completed in its first phase in 1973–1985 and will be completed in a second phase in 1985–1995. Among the outstanding individual buildings in Iran is the stadium in Teheran by the architect Djahanguir Darvich, in collaboration with the French engineer René Sarger, of 1977.[58]

Architecture in Pakistan Since 1970

Architecture in Pakistan in the 1960s was largely dominated by foreign plans and buildings, such as the urban plans by Doxiadis in Islamabad, which resulted in large-scale residential settlement projects, administration buildings, and hotels. Within this plan, the Italian architect Gio Ponti built the Government Center in Islamabad of 1978. Louis I. Kahn designed the Capitol Complex in Islamabad of 1965, an ingenious plan that unfortunately was never realized. Since the early 1970s, there has been stronger emphasis on the challenges

244 Kamran Diba: Museum of Contemporary Art, Teheran (1977)

of mass housing, and in some parts of the country, outstanding results have been achieved in this area. Yasmeen Lari's (* 1942) low-cost housing complexes in Lahore of 1973–1979 are solutions not only in regard to the area's extreme needs, but are also based on the principle of self-help and the efforts of women cooperatives. Yasmeen Lari also built office buildings (Finance and Trade Center in Karachi), hotel buildings (Taj Mahal Hotel in Karachi), and tourist villages (Keenjhar Lake Tourist Resort, Clifton, and Nowshera), the latter completed in 1980. Habid Fida Ali (* 1936) had a strong impact on shaping the skyline of Karachi with office buildings (Commercial Union Building in Karachi of 1989–1991), banks, and restaurants in a contemporary architectural language. The work of Kamil Khan Mumtaz is also devoted to contemporary forms of a local vernacular, in which low-tech elements are explored in order to find solutions for a wide variety of building types (doctor's residence in Lahore of 1976).[59]

Architecture in India Since 1970

Indian architecture in its vast regional manifestations is strongly shaped by Le Corbusier (Fig. 189) and Louis I. Kahn (Fig. 191), who, in their very different ways, influenced numbers of Indian architects. In spite of criticism by Indian architects, Le Corbusier's Chandigarh and Kahn's Institute of Management in Ahmedabad continue to influence current development. The three major contemporary architects practicing in India are Balkrishna V. Doshi (Fig. 190), Charles Correa, and Uttam C. Jain, each of whom has an individual way of defining the regional character of India. In the years after 1970, Doshi (* 1927) designed and built worker settlements with so-

245 *Uttam C. Jain: Indira Gandhi Institute for Development Research, Bombay (1985–1987)*

cial and cultural amenities in Hydera-bad (completed 1971), and Kalol in North Gujarat (1973–1976). Among his most recent works are the Gandhi Labour Institute in Ahmedabad of 1984 and his own architectural office, "Sangath," in Ahmedabad; both explored appropriate ways to develop a low-tech method of building in harmony with the climate and cultural tradition of India.

The work of Charles Correa (* 1930) has stronger affinities with urban context and international architecture. His various forms of housing, such as his high-rise Kanchanjunga Apartments in Bombay of 1980, Tara-Group Housing in New Delhi of 1979, and Belapur Housing of 1983–1986, experiment with alternatives for mass housing in the Indian context. Correa's major work is the creation of Vashi, a new satellite town of Bombay that was begun in 1970 and is planned for a population of 2 million inhabitants (Fig. 246). Here, a large number

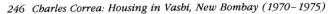

246 *Charles Correa: Housing in Vashi, New Bombay (1970–1975)*

of housing types for all income groups are combined with social and communal facilities in order to create a new community.

In his early work, the Indian architect Uttam C. Jain (* 1934) concentrated on educational buildings in the provinces of Gurajat and Rajasthan, among them buildings for the University of Jodhpur (Printing Plant of 1971 and Lecture Hall of 1971, and Faculty for Social Sciences of 1979–1980). More recent works are the Oberoi Bagmalo Beach Hotel in Goa of 1977 and the Indira Gandhi Institute for Development Research in Bombay of 1985–1987, the latter a complex and sophisticated architectural ensemble of high quality (Fig. 245).

Today, a large number of other Indian architects are actively building, for example, Kanvinde and Rai with buildings for education, Satish Grover with hotel buildings, Anil Laul and Arvind Talati with low-cost housing, and Fariburz Sabha with religious buildings (Bahai Temple in New Delhi of 1986). Raj Rewal completed the Delhi Olympic Village for the Asian Games in the shape of a neighborhood in 1982 and, more recently, the Central Institute of Education and Technology and the National Institute of Immunology in New Delhi.[60]

New Architecture in Bangladesh

The overwhelming urbanistic and architectural achievement in Bangladesh is the planning and building of the capitol complex of Dacca by Louis I. Kahn, which is exemplary in its articulation of the aspirations and values of the entire country (Fig. 191). Built between long interruptions and in an environment of crisis, the complex was executed during 1962–1982 and today stands as a symbol of meaningful architecture unrivaled in any other country of the world. Other architects practicing in Bangladesh are Muzharul Islam (Institute of Fine Arts, Dacca; National Archive, Dacca; Student Hostel of the Jahangir University in Sarar), Rabiul Hussain (Bangladesh Agricultural Research Council in Dacca and Central Mosque RDA in Bogra), Shah Alam Zahiruddin (Mohila Polytechnic in Dkala; Ministers Housing, Minto Road, Dacca), and Raziul Ahsan (SOS Youth Village in Dacca).[61]

Architecture in Southeast Asia

Recent architecture in the countries of Southeast Asia, Malaysia, Singapore, the Philipines, Indonesia, and Thailand has taken on new importance, due to interrelated economic importance for international trade and individual approaches toward a regional identity, which is based on a multiracial reality.

In Malaysia, a rich development is in progress, one dominated by such local architects as Lim Chong Keat (* 1930), the chief designer of the Jorubena Bertiga firm, Hijjas by Kasturi (* 1936), Lai Lok Kun (* 1934), Ruslan Khalid (* 1933), and Ken Yeang (* 1948). Because of the religious movement in the country, emphasis is placed on mosques, especially new mosques by Jorubena Bertiga (mosque in Petaling Jaya of 1975) and Haji

Hajeedar (Abu Baker Mosque in Kuala Lumpur of 1981), as well in individual houses and housing complexes by Lai Lok Kun (condominiums in Kuala Lumpur of 1980), in buildings for social purposes by Fawizah Kamal (student hostel in Penang of 1981), and high-rise apartment buildings by Ken Yeang (Plaza Atrium of 1983 in Kuala Lumpur). Pahang, the new second capital city of Malaysia, was planned by Kenzo Tange in 1983.

Architecture in Singapore is in a high stage of expansion and refinement. Many foreign architects, such as Kenzo Tange (Nanyang Technical Institute of 1981–1986, GB Building of 1981–1986, OUB Building of 1986), I. M. Pei (Oversea Chinese Bank of 1976), Skidmore, Owings, and Merrill (Singapore International Airport of 1974), and Moshe Safdie (Ardmore Apartments of 1984–1985) have contributed large-scale works. The Australian architect Geoffrey T. Malone (* 1943) added a high-technological component with his Crystal Court building of 1984. The most important architect in Singapore is William Lim (* 1932), who created the Golden Mile Shopping Center in 1970–1973, the St. Andrew's Junior College in 1978, the luxury apartment complex unit 8 in 1985, as well as several industrial buildings, residences, and commercial buildings. Other Chinese architects practicing in Singapore are Akitek Tenggara with chief designer Tay Kheng Soon (Chee Tong Temple of 1987), Alfred Wong (Singapore Polytechnic of 1979), and Paul Tsakok (restorations on Emerald Hill Road of 1982–1984).

Since 1970, Indonesian architecture has produced a large number of major buildings, most of them designed by architects from Indonesia, for example, Suyudi (Conference Hall of the National Parliament in Jakarta of 1970; Ministry of Forestry in Jakarta of 1978–1983), Robi Sularto (bank in Densapar on Bali of 1984), and Moersid (Lipi Headquarters in Jakarta of 1980–1983). The new University of Indonesia in Depok, begun in 1986 and expected to be completed in 1996, was designed by Suwondo B. Sutedjo, Gunawan Tjahjono, Budi A. Sukada, and Triatno Y. Hardjoko. Most of the Indonesian architects work in large firms and are in charge of the major commissions given by the government. Only a relatively small number of buildings are by foreign architects, among them the Americans Skidmore, Owings, and Merrill (Hyatt International Hotel in Surabaya of 1978), and Anthony Lumsden (Bank Bumi Daya in Jakarta of 1972–1976), and the Australian Peter Muller (Kayu Aya Hotel in Bali of 1975).

Under the government of Ferdinand Marcos, architecture in the Philippines was represented by buildings of monumental scale and gigantic dimensions reflecting the ambitions of its clients. The leading architect during those years was Leandro V. Locsin (* 1928), who designed the Ayala Museum in Manila Makati of 1974, the Theater of Mount Makeling in Los Banos, Laguna, of 1976, and the new international airport of Manila of 1980. Locsin also did several luxurious residences and restorations of old buildings, such as the Manila Hotel of 1976. Architects working in the Philippines besides Leandro V. Locsin are Francisco Manosa, Santos R. Alfon, and Jorge Ramos.

The recent architecture in Thailand is dominated by the country's two leading architects: Sumet Jumsai and Satrabandhu Ongard. Sumet Jumsai (* 1939) has built a rich variety of building types, among them the School for the Blind in Bangkok of 1970, the Science Museum in Bangkok of 1975, the Ban Saray Seaside Resort of 1982, the Thammasat University Campus of 1984–1986, and the Bank of Asia Headquarters in Bangkok of 1983–1986. The work of Satrabandhu Ongard (* 1943) is concentrated on luxurious residences (Suriyasat residence of 1976–1978, Fig. 247); Khun V. Ed residence of 1982–1983) in which a combination of the American influence of Charles Moore, the architect's teacher at Yale University, and authentic traditional Thai elements merge into a form of fascinating eclectic architecture. Western and Eastern traditions are fully united in his Marble Showroom in Bangkok of 1982.

Besides Jumsai and Ongard, other architects working in Thailand are Boonyawat and Pussadee Tiptus, Chulathat Kitbutr, and Nitt Chaurorn, as well as the Japanese architect Kisho Kurokawa (Japanese Studies Institute of Thammasat University of 1985).[62]

Architecture in Australia and New Zealand

In the last decades, Australian architecture has been dominated by the works of Harry Seidler (* 1923) and John Andrews (* 1933), both engaged in a large number of office buildings, government centers, and houses. Andrew's Cameron Offices in Belconnen of 1977 set a new Australian standard.

247 Satrabandhu Ongard: Suriyasat residence, Bangkok (1976–1978)

Other Australian architects are Cameron, Chisholm, and Nicol (Allendale Square in Perth of 1973–1976), Glen Murcutt (artist's house and studio in Sydney of 1982–1983), and Philip Cox, Richardson, and Taylor (Yulera Tourist Village, Uluru Park, Ayers Rock of 1982–1983; Sydney Football Stadium of 1986–1988). In collaboration with Rice and Daubney, Kenzo Tange designed the World Square in Sydney (1981).

In New Zealand, architects such as Ian Athfield (* 1940) and Roger Walker (* 1942) in Wellington (housing for the elderly, Lower Hutt, of 1992), and Miles Warren (* 1929) in Aukland, have created a regional architectural language in which the organic qualities relate harmoniously to the given landscape.[63]

Architectural Alternatives in China

Contemporary architecture in China is shown in a variety of articulations, in strong contrasts, and in multiple forms, including the People's Republic of China, Hong Kong, Taiwan, and Macau. The enormous diversity within the People's Republic of China constitutes architecture in nearly all possible forms, from cave buildings cut directly into the earth, to low-technology structures, often built by the users themselves, buildings within the tradition of Chinese monumental architecture, to modern constructions with materials such as steel, glass, and concrete, often designed by foreign architects (Fragrant Hill Hotel in Beijing by I. M. Pei of 1982).

Today, all of these forms of architecture co-exist side by side, so that monumental tasks for political meeting halls (Memorial Hall for Mao Tse-Tung in Beijing of 1979, Fig. 195) and agricultural settlements, elementary schools carved into the earth of mountains, and simple units for worker's or farmer's houses constitute the totality of contemporary Chinese architecture. Among the young architects practicing in China today are Wu Changfu (* 1959), who built terraced housing in Gudao New Town in the Shandong Province in 1985 (Fig. 247a), and Huang Xiang-Ming, who built a kindergarten for the housing quarters of Tongji University in Shanghai.

This is in extreme contrast to the situation in Hong Kong, which reflects, besides the temporary self-help structures and house boats, the highest possible technological articulation of architecture today, for example, Norman Foster's Bank of Hong Kong of 1979–1985 (Fig. 248) and I. M. Pei's Bank of China of 1991 (Fig. 249), both landmark buildings that will dominate the skyline of Hong Kong for decades to come. Other foreign architects contributing with major works to the architecture in Hong Kong are Harry Seidler (Hong Kong Club of 1981), Palmer and Turner (Hong Kong Polytechnic of 1973–1979), Paul Rudolph (Bond Center of 1988), and William Turnbull (American Club of 1987).

The leading Chinese architects practicing in Hong Kong are Wong, Tung, and Partners (First National Bank on Queen's Road Central of 1974); Simon Kwan (Academy for Performing Arts of 1989); and Tao Ho (* 1936), who in his Hong Kong Art Center of 1974 searched for a unity of Chinese and Western elements. Ho's most recent buildings are the Arcadia of 1988 and Hong Kong Baptist College of 1990. Other variations of Chinese contemporary architecture can be seen in the developments in Tai-

247a Wu Changfu: Terraced housing of Gudao New Town of Shengli oilfield, Shandong Province (1985)

248 Norman Foster: Bank of Hong Kong, Hong Kong (1979–1985)

249 I. M. Pei: Bank of China, Hong Kong (1982-1990)

wan and Macau. Foreign contributors in Taiwan are I. M. Pei, Kenzo Tange, and Skidmore, Owings, and Merrill (World Trade Center in Taipei of 1985). The architecture in Macao is dominated by mass housing by the architect Manuel Vicente.[64]

Contemporary Architecture in Korea

Contemporary architecture in Korea is distinctly different from the development in China and Japan and has an independent tradition of its own. A large number of buildings by the leading architect Swoo Geun Kim (1931-1986) are devoted to cultural centers and churches (Korean Culture and Arts Center in Seoul of 1979; Masan Cathedral in Seoul of 1979). Among younger architects practicing in Korea are Sung-Yong Joh (* 1944). Some of Sung-Yong Joh's works are houses in

Seoul and the student center of Inha University in Inchon of 1984-1987.[65]

Japanese Architecture Between 1970 and 1990

By 1970, Japanese architecture had already achieved its independence with works by such highly significant architects as Kenzo Tange (Fig. 197), Kunio Mayekawa (Fig. 196), Junzo Sakakura, Kazuo Shinohara, and the representatives of the next generation, Fumihiko Maki, Kisho Kurokawa (Figs. 198 and 202), Kiyonori Kikutake (Fig. 199), and Arata Isozaki (Fig. 201). Early developments have been accelerated with energy and have produced an environment of experimentation and achievement that is internationally unique. No other country today has been able to achieve the synthesis of contemporary requirements and traditional roots as has Japan.

The Osaka world's fair of 1970 was a significant event for Japanese architecture. The various buildings designed for the fair by Kenzo Tange in collaboration with Kurokawa, Kikutake, and Isozaki were signals of Japan's ability to rethink structures of high technological efficiency. Individual works by Tange since 1970, to a large extent outside of Japan, have established him as the grand master of Japanese architecture. A large number of his buildings, such as the Toin School in Kanagawa (1982-1986, Fig. 250), the Yokohama Art Museum (1983), the United Nations University in Tokyo (1986), Tokyo City Hall of 1986, and the Akasaka Prince Hotel of 1983, have become landmarks, as

250 *Kenzo Tange: Toin School, Kanagawa (1982–1986)*

have his buildings in Singapore, Malaysia, Nigeria, Algeria, Saudi Arabia, Italy, France, and many other countries.

The next generation of Japanese architects, such as Maki, Kikutake, Kurokawa, and Otaka, who were at one time referred to as the Metabolists, went in many different directions. Maki built St. Mary's International School in Tokyo (1972), the Kindergarten in Noba and the Aquarium in Okinawa (both of 1975), and the Fuisawa Municipal Gymnasium (1982–1984). Kurokawa built a large number of commercial and cultural buildings such as the Sony Tower in Osaka (1973–1976), the Nagakin Tower in Tokyo (1970–1972, Fig. 198), the Museum of Modern Art in Saitama (1982), and the Museum of Contemporary Art in Hiroshima (1988), and was active in such other countries as the United States, Germany, Libya, Bulgaria, and Thailand.

Kiyonori Kikutake built several city halls and religious buildings and also explored the area of housing (Pasadena Heights Housing in Mishima of 1974). Arata Isozaki explored a rich and comprehensive system of cultural buildings in Kitakyushu (Art Museum and Library in 1975, Fig. 201) and, in the Tsukuba Center of 1979–1983, created an imaginative urban center, including an information complex, a concert hall, a shopping center, and an outdoor plaza, which has significant references to Michelangelo's Piazza del Campidoglio in Rome. Among his most recent realizations — several in other countries, including America, Germany, Poland, and Spain — is the International Conference Center in Kitakyushu (1989–1990).

A large number of Japanese architects came up with their own architectural results in other areas: Kazuo Shinohara (* 1925), with buildings in which a new sense of traditional energies are displayed (House on a Curved Road in Tokyo of 1978); Takamitsu Azuma (* 1933), with an architecture of complexity and contradictions of a new kind (House in Hanagi of 1982); Koichi Nagashima, with large-scale buildings using new technology; Minoru Takayama (* 1934), with buildings for youth organizations (Beverly Tom in Hokkaido of 1973 and Tokyo International Port Terminal of 1991); Osamu Ishiyama (* 1944), with the new Chobachi Art Museum in Matsuzaki of 1986; Takefumi Aida (* 1937; with the PL Institute Kindergarten in Osaka of 1972–1973 and the Tomo's Dental Office in Yamagushi of 1978–1979); Tooyo Ito (* 1941) (White W-House in Tokyo of 1976) — all contributing to the rich architectural scene in Japan.

The work of Tadao Ando (* 1941) reached a level of quality in which the old patterns of Japan and new requirements of our time are fully united in a classical serenity. (Koshino residence in Ashiya of 1981, Fig. 252; "Times" in Kyoto; Okinawa Shopping Center; Hyogo Children's Museum of 1987–1989; Chapel at Mount Rokko of 1987; Japanese pavilion for Expo '92 in Seville, Fig. 253).

At present, Japanese architecture is represented in buildings by Atsuko Hasegawa (* 1941; Shonandai Cultural Center, Fujisawa City of 1989), Shin Takamatsu (* 1948), Atsushi Kitagawara (* 1951; "Rise" in Tokyo of 1986), Kiyoshi Sei Takeyama (* 1954) and Hiroyuki Wakabayashi (* 1949)

247

("Life in Kyoto" of 1986), as well in housing schemes and urban complexes by Kunihiko Hayakawa (* 1941) and Hiroshi Hara (* 1936) (Yamato International in Tokyo of 1984–1987).

The Japanese situation today is further enriched with contributions by such foreign architects as Aldo Rossi (Hotel Il Palazzo in Fukuoka of 1990), Peter Eisenman (Koizuma Lighting Theatre/IZM in Tokyo of 1990), the Cambridge Seven Associates (Tempozan Harbour Village in Osaka of 1990), Christopher Alexander (New Eishin University in Tokyo of 1985), Rafael Vinoly (Tokyo International Forum of 1989–1995, Fig. 251), Harry Weese, Philippe Starck, Zaha Hadid, Steven Holl, Rem Koolhaas, Christian de Portzamparc, Mark Mack, Mario Botta, Oscar Tusquets, Mario Bellini, Richard Rogers, Stanley Tigerman, and Daniel Libeskind (Folly in Osaka of 1990).[66]

252 Tadao Ando: Koshino residence, Ashiya (1981)

253 Tadao Ando: Japanese pavilion for Expo '92 in Seville (1992)

251 Rafael Vinoly: Tokyo International Forum (1989–1995)

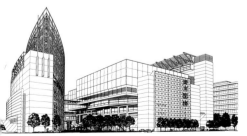

Conclusion

More than ever before, the development of architecture in the twentieth century has expanded all over the world, and this expansion defies a linear historical description. The major role played by the ever-changing political and social differences is shown in the often contrasting building tasks and their architectural articulation. Form and anti-form, fixed and non-fixed structures, buildings that resemble historical models and buildings that solve only the immediate needs of their users, all exist side by side. Eclecticism has both formal and ideological underpinnings and has been established as a positive alternative to the earlier fixed and often power-based notions of style.

Previous books on twentieth-century architecture were, in nearly all cases, written from the Western perspective, and developments, values, and materials were presented exclusively with European and American works in mind. Only in recent years have attempts been made to integrate buildings from Latin-America and Japan, and even then they were mostly seen with evaluative criteria derived from Western models. In this regard, architecture of the Third World has generally been distorted. It has been misrepresented as an appendix of Western architecture and considered of lower quality than Western architecture. As in the periods of colonialism, this remains for many historians the dominant view today. A practicing Third World architect, in objecting to the term "Third World," ironically referred to Dostoyevski's "underground man" in characterizing the distorted reality.

One of the worst consequences of this widely existing distortion is that misrepresenting contemporary Third World architecture also extends to the architectural tradition of Southern Hemisphere. There is an inexcusable gap between the research devoted to European architectural tradition and the traditions of India, Africa, China, Southeast Asia, and Latin America. And, as if the old architectural monuments in the Southern Hemisphere are of no value, much of its architectural heritage, with few exceptions, has been and continues to be destroyed. This negative value judgment has led to the physical annihilation of the cultural heritage of entire civilizations.

The four sections of this book attempt to document twentieth-century architectural developments under these existing conditions. The result is not based on stylistic, formalistic, or other surface categories, but rather on a fundamental revelation of truth. Architecture is not seen as a matter of taste or preference, or restricted to selected parts of the world; rather, it is programmatically described as the universal articulation of society and the conditions of our world as it exists in the twentieth century.

Architecture in this context is seen as the art of building individual structures as well as total environments. The goal is to understand the totality of the constructed milieu as part of a larger human and social fabric from which each part receives meaning.

The book is organized chronologically, according to four generations of architects who emerged at specific turning points in twentieth-century history with their significant and innovative works. These crucial turning points took place around 1910, 1930, 1950, and 1970, and each defined a different task in the development of society at that time.

Around 1910, the emphasis was on architecture, science, and technology, with factories and machine-oriented buildings as the dominant building types. The changes around 1930 resulted in an important shift toward organic building projects, such as hospitals, open-air schools, and buildings for sports and recreation. The third phase began around 1950 and was directed toward new forms of technology, such as nuclear power plants, airports, and launching pads for space travel, a time during which a second machine age developed. The last phase began around 1970, and turned to building types related to social responsibility, such as homes and institutions for handicapped people and children and alternative solutions to the appropriate use of technology in the service of humankind.

The four phases covered in the book are interrelated in complex ways, and specific affinities exist between Parts I and III and Parts II and IV. All sections reflect the historic laws of generational precedents as they occur in other fields of human developments, such as literature, music, and the arts.

It is not possible to predict the developments of the next generation. Perhaps new beginnings around 1990 will merge the elements of the previous periods of twentieth-century architecture, possibly with a special focus on solving the problems of the city, in particular those of the inner city, which in all parts of the world has become one of the major problems in terms of urban, social, political, and cultural matters.

It will be an important challenge for architects, and society in general, to face the vast numbers of unsolved problems in both a pragmatic and imaginative manner. It is no longer possible to live with the illusions and ideologies that have dominated and veiled public debate. Architecture will have to be redefined according to the changes in the macro scale of worldwide transformations, as well as in those in the micro scale of human interrelations. Urban problems can no longer be separated from problems of social and political equality.

The notion of style and the continuation of social domination and degradation of parts of human society by means of economic, political, and cultural subjection will have to be questioned in order to open up new possibilities necessary for the survival of mankind. The value of tradition as the values freedom and economic independence should be accessible to every individual, and the achievements of earlier centuries used as tools in solving the new challenges. It is in this sense that the continuation of human civilization is at stake. Goethe's wisdom envisioned this and the creation of a better reality: "There is no past which one can want to have back, there is only something permanently new, which creates itself out of the broadened elements of the past, and the true search must always be to produce a better new."

Notes

Preface (pp. vii – viii)
1. H. Sedlmayer: "Zu einer strengen Kunst-
   wissenschafr," *Kunstwissenschaftliche
   Forschungen* I, 1931, goes further and demands an appropriate attitude, in the
   sense of scientific predestination.
2. C. Jencks and G. Baird, eds.: *Meaning in
   Architecture*, London, 1970.
3. Hommage à Giedion, Basel 1971.

Part I (pp. 1 – 71)
1. G. Semper: *Wissenschaft, Industrie und
   Kunst*, new ed., Mainz, 1966.
2. U. Kultermann: "Brauchen wir Tradition?
   Über die Notwendigkeit des Architektur-
   geschichte," *Die Tat* 6-25-1968.
3. Appeared first in: Grosstadtarchitektur,
   Berlin, 1924. Reprinted in *Berliner Architektur des 20er Jahre*, Mainz, 1967, p. 55.
4. *Von Material zu Architektur*, new ed.,
   Mainz, 1958, p. 213.
5. C. Gibbs-Smith: *Early Flying Machines*,
   London, 1975. The fact itself is a surprising parallel: that Orville Wright, as well as
   Frank Lloyd Wright, went to Berlin in
   1909 in order to acquaint the inexperi-
   enced German aviation pioneers with the
   new machine.

6. "I cannot tell you how I hate this innocent
   monster which is going to destroy the
   world I love. It will destroy the world I
   love, the world of level vision or vision
   from down upwards, in other words, the
   whole way of looking at things that the artist has been taught to expect, all the rules
   of perspective, the sense of looking at
   solid objects from one fixed place on the
   earth. . . ." Quoted in J. R. Killian:
   *Toward a Working Partnership of the
   Sciences and Humanities,* in *Approach-
   ing the Benign Environment,* University
   of Alabama, 1970, p. 109.
7. H. P. Berlage: *Fundamentals and Development of Architecture*, Berlin, 1908,
   p. 7.
8. ". . . Le Corbusier's work was to be characterized most essentially by a search for
   generalization, universality, and absolute
   formal truths which would put Man in
   touch with a harmony underlying nature
   —a divine 'axis', as he called it, which
   leads us to assume a unity of direction in
   the universe, and to admit a single will at
   its source." Quoted in P. Turner: *The Beginnings of Le Corbusier's Education:
   1902 – 1907, The Art Bulletin* June 1971,
   p. 224. The quotation comes from Le Cor-

busier's book, *Vers une Architecture*, of 1923.

9. J. J. P. Oud: *My Path in "De Stijl,"* Rotterdam, n.d. (c. 1958), p. 13.

10. R. Banham: "The Machine Aesthetics," *The Architectural Review* 4, 1955.

11. "If a machine does the work, it should be allowed to leave its mark, to imprint its mode of expression on the things it produces." Quoted in Rioux de Maillou: *The Decorative Arts and the Machine*, reprinted in T. and C. Benton, eds.: *Architecture and Design, 1890–1939*, New York, 1975, p. 5.

12. ". . . a book is a machine to think with." Quoted in C. Jencks: *Modern Movements in Architecture*, Garden City, N.Y. 1973, p. 32; see also R. Banham: *The Revolution of Architecture: Theory and Design During the First Epoch of the Machine*, Hamburg, 1964 (London, 1960); K. Rowland: *A History of the Modern Movement*, London, 1973, p. 129ff; P. Portoghesi: *Infanzia delle macchine*, Rome, 1965.

13. *De Stijl* V, 33–34. Quoted in H. L. C. Jaffé: *Mondrian and De Stijl*, Cologne, 1967, p. 164.

14. *De Stijl* V, 201. Quoted in H. L. C. Jaffé: *De Stijl*, Amsterdam, 1956, p. 165.

15. O. Stelzer: "Outline of a Creative Experiment," Epilogue to *Moholy-Nagy: From Material to Architecture*, Mainz, 1968, p. 245. It is uncertain as to the reality of a connection to Einstein's 1905 publication, "Electrodynamics of Matter in Motion" or Minkowski's report, "Space and Time" of 1909.

16. H.-R. Hitchcock: *In the Nature of Material: The Buildings of Frank Lloyd Wright*, New York, 1942, is still basic. No comprehensive documentation of the achievement has been published since. N. K. Smith expressed a new perspective, pointing to the content of Wright's buildings: *Frank Lloyd Wright*, Englewood Cliffs, N.J., 1966.

17. "Standardization was either the enemy or a friend to the architect. He might choose." Quoted in Frank Lloyd Wright: *An Autobiography*, New York, 1943, p. 148.

18. J. Rewald, ed.: *Paul Cézanne, Correspondence*, London, 1941.

19. Wright's mother had purchased the Fröbel toy at the 1876 Philadelphia World's Fair and had given it to her son, who had been interested in the profession of architect since his early youth.

20. The 1892 house for Thomas H. Gale in Oak Park cost $3,000; the one for R. P. Parker in Oak Park in 1892, $3,000; the famous Joseph Husser house in Chicago of 1899 had a price tag of $4,500. These extremely low prices have not been sufficiently considered regarding an evaluation of Wright. See H. Allen Brooks: *The Prairie School*, New York, 1976.

21. C. Gibbs-Smith: *Early Flying Machines*, London, 1975.

22. See Wright's notes on hot-water heating in the 1910 Wasmuth publication, F. Gutheim: *Frank Lloyd Wright on Architecture*, New York, 1914, p. 72. William Hogarth linked the concept of beauty with the building of ships in his "Analysis of Beauty" as early as 1753.

23. Eduard Waller was the builder. The total cost amounted to $25,000, rent for an apartment, $12 a month. The building was torn down in 1974. D. Bowley, Jr.: "Saving the idea of Wright's 1895 'model tenement,'" *Inland Architect*, Feb. 1976, pp. 18–20. See also G. C. Manson: *Frank Lloyd Wright to 1910*, New York, 1958, p. 83.

24. The aftereffect of this principle is especially visible in the Dutch social housing projects of J. J. P. Oud in Rotterdam (for example, the housing project Tusschendijken of 1919).

25. Frank Lloyd Wright: *An Autobiography*, New York, 1943, p. 150.

26. Frank Lloyd Wright: *An Autobiography*, New York, 1943, p. 151; C. Lancaster: "Transportation Design Elements in American Architecture," *American Quarterly* 8, Fall 1956.

27. R. Banham: *The Architecture of the Well-Tempered Environment*, Chicago, 1969, p. 92.

28. ". . . the first concrete monolith in the world." Quoted by Frank Lloyd Wright in *An Autobiography*, New York, 1943, p. 150.

29. Frank Lloyd Wright: "Designing Unity Tempel," in Frank Lloyd Wright: *Writings and Buildings*, New York, 1960, p. 74–83.

30. F. L. Dyer and T. C. Martin in cooperation with W. H. Meadowcroft: *Edison: His Life and Inventions*, 2 vols., New York, 1929. See especially vol. 2, pp. 506–526. See also B. Kelley: *The Prefabrication of Houses*, Cambridge (Mass.), 1951, p. 14.

31. The ground floor was slightly elevated in order to let daylight into the basement.

32. Interview with Allan L. Benson; quoted in "Thomas A. Edison: Benefactor of Mankind," *Munsey's* 1909, pp. 419–425.

33. New research in New Jersey is urgently needed. See U. Kultermann: "Thomas Alva Edison et la prefabricazione," *Domus*, March 1979, p. 594.

34. Patent for "Waterproofing Paint for Portland Cement Structures," Washington Patent Office, submitted 6-1-1908, accepted as patent on Jan. 12, 1909.

35. ". . . what invention can do for the poor." Quoted in "Thomas A. Edison. Benefactor of Mankind," *Munsey's* 1909, pp. 419–425.

36. Quoted in "Thomas A. Edison. Benefactor of Mankind," *Munsey's* 1909, pp. 419–425.

37. Quoted in *Edison Cast Concrete House,* Orange, N. J., 1920 (?), p. 11. Other inventors besides Edison were occupied with prefabricated houses, as was Grosvenor Atterbury, who arrived at a system of "precast hollowcore panels" for walls, floors, and roofs. Numerous houses were built with this system between 1910 and 1918. Atterbury recognized, like Edison, the social significance of his invention and was able to execute the construction of a number of houses for workers in Forest Hills Gardens, L.I. See F. S. Onderdonk: *The Ferro-Concrete Style,* New York, 1928, pp. 45–49. Subsequent methods were the Merrill System, the Simpson Craft System (1917), the Lakeolith System (1918), and the Hahn Concrete Lumber System (1919).

38. I could not find any verification for this.

39. ". . . successful flying machine was a possibility in the near future." Quoted in C. Mackenzie: *Alexander Graham Bell: The Man Who Contracted Space,* Boston, 1928 (in German, Wiesbaden 1959); K. Wachsmann: *Wendepunkt im Bauen,* Wiesbaden, 1959, pp. 29–34.

40. A. G. Bell: "The Tetrahedral Principle in Kite Structure," *National Geographic Magazine* 1903.

41. J. H. Parkin: *Bell and Baldwin,* Toronto, 1964, pp. 32–33. Curtiss, Baldwin, McCurdy, and Selfridge were in Beinn Breagh during the summer of 1907 and participated in the experimentation. See B. Busfield: "Alexander Graham Bell," *Architectural Design* 8, 1970.

42. Quoted in J. H. Parkin: *Bell and Baldwin,* Toronto, 1964, pp. 32–33.

43. Bell introduced the tower to the public in a ceremony on August 31, 1907. It remained for more than 10 years and was then torn down.

44. R. Buckminster-Fuller: *Ideas and Integrities. A Spontaneous Autobiographical Disclosure,* R. W. Marks, Englewood Cliffs, N. J., 1963.

45. C. Gibbs-Smith: *Early Flying Machines,* London, 1975.

46. C. H. Gibbs-Smith: *A History of Flying,* New York, 1954; P. Supf: *Airman's World,* New York, 1933; B. Newhall: *Airborne Camera,* New York, 1969; H. Reich: *The Earth from Above,* New York, 1966. The first motorized flight of the Wright brothers in an airplane that was heavier than air took place on Dec. 17, 1903, and reached a distance of approximately 385 yd. (350 m).

47. C. W. Condit: *The Chicago School of Architecture,* 2d ed., Chicago, 1962.

48. Steel was previously used for shipbuilding. To date, there is no monograph about Jenney, not even comprehensive documentation of his work in magazines.

49. F. Washburn: *Gigantic Buildings in America,* Zürich and Leipzig, 1950.

50. The International Competition for a New Administration Building for the Chicago Tribune, Chicago, 1923.

51. A. T. North: *Raymond Hood,* New York, 1931.

52. H.-R. Hitchcock and P. Johnson: *The International Style,* New York, 1932.

53. T. James, Jr.: *The Empire State Building,* New York, 1975; R. Hood: "The Design of Rockefeller Center," *Architectural Forum,* Jan. 1932.

54. C. Lancaster: *The Japanese Influence in America,* New York, 1963.

55. J. M. Woodbridge: "Bay Region Style," *Casabella* 322, Oct. 1959.

56. E. McCoy: *Five California Architects,* New York, 1960.

57. D. Gebhard and H. von Breton: *Architecture in California,* Santa Barbara, Cal., 1968.

58. R. Banham: *Los Angeles: The Architecture of Four Ecologies,* London, 1971.

59. E. McCoy: *Five California Architects,* New York, 1960. W. H. Jordy: *American Buildings and Their Architects,* Garden City, N.Y., 1972, p. 246 ff.

60. W. H. Jordy: *American Buildings and Their Architects,* Garden City, N.Y., 1972, p. 246 ff. Schindler's Lovell beach house in Newport Beach of 1925–1926 remains one of the most outstanding examples of

this tradition. The Dodge House by Gill was torn down in 1970.

61. W. H. Jordy: *American Buildings and Their Architects*, Garden City, N.Y., 1972, p. 217 ff.; K. Current: *Greene and Greene*, Fort Worth, Texas, 1974.

62. Neutra's "Rush City Reformed" of 1925 is an outstanding example of the integration of architecture and industry.

63. D. Gebhard and H. von Breton: *Lloyd Wright*, exhibition catalogue, Santa Barbara Art Gallery, 1971.

64. F. S. Onderdonk: *The Ferro-Concrete Style*, New York, 1928, pp. 47 and 98.

65. C. Tyler: *An Annotated Bibliography of Julia Morgan, California Architect, and Her Work*. Dissertation, University of California, Berkeley, 1964; R. W. Longthrath: "Julia Morgan," *Perspecta* 15, 1975.

66. P. Laporte: *Simon Rodia's Towers in Watts*, Los Angeles, 1962.

67. D. Wiebenson: *The Cité Industrielle*, New York, 1969.

68. Badovici and Morancé, eds.: *L'Œuvre de Tony Garnier*, Paris, 1938; C. Pawlowski: *Tony Garnier*, Paris, 1967.

69. W. Ostrowski: *Contemporary Town Planning*, The Hague, 1970, p. 51 ff.

70. A subsequent difference and division of industry, which was detrimental to housing and industry, is clearly visible.

71. "The simpler the molds, the easier will be the construction, and consequently the less the cost." Quoted in D. Wiebenson: *The Cité Industrielle*, New York, 1969, p. 112.

72. Peet and Wooley: *The City of Akhenaten*, Boston, 1923, Fig. 155: suburban housing area in Tel-el-Amarnah.

73. L. Mensch: "The Hennebique System," *American Architect and Building News* 1902.

74. S. Giedion: *Bauen in Frankreich*, 2d ed., Leipzig, 1928.

75. P. Jamot: *A.-G. Perret et l'architecture du beton armé*, Paris, 1927; P. Collins: "The Doctrine of Auguste Perret," *The Architectural Review*, 1953; P. Collins: *Concrete*, New York, 1959; S. Giedion: *Raum, Zeit, Architektur*, Ravensburg, 1965.

76. This architectural style, which today has deteriorated into mostly decorative clichés, became internationally known due to the provision of Antonin Raymond and numerous other collaborators of Perret.

77. M. Besset: *Eugène Freyssinet*, Paris, 1959; B. Günschel: *Grosse Konstrukteure*, vol. 1, Berlin, 1966.

78. Le Corbusier's publication of the design of one of these halls in "Vers une architecture" of 1923 shows the construction with a gigantic isolated parabolic arch. The structure, i.e., the illustration in Le Corbusier's book, has possibly not only influenced his own project of the Palace of the Soviets in Moscow of 1931, but also Adalberto Libera's monumental arch of EUR in Rome of 1938 and the subsequent Gateway Arch by Eero Saarinen in St. Louis (1947–1965).

79. S. von Moos: "Aspects of the More Recent Architecture in Paris," *Werk* 2, 1965.

80. It has not been determined if these projects are connected to Italian Futurism.

81. "Richard Becherer: Monumentality and the Rue Mallet-Stevens," *Journal of the Society Architectural Historians*, March 1981. Subsequent architects of this time period are Pierre Chareau (1883–1950), J. J. Honegger and A. Lurcat (* 1894). See P. Lavedan: L'Architecture Française, Paris, 1944.

82. Basic concerning Le Corbusier are the seven-volume *Oeuvre Complète*, Zürich, since 1929, the magazine *L'Esprit Nouveau*, 1919–1925, published by Le Corbusier and A. Ozenfant; more recently, S. von Moos: *Le Corbusier*, Frauenfeld, 1968; C. Jencks: *Le Corbusier*, London, 1973; S. Gardiner: *Le Corbusier*, New York, 1974; P. Sereny, ed.: *Le Corbusier in Perspective*, Englewood Cliffs, N.J., 1975; M. P. M. Sekler: *The Early Drawings of Charles-Eduoard Jeanneret (Le Corbusier): 1902–1908*, New York, 1977; Paul Venable Turner: "Frank Lloyd Wright and the Young Le Corbusier," *Journal of the Society of Architectural Historians*, December 1983.

83. P. Turner: "The Beginnings of Le Corbusier's Education," *The Art Bulletin* 53, 1971.

84. Quoted in S. Gardiner: *Le Corbusier*, New York, 1974, p. 51. Colin Rowe points to a relationship between Le Corbusier and Mannerist architecture of the 16th century in C. Rowe: "Mannerism and Modern Architecture," *The Architectural Review* 107, May 1950.

85. Quoted in D. Wiebenson: *Tony Garnier: The Cité Industrielle*, New York, 1969, p. 99.

86. U. Conrads: *Programme und manifeste zur Architektur des 20. Jahrhunderts*, Berlin, 1964, p. 59.

87. The idea developed as early as 1914 with the project of the Domino Houses. The

motivation for the system was the quick and inexpensive reconstruction of the housing areas in Flanders, which had been destroyed during the war.

88. Quoted in P. Serenyi: *Le Corbusier, Fourier, and the Monastery of Ema, The Art Bulletin* 49, 1967. Reissued in P. Serenyi, ed.: *Le Corbusier in Perspective*, Englewood Cliffs, N.J., 1975, p. 104 ff.

89. Le Corbusier: *Observations Regarding Architecture and City Planning*, Berlin, 1964, p. 39 (initially, Paris, 1929).

90. Between 1910 and 1930, Frank Lloyd Wright also had a phase in his development when he was mainly occupied with the Imperial Hotel in Tokyo as well as with houses for single patrons, this being the time of his own private crisis. See N. K. Smith: *Frank Lloyd Wright*, Englewood Cliffs, N.J., 1966, p. 110.

91. C. Jencks, *Le Corbusier*, London, 1973, p. 67.

92. C. Jencks: *Le Corbusier*, London, 1973, p. 72.

93. A. Roth: *A Meeting With Pioneers*, Basel, 1973, p. 187.

94. S. von Moos: *Le Corbusier*, Frauenfeld, 1968, p. 279.

95. C. Rowe and R. Slutzky: "Transparency, Literal and Phenomenal," *Perspecta* 8, 1968, pp. 45–54.

96. Le Corbusier's design for the international contest differs from the rest (for example, those of Gropius, Perret, Poelzig) by the openness of the building units and their proximity to each other: "Le Corbusier left it to these crowd movements, it would seem, to create that unity, which the other projects sought to attain by the play of architectural form." M. Besset: *Who Was Le Corbusier?*, Cleveland, 1968, p. 117.

97. The motive which stems from Freyssinet returns characteristically in the project of Adalberto Libera of 1939 for EUR, as the principal symbol and is used again with a symbolic content in the Gateway Arch by Saarinen (1947–1965) in St. Louis.

98. Jörn Utzon viewed the project of Le Corbusier as immediate stimulation for his Opera House in Sydney. See S. Giedion: *Space, Time, Architecture*, Ravensburg, 1965, p. 412.

99. M. Besset: *Who Was Le Corbusier?*, Cleveland, 1968, p. 117.

100. H. Eckstein, ed.: *50 Jahre Deutscher Werkbund*, Berlin, 1958, p. 34.

101. J. Posener: "Muthesius come architetto," *Lotus* 9, 1975.

102. U. Kultermann: *Die Wright-Publikation von 1910 im Verlag Ernst Wasmuth*, Festschrift Günter Wasmuth, Tübingen 1968. Ludwig Hilberseimer recognized the Wright influence: "His work was fascinating. It was as if someone opened the window shades in a dark room and flooded it with light." Quoted in: *Berliner Architektur der 20er Jahre*, ed., H. M. Wingler, Mainz, 1967, p. 15.

103. F. Höber: *Peter Behrens*, Munich 1913; T. Buddensieg: "Riegl, Behrens, Rathenau," Kunstchronik 23, 1970.

104. Wilhelm Worringer articulated related ideas in an analogous area, see his book *Abstraktion und Einfühlung* of 1908. U. Kultermann: *Geschichte der Kunstgeschichte*, Düsseldorf, 1966, p. 357–359.

105. S. Anderson: "Behrens' Changing Concept," *Architectural Design* 2, 1969, p. 73.

106. R. Breuer: Peter Behrens, *Werkkunst* 3, Feb. 1908.

107. Jahrbuch des Deutschen Werkbundes 1914. See also F. Schuhmacher: *Lesebuch für Baumeister*, Berlin, 1947, pp. 127–431.

108. U. Kultermann: "Il primo periodo dell' architettura industriale in Germania," *Casabella* 311, 1967.

109. G. A. Platz: *Baukunst der neuesten Zeit*, Berlin, 1927, p. 29. The hall was originally 121 yd. (110 m) in length, which was later increased to 228 yd. (207 m), according to the original plan. Front width is 43¼ yd. (39.3 m).

110. Ludwig Hilbersheimer: *Grosstadtarchitektur*, Stuttgart, 1927, p. 91.

111. Erich Mendelsohn: *Das Gesamtschaffen des Architekten*, Berlin, 1930, p. 16. Speech from the year 1919.

112. Le Corbusier: "Etude sur le Mouvement d'Art Décoratif en Allemagne," *La Chaux de Fonds* 1912. Translation by S. von Moos: Peter Behrens. *Exhibition Catalogue Kaiserslautern*, 1966, p. 22.

113. The motto of the opening ceremony of the Architecture colony in Darmstadt on May 15, 1901, was the festival performance of the play *The Sign*. S. Anderson: "Behrens' Changing Concept, *Architectural Design* 2, 1969, p. 73.

114. Emperor Wilhelm II took part in the festive opening of the AEG Pavilion in 1909 and thus emphasized the intent of the nationalistic component of the new industrial architecture.

115. Nationalistic tendencies occurring in Italy and France, as well as in Germany, were the seed for the subsequent devel-

opment. See R. Soucy: *Fascism in France,* Berkeley, 1972.

116. W. Pehnt wrote about men like Eberhard von Bodenhausen and Harry Count Kessler: "Some of these artistic managers were equally suited to be in charge of arms factories or to be the head of an art museum." Quoted in *Die Architektur des Expressionismus,* Stuttgart, 1973, p. 24.

117. U. Kultermann: "Der Baumeister Walter Gropius," *Der Fortschritt,* Dec. 1955.

118. Gropius designed a railroad car for the Königsberg factory for railroad card in 1913, in which the laws of air resistance were already used as the basis for the design. S. Giedion: *Walter Gropius,* Stuttgart, 1954.

119. H. Weber: *Gropius und das Faguswerk,* Munich, 1961; U. Kultermann: "Il primo periodo dell' architettura industriale in Germania," *Casabella* 311, 1967.

120. W. Schadendorf: *Das Fagus-werk Karl Benscheidt,* Alfeld/Leine, Göttingen, 1954.

121. W. Hofmann and U. Kultermann: *Baukunst in unserer Zeit,* Essen, 1969, plate 43.

122. The Werkbund Theater by Henry van de Velde was developed within the framework of the same exhibit, as was the Austrian Pavilion by Josef Hoffmann and the pavilion of the glass industry by Bruno Taut.

123. *The Architectural Review,* August 1924.

124. V. Scully: *Modern Architecture,* 5. Rev. ed., New York, 1974, Fig. 59 and 60.

125. Quoted in A. Busignani: *Gropius,* London, 1973, p. 20. Gropius had pointed out the excellence of the anonymous American industrial buildings very early on. See his writings: *Der stilbildende Wert industrieller Bauformen, Jahrbuch des Deutschen Werkbundes,* 1914.

126. H. M. Wingler, ed.: *Das Bauhaus 1919–1933,* Weimar Dessau Berlin, Bramsche, 1962.

127. W. Gropius: *The New Architecture and the Bauhaus: Basic Elements of Its Development and Conception,* Mainz, 1965, p. 22.

128. H. von Erffa: "Bauhaus: First Phase," *The Architectural Review* 132, August 1957. The views of John Ruskin and Walter Gropius are nearly identical in regard to this topic.

129. B. Adler: *Das Weimarer Bauhaus,* Darmstadt, 1966; W. Pehnt: "Gropius the Romantic," *The Art Bulletin,* Sept. 1971, p.

379–392; K. Hüter: *Das Bauhaus in Weimar,* Berlin, 1976.

130. M. Franciscono: *Walter Gropius and the Creation of the Bauhaus,* Urbana, Ill. 1971; E. Neumann: *Bauhaus und Baühausler,* Bern, 1971. In 1922, Oskar Schlemmer clearly articulated this change: ". . . withdrawal indeed . . . from the notion of crafts in the middle ages and in the end from the craft itself, only used as a means to the end, i.e., the design."

131. B. Miller-Lane: *Architecture and Politics in Germany, 1918–1945,* Cambridge (Mass.), 1968.

132. The city parliament of Dessau had approved the suggestion of the Mayor, Dr. Hesse, for the construction cost of over 850,000 marks as well as the yearly budget of 100,000 marks for 24 teachers and approximately 180 to 200 students.

133. The idea of the school can be compared to Wright's architectural office Taliesin-North, which was founded in 1910, as well as with yet earlier offices of Eliel Saarinen in Finland. The project by Bruno Taut of 1916 for a Bauhof, may also have contributed to the development of this basic idea.

134. W. Hofmann and U. Kultermann: *Baukunst in unserer Zeit,* Essen, 1969, Plate 50. The ship metaphor, which has been used since Wright, is typically returning at this time.

135. C. Schnaidt: *Hannes Meyer: Buildings, Projects and Writings,* Teufen, 1965. For the views of Hannes Meyer, see: W. Herzogenrath, "About the Establishment of the Bauhaus, in *Contributions Towards the Survey of the 19th and 20th Centuries,"* edited by W. Schadendorf, Munich, 1975, p. 133. New perspectives for the evaluation of the work of Hannes Meyer are provided by K. Michael Hays: *Modernism and the Posthumanist Subject: The Architecture of Hannes Meyer and Ludwig Hilberseimer,* Cambridge, Mass., 1992.

136. The documents by H. M. Wingler, ed.: *The Bauhaus 1919–1933,* Bramsche, 1962.

137. U. Conrads, ed.: *Programme und Manifeste zur Architektur des 20. Jahrhunderts,* Berlin, 1964, p. 67; P. Johnson: *Mies van der Rohe,* Stuttgart, 1956; L. Hilberseimer: *Mies van der Rohe,* Chicago, 1956; W. Blaser: *Mies van der Rohe: The Art of the Structure,* Zürich, 1965.

138. U. Conrads, ed.: *Programme und Manifeste zur Architektur des 20. Jahrhunderts*, Berlin, 1964, p. 76.

139. U. Conrads, ed.: *Programme und Manifeste zur Architektur des 20. Jahrhunderts*, Berlin, 1964, p. 108.

140. Bruno Taut himself suggested dictators in the field of art. He said at the Werkbund exhibition in 1914 in Cologne, while being applauded vigorously: "I therefore suggest that for any artistic question a prominent artist should be chosen as dictator for the organizational tasks, who is absolutely decisive. His time can be limited to approximately three years. But a dictatorship with regard to art . . . that this is the only possible way to succeed with the goodness and art. If I may mention names, I would suggest names like van de Velde or Poelzig for such a dictatorship." J. Posener, ed.: *Hans Poelzig: Gesammelte Schriften und Werke*, Berlin, 1970, p. 13.

141. U. Kultermann: *Paul Scheerbart und die Architektur im 20. Jahrhundert*, Stuttgart, 1963. U. Kultermann, ed.: *Paul Scheerbart*, Exhibition Catalogue, Museum Leverkusen, 1963; U. Kultermann: "Glass Architecture," *Byggekunst* 3, 1966.

142. The Lange House in Krefeld of 1928 was changed into a museum. See W. Hofmann and U. Kultermann: *Baukunst in unserer Zeit*, Essen, 1969, Fig. 54.

143. R. Döcker: "25 Jahre Werkbundsiedlung," *Die Neue Stadt* 1951; J. Joedicke and C. Plath: *Die Weissenhofsiedlung*, Stuttgart, 1968.

144. For an illustration of the photomontage of L. Hilberseimer, see: *Berliner Architektur 20er Jahre*, Mainz, 1967, p. 91. The roofs of the various houses were characteristically equipped with gables after 1933. Only in more recent times were they restored to the original forms. The review of Schwitters reprinted in *Oppositions* 7, 1976: "The Dwelling."

145. U. Kultermann: *Wassili and Hans Luckhardt*, Tübingen, 1958; D. Sharp: *Modern Architecture and Expressionism*, London, 1966; W. Pehnt: *Die Architektur des Expressionismus*, Stuttgart, 1973.

146. J. Posener, ed.: *Hans Poelzig: Gesammelte Schriften und Werke*, Berlin, 1970; T. Heuss: *Hans Poelzig*, Berlin, 1939.

147. W. Hofmann and U. Kultermann: *Baukunst in unserer Zeit*, Essen, 1969, p. 42.

148. Hans Poelzig: "Festspielhaus in Salzburg," *Das Kunstblatt* 5/3, 1921, p. 79.

149. W. Pehnt: *Die Architektur des Expressionismus*, Stuttgart, 1973.

150. H. Sörgel: *Wright, Dudok, Mendelsohn*, Munich 1926; A. Whittick: *Eric Mendelsohn*, 2nd ed., London, 1965; W. von Eckardt: *Erich Mendelsohn*, Ravensburg 1962; B. Zevi: *Erich Mendelsohn: Opera completa*, Milan, 1970.

151. G. K. Koenig: "Mendelsohn e l'Einsteinturm," *Casabella* 303, 1966.

152. G. A. Platz: *Die Baukunst der neuesten Zeit*, Berlin, 1927, p. 70.

153. Quoted in R. Blomfield: *Modernism*, London, 1934; reprinted in: H. T. and C. Benton, eds.: *Architecture and Design: 1890 to 1939*, New York, 1975, p. 175. The metaphor of the battleship is newly revived at this point.

154. Exhibition catalogue of Eric Mendelsohn, Akademie der Künste, Berlin, 1968, p. 9.

155. K. Rühl: "Erinnerungen an Bruno Taut," *Baukunst und Werkform* 12, 1959; K. Junghans: *"Bruno Taut, 1880–1938,"* Berlin, 1970; Bruno Taut: *Architekturlehre, Grundlagen: Theorie und Kritik aus der Sicht eines sozialistischen Architekten*, edited by G. Peschken and T. Heinrich, Hamburg, 1977.

156. U. Kultermann: "Paul Scheerbart und die Architektur im 20. Jahrhundert," *Handbuch der Bauwesens*, Stuttgart, 1963; R. Haag Bletter: *Bruno Taut and Paul Scheerbart's Vision: Utopian Aspects of German Expressionistic Architecture*, New York (Columbia University), 1973.

157. K. Junghanns: *Bruno Taut: 1880–1938*, Berlin, 1970, p. 26.

158. H. G. Scheffauer: "Bruno Taut: A Visionary in Practice," *The Architectural Review*, 12, 1922. The series of books was later continued for practical use: *Die neue Wohnung*, 1924; *Ein Wohnhaus*, 1927; *Die neue Wohnbau*, 1927, and climaxed in the encyclopedia, *Die neue Baukunst in Europe und Amerika*, 1929.

159. U. Kultermann and O. M. Ungers, eds.: *Die Gläserne Kette*, Exhibition Catalogue of the Museum Leverkusen and the Academy of Arts, Berlin, 1963; U. M. Schneede and Maria Schneede-Szessny: *Hermann Finsterlin*, Catalogue Württembergischer Kunstverein, Stuttgart, 1973.

160. M. Tafuri: *Sozialdemokratie und Stadt in der Weimarer Republik 1923–1933*, vol. 3, 1974. Taut had already previously dealt with the garden city of Falkenberg in Berlin-Grünau (1913–1914) and social

housing, and had built two-story, low-income row houses.

161. Due to the mediation of Bruno Taut,
housing blocks by Mies van de Rohe, Gropius, Scharoun, Häring, Salvisberg, and
many others were built.

162. The second phase was built 1930–1931;
L. Adler: "Siedlungen in Berlin-Britz,"
Wasmuth's Monatshefte für Baukunst II,
1927.

163. K. Junghanns: *Bruno Taut,* Berlin, 1970,
p. 68.

164. U. Kultermann: *Das Werk des Architekten
Hans Scharoun: Theater der Stadt Wolfsburg,* Wolfsburg, 1973; M. Hennig-Sche-
fold and I. I. Schäfer: *Frühe Moderne in
Berlin,* Winterthur, 1967, pp. 50–52.

165. "A proud, dark banner of socialist solidar-
ity." Quoted in *Modern Architecture,* rev.
ed., New York 1974, p. 54. Jörg Mauthe:
"The Fantastic Community Building,"
Alte und moderne Kunst 44, 1961; O. M.
Ungers: "Die Höfe," *Lotus* 10, 1975.

166. The Törten housing project comprised
316 houses of 4 to 5 rooms each with
bathroom and central heating, affordable
for people with low income: a 1½ room
apartment with kitchen, bath, and fittings
rented for 37.50 marks a month.

167. L. Hilberseimer: *Berliner Architektur der
20er Jahre,* Mainz, 1967, p. 89 ff.

168. U. Conrads, ed.: *Programme und Manifeste zur Architektur des 20. Jahrhunderts,* Berlin, 1964, p. 117. The text is
from 1932. See also H. Lauterbach and J.
Joedicke, eds.: *Hugo Häring,* Stuttgart,
1965.

169. H. Lauterbach and J. Joedicke, eds.: *Hugo
Häring,* Stuttgart, 1965, p. 152.

170. C. Kemper: *Der Bau,* Stuttgart, 1963; R.
Steiner: *Mein Lebensgang,* Dornach,
1962; W. Pehnt: *Die Architektur des Expressionismus,* Stuttgart, 1973, pp.
137–148.

171. W. Pehnt: *Die Architektur des Expressionismus,* Stuttgart, 1973, p. 148. A
former building, which was begun in
1913, burnt down in the night of the New
Year of 1922–1923. See also F. Durach:
"Das Goetheanum in Dornach,"
Deutsche Bauzeitung 8, 1961. The artistic
design, which stemmed exclusively from
Rudolf Steiner, was translated into the
second Goetheanum, while remaining
true to the model, which was executed by
Ernst Aisenpreis, who was the architect in
charge.

172. J. Joedicke: *Schalenbau,* Stuttgart, 1962;

173. The cupola of the Pantheon had also
reached such an extraordinary span
through the use of Roman concrete.

174. G. Günschel: *Grosse Konstrukteure,* Berlin, 1966.

175. The ratio of the cupola strength to the
span of St. Peter's in Rome is 1/13.

176. G. Günschel: *Grosse Konstrukteure,* Berlin, 1966, p. 180–184.

177. R. T. Clough: *Futurism,* New York, 1961;
M. W. Martin: *Futurist Art and Theory,*
Oxford, 1968; U. Apollonio: *Futurism,*
Cologne, 1972; N. Lynton: "Der Futurismus," in T. Richardson and N. Stangos,
eds.: *Concepts of Modern Art,* New York,
1974, p. 96–104.

178. A comparable enthusiasm for machines
had already been articulated by Henry
Adams, after forerunners during the 19th
century (Whitman, Verhaeren, Jarry): *The
Education of Henry Adams, An Autobiography,* Boston, 1918, p. 380. The first publication of the volume in 1906 may have
been known to Marinetti. A second forerunner was Mario Morasso, who wrote
provocative essays between 1902 and
1905 for the magazine, *Marzocco,* where
such topics as "Aesthetics of Speed,"
"The Heroes of the Machine," and "The
Great Flight" were especially relevant for
futuristic ideas.

179. Quoted in *Futurismus 1909–1917,* exhibition catalogue of the Kunsthalle in Düsseldorf, 1974, no pagination. W. Ley:
Bombs and Bombing, New York, 1941, p.
83, attributed in his chapter "Bombing as
a Fine Art" the invention of the air war to
the Italians: "The first modern air raid—
though a very ineffective one—was carried out by the Italians in 1911. The Italian
fliers used Farman biplanes to bombard
Arabs at Benghazi and in the vicinity of
Derna."

180. A parallel to the tendencies of nationalistic development can at the same time be
observed in Germany, France, and Russia.
A glorification of the war can, however, already be seen with Maurice Barrès, whose
followers saw in war "an aesthetic ideal of
energy and strength." See Agathon
(pseudonym of Henry Massis and Alfred
de Tarde): *Les jeunes gens d'aujourd'hui,*
Paris, 1913. Quoted in R. Soucy: *Fascism
in France: The Case of Maurice Barrès,*
Berkeley, 1972, p. 8.

181. M. Piacentini: *Sant'Elia: Rassegna di Ar-*

chitettura, 1926; A. Sartoris: *Antonio Sant'Elia,* Milan, 1930; R. Banham: "Sant'Elia," *The Architectural Review,* May 1955; L. Caramel and A. Longatti: *Antonio Sant'Elia,* Como, 1962; J. P. Schmidt-Thomson: *Floreale und futuristische Architektur,* Berlin, 1967.

182. A few drawings by Sant'Elia were exhibited in 1914 within the framework of the group "Nuove Tendenze." Also sketches by Mario Chiattone were shown.

183. Quoted in exhibition catalogue, Düsseldorf, 1974; and C. Baumgart: *Geschichte des Futurismus,* Reinbek, 1966.

184. Quoted in R. Banham: *Die Revolution der Architektur,* Reinbek, 1964, p. 105.

185. Leon Trotsky: *Der Futurismus,* Zürich, 1971.

186. G. Veronesi and G. Dalli Regoli: *L'opera di Mario Chiattone,* Pisa, 1965; V. Marchi: "Architettura Futurista," *Foligno* 1919; V. Marchi: *Italia Nuova—Architettura Nuova,* Rome, 1931.

187. W. Hofmann and U. Kultermann: *Baukunst in unserer Zeit,* Essen, 1969, Plate 45.

188. Berlage had traveled to the United States in 1912 and referred to Sullivan and Wright repeatedly and with enthusiasm in his talks after his return. Also Robert van't Hoff had been in America in 1910 and had direct contact with Frank Lloyd Wright.

189. Quoted in B. Taut: *Modern Architecture,* London, 1929, p. 70. Also, Mies van der Rohe was strongly influenced by Berlage about 1911–1912.

190. R. Banham: *Age of the Masters,* New York, 1975, p. 66–67.

191. R. F. Jordan: "Dudok," *The Architectural Review* 115, 1954; *Willem M. Dudok,* 2d ed., Amsterdam, 1975.

192. H. L. C. Jaffé: *De Stijl: 1917–1931,* Berlin 1965; exhibition catalogue, *Theo van Doesburg 1883–1931,* Kunsthalle Nürnberg, 1969; K. Frampton: "De Stijl," in T. Richardson and N. Stangos, eds.: *Concepts of Modern Art,* New York, 1974, pp. 140–158.

193. Theo van Doesburg: *Grundbegriffe der neuen gestaltenden Kunst,* H. M. Wingler, ed., Mainz, 1966, p. 71. The thoughts of Theo van Doesburg are influenced by the writings of Dr. Schoenmaeker, such as "Het nieuwe Wereldbeeld," 1915; and "Beeldende Wiskunde," 1916.

194. L'Aubette was destroyed during the Second World War.

195. T. M. Brown: *The Work of G. Th. Rietveld,* Utrecht 1958; T. M. Brown: "Rietveld's Egocentric Vision," *Journal of the Society of Architectural Historians* 24, 1965; U. Kultermann: "Der Rot-Blau-Stuhl von Rietveld," *Alte und Moderne Kunst* 141, 1975, pp. 20–22.

196. However, due to restrictions by the building authorities, Rietveld was restricted in his planning with regard to the upper floor. The ground floor has traditional divisions of space.

197. J. J. P. Oud: *Mein Weg in "De Stijl,"* The Hague, 1960.

198. H.-R. Hitchcock: *J. J. P. Oud,* Paris, 1931.

199. L. Benevolo: *Geschichte der Architektur im 19. und 20. Jahrhundert,* vol. 2, Munich, 1964, p. 98. W. Hofmann and U. Kultermann: *Baukunst in unserer Zeit,* Essen, 1969, Plate 51.

200. G. Oorthuys: *Mart Stam,* London, 1970.

201. "ABC Demands the Dictatorship of the Machine" of 1928. See U. Conrads, ed.: *Programme und Manifeste zur Architekur des 20. Jahrhunderts,* Berlin, 1964, p. 108.

202. R. Vickery: "Bijvoet and Duiker," *Architectural Association Quarterly,* Jan. 1970.

203. V. de Feo: *USSR Architettura: 1917–1936,* Rome, 1963; V. Quilici: *L'architettura del construttivismo,* Bari, 1969; O. A. Shidkovsky, ed.: *Building in the USSR: 1917–1932,* New York, 1971; M. Tafuri, ed.: *Socialismo, città, architettura USSR, 1917–1937,* 2d ed., Rome, 1972.

204. I. Ehrenburg: *First Years of Revolution: 1918–1921,* London, 1962.

205. C. Gray: *Die russische Avantgarde der modernen Kunst, 1863–1922,* Cologne, 1963.

206. B. Taut: *Russlands architektonische Situation,* original text: reprinted by El Lissitzky: *Russland: Architektur für eine Weltrevolution,* Berlin, 1965, p. 147.

207. V. Quilici: "The Residential Commune," *Lotus* 8, 1974; M. J. Ginsburg: "Zeitgenössische Architekur in Russland," *Die Baugilde,* Oct. 1928, reprinted in El Lissitzky: *Russia: Architecture for a World Revolution,* Berlin, 1965, pp. 135–199.

208. A. Rodtschenko: "Vladimir Tatlin," *Opus International* 4, 1967; Exhibition catalogue: *Vladimir Tatlin,* Moderna Museet, Stockholm, 1968; S. Lissitzky-Küppers: *El Lissitzky,* Dresden, 1967.

209. M. A. Il'Bin: *Vesnini,* Moscow, 1960.

210. M. Tafuri, ed.: *Socialismo, città, architet-*

tura USSR, 1917–1937, Rome, 1972, Fig. 72.

211. F. Starr: "Melnikov," *Architectural Design* 7, 1969.
212. U. a. A. Whittick.
213. Among the designs also submitted for the contest are those of Le Corbusier, Gropius, Poelzig, Perret, Mendelsohn, and Brasini as well as those by the Russian architects Ginzburg, Lubetkin, Barchin, Vlasov, and Sholtovski. There were 272 designs in all. See M. Piacentino: "Un grande avvenimento architettonico in Russia: Il Palazzo dei Soviet a Mosca," *Architettura,* March 1934.
214. A. Gutnov et al.: *The Ideal Communist City,* New York, 1970.
215. K. N. Afanasjew: *Das Leninmausoleum, Ideen-Projekte-Bauten: Sowjetische Architektur 1917–1932,* Dresden, 1973, pp. 148–152.
216. The division into conservative and progressive wings with regard to the architectural development during the twenties is a general occurrence and not just limited to Russia. This can be observed in the same manner in Italy, Germany, France, and the United States. Shchusev's position can be compared to Marcello Piacentini's in Italy. Both were famous architects prior to the new regime and were therefore able to negotiate between the conservative and progressive powers. See also G. K. Loukomski: "Il ritorno dell'architettura classica in Russia," *Rassegna d'Architettura,* April 1933.

Part II (pp. 73–183)

1. U. Kultermann: Architektur der *Gegenwart,* Baden-Baden, 1967, p. 95 ff.
2. U. Conrads, ed.: *Programme und Manifeste zur Architektur des 20. Jahrhunderts,* Berlin, 1964, p. 108.
3. Quoted in "The New Empiricism," *The Architectural Review,* Jan. 1948.
4. Frank Lloyd Wright: *Humane Architektur,* ed. by W. Braatz, Gütersloh, 1969, p. 162.
5. Quoted in *The Architectural Review,* March 1973, p. 100.
6. P. Hofer: *Fundplätze Bauplätze: Aufsätze zu Archäologie, Architektur und Städtebau,,* Basel, 1970, p. 136.
7. *Modern Times.* Reprinted in U. Conrads, ed.: *Programme und Manifeste zur Architektur des 20. Jahrhunderts,* Berlin, 1964, p. 114.

8. U. Kultermann: "Geschichte des modernen Ingenieurbaus," unpublished manuscript 1967, p. 17. The quotation is by Eugène Freyssinet.
9. P. Bürger: *Der Französische Surrealismus,* Frankfurt, 1971, p. 13; H. M. Enzensberger: *Die Aporien der Avantgarde, Einzelheiten II,* Frankfurt, n.d.
10. The new evaluation of the organic and of nature is manifested especially in the obvious changes of film of the epoch—for example, in Alexander Dovshenko's *The Earth* of 1930, in Pare Lorentz' *The Plow That Broke the Plains* of 1936, and Robert Flaherty's *The Land* of 1941.
11. A. Speer: *Erinnerungen,* Berlin, 1969, p. 95. Speer mentions referring to a footnote by John Burchard and Bush-Brown, as American neoclassic buildings of the time: Cret's Federal Reserve Building of 1937, Pope's Jefferson Memorial of 1937, and Pope's National Gallery of 1939, all in Washington, D.C.
12. R. R. Taylor: *The Word in Stone,* Berkeley, 1972, p. 72. Also, the expansion of the Fascist ideology nearly at the same time should be considered: 1932 marks the founding of the British Union of Fascists by Sir Oswald Mosley, the Falange Española was founded in 1932 in Spain, and in Hungary the takeover of power by Fascism by Gyula Gömbös took place in 1932.
13. Alfred Rosenberg: *Der Mythos des 20. Jahrhunderts,* Munich, 1934, pp. 385–386.
14. Alfred Rosenberg: *Der Mythos des 20. Jahrhunderts,* Munich, 1934, p. 386. Alvar Aalto spoke during the same time period of "humanizing the mechanically produced type of material." See H. Lauterbach in *A. Aalto,* exhibition catalogue of the Akademie der Künste, Berlin, 1936, p. 8.
15. G. R. Clapp: *The TVA. An Approach to the Development of a Region,* Chicago, 1955; J. H. Kyle: *The Building of TVA: An Illustrated History,* Baton Rouge, 1958.
16. *Raum, Zeit, Architektur,* Ravensburg, 1965, p. 618. About further connections between architecture and technology: D. J. Bush: *The Streamlined Decade,* New York, 1975, pp. 128–140.
17. Ralph Barsodi: *Flight From the City,* New York, 1933. Barsodi continued his activities in his late books, "Inflation is Coming and What to do About It" (1945) and "Social Pluralism" (1952), as well as in his experiment in Exeter, N.H. A typical parallel of these efforts is possibly also the farm cooperative in Chandler, Arizona, by Vernon

de Mars (* 1908) and Burton D. Cairns (1909–1937), built in 1936–1937.

18. C. S. Stein: *New Towns for America*, Liverpool, 1950.

19. B. Zevi and E. Kaufmann: "La casa sulla cascata di Frank Lloyd Wright" *L'Architettura*, Aug. 1962.

20. Quoted in *House Beautiful*, Nov. 1955, "The Man Who Liberated Architecture."

21. An exhibition by this title was held at the Museum of Modern Art in New York in 1932. The catalogue by H.-R. Hitchcock and Ph. Johnson had a far-reaching influence on the development of architecture in the United States (2d ed., 1966).

22. G. Barbey: "William Lescaze," *Werk* 8, 1971; R. A. M. Stern: *George Howe*, New Haven, 1975.

23. R. Hood: "The Design of Rockefeller Center," *Architectural Forum* I, 1932; W. Weissman: "Who Designed Rockefeller Center?," *Journal of the Society of Architectural Historians* 10, 1951; W. H. Jordy: *American Buildings and Their Architects*, New York, 1972.

24. D. Gebhard and H. von Breton: *L.A. in the Thirties, 1931–1941*, New York 1975; R. Banham: *Los Angeles, The Architecture of Four Ecologies*, London, 1971.

25. The construction of the house took place within the framework of a large scale process of change from the airplane industry, which was concentrated in Wichita, to the production of housing.

26. O. H. Ammann and F. C. Kurz: *Design of Steel Bridges*, New York, 1915; F. Stüssi: *Othmar H. Ammann: Sein Beitrag zur Entwicklung des Brückenbaus*, Basel, 1974.

27. P. Goodwin: *Brazil Builds*, New York, 1943; G. Ferraz: *Warchavchik*, São Paulo, 1965; S. Bracco: *L'architettura moderna in Brasile*, Bologna, 1967.

28. S. Papadaki: "Oscar Niemeyer." *Works in Progress*, New York, 1956; S. Papadaki: *Oscar Niemeyer*, Ravensburg, 1962.

29. M. Bill and R. Rigoli: "The Work of Amancio Williams," *Zodiac* 16, 1966.

30. E. Born: *The New Architecture in Mexico*, London, 1938.

31. W. D. Howie: *Contemporary Architecture in South Africa*, Johannesburg, 1958.

32. A. S. G. Butler: *The Architecture of Sir Edwin Lutyens*, 3 vols., London, 1950.

33. J. M. Freeland: *Architecture in Australia*, Melbourne, 1968.

34. K. Abe: "Early Western Architecture in Japan," *Journal of Society of Architectural Historians* 13, 1954; U. Kultermann: "Tetsuro Yoshida," *Baukunst und Werkform* 2, 1957.

35. U. Kultermann: *Neues Bauer in Japan*, 2d ed., Tübingen, 1967.

36. P. Suhonen: *New Architecture in Finland*, Helsinki, 1967; M. L. Borràs: *Arquitectura Finlandese en Otaniemi*, Barcelona, 1967.

37. Alvar Aalto *Synopsis*, ed. by B. Hösli, Basel 1970; Alvar Aalto, *Gesamwerk* 2d ed., Zürich, 1963–1965; H. Scharoun and H. Lauterbach: *Alvar Aalto*, exhibition catalogue, Academy of Arts, Berlin, 1963.

38. S. Giedion wrote about the ceiling in Viipuri: "Its small band of reddish pine wood starts at the floor behind the speaker, curves up and cuts through the glass front in an irrational manner, like a whirlpool. . . . The healthy part of this bold endeavour is that scientific thought and fantasy are combined, to loosen up an architecture, which was becoming too rigid." Quoted in *Raum, Zeit, Architektur*, Ravensburg, 1965, p. 384.

39. F. Gutheim: *Alvar Aalto*, Ravensburg 1961.

40. W. Hofmann and U. Kultermann: *Baukunst in unserer Zeit*, Essen, 1969, Plate 72.

41. T. Faber: *Arne Jacobsen*, Stuttgart 1964.

42. E. de Maré: *Gunnar Asplund*, London, 1955; G. Johansson: "Sven Markelius architetto svedese e internationale," *Casabella* 201, 1954; E. Thelaus: *New Architecture in Sweden*, Stockholm, 1962; N.-O. Lund: "Arne Korsmo und der norwegische Funktionalismus," *Bauen und Wohnen* 3, 1966; S. Ray; *Il contributo svedese all'architettura contemporanea e l'opera di Sven Markelius*, Rome, 1969.

43. For example, Saarinen's building activity in America; Aalto's works in America, Germany, Switzerland, and France; Viljo Revell's building in Canada; Jacobson's works in England, Germany, and India; Utzon's building in Australia. These are only a few examples for the intensive expansion of Scandinavian architecture in the world.

44. H.-R. Hitchcock und C. Bauer: *Modern Architecture in England*, New York, 1937; T. Dannatt: *Modern Architecture in Britain*, London 1959; F. Elgohary: *Wells Coates and His Position in the Beginning of the Modern Movement in England*, Diss. London, 1966.

45. The firm Tecton, which was founded by Lubetkin in 1932, was important for the further development of English architecture.

46. G. C. Argan: *Marcel Breuer*, Milan, 1957; U. Kultermann: *Marcel Breuer*, "Architekt

und Möbelgestalter," *Bauer und Wohnen*, Jan. 1959.

47. A. Roth: *Die neue Architektur*, 4th ed., Zürich, 1948.

48. H. Spieker: "Bauten von Joannes Duiker," *Bauwelt*, Feb. 12, 1968; R. Vickery: "Bijvoet and Duiker," *Architectural Association Quarterly*, Jan. 1970.

49. " . . . a building that, as it were, opens its arms to a typical street scene, while enclosing a private landscape of its own." S. Giedion: *A Decade of New Architecture*, Zürich, 1951, p. 112.

50. A. Roth: *Die neue Architektur* 4th ed., Zürich, 1948.

51. S. Giedion: *A Decade of New Architecture*, Zürich, 1951, p. 184.

52. M. Bill: *Moderne Schweizer Architektur*, Basel, 1949.

53. A. Roth: *Die neue Architektur*, 4th ed., Zürich, 1948, pp. 71–90.

54. M. Bill: *Robert Maillart*, Zürich, 1949; G. Günschel: *Grosse Konstrukteure*, Berlin, 1966.

55. The exceptionally low cost of this bridge (it amounted to 47,300 Swiss Francs) labels this work as an ideal solution for public construction projects.

56. S. Giedion: *Raum, Zeit, Architektur*, Ravensburg, 1965, p. 303. Lately, reservations were voiced from the engineer's point of view, against the "art-historical" evaluation of Maillart, see Billington: *Meaning in Maillart*. Background Papers for the First National Conference on Civil Engineering. History, Heritage and the Humanities, Princeton, 1970.

57. O. Bohigas: *Arquitectura española de la segunda Republica*, Barcelona, 1970.

58. E. Torroja: *The Philosophy of Structures*, Berkeley, 1958.

59. W. Hofmann and U. Kultermann: *Baukunst in unserer Zeit*, Essen, 1969, Plate 61.

60. Eduardo Torroja: *Logik der Form*, Munich, 1961.

61. H. H. Reed: "Rome, the Third Sack," *The Architectural Review* 107, 1950, p. 110. Subsequent programmatic speeches of Mussolini in: *Rome of Mussolini*, Rome, 1933. About general Italian architecture of the time, see G. Accastro, V. Fraticelli, and R. Nicolini: *L'architettura di Roma Capitale 1870–1970*, Rome, 1971; S. de Paolis and A. Ravaglioli: *La Terza Roma*, Rome, 1971; H. Frank, ed.: *Faschistische Architekturen: Planen und Bauen in Europa 1930–1945*, Hamburg, 1985.

62. A. Brasini: *Relazione sul progetto P. R. di Roma studiato dal '25 al '30*, Rome, 1930.

63. A. Muñoz: "Marcello Piacentini," *Architettura e arte decorativi*, 1925; G. Veronesi: *Difficoltà politiche dell'architettura in Italia 1920–1940*. Milan, 1953.

64. P. D. Eisenman: "From Object to Relationship: The Casa del Fascio by Terragni," *Casabella* 344, Jan. 1970, p. 38, arrived at a new evaluation of the work and considered it to be a pioneering contribution, "one which has gone virtually unnoticed in the architectural history, theory and criticism of the intervening years." See also M. Labo: *Giuseppe Terragni*, Milan, 1947; W. Hofmann and U. Kultermann: *Baukunst in unserer Zeit*, Essen, 1969, Fig. 62.

65. *Italy Builds*, New York, 1954, p. 118.

66. Numerous projects were received for the contest of 1939, among them the one by Pascoletti, which is oriented on styles of the antiquity. The railroad station was only completed in 1950 after a new contest won by the architects Montuori and Calini.

67. P. L. Nervi: *Neue Strukturen*, Stuttgart, 1962.

68. M. Albini: "Modern Italy: The National Style and the International Style," *The Architectural Review*, Jan. 1937.

69. The building is used today for the Ministry of the Exterior.

70. H.-R. Hitchcock: *Architecture: Nineteenth and Twentieth Centuries*, Harmondsworth, 1958, p. 409, however—"the final nonsense of La Padulla's (sic) Palace of Italian Civilization." New evaluations by S. Kostof: *The Third Rome*, Berkeley, 1973; L. Benevolo: *Roma: Un centro Direzionale Sbagliato. Le avenute della città*, Bari, 1974, p. 86. The new city of Sabaudio, a major example of Fascist city planning, was initiated by Eugenio Montuori in 1933.

71. U. Kultermann: "Wassily and Hans Luckhardt," *Bauten und Entwürf*, Tübingen, 1958.

72. A. Teut, ed.: *Architektur im Dritten Reich, 1933–1945*, Berlin, 1967, pp. 136–137. See also G. Bussmann, ed.: *Kunst im Dritten Reich. Dokumente der Unterwerfung*, exhibition catalogue, Frankfurter Kunstverein, 1974.

73. Ph. Johnson: *Architecture in the Third Reich* (1933), reprinted in: T. and C. Benton, eds. *Architecture and Design: 1980 to 1939*, New York, 1975, pp. 207–208; G. Troost: *Das Bauen im Neuen Reich*, Bayreuth, 1938; K. W. Straub: *Architektur im*

Dritten Reich, Stuttgart, 1932; H. Stephan: *Baukunst im Dritten Reich*, Berlin, 1939; H. Schrade: *Bauten des Dritten Reiches*, Leipzig, 1937; A. Speer, ed.: *Neue deutsche Baukunst*, Prague, 1943; R. Wolters: *Albert Speer*, Oldenburg, 1943; G. Janssen: *Das Ministerium Speer*, Berlin, 1968; R. R. Taylor, *The Word in Stone*, Berkeley, 1974; "A. Speer," *Current Biography*, Oct. 1976.

74. A. Dressler: *Das Braune Haus und das Verwaltungsgebäude der Reichsleitung der NSDAP*, Munich, 1939.

75. H.-G. Seraphim: *Das politische Tagebuch Alfred Rosenbergs, 1934/35 and 1939/40*, Göttingen, 1956, p. 125.

76. H. Lehmann-Haupt: *Art Under Dictatorship*, New York, 1954, p. 57; E. Schönleben: *Fritz Todt*, Oldenburg 1943; K. Kaftan: *Der Kampf um die Autobahn*, Berlin, 1953. Alfons Leitl still attempted to see the ideals of the National Socialist regime in unison with the new construction, as expressed in his book *From Architecture to Building*, published in 1936 in Berlin.

77. H.-G. Seraphim: *Das politische Tagebuch Alfred Rosenbergs, 1934/35 and 1939/40*, Göttingen, 1956, pp. 124–125. Note in diary Dec. 10, 1940.

78. A. Teut, ed.: *Architektur im Dritten Reich, 1933-1945*, Berlin, 1967, pp. 271–279.

79. W. March: *Bauwerk Reichssportfeld*, Berlin, 1936; R. R. Taylor: *The Word in Stone*, Berkeley, 1974, pp. 161–164; W. Götz: *Die Reaktivierung des Historismus*, in: *Beiträge zur Rezeption des 19. und 20. Jahrhunderts*, W. Schadendorf, ed., Munich, 1975, p. 51.

80. Review of the book by A. Speer: *Inside the Third Reich*, New York, 1970, in *Journal of the Society of Architectural Historians* 32, 1973. See also W. Lotz: "Das Reichsparteitagsgelände in Nürnberg: Die Kunst im Dritten Reich," Issue No. 9, 1938; G. K. Koenig: "Un Colosso inedito," *Casabella* 382, 1973; K. Arndt: *Baustelle Reichsparteitagsgebäude 1938/1939*, Göttingen, 1973.

81. A. Speer: *Erinnerungen*, Berlin, 1969, p. 71.

82. A. Speer: *Erinnerungen*, Berlin, 1969, p. 95; A. Hoffmann: *Deutschland in Paris*, Munich, 1937; see also the presentation by Paul Bonatz: *Leben und Bauen*, Stuttgart, 1950, pp. 170–173.

83. Quoted in R. R. Taylor: *The Word in Stone*, Berkeley, 1974, p. 137; A. Speer: "Die neue Reichskanzlei," *Moderne Bauformen* 38,

1939. The building was destroyed during World War II; in May 1945 it was completely demolished by the Russian occupation of East Berlin and the marble blocks were used for the construction of the Russian War Memorial in Berlin-Treptow; Ref. also K. Herding and E. Mittig: *Kunst und Alltag im NS-System: Albert Speers Berliner Strassenlaternen*, Giessen, 1975.

84. In A. Speer: *Die neue Reichskanzlei*, Munich, 1940.

85. A. Speer: *Erinnerungen*, Berlin, 1969, pp. 167–168. About a different analogy of history, Speer writes: "The railroad station plaza of a thousand meters length and three hundred meters width, would have been lined with captured weapons following the example of the Ram Boulevard from Karnak to Luxor." *Erinnerungen*, Berlin, 1969, p. 149; L. O. Larsson: *Die Neugestaltung der Residenzhauptstadt: Albert Speers Generalbebauungsplan für Berlin*, Stockholm, 1977. Hitler's plan for the expansion of the city of Linz into a "European Cultural Center," with designs by the architect Roderich Fick, provided for a huge art gallery. H. Brenner: *National Socialist Art Politics*, Hamburg, 1963, p. 154 ff. See also G. Masur: *Imperial Berlin*, New York, 1970.

86. G. Masur: *Imperial Berlin*, New York, 1970; C. Partridge: *Hitler's Atlantic Wall*, Guernsey, 1976; M. Ludwig: *Neuzeitliche Festungen*, Berlin, 1938.

87. M. Major: *Geschichte der Architektur*, vol. 3, Berlin, 1966, p. 54 ff. W. A. Shchuko already stood out as an architect in 1910 because of an apartment house buildt in St. Petersburg.

88. H. Aurenhammer: *J. B. Fisher v. Erlach*, London, 1933, p. 79 ff. *Sowjetische Architektur*, Moscow, 1962 (in Russian); V. Quilici: *Architettura sovietica contemporanea*, Bologna, 1965.

89. M. Major: *Geschichte der Architektur*, vol. 3, Berlin, 1966, pp. 555–556.

90. W. Hofman and U. Kultermann: *Baukunst in unserer Zeit*, Essen, 1969, Fig. 68. Subsequent constructions of the Unité d'Habitation were realized with minor variation in Nantes, Meaux, Brieyen-Forêt, and Berlin.

91. Le Corbusier maintains that his concept is influenced by biological considerations: *Creation Is A Patient Search*, New York, 1960; especially p. 138 ff. See also H. Higuchi: "Le Corbusier and Modern Architecture," *The Japan Architect*, March 1968.

92. M. Dormoy: *L'Architecture Française*, Paris, 1938; P. Lavedan: *L'Architecture Française*, Paris, 1944.
93. A. Roth: *Die Neue Architektur*, 4th ed., Zürich, 1948, pp. 115–130; M. Schiedhelm: "Marcel Lods," *Architectural Design* 10, 1974.
94. M. Major: *Geschichte der Architektur*, vol. 3, Berlin 1966, p. 400; S. Giedion: *A Decade of New Architecture*, Zürich, 1951, p. 129.

Part III (pp. 107–183)

1. U. Kultermann: *Neues Bauen in der Welt*, 2d ed., Tübingen, 1976.
2. R. Dent: *Principles of Pneumatic Architecture*, London, 1971.
3. U. Kultermann: "Der neue Dynamismus," *Bauen und Wohnen*, May 1958; U. Kultermann: "Elementare Architektur," *Europäisches Bauforum* 7, 8, and 9, 1964, and 1, 1965.
4. S. Anderson: "Planning for Fullness," *Arena*, March 1967, p. 209 ff.
5. H. Hardy: *The Energy of Reuse: On Site on Energy*, ed. by A. Sky and M. Sonte, New York, 1974, p. 69 ff.; S. Cantacuzino: *New Uses for Old Buildings*, London, 1975.
6. *New Uses for Old Buildings*, London, 1975; E. Kendall Thompson, ed.: *Recycling Buildings*, New York, 1977.
7. Examples of similar types of sculpture as the sun telescope of Kitt Peak, Arizona, by Skidmore, Owings and Merrill are the copy "Tapanga" by Robert Grosvenor (1965), Derek Boshier's "Kenzo" series of sculptures and Richard Hamilton's "Guggenheim Museum."
8. Quoted in T. Wolfe: *"Electrographic Architecture," Architectural Design* 7, 1969, p. 382.
9. F. Maki: *Investigations in Collective Form*, St. Louis, Mo., 1964.
10. P. and A. Smithson: "Die offene Stadt," *Bauen und Wohnen* 1, 1964.
11. Frei Otto: "Städtebau und Anpassungsfähigkeit, *Der Architekt*, special issue, 1965, p. 2.
12. U. Kultermann: *Neues Bauen in der Welt*, 2d ed., Tübingen, 1976, vii.
13. I. McCallum: *Architecture USA*, New York, 1959; U. Kultermann: "Moderne amerikanische Architektur," *Die Innenarchitektur*, June 1959; E. Burchard and A. Bush-Brown: *The Architecture of America*, Boston, 1961; A. Mendini: "Li-

mite nell'architettura americana," *Casabella* 301, 1966; R. A. M. Stern: *New Directions in American Architecture*, New York, 1968; V. Scully: *American Architecture and Urbanism*, New York, 1969.
14. U. Kultermann: "Frank Lloyd Wright und seine Nachfolge," *Bauen und Wohnen*, Oct. 1958; K. Higuchi: "The Significance for Today of Wright's Architecture," *The Japan Architect*, Oct. and Nov. 1967.
15. *Knaur's Lexikon der modernen Architektur*, Munich, 1963, p. 297.
16. J. M. Fitch: *American Building: The Historical Forces That Shaped It*, Cambridge, 1966, pp. 270–271.
17. W. Gropius and S. P. Harkness, eds.: *The Architects Collaborative*, Zürich, 1966; S. Giedion: *Walter Gropius*, Stuttgart 1954; U. Kultermann: "Der Baumeister Walter Gropius," *Der Fortschritt*, Dec. 1955; J. M. Fitch: *Walter Gropius*, Ravensburg, 1962.
18. U. Kulterman: "Marcel Breuer," *Bauen und Wohnen*, Jan. 1959; C. Jones: *Marcel Breuer, 1921–1962*, Stuttgart, 1962.
19. P. Johnson: *Mies van der Rohe*, New York, 1947; U. Kultermann: "Der Klassiker Mies van der Rohe," *Die Innenarchitektur*, Feb. 1956; L. Hilberseimer: *Mies van der Rohe*, Chicago, 1956; W. Blaser: *Mies van der Rohe*, Zürich, 1965.
20. U. Kultermann: "The Miesians," *Das Kunstwerk*, 1955/1956.
21. U. Kultermann. "O classico L. Mies van der Rohe e os Miesianos," *Habitat*, 1957.
22. H.-R. Hitchcock: *Architektur von Skidmore, Owings und Merrill*, Stuttgart, 1962; M. Goldsmith: "Struttura, scale e architettura," *Casabella* 418, Oct. 1976.
23. S. Giedion: "Das Carpenter Center für Visual Arts der Harvard University in Cambridge," *Bauen und Wohnen* 8, 1964.
24. K. Bastlund: *José Luis Sert*, New York, 1967.
25. U. Kultermann: "Architektur als angewandte Physiologie," *Das Kunstwerk* 6, 1961; E. McCoy: *Richard Neutra*, Ravensburg, 1962.
26. U. Kultermann: "Das Wohnhaus und die Erziehung zum Glück," *Innenarchitektur* 2, 1958; U. Kultermann: "Ein Ferienhotel von Neutra," *Innenarchitektur* 1, 1959.
27. "Congregation B'Nai Amoona Synagoge and Community Center," *Architectural Forum* 98, April 1953.
28. F. Otto: "Die Raleigh Arena," *Bauwelt* 5, 1953; L. Mumford: "The Life, the Teaching and the Architecture of Matthew No-

wicki," *Architectural Record* 6-9, 1954; U. Kultermann: "Der neue Dynamismus," *Bauen und Wohnen*, 1958.

29. A. B. Saarinen, ed.: *Eero Saarinen and His Work*, New Haven, 1962; U. Kultermann: "Eero Saarinen," *Deutsche Bauzeitung*, 1961; A. Temko: *Eero Saarinen*, Ravensburg, 1964.

30. U. Kultermann: "Der neue Dynamismus," *Bauen und Wohnen*, 1958; U. Kultermann: "Une architecture autre," *Baukunst und Werkform* 8, 1958; Eero Saarinen: letter to the editor in regard to "Une architecture autre," *Baukunst und Werkform* 8, 1958; U. Kultermann: "Eine neue Figuration in der Architektur," *Deutsche Bauzeritun* 4, 1963; R. Spade: *Eero Saarinen*, New York, 1971. Saarinen's monumental Gateway Arch in St. Louis (1959-1964), which was designed in 1947, again takes up a motif of Adalberto Libera for EUR in Rome.

31. Kevin Roche, *John Dinkeloo*, Tokyo, 1974.

32. S. Moholy-Nagy: *The Architecture of Paul Rudolph*, New York, 1970; R. Spade: *Paul Rudolph*, New York, 1971.

33. J. Jacobus: *Philip Johnson*, Ravensburg, 1963; H.-R. Hitchcock: *Philip Johnson*, New York, 1966.

34. W. H. Jordy: "The Mies-less Johnson," *Architectural Forum* 9, 1959; U. Kultermann: "Philip Johnson's Museum," *Artis*, 1966.

35. J. M. Johansen: "The Mummers Theater: A Fragment Not a Building," *Architectural Forum* 5, 1968.

36. R. Giurgola: "Reflections on Buildings and the City," *Perspecta* 9/10, 1965.

37. J. Jacobus: "Beyond the Seagram Building: Architecture Now," *Artforum* 1, 1966; H. Klotz: "Bertrand Goldberg," *Perspecta* 13/14, 1971.

38. V. Scully: *Louis I. Kahn*, Ravensburg, 1963; R. Giurgola and J. Mehta: *Louis I. Kahn*, Zürich, 1975; A. E. Komendant: *18 years with Architect Louis I. Kahn*, Englewood Cliffs, N.J., 1975; H. Ronner, S. Jhaveri, and A. Vasella: *Louis I. Kahn. The Complete Works. 1935-1974*. Boulder, Col., 1977.

39. Quoted in J. C. Rowan: "Wanting To Be," *Progressive Architecture* 4, 1961.

40. W. Hofmann and U. Kultermann: *Baukunst in unserer Zeit*, Essen, 1969, Fig. 81; W. H. Jordy: *American Buildings and Their Architects*, Garden City, N.Y., 1972, pp. 361-426.

41. A. Smithson: "Review of Recent Work: Louis Kahn," *Architectural Design* 8, 1973. Subsequent projects of Kahn are the Palace of the President in Islamabad (1963), the Ayup Central Hospital in Dacca (1963), and the Philadelphia College of Art (1964).

42. R. Venturi, D. Scott Brown, and S. Izenour: *Learning From Las Vegas*, Cambridge, Mass., 1972.

43. C. Moore: "After a New Architecture: The Best Shape for a Chimera," *Oppositions* 3, 1974; C. Moore: "Sea Ranch. A Second Look," *Architectural Records* 9, 1974; Moore, Allen, Lyndon: "The Place of Houses, Lotus 8, 1974; R. A. M. Stern: Burns House, Santa Monica Canyon, Los Angeles," *Progressive Architecture* 5, 1975; C. Moore and G. Allen: *Space, Shape and Scale*, New York, 1977.

44. S. Cantacuzino: *New Uses for Old Buildings*, London, 1975; U. Kultermann: *Neues Bauen in der Welt*, 2d ed., Tübingen, 1976, pp. 72-73.

45. C. Moore: "You Have To Pay For Public Life," *Perspecta* 9/10, 1965.

46. "The House That Walt Built," *Progressive Architecture* 8, 1971; P. Goldberger: "Mickey Mouse Teaches the Architect," *New York Times Magazine* Oct. 23, 1972; C. Jencks: "Ersatz in L. A.," *Architectural Design* 9, 1973.

47. Quoted in H. C. Schulitz: "The Message as an Architectural Medium," *Architectural Forum* 5, 1970; Tom Wolfe: *The Kandy-Kolored, Tangerine-Flake, Streamline Baby*, New York, 1965; Tom Wolfe: "Electrographic Architecture," *Architectural Design* 7, 1969.

48. P. Blake: "Fantastic World of Paolo Soleri," *Architectural Forum* 2, 1961; P. Soleri: *Arcology: The City in the Image of Man*, Cambridge, Mass., 1969; P. Soleri: "Simulation and Becoming," *Architectural Association Quarterly* 3, 1972; P. Soleri: "Utopia and/or Revolution," *Perspecta* 13/14, 1971; "Job Site for Utopia," *Progressive Architecture* 4, 1973; S. Moholy-Nagy: "The Arcology of Paolo Soleri," *Architectural Forum* 5, 1970; R. Jensen: "The Arcosanti Antithesis. Paolo Soleri and the Counter Culture," *Architectural Record* 8, 1974.

49. J. Hix: *The Glass House*, Cambridge, Mass., 1974, pp. 192; W. Bird: "Air Structures," *Building Research* 1/2, 1972.

50. P. Eisenman: "Cardboard Architecture," *Casabella* 374, 1973; P. Eisenman: "Notes

on Conceptual Architecture," *Casabella* 359–360, 1971; Five Architects," *Lotus* 9, 1975; *Five Architects*, New York, 1975; E. McCoy: "High Tech Images: San Bernadino City Hall," *Progressive Architecture* 2, 1974; C. Moore: "After a New Architecture," *Oppositions* 3, May 1974; J. Burns: *Anthropods*, New York, 1972, 101–110; S. E. Cohen: "Hardy, Holtzman, Pfeiffer on America, "*Progressive Architecture* 2, 1975.

51. A. Gowan: *Building Canada*, Toronto, 1966; C. Moore Ede: *Canadian Architecture*, 1960/1970, Toronto, 1971.

52. The total cost of the expandable complex amounted to 11.7 million U.S. dollars. The first phase of construction was intended for 500 students.

53. P. Blake: "Half-Mile Gangplank," *Architectural Forum* 3, 1970; P. Drew: *The Third Generation*, New York, 1972, pp. 144–151.

54. M. Safdie: *Beyond Habitat*, Cambridge, Mass., 1970

55. M. Safdie: *For Everyone a Garden*, Cambridge, Mass., 1974. The German pavilion by Frei Otto and the American pavilion by Buckminster-Fuller should be pointed out among the buildings for the World Exhibit in Montreal in 1967. The Buckminster-Fuller building burned down in May 1976.

56. G. E. Kidder Smith: *The New Architecture of Europe*, London, 1961; A. Whittick: *European Architecture in the Twentieth Century*, New York, 1974.

57. The cities of Rotterdam, with the grand-scale planning of a pedestrian center by van den Bakema and Behrens, and Hannover, with Rudolf Hillebrecht's solution to traffic circulation, can be viewed as exceptions.

58. The New Town Act of 1946 afforded the necessary legal basis.

59. Milton Keynes, *Architectural Design* 1975; F. J. Osborne and A. Whittick: *The New Towns*, London, 1969; E. Y. Galantay: *New Towns*, New York, 1975, pp. 57–62.

60. "Concert Hall, South Bank London," *Bauen und Wohnen* 12, 1967; *Zodiac* 18, 1968; D. Lasdun: "Humanising the Institution," *The Architectural Review*, Jan. 1977

61. Leslie Martin on the bridges between two cultures, *RIBA Journal* 8, 1973.

62. L. Biscoglia: "L'opera di James Stirling," *Casabella* 315, 1967; James Stirling, *Bauten und Projekte*, Stuttgart, 1975; W. Se-ligman: "Runcorn," *Oppositions* 7, 1976. Stirling and Gowan stood out previously with low-income apartments in Preston, Lancashire.

63. *Zodiac* 18, 1968; "Forward Through the Past," *Progressive Architecture* 5, 1973.

64. P. and A. Smithson: "Die offene stadt," *Bauen and Wohnen* I, 1964; P. and A. Smithson: *Urban Structuring*, London, 1967.

65. Ron Herron's Walking City (Fig. 145) of 1964 and Warren Chalk's Plug In City of 1964 are spectacular examples of the group.

66. J. Burns; ed.: *Anthropods*, New York, 1972, pp. 58–63.

67. E. Y. Galantay: *New Towns*, New York, 1975.

68. M. F. Borràs: *Arquitectura finlandesa en Otaniemi*, Barcelona, 1967. Aalto had developed a comprehensive plan for a contest for the Technical University in Otaniemi in 1949, for which he received first prize.

69. P. Hodgkinson: "Finlandia Hall, Helsinki," *The Architectural Review* 6, 1972.

70. J. M. Richards: *A Guide to Finnish Architecture*, London 1966; A Solokorpi: *Modern Architecture in Finland*, New York, 1970.

71. C. Norberg-Schulz, U. Kultermann, O. Hansen: "Arvio inteja Dipolista," *arkkitehti/arkitekten* 9, 1967; U. Kultermann: "Reima Pietilae," *Allgemeine Bauzeitung* 52, 1968. The total capacity of the building affords space for activities for 3,000 people; the kitchen can serve 2,000 people per meal.

72. G. Johansson: "Sven Markelius: architetto svedese e internazionale," *Casabella* 201, 1954; U. Kultermann: "Ein Wohnhaus van Ralph Erskine in Skoevede," Die Innerarchitektur 2, 1958.

73. G. Kavli: *Norwegian Argriculture,* Oslo, 1958; N.-O. Lund: "Arne Korsmo and Norwegian Architecture," *Bauen und Wohnen* 3, 1966.

74. T. Faber: *Arne Jacobsen*, Stuttgart, 1964.

75. U. Kultermann: "Zwei dänische Einfamilienhauser," Die Innenarchitektur 3, 1959.

76. For J. Bo and V. Wohlerts Louisiana Museum in Humlebaek of 1958, see M. Brawne: *The New Museum*, New York, 1965, p. 79.

77. S. Giedion: "Jörn Utzon and the Third Generation," *Zodiac* 14, 1965, "The Works of Jörn Utzon," *Arkitektur* 1, 1970.

78. J. Utzon: "The Sydney Opera House," *Zodiac* 14, 1965; M. Takeyama: *Jörn Utzon and His Intention*, Tokyo, 1966; E. Derek-Cohen: *Utzon and the Sydney Opera House*, Sydney, 1967; M. Baume: *The Sydney Opera House Affair*, Sydney, 1967.

79. J. H. van den Broeck: *Guide to Dutch Architecture*, Rotterdam, 1959; *Building in the Netherlands*, The Hague, 1964.

80. J. Joedicke: *Architektur und Städtebau Das Werk der Architekten van den Broek and Bakema*, Stuttgart, 1963; L. Mumford: "Der Wiederaufbau Rotterdams," *Der Monat* 1958.

81. U. Kultermann: Haus "Uitenbroek in Holland," *Architektur und Wohnform* 8, 1959.

82. H. J. Habraken: *Supports: An Alternative to Mass Housing*, New York, 1972.

83. D. Mellor: "Hertzberger's Office Complex Apeldoorn." *Architectural Design* 2, 1974; H. Hertzberger: "Old People's Centre Amsterdam," *The Architectural Review* 2, 1976.

84. A. van Eyck: "Team 10 Primer," *Architectural Design* 12, p. 196.

85. *Progressive Architecture* 9, 1962, p. 155.

86. U. Kultermann: *Der Schlüssel zur Architektur von heute*, Düsseldorf, 1963; pp. 160–162. Among the recent works of van Eyck are the art gallery in Düsseldorf, the experimental houses in Lima, and the project for a church in the Hague. P. Smithson: "Church at the Hague by Aldo van Eyck," *Architectural Design* 6, 1975.

87. "I. Schein: Architecture in France, 1944–1964," *Architectural Design* 1, 1965; G. Piccinato: *L'architettura contemporanea in Francia*, Bologna, 1965; M. Besset: *New French Architecture*. New York, 1967; D. Amouroux, M. Crettol and J. P. Monnet: *Guide d'architecture contemporaine en France*, Paris, 1972.

88. Between the outer skin of the roof and the ceiling of the interior is a difference of 2½ yd. (2.26 m). The interior is 27½ yd. (25 m) long and 14 yd. (13 m) wide. It provides room for approximately 200 people. The floor slopes considerably toward the main altar.

89. U. Kultermann: *Der Schlüssel zur Architektur von heute*, Düsseldorf, 1963, pp. 141–143.

90. E. Chowdhury "Le Corbusier in Chandigarh," *Architectural Design* 10, 1965; N. Evenson: *Chandigarh*, Berkeley, 1966.

91. S. Woods: *Candilis, Josic, Woods*, New York, 1968; J. Hermann: "Was ist aus Le Mirail?," *Deutsche Bauzeitung 3*, 1976; M. Besset: *New French Architecture*, New York, 1967, 1965.

92. M. Tournon Branly: "History of ATBAT and Its influence on French Architecture," *Architectural Design* 1, 1965.

93. Piano and Rogers also stood out with a factory building in Tadworth, Surrey, see: *Architectural Review* 12, 1974; *Architectural Design* 5, 1975; *Zodiac* 22, 1973.

94. Y. Friedman: "Mobiler Städtebau," *Der Architekt*, 1965; Y. Friedman: "La città come meccanismo," *Casabella* 326, 1968; Y. Friedman: *Pour l'architecture scientifique*, Paris, 1971.

95. U. Kultermann: "Na-oorlogse architectuur in Duitsland," *Kronick van Kunst en Kultuur* 1, 1958; A. Giefer and F. F. Meyer: *Planen und Bauen im neuen Deutschland*, Cologne, 1960; U. Kultermann: *Deutsche Nachkriegsarchitektur*. Handbuch des Bauwesens, Stuttgart, 1961; U. Conrads: *Neue deutsche Architektur 2*, Stuttgart, 1962; U. Kultermann: "Architettura tedesca del dopoguerra," *La Biennale di Venezia* 48, 1963; G. K. Koenig: *Architettura tedesca del Secondo Dopoguerra*, Bologna, 1965; J. E. Burchard: *The Voice of the Phoenix*, Cambridge, Mass., 1966.

96. P. Blundell Jones: "Late Works of Scharoun," *The Architectural Review* 3, 1975; U. Kultermann: *Das Werk des Architekten Hans Scharoun: Theater der Stadt Wolfsburg*, Wolfsburg, 1973. Subsequent works of Scharoun are the school in Lünen, the German Embassy in Brasilia, the theater in Wolfsburg, and the State Library in Berlin.

97. U. Kultermann: *Wasili und Hans Luckhardt*, Tübingen, 1958

98. W. Schwagenscheid: *Die Raumstadt und was daraus wurde*, Stuttgart, 1971.

99. P. Serenyi: "Spinoza, Hegel and Mies: The Meaning of the New National Gallery in Berlin," *Journal of the Society of Architectural Historians* 30, 1971.

100. U. Kultermann: "Restrospective statt Zukunftsplanung," *Das Werk*, August 1957. The architects Oscar Niemeyer, Alvar Aalto, Pierre Vago, Le Corbusier, Fritz Jaenecke, Sten Samuelson, and Walter Gropius participated, among others.

101. Subsequent Swiss architects working in Germany were Atelier 5, Stucky and Meuli, and Walter M. Förderer.

102. U. Kultermann: "Fritz Schupp," *Deutsche Bauzeitung* 3, 1961.

103. H.-R. Hitchcock: *Hentrich and Petschnigg; Bauten und Entwürfe*, Düsseldorf, 1973.

104. H.-R. Hitchcock: "Germany 1955–1965: More Specially Düsseldorf," *Zodiac* 14, 1965; U. Kultermann: "Mathematische Masken: Hochhäuser im Rheinland," *Neues Rheinland,* Feb.-March 1965.

105. Hentrich and Petschnigg started a second office in South Africa, which executed such buildings as the Diamond Sorting Building of de Beers in Kimberly (1970–1974) and high rises in Johannesburg.

106. U. Kultermann: "Das neue Theater in Gelsenkirchen," *Die Innenarchitektur* 3, 1960; U. Kultermann: "Harald Deilmann," *Deutsche Bauzeitung* 4, 1961; U. Kultermann: "Das mobile Theater," *Möbel und Decoration,* 1961.

107. "Märkisches Viertel," *Architectural Design* 1, 1964.

108. Olympic Village in Munich, 1972.

109. C. Roland: *Spannweiten*, Berlin, 1965; U. Kultermann: "Der Architekt Frei Otto," *Der Egoist* 2, 1967; P. Drew: *The Third Generation*, New York, 1972, pp. 114–129; P. Drew: *Frei Otto: Form and Structure*, Boulder, Colo., 1976. The total cost of the pavilion of 2.4 million DM was less than estimated.

110. E. Happold and M. Dickson: "The Story of Munich," *Architectural Design* 6, 1974.

111. U. Kultermann: *Neues Bauen in der Welt*, 2d ed. Tübingen, 1976, pp. 26–27. The Hoechst Stadium at Hannover was a similar structure, realized in 1970.

112. R. Doernach: "Studien zum 'Instrumentalen Bauen,'" *Der Architekt*, 1965; "Gernot Minke," *Zodiac* 22, 1973; Rob Krier: "Siemer House, Warmbronn (1969–1973)," *Lotus* 9, 1975; A. Colquhoun: "Rational Architecture," *Architectural Design* 6, 1975; Rob Krier: *Stadtraum*, Stuttgart, 1975; A. Grumbach: "The Krier Brothers," *Lotus* 11, 1976; "Architectural Exhibit of Dortmund 1976," *Dortmunder Architekturhefte* 3, 1976; R. Krier: "Il ne faut plus longtemps renoncer à l'architecture," *Architecture et Technique* 312, Dec. 1976.

113. A. Altherr: *Neue Schweizer Architektur*, Teufen, 1965; J. Bachmann and S. von Moos: *New Directions in Swiss Architecture*, New York, 1968.

114. J. Dahinden: *Denken — Fühlen — Handeln*, Lausanne, 1973, pp. 65–70.

115. The integration of works by sculptors in regard to the conception of the University of Trade was important (Calder, Arp, Giacommetti, Hajdu, Tàpies, Penalba, Stahly, Kemeny).

116. G. E. Kidder Smith: *Switzerland Builds*, New York, 1950.

117. M. Brawne: *The New Museum*, New York 1965, pp. 121–123; O. Uhl: *Moderne Architektur in Wien*, Vienna, 1966; J. S. Margolies: "Art Machines for the 70s," *Architectural Forum* 1/2, 1970; D. Steiner: "Experimentelle Architektur in Österreich," *Bauen und Wohnen* 4, 1976.

118. J. Burns: *Anthropods*, New York, 1972, pp. 78–85.

119. A. Galardi: *Neue Architektur in Italien*, Stuttgart, 1967; V. Gregotti: *New Directions in Italian Architecture*, New York, 1968.

120. J. Rykwert: "The Work of Gino Valle," *Architectural Design* 3, 1964; U. Kultermann: "Enrico Castiglioni, *Bauen und Wohnen* 9, 1959.

121. G. de Carlo: *An Architecture of Participation*, Melbourne, 1972; G. de Carlo: "Statement, Architecture," *Formes Fonctions* 16, 1971, p. 175.

122. G. Mazzariol: "Un Progetto per Venezia," *Lotus* 8, 1969.

123. "MOMA Italian Style," *Progressive Architecture* 3, 1975.

124. L. Savioli, "Florenz 1967," *Zodiac* 22, 1973.

125. J. Burns: *Anthropods*, New York, 1972, pp. 86–98, pp. 144–151; A. Rossi: *Die Architektur der Städt*, Düsseldorf, 1973; A. Savio: *L'architettura di Aldo Rossi*, Milan, 1976.

126. L. Domenech Girbau: *Arquitectura Epañola Contemporanea*, Barcelona, 1968; O. Bohigas: *Contra una arquitectura adjetivada*, Barcelona, 1969; O. Bohigas: *Proceso y Erotica del Diseño*, Barcelona, 1972.

127. U. Kultermann: "Ein studentenwohnheim in Madrid," *Die Innenarchitektur* 10, 1958; P. Hodgkinson: Xanada," *Architectural Forum* 6, 1968; P. Hodgkinson: Kafka's Castle," *Architectural Forum* 11, 1969.

128. V. Gregotti: "La passion d'Aivaro Siza," *L'Architecture d'Aujourd'hui* 185, 1976.

129. A. Voyce: *Russian Architecture*, New York, 1948; U. Kultermann: "Abkehr vom Zuckerbäckerstil," *Christ and Welt*, Feb. 5, 1965; U. Kultermann: "Suche nach neuen Städten," *Christ und Welt,*

2-19-1965; N. D. Kolli: "Recent Soviet Architecture," *Architectural Design* 10, 1962; A. Aman: "Sovjetarkitektur," *Kunstrevy* 3, 1968; V. Quilichi: *Architettura sovietica contemporanea*, Bologna, 1965.

130. G. Minervin: "Recent Development in Soviet Architecture," *Progressive Architecture* 6, 1961.

131. P. Cook: "The NER Group," *Architectural Design* 10, 1968; A. Gutnow: *The Ideal Communist City*, New York, 1970.

132. G. Borisowski: *Form and Uniform*, Stuttgart, 1967, p. 113; G. Borisowski: "Architecture and Technical Progress," *Annual of Architecture, Structure and Town Planning* 3, 1962.

133. U. Kultermann: *Neues Bauen in der Welt*, 2d ed., Tübingen, 1976, pp. 32-33.

134. W. Hofmann and U. Kultermann: *Baukunst in unserer Zeit*, Essen, 1969, Fig. 83. The platform has a free span of 81½ yd (74.25 m) and provides space for 31,500 vocalists. A similar platform was created in Vilnius shortly thereafter.

135. M. Bicher: *Architecture in Bulgaria*, Sofia, 1961; P. Peters: "Über Architektur und Architekten im Ungarn," *Der Baumeister* 1964; F. Merényi: *Cento Anni Architettura Ungharese*, Rome, 1965; Z. Dmochowski: *The Architecture of Poland*, London, 1965; G. Gusti: *Architectura in Romania*, Bucharest, 1965; K. Gavlas: "On Housing in Czechoslovakia," *Lotus* 10, 1975; I. Horky: "Quelques aspects de la creativité architecture," March 1975.

136. B. Szmidt: "Modern Architecture in Poland," *Architectural Design* 10, 1962; P. Trzeciak, ed.: *Building and Architecture in Poland: 1945-1966*, Warsaw, 1968.

137. U. Kultermann: *Neues Bauen in der Welt*, Tübingen, 1965.

138. U. Ramseger: "Architektur in Jugoslawien," *Werk* 8, 1963.

139. U. Kultermann: *Neues Bauen in der Welt*, Tübingen, 1965, p. 178.

140. U. Kultermann: *Kenzo Tange: Architektur und Städtebau*, Zürich, 1970, pp. 262-281.

141. H. v. Huyck: *Urban Planning in the Developing Countries*, New York, 1968; N. Wright: "Science and Technology in the Less Developed Countries," *Arena* 4/5, 1968; R. Martin: "The Architecture of Underdevelopment," *Architectural Design* 10, 1974.

142. C. Abrams: *Man's Struggle for Shelter in an Urbanizing World*, Cambridge, 1964; C. Abrams: *Squatter Settlements: The Problem and the Opportunity*, Washington, D.C., 1966; A. Farroukh, A. Cain and J. Norton: "Indigenous Building and the Third World," *Architectural Design* 4, 1975.

143. H.-R. Hitchcock: *Latin-American Architecture Since 1945*. New York, 1955.

144. H. Meyer: "Schulbau in Mexiko," *Bauen und Wohnen* 1, 1951; M. L. Cetto: *Moderne Architektur in Mexiko*, Stuttgart, 1961; C. B. Smith: *Builders in the Sun*, New York, 1967; J. Katzmann: *La arquitectura contemporanea Mexicana*, Mexico City, 1964.

145. T. Sharp: "Mexico University," *The Architectural Review* 11, 1953. The stadium was enlarged for the Olympic Games in 1968.

146. Ramirez Vasques had previously executed the Museum of Modern Art in Mexico City.

147. H.-R. Hitchcock: *Latin American Architecture Since 1945*, New York, 1955, pp. 123-125.

148. C. Faber: *Felix Candela*, Munich, 1964.

149. W. Hofmann and U. Kultermann: *Baukunst in unserer Zeit*, Essen, 1969, Fig. 110. The hall has 22,370 seats. Candela, was more recently occupied with the work of a sports center in Kuwait.

150. A. A. Raafat: *Reinforced Concrete in Architecture*, New York, 1958, pp. 343ff.; R. Segre: "Cuba. L'Architettura della revoluzione," Padua, 1970; S. Torre: "Architecture and Revolution: Cuba 1959-1974," *Progressive Architecture* 10, 1974.

151. "Housing for the Elderly: Cidra, Puerto Rico," *Progressive Architecture* 6, 1969.

152. Previ/Lima: "Low-Cost Housing Project," *Architectural Design* 4, 1970. O. Hansen and S. Hatloey: "Pilot Project and Testhouses in Lima, Peru," *Lotus* 8, 1974. Participants of the international contest, among others, were A. van Eyck, K. Kurokawa, A. Kikutake, F. Maki, C. Correa, O. Hansen, J. Stirling, H. Ohl, C. Alexander, and Atelier 5. The first prize was bestowed upon the Swiss team, Atelier 5.

153. C. Martinez: *Arquitectura in Colombia*, Bogotá, 1963.

154. U. Kultermann: "Universitetsbyen y Caracas," *Arkitekten*, 1957; S. Moholy-Nagy: *Carlos Raul Villanueva und die Architektur in Venezuela*, Stuttgart, 1964.

155. Quoted in U. Kultermann: *Der Schlüssel*

zur Architektur von heute, Düsseldorf, 1963, p. 116.

156. About the evaluation of this mass housing project, see F. Bullrich: *New Direction in Latin American Architecture*, New York, 1969, p. 119.

157. *The Bridge Spanning Lake Maracaibo in Venezuela*, Berlin, 1963.

158. H. E. Mindlin: *Modern Architecture in Brazil*, New York, 1956; S. Bracco: *L'Architettura moderna in Brasile*, Bologna, 1967.

159. J. M. Richards: "Brasilia," *The Architectural Review* 2, 1959; S. Giedion; "Stadform und Gründung von of Brasilia," *Bauen und Wohnen*, 1960; W. Stäubli: *Brasilia*, Stuttgart, 1965.

160. O. Niemeyer: *Minha experiencia em Brasilia*, Rio de Janeiro, 1961.

161. H.-R. Hitchcock: *Latin-American Architecture Since 1945*, New York, 1955, pp. 126–131; S. Giedion: *The Works of Affonso Eduardo Reidy*, New York, 1960. A subsequent major work of Reidy is the Museum for Modern Art in Rio de Janeiro (1945 to 1958).

162. P. M. Bardi: *The Tropical Gardens of Burle-Marx*, New York, 1964.

163. U. Kultermann: *Neues Bauen in der Welt*, 2d ed., Tübingen, 1976, Fig. 14.

164. F. Bullrich: *New Directions in Latin American Architecture*, New York, 1969, pp. 98–99.

165. F. Bullrich: *Arquitectura Argentina Contemporanea*, Buenos Aires 1963; P. Nicolin und B. Viganò: "Argentine Idiom," *Casabella* 394, 1974.

166. In Chile, residential buildings by Carlos Bresciani, Hector Valdes, and Garcia Huidobro should be pointed out, as well as the United Nations building in Santiago, Chile, by Emilio Duhart (* 1917); J. Bellalta: "Architecture in Chile," *Architectural Design* 4, 1964, U. Kultermann: *Neues Bauen in der Welt*, 2d ed., Tübingen, 1976, Figs. 1–3.

167. A. Sharon: *Physical Planning on Israel*, Tel Aviv, 1951.

168. E. Perry: "The Architecture of Israel," *Progressive Architecture* 3, 1965.

169. E. Spiegel: *Neue Städte in Israel*, Stuttgart, 1966.

170. U. Kultermann: "The Renaissance of Contemporary Arab Architecture" (in progress).

171. M. Ragon: *Histoire mondiale de l'architecture et d'urbanisme moderne*, Paris, 1972, vol. 2, p. 356.

172. "Flughafengebäude in Dharan, Saudi Arabien," *Deutsche Bauzeitung* 4, 1963.

173. U. Kultermann: *Kenzo Tange, Architektur und Städtebau*, Zürich, 1970.

174. Dannatt at Riyadh, "*The Architectural Review*" 4, 1975.

175. "Gutbrod at Mecca," *The Architectural Review* 4, 1975.

176. Mohamed Scharabi: "Civic Center in Djeddah, Saudi Arabia," *Deutsche Bauzeitung* 17, 1964.

177. "Leslie Martin on the Bridges between the Cultures," *Riba Journal* 8, 1973.

178. "Sports Center of Kuwait," *Zodiac* 22, 1973.

179. K. Jamal: "Immigrant Worker's Settlements in Kuwait," *Architectural Design* 7, 1974.

180. U. Kultermann: *Neues Bauen in Africa*, Tübingen, 1963; U. Kultermann: *In einem ganz anderen Land: Die Kunst zu Hause zu sein*, Munich, 1965; U. Kultermann: *New Directions in African Architecture*, New York, 1969.

181. U. Kultermann: *New Directions in African Architecture*, New York, 1969; A. Wells: "Low-cost Housing in Casablanca," *Architectural Association Quarterly* 10, 1969.

182. W. Hofmann and U. Kultermann: *Baukunst in unserer Zeit*, Essen, 1969, Fig. 111.

183. *The Architectural Review* 12, 1974; R. Simounet: "La double notion de tissu," *Techniques et Architecture* 306, 1975.

184. R. S. McConnell: "Asswan. Egypt's Third City," *The Architectural Review* 8, 1966; H. Fathy: *Gourna: A Tale of Two Villages*, Cairo, 1969, English edition title: *Architecture for the Poor*, Chicago, 1973; J. M. Richards: "Gourna: A Lesson in Basic Architecture," *The Architectural Review* 2, 1970; Y. Blumenfeld: "Interview with Hassan Fathy," *Architectural Association Quarterly* 6, 1974.

185. E. Maxwell Fry and J. Drew: *Tropical Architecture*, New York, 1956.

186. U. Kultermann: "Repräsentation oder Formmalismus? Das Zentrum der französischen Verwaltung für Westafrika in Daka," *Die Innerarchitektur* 1, 1959.

187. U. Kultermann: *New Directions in African Architecture*, New York, 1969.

188. U. Kultermann: *New Directions in African Architecture*, New York, 1969, p. 29.

189. U. Kultermann: *Neues Bauen in der Welt*, 2d ed., Tübingen, 1976, pp. 50–51.

190. U. Kultermann: *New Directions in African Architecture*, New York, 1969, p. 87.

191. Quoted in: U. Kultermann: *New Directions in African Architecture*, New York, 1969, pp. 101–103.

192. J. Dahinden: *Deuken — Fühlen — Handeln*, Lausanne, 1973, p. 261ff.

193. W. D. Howie: *Contemporary Architecture in South Africa*, Johannesburg, 1958; N. Pevsner: "Johannesburg," *The Architectural Review* 6, 1953.

194. J. Tyrwitt: *Patrick Geddes in India*, London, 1947; A. Mayer and N. V. Modak: *An Outline of the Master Plan for Greater Bombay*, Bombay, 1948.

195. For example, the population density of Bombay is 164.8 per acre, 124.4 per acre in Calcutta, in comparison with 41 per acre in London and 20 per acre in Paris. C. Correa: "Third World Housing. Space as a Reserve." *Ekistics* 41, Jan. 1976.

196. A. Volwahsen: *Architektur in Indien*, Freiburg, 1968; C. Correa: "India Today," *The Architectural Review* 12, 1971; U. C. Jain: "Modern Architecture in India," *Journal of the Indian Institute of Architects*, Jan.-Mar. 1971.

197. N. Evenson: Chandigarh, Berkeley 1966; H. Schmetzer and P. I. Wakely: "Chandigarh Twenty Years Later," *Architectural Design* 6, 1974.

198. P. Hofer: *Le Corbusier und die Stadt: Fundplätze Bauplätze*, Basel, 1970, p. 150.

199. U. Kultermann: *Der Schüssel zur Architektur von heute*, Düsseldorf, 1963, pp. 117–119.

200. V. Z. Newcombe: "Auroville cradle of a new man," *Architectural Association Quarterly* 6, 1973; G. S. Troller: "Auroville," *Bauwelt* 40, 1974.

201. R. Giurgola und J. Mehti: *Louis I. Kahn*, Zürich, 1975; "Kahn at Dacca," *Domus* 7, 1975.

202. B. V. Doshi: "The Ahmedabad Projects of Le Corbusier," *The Indian Builder* 4, 1956.

203. M. Brawne: *The New Museum*, New York, 1965, pp. 168–169.

204. E. D. Stone: *The Evolution of an Architect*, New York, 1962.

205. M. W. Newman: "Stanley Tigerman in Bangladesh: Adventure, Adversion, Achievement," *The Inland Architect* 2, 1973.

206. U. Kultermann: *Neues Bauen in der Welt*, 2d ed., Tübingen, 1976, p. 40, pp. 48–49.

207. C. M. Correa: "New Bombay," *The Architectural Review* 12, 1971; A. Monroy: "India," *Lotus* 8, 1974.

208. S. Ghosh: "L'architecture en Inde," *Architecture Formes Fonctions* 12, 1965/1966.

209. Harry Seidler, *1955/1963*, Sydney, 1963; P. Blake: *Architecture for the New World: The Work of Harry Seidler*, Sydney, 1973.

210. E. Duek-Cohen: *Utzon and the Sydney Opera House*, Sydney, 1967; M. Baume: *The Sydney Opera House Affair*, Sydney, 1967.

211. J. M. Freeland: *Architecture in Australia*, Melbourne 1968; H. Sowden: *Toward an Australian Architecture*, Sydney, 1968; D. Saunders: "So I Decided to go Overseas," *Architecture in Australia*, Feb.–Mar. 1977.

212. A. Hsia: *Die chinesische Kulturrevolution*, Berlin, 1971.

213. J. Wilson-Lewis, ed.: *The City in Communist China*, Stanford, 1971; Ching-chih Hsu: *Chinese Architecture: Past and Present*, Hong Kong, 1964.

214. O. J. Golger: "Hongkong oder das Hausen von Massen," *Werk* 12, 1966; A. Mendini: "Edilizia contemporanea in Cina," *Casabella* 304, 1966; U. Hausmann: "China: Architecture for the People," *Architectural Association Quarterly* 1, 1980.

215. U. Kultermann: *Der Schlüssel zur Architektur von heute*, Düsseldorf, 1963, pp. 130–132.

216. R. T. F. Skinner: "Peking 1953," *The Architectural Review*, Oct. 1953; J. T. A. Lee: "The New China," *Architectural Record* 10, 1973; J. Deleyne: *Die chinesische Wirtschaftsrevolution*, Hamburg, 1971; A. Moravia: *Die Kulturrevolution in China*, Hamburg, 1971; G. Mathiessen: *Kritik der philosophischen Grundlagen und der gesellschaftspolitischen Entwicklung des Maoismus*, Cologne, 1973.

217. U. Kultermann: "Tanges Bau auf Formosa," *Die Tat* 146, June 24, 1969.

218. S. Koike: *Contemporary Architecture in Japan*, Tokyo, 1956; U. Kultermann: *Neue Bauen in Japan*, Tübingen, 1960, 2d ed., 1967; P. Riani: *Contemporary Japanese Architecture*, Florence, 1969; E. Tempel: *Neue japanische Architektur*, Stuttgart, 1969.

219. J. Hayashida: "Kunio Mayekawa and His Associates," *Sinkentiku* 8, 1957.

220. U. Kultermann: *Kenzo Tange: Architektur und Städtebau*, Zürich, 1970.

221. U. Kultermann: "The Residence of Kenzo

Tange," *Innenarchitektur* 5, 1958; U. Kultermann: "Kenzo Tange," *Bauen und Wohnen* 1, 1960, P. Thiel: "Kurashiki Town Hall by Tange," *The Architectural Review* 1, 1961.

222. V. C. Mahler: "Miniature Megastructure," *Architectural Forum* 9, 1967; W. Hofmann and U. Kultermann: *Baukunst in unserer Zeit*, Essen, 1969, Fig. 112.

223. K. Tange: "A Plan for Tokyo," *Bauen und Wohnen* 1, 1964.

224. P. Riani: 'Bologna bis, "*Casabella* 345, 1970; U. Kultermann: *Kenzo Tange: Architektur und Städtebau*, Zürich, 1970; *The Japan Architect* Aug.–Sept. 1976.

225. *Metabolism: The Proposals for New Urbanism*, Tokyo, 1960; U. Kultermann: "Metabolismo oggi," *Casabella* 318, 1967; U. Kultermann: "Metabolismus: Japans Beitrag zum Städtebau der Zukunft" *Die Tat*, April 30, 1968; K. Kurokawa: *Metabolism in Architecture*, Boulder, Colo., 1977.

226. "Campus of Many Spaces," *Architectural Forum* 5, 1970.

227. M. Speidel: "Kiyonari Kikutake," *Bauen und Wohnen* 7, 1967; *The Japan Architect* Oct.–Nov., 1975.

228. C. Jencks: Enigma of Kurokawa, *The Architectural Review* 3, 1976.

229. R. Boyd: "A Glimpse of the Future," *Architectural Forum* 3, 1970.

Part IV (pp. 185–249)

1. The names and years of birth of the leading architects born between 1925 and 1950, are: Moore, Venturi, Shinohara, Porro, Otto, Bohigas (1925); Aymonino, Stirling, Ungers, Taillibert, Pelli (1926); Doshi, Kroll, Aulenti (1927); Maki, Strauss (1928); Hejduk, Gehry, Sramkova, Stoilov, Mutnjakovic (1929); Tigerman, Correa, Holzbauer, Magas, Lim Chong Keat (1930); Isozaki, Scott Brown, Rossi, Portoghesi (1931); Eisenmann, Hertzberger, William Lim (1932); Andrews, Siza Vieira, Rogers, Kleihues (1933); Graves, Hollein, Jain, Kurokawa, Meier (1934); Foster, Grassi, Makovesz (1935); Lyndon, Ho, Hara (1936); Moneo (1937); Taveira, Safdie, Naudé Santos (1938); R. Krier, Jumsai, Bofill (1939); Athfield, Rein, Jahn, Cynthia Weese (1940); Hasegawa, Ando, Reichlin, Natalini, Purini (1941); Lari, Nuñez-Yanowsky (1942); Botta, Thermes, Reinhardt,

Ongard (1943); Tschumi, Vinoly, Koolhaas, Portzamparc, Hrzic, Mayne, Torre (1944); Badran (1945); Hall (1947); Yeang, Takamatsu (1948); Mack Rotondi (1947); Hadid, Wilson (1950); Kitagawara, Koyama, Calatrava (1951).

Names of such stylistic references as Postmodernism, Late Modernism, Deconstructivism, etc., have been avoided, as they are misleading in the debate about contemporary architecture and its meaning.

2. The term "Multiculturalism" has frequently been used in order to understand the growing complexity of the present situation and as a critique of earlier, more superficial, approaches.

3. About the responsibility of the architect for his environment, see: A. Tzonis: *Towards a Non-aggressive Environment*, Boston, 1972.

4. W. Graboury: "American Indian Identity," *The Architectural Review* 8, 1980.

5. For the term "deconstruction," according to the notion of Jacques Derrida, see: U. Kultermann: "Die Wiederherstellung des Problems: Jacques Derrida (geb. 1930)," in: *Kunst und Wirklichkeit; Von Fiedler bis Derrida. Zehn Annäherungen*, Munich, 1991.

6. Jack Travis, ed.: *African American Architects in Current Practice*, Princeton, 1991.

7. U. Kultermann: "Redefining American Architecture," *Architektur* (Berlin) 12, 1992.

8. About Philip Johnson and the I. T. and T. Building in New York, see M. Filler: "High Rise, Part I," *Art in America*, Sept. 1984.

9. About the work of Skidmore, Owings, and Merrill, and Hellmuth, Obata, and Kassabaum, see: A. Drexler, ed.: *Architecture of Skidmore, Owings, and Merrill*, New York, 1974; Walter McQuade: *Architecture of the Real World: The Work of H.O.K.*, New York, 1984.

10. Carter Wiseman: *Ieoh Ming Pei. A Profile in American Architecture*, New York, 1990.

11. John Pastier: *Cesar Pelli*, New York, 1980. For Cesar Pelli's Rainbow Center Mall and Wintergarden in Niagara Falls, see: U. Kultermann: "Glas als Strukturelement im Städtebau. Cesar Pelli's Rainbow Center Mall und Wintergarten in Niagara Falls," *Glasforum* 3, 1982; Pelli's admiration for Paxton's Crystal Palace is articulated in: Cesar Pelli: "Joseph Paxton's Crystal Palace," *architecture + urbanism* 2, 1980.

12. Kallmann, McKinnell, and Knowles: "Ath-

letics Center, Harvard University," *Architectural Review* 2, 1991.

13. Kahn's decisive impact on international architecture became most evident in 1991 in the exhibition in Philadelphia: David B. Brownlee and David G. DeLong: *Louis I. Kahn: In the Realm of Architecture*, New York, 1991. See also: U. Kultermann: "The Hollow Column and the Family of Human Institutions. Kahn's National Assembly in Dacca and Its Meaning" (unpublished manuscript).

14. It is significant that none of the contemporary promoters of style terminology claim Kahn as a stylistic originator. See: Philip Johnson and Mark Wigley: *Deconstructivist Architecture*, New York, 1988; Charles Jencks: *Late Modern Architecture*, London, 1980; *Contemporary Architects*, ed. by Muriel Emanuel, New York, 1980, p. 850.

15. In 1992, under construction are the Children's Museum in Houston, Texas (since 1989), and the National Museum for the American Indian (since 1990), significant commissions in regard to the newly expanded articulation of contemporary American architecture. See Robert Venturi and Rauch: *The Public Buildings*, London, 1978. About Venturi and Kahn, see: J. Lobell: "Kahn and Venturi," *Artforum*, Feb. 1978. *Publications by Robert Venturi: Complexity and Contradiction in Architecture*, New York, 1966; Robert Venturi and Denise Scott Brown: "Learning from Lutyens," *RIBA Journal* 8, 1969; Robert Venturi, Denise Scott Brown, and S. Izenour: *Learning from Las Vegas*, Cambridge, Mass., 1972; V. Carroll, Denise Scott Brown, and Robert Venturi: "Styling," *Lotus* 9, 1975; Robert Venturi: "A Definition of Architecture as Shelter Decoration on It, and Another Plea for Symbolism of the Ordinary in Architecture," *architecture + urbanism* 1, 1978.

16. Charles Moore and Gerald Allan: *Dimensions*, New York, 1976; Charles Moore, Gerald Allan, and Donlyn Lyndon: *The Place of Homes*, New York, 1974; Charles Moore: *Architecture and Fairy Tales*, New Orleans, 1975.

17. Moshe Safdie reflected about his concept in *Beyond Habitat*, Cambridge, Mass., 1970; *For Everyone a Garden*, Cambridge, Mass., 1974, and "Collective Consciousness in Making Environment," in *Frontiers of Knowledge*, Garden City, N.Y., 1975.

18. Kenneth Frampton: *Richard Meier*, New York, 1976. E. Kupper: "Meier's Type-Forms," *Progressive Architecture* 7, 1979; M. K. Frampton and Joseph Rykwert: *Richard Meier Architect: 1985–1991*, New York, 1991.

19. D. Dunster, ed.: *Michael Graves*, New York, 1979; Vincent Scully: *Michael Graves*, New York, 1982. In his low-income and elderly housing in Coatsville, Penn., of 1967–1968, Graves, also, like Meier in those years, gave solutions to the then-considered unsolvable tasks, and — in his Newark Children's Museum of 1978 — a visionary anticipation of the tasks of the future.

20. S. Abercrombie: *Gwathmey/Siegel*, New York, 1981; Peter Arnell and Ted Bickford, eds.: *Charles Gwathmey and Robert Siegel: Buildings and Projects, 1964–1984*, New York, 1984.

21. John Hejduk, *Architect*, Zürich, 1973; Martin Filler: "The Practice of Theory," *Art in America* 2, 1980; John Hejduk: *The Silent Witness and Other Poems*, Institute of Architecture and Urbanism, New York, 1980.

22. The early conceptual writings by Peter Eisenman are: "Notes on Conceptual Architecture," *Casabella* 359/360, 1970; "The Future of the Architectural Past," *Casabella* 345, 1970; and "Cardboard Architecture," *Casabella* 374, 1973. See also: R. Moneo and A. Vidler: *Wexner Center for the Visual Arts*, New York, 1989.

23. E. Gaboury: "Amerindian Identity," *The Architectural Review* 8, 1980.

24. About Predock, Greene, and Morgan see: Dominic Marti: "Klimagerechte Architektur in regionaler Bauweise," *Werk, Bauen und Wohnen* 3, 1984.

25. Jack Travis, ed.: *African American Architects in Current Practice*, Princeton, 1991.

26. P. Restany and B. Zevi: *Site: Architecture as Art*, London, 1981.

27. William Bernstein and Ruth Cawker: *Contemporary Canadian Architecture: The Mainstream and Beyond*, Toronto, 1982; Leon Whiteson: *Modern Canadian Architecture*, Edmonton, 1983. For the work of Arthur Erickson: *The Architecture of Arthur Erickson*, New York, 1988. The quotation from Douglas Cardinal is from Ann Lee Morgan and Colin Naylor, eds.: *Contemporary Architects*, Chicago and London, 1987, p. 136.

28. U. Kultermann: "Viel Herz für Hinz und Kunz." *Die grossen Architekten von heute*, 2, "James Stirling, der Brutalist aus Glasgow," *Die Welt*, Feb. 3, 1979; Jonathan

Glancy: *New British Architecture*, London, 1989; Colin Davis: *High Tech Architecture*, London, 1991.

29. S. Poole: *The New Finnish Architecture*, 1991; Markku Komonen, ed.: "Finnish Architecture Now," *Process Architecture* 37, 1983; Christian Norberg Schulz: *Modern Norwegian Architecture*, Oslo, 1986; the quotation by Romaldo Giurgola is from Ann Lee Morgan and Colin Naylor, eds.: *Contemporary Architects*, 2d ed., Chicago and London, 1987, p. 928.

30. About recent architecture in the Netherlands, see Francis Strauven, ed.: *Aldo van Eyck*, Antwerp, 1985; H. Hertzberger: "Old People's Centre: Amsterdam," *The Architectural Review* 2, 1976.

31. The quotation by Lucien Kroll is from Ann Lee Morgan and Colin Naylor, eds.: *Contemporary Architects*, 2d ed., Chicago and London, 1987, p. 504.

32. About the contemporary situation of architecture in Germany, see U. Kultermann: *Das Werk des Architekten Hans Scharoun: Theater der Stadt Wolfsburg,* Wolfsburg, 1973; H. and M. Bofinger: *Architektur in Deutschland,* Stuttgart, 1979; U. Kultermann: "Das Werk des Architekten Gottfried Böhm" (unpublished manuscript).

33. About Austrian contemporary architecture: D. Steiner: "Experimentelle Architektur in Österreich," *Bauen und Wohnen* 4, 1976. Peter M. Bode and Gustav Peichl: *Architektur aus Österreich seit 1960,* Salzburg, 1980.

34. About Swiss Contemporary architecture, see J. Dahinden: *Denken — Fühlen — Handeln,* Lausanne, 1973; Blaser, Werner: *Architecture 70/80 in Switzerland,* Basel, 1982. Francesco Dal Co: *Mario Botta: Architecture 1960-1985,* London, 1987.

35. U. Kultermann: "Roland Simounet, ou une Architecture de l'urbanité," in Roland Simounet: *Pour une invention de l'espace,* Paris, 1986. For French contemporary architecture, see W. Lesnikowski: *The New French Architecture,* 1990; J.S.: *Young French Architecture, AD Aspects of Modern Architecture,* London, 1991.

36. For Italian contemporary architecture: A. Savio: *L'Architecttura di Aldo Rossi*, Milan, 1976; Gianni Braghieri: *Aldo Rossi*, Bologna 1981; Lamberto Rossi: *Giancarlo de Carlo: Architecture,* Milan, 1988.

37. Helio Piñon: *Arquitecturas Catalanas,* Barcelona, 1978; E. Bru and J. L. Mateo: *Spanish Contemporary Architecture,* 1984; K. Frampton, ed.: *Contemporary Spanish Architecture: An Eclectic Panorama,* New York, 1986; Thomas Reese: "Figures canonicas. La imagen de la España reciente," *A + U* 24, 1990; William Curtis et al: "El Croquis," special issue, 49-50, 1991.

38. Alvaro Siza: *Esquissos de Viagem/Travel Sketches,* Porto, 1988; Laurent Beaudouin: *Alvaro Siza, L'Architecture d' Aujourd'hui,* Dec. 1991.

39. Oleg Shvidovsky: "Soviet Architecture and the Essence of National Traditions," *Architectural Association Quarterly* 11, no. 2, 1979; Mikhail V. Posokhin: *Towns for People,* Moscow, 1980; Catherine Cooke: "Russian Reaction to Post-Modernism: The 'Meaningful Messages' of Post-Modernism" *Architectural Design* 51, May 1981; U. Kultermann: *Zeitgenössische Architektur in Osteuropa,* Cologne, 1985; U. Kultermann: "La 'perestroika' anunciada. Europa Oriental en los ochenta," *Arquitectura viva* 13, Jul.-Aug. 1990.

40. M. Elvseyeva: "Rural Construction in Estonia," *Architektur USSR* Jan. 1971; U. Kultermann: "Tomas Rein: Towards an Estonain Identity," *Space and Society* 19, 1982; U. Kultermann: "Looking East," *Space and Society*, June 1985.

41. Simon Kintsurashvili: *The Architecture of Soviet Georgia,* Moscow, 1974; U. Kultermann: "Giorgi Chakhava: Un Architetto Georgiano," *Space and Society* 37, 1987.

42. Alfred Max: *The Siberian Challenge*, Englewood Cliffs, N. J., 1977; Murad Adzhiyev: *Tapping Siberia's Resources,* Moscow, 1980.

43. P. Szafer: *Nova Architektura Polska,* Warsaw 1972; Zbigniew Pininsky: "Poland," in Warren Sanderson, ed.: *International Handbook of Contemporary Developments in Architecture,* Westport, Conn., 1981. T. Czaplinska-Archer: "Polish Architecture," *Architectural Association Quarterly* 10, 1981.

44. Jan Michl: *Realizace a Projekty v Soucasne Architecture,* Prague, 1978; Vladimir Slapeta: *Praha 1900-1978,* Prague, 1978; U. Kultermann: "Das Werk der Architektengruppe SIAL. Zeitgenössiches Bauen in der Tschechoslowakei, AIT Architektur," *Innenarchitektur, Technischer Ausbau* 1, 1985; Josef Pechav: "Czechoslovakia," in *Handbook of Contemporary Developments in Architecture,* ed., Warren Sanderson, Westport, Conn., 1981; Rostislav Svacha: "Contemporary Czech Architecture" (unpublished manuscript).

45. J. Glancy: "Imre Makovecz and Corvina Muterem," *The Architectural Review* 3, 1981; U. Kultermann: *György Keves*, exhibition catalogue, Sopron, 1982; U. Kultermann: "Architecture as Folk Architecture: The Work of the Hungarian Architect Imre Makovecz," *architecture + urbanism*, March 1984.

46. Siegfried Wagner: "Internationaler Erfahrungsaustausch der Architekten in Rumänien 1980," *Architektur der DDR* 6, 1981.

47. William Malchev: *Bulgarian Architecture*, Sofia, 1981.

48. Mihajlo Mitrovic: *Modern Belgrade Architecture*, Belgrade, 1975; Zdenko Kolacio: "Zeitgenoessische Architektur in Jugoslawien," in *Cahiers Europeenne*, Apr. 1981; U. Kultermann: "Bauen fuer Kroatia: Der Architekt Boris Magas," *Architektur, Innenarchitektur, Technischer Ausbau* 5, 1984; Tomislav Premerl: *Hrvatska moderna arhitektura izmedu dva rata*, Zagreb, 1989; Ivan Straus: *Arhitektura Jugoslavije*, Sarajevo, 1991; Drago Galic, ed. *Arhitekti Clanovi Jazu*, Zagreb; U. Kultermann: "A Masterpiece of Contemporary Macedonian Architecture" (unpublished manuscript).

49. U. Kultermann: *Architekten der Dritten Welt*, Cologne, 1980.

50. Mexico: *Nueva Arquitectura*, Barcelona, 1991.

51. Susana Torre: "Architecture and Revolution: Cuba 1959–1974," *Progressive Architecture* 10, 1974.

52. F. Bullrich: *New Directions in Latin-American Architecture*, New York, 1969; Damian Bayon and Paolo Gasparini: *The Changing Shape of Latin-American Architecture*, Chichester, 1979; Anne Berty: *Architecture Colombiennes*, Paris, 1981; Jorge Glusberg: *Miguel Angel Roca*, London, 1981.

53. U. Kultermann: *New Directions in African Architecture*, New York, 1969.

54. U. Kultermann: "Aqua per Arabia," *Domus* 595, 1979; U. Kultermann: "Arabische Architektur, Zeitgenoessische Arabische Architektur: Eine Einführung," *Werk-Bauen und Wohnen* 12, 1981; U. Kultermann: "The Renaissance of Contemporary Arab Architecture" (unpublished manuscript).

55. U. Kultermann: "Contemporary Architecture in Jordan," *Mimar* 39, 1991.

56. U. Kultermann: "Contemporary Arab Architecture: The Architects in Saudi Arabia," *Mimar* 16, 1985; U. Kultermann: "Riyadh

—The Arab Capital of the 20th Century," *arcus* 2, March/April 1985.

57. E. Spiegel: *Neue Staedte in Israel*, Stuttgart, 1966; Amiram Harlap: *New Israeli Architecture*, London, 1982.

58. For the new university of Kernan, see: *Mimar* 42, 1992.

59. Kamil Khan Mumtaz: *Architecture in Pakistan*, Singapore 1985; U. Kultermann: "Yasmeen Lari," in *Architekten der Dritten Welt*, Cologne, 1980.

60. Uttam C. Jain: "Modern Architecture in India," *Journal of the Indian Institute of Architects*, Jan.–March 1971; U. Kultermann: "'Sangath' de Balkrishna Doshi, o la cooperacion creativa en arquitectura," *Goya* 225, Nov.–Dec. 1991.

61. M. W. Newman: "Stanley Tigerman in Bangladesh," *The Inland Architect* 2, 1973; Shah Alam Zahiruddin, Abu H. Imamuddin, and M. Mohiuddin Khan, eds.: *Contemporary Architecture in Bangladesh*, Dacca, 1990; U. Kultermann: "The Hollow Column and the Family of Human Institutions: About Kahn's National Assembly in Dacca and Its Meaning" (unpublished manuscript).

62. D. J. Steinberg, ed.: *In Search of Southeast Asia*, New York, 1976, 4th ed.; J. F. Sunandar: "Wandel in Indonesien," *Bauen und Wohnen* 9, 1978; Winand Klassen: "Towards a Filipino Architecture," *Philippine Quarterly of Culture and Society* 6, 1978; U. Kultermann: "Sumet Jumsai: Profil eines jungen Architekten aus Thailand," *Architektur Aktuell* 76, 1980; Robert Powell: *Innovative Architecture of Singapore*, Singapore, 1989; U. Kultermann: "Southeast Asian Architecture," in *Encyclopedia of Architecture: Design, Engineering and Construction*, ed. by J. Wilkes, vol. 4, New York, 1989. For the new university of Depok, see *Mimar* 42, 1992.

63. J. M. Freeland: *Architecture in Australia*, Melbourne, 1968; Jennifer Taylor: *An Australian Identity*, Sydney, 1972; D. Saunders: "So I Decided to Go Overseas," *Architecture in Austria*, Feb.–Mar. 1977; Philip Drew: *Leaves of Iron: Glenn Marcutt, Pioneer of an Australian Form*, Sydney, 1985.

64. A. Mendini: "Edilizia contemporanea in Cina," *Casabella* 304, 1966; U. Kultermann: "Tanges Bau auf Formosa," *Die Tat* June 24, 1969; J. T. A. Lee: "The New China," *Architectural Record* 10, 1973; Tao Ho: "Hong Kong: A City Prospers

Without a Plan," *Process Architecture* 20, 1980; U. Kultermann: "Architecture in Southeast Asia: Hong Kong," *Mimar* 33, 1989.
65. U. Kultermann: "Swoo Geun Kim" in *Architekten der Dritten Welt*, Cologne, 1980.
66. U. Kultermann, ed., *Kenzo Tange*, Zürich, 1970 (paperback, Zürich 1978); U. Kultermann: "Coincidentia oppositorum. About the Work and Philosophy of Takamitsu Azuma," *Shinkenshiku* 4, 1982; Charles Jencks: "Enigma of Kurokawa," *The Architectural Review* 3, 1976; Kisho Kurokawa: *Metabolism in Architecture*, Boulder, Colo., 1977; R. Pommer: "The New Architectural Suprematists," *Artforum*, Oct. 1976; U. Kultermann: "Kisho Kurokawa: Einheit von Technik and Architektur," *Architektur, Innenarchitektur, Technischer Ausbau* 88, 1980; Kenzo Tange Associates, special issue, *Space Design* 4, 1987; Kenzo Tange: "Recollections," *The Japan Architect*, April 1985–June 1986; Itsuko Hasegawa: *Architecture as Another Nature, AD Aspects of Modern Architecture*, London, 1991.

Critical Bibliography

Part I

Research about the phase from 1900 to 1930 is most extensive, although a comprehensive overview and visionary explanation do not yet exist. G. Kokkelink remarked two decades ago: "Up to date there does not exist a descriptive and interpretative treatment of the history of architecture and city planning which reaches into the present." (The Art Historian as Partner of the City Planner, Architectural 2, 1973, p. 101.) There are comprehensive descriptions of architecture of the twentieth century, which deal extensively with the tendencies of the first three decades, the earliest compendium being the book by G. A. Platz: Die Baukunst der neuesten Zeit, Berlin, 1920; also H.-R. Hitchcock: Architecture — Nineteenth and Twentieth Centuries, 3rd edition, Baltimore, 1969 (first published 1958); yet here the developmental lines are described separately, and architectural engineering, historicism, and rational architecture are not seen as a continuous unity. Siegfried Giedion: Raum, Zeit, Architektur, Ravensburg 1965 (English edition, Space, Time, Architecture, 1941), presents polemic and selective features of more contemporary architecture, as seen in the context of CIAM, but a balancing view of the various possibilities has not been attempted. Nikolaus Pevsner: Wegbereiter moderner Formgebung: Von William Morris Zu Walter Gropius, Hamburg, 1957 (English edition, Pioneers of Modern Design, 1936), is an explanation of the more contemporary architecture, leading from Morris to Gropius, as suggested by the subtitle, which must necessarily leave out the irrelevant tendencies not fitting into the argument.

Research about the younger generation is less resourceful and more geared toward an objective balance; Reyner Banham: Theory and Design in the First Machine Age, London, 1960 (German edition, Die Revolution des Architektur, Hamburg, 1964), views the development newly under the aspect of the techno-constructive components; Leonard Benevolo: Geschichte der Architektur im 19. und 20. Jahrhundert, Munich, 1964 (English edition, History of Architecture of the 19th and 20th Century, 1960), more under the sociopolitical aspect; Michel Ragon: Histoire mondiale de l'architecture et de l'urbanisme moderne, Paris, 1972, and Dennis Sharp: A Visual History of Twentieth-Century Architecture, London, 1972, present summaries of earlier results. The latest research is represented in: Kenneth Frampton: Modern Architecture, A Critical History, London, 1980; Adolf Max Vogt, Ulrike Jehle-Schulte Strathaus, and Bruno Reichlin: Architektur 1940–1980, Frankfurt, 1980; and Vittorio Magnago Lampungnani: Architektur und Staedtebau des 20. Jahrhundert, Stuttgart, 1980. My own results are presented in: Baukunst der Gegenwart, Tübingen, 1958; Dynamische Architektur, Munich, 1959; Der Schlüssel zur Architektur von heute, Vienna and Düsseldorf, 1963; Neues Bauen in der Welt, Tübingen, 1965 (expanded new edition 1975); Architektur der Gegenwart, Baden-Baden, 1967; Die Baukunst in unserer Zeit — Die Entwicklung seit 1850, Essen, 1969 (in cooperation with Werner Hofmann).

Several of the basic works offer convincing introductions to the epoch: Frank Lloyd Wright: Ausgeführte Bauten und Entwürfe, Berlin, 1910; Le Corbusier: Vers une architecture, Paris, 1923; Walter Gropius: Internationale Architektur, Munich, 1925; L. Hilberseimer: Internationale neue Baukunst, Stuttgart, 1926; Bruno Taut: Die neue Baukunst in Europa und Amerika, Berlin, 1927. The following contributions are more strongly geared toward certain concepts of modern architecture: M. Casteels: The New Style, London, 1931; A. Sartoris: Gli elementi dell'architettura razionale, Milan, 1932; H.-R. Hitchcock and P. Johnson: The International Style, New York, 1932; B. Zevi: Storia dell' architettura moderna, Turin, 1950; V. Scully: Modern Architecture, New York, 1961. The movement contrary to rationalism or the international style found adequate documentation relatively late: D. Sharp: Architecture and Expressionism, London, 1966; F. Borsi and G. K. Koenig: Architettura dell'Espressionismo, Paris, 1967; W. Pehnt: Die Architektur des Expressionismus, Stuttgart, 1973.

Monographs concerning the latest research of the work of single architects in this period are limited, in spite of the great number of publications. The following are noteworthy, listed in chronological order:

H.-R. Hitchcock: In the Nature of Materials, New York, 1942

P. Johnson: Mies van der Rohe, New York, 1947

S. Giedion: Walter Gropius, New York, 1954

T. M. Brown: The Work of G. T. Rietveld, Utrecht, 1958

U. Kultermann: Wassili und Hans Luckhardt, Tübingen, 1958

G. C. Manson: Frank Lloyd Wright to 1910, New York, 1958
P. Collins: Concrete, New York, 1959
J. Buekschmitt: Ernst May, Stuttgart, 1963
J. Birrell: Walter Burley Griffin, Brisbane, 1964
W. Blaser: Mies van der Rohe, Zürich, 1965
C. Schnaidt: Hannes Meyer: Teufen, 1965
S. von Moos: Le Corbusier, Frauenfeld, 1968
K. Junghanns: Bruno Taut, Berlin, 1970
B. Zevi: Erich Mendelsohn, Mailand, 1970
C. Jencks: Le Corbusier, London, 1913
W. H. Kilham: Raymond Hood, New York, 1974
P. Pfankuch, Ed.: Hans Scharoun. Bauten, Entwürfe, Texte, Berlin, 1974

More recent research is missing of even some of the most important architects of the twentieth century, such as Peter Behrens, Konstantin Melnikov, and Tony Garnier, as well as for the midphase of Frank Lloyd Wright. Detailed research of single buildings remains at its inception. Examples to be mentioned are: H. Weber: Walter Gropius und das Faguswerk, Munich, 1961; P. Boudon: Lived-In Architecture, Le Corbusier's Pessac Revisited, Cambridge, Mass., 1972; J. P. Bonta: Mies van der Rohe, Barcelona, 1929, Barcelona, 1975 and T. James, Jr.: The Empire State Building, New York, 1975.

Up to now, city planning of the twentieth century with its complexity and problems has hardly been expressed in a relevant manner. W. L. Creese: In Search for Environment, New Haven, 1966, gave an extensive account of the concept of the garden city; L. Benevolo researched Die sozialen Ursprünge des modernen Städtebaus, Gütersloh, 1971. The similarly significant conceptions of the linear city, of the urbanism of the Bauhaus, of the early city plans of Le Corbusier and Wright's Broadacre City have not been researched sufficiently to date.

The relationship between architecture and society, i.e., sculpture and painting, have also only been researched allusively, to say nothing of the relationship between literature, dance, music, theater, and architecture. H. L. C. Jaffé: De Stijl, 1917–1931, Berlin, 1956; U. Kultermann: Paul Scheerbart und die Architektur im 20. Jahrhundert, in Handbuch des Bauwesens, Stuttgart, 1963; J. Petsch: Architektur und Gesellschaft, Cologne, 1973; Kurt Rowland: A History of the Modern Movement. Art, Architecture, Design, London 1973, are first steps toward an interdisciplinary research.

Part II

Little has been done so far to analyze the extraordinarily complex situation of architecture between 1930 and 1950. Early documentation of select singular examples by A. Roth: The New Architecture, Zürich 1940, and S. Giedion: Ein Jahrzehnt moderner Architektur, Zürich, 1951, are still of value, although one-sided and chosen to exclude German, Italian, and Russian Architecture. The contemporary politically oriented presentations of these countries, however, are based on preconceived ideological hypotheses.

Bruno Zevi attempted a comprehensive presentation in his books, for example, in: Towards an Organic Architecture, London, 1950, and Storia dell' architettura moderna, Turin, 1950; his view is influenced strongly by the work and concept of Frank Lloyd Wright. J. M. Richards presents an introduction which is written from the viewpoint of functionalism: An

Introduction in Modern Architecture, London, 1940.

While Stalinistic architecture is still a blind field regarding recent international research, there are more and more inquiries concerning German and Italian architecture of the 1930s and 1940s. S. de Paolis and A. Ravaglioli: Le Terza Roma, Rome, 1971, concentrated on the capital and gathered an abundance of material, which is still waiting to be analyzed in detail. P. E. Eisenman wrote as architect about Terragni and arrived at a new perspective with regard to his historical position: From Object to Relationship, Casabella 344, 1970. There are two accounts of National Socialist architecture, which obviously include the political reality, yet are an objective analysis: B. Miller Lane: Architecture and Politics in Germany, 1818–1945, Cambridge, Mass., 1968, and R. R. Taylor: The Word in Stone, Berkeley, 1974. The international connection to neoclassicism was occasionally mentioned but were, however, not yet systematically analyzed.

The architecture of individual countries during this phase is comprehensively documented in:

P. Goodwin: Brazil Builds, New York, 1943
M. Bill: Moderne Schweizer Architektur, Basel, 1949
T. Dannatt: Modern Architecture in Britain, London, 1959
E. Thelaus: New Architecture in Sweden, Stockholm, 1962
J. M. Freeland: Architecture in Australia, Melbourne, 1968
O. Bohigas: Arquitectura española de la segunda Republica, Barcelona, 1970
A. Senkevitch, Ed.: Soviet Architecture, Charlottesville, 1973

Several noteworthy monographs about individual architects are:

M. Bill: Robert Maillart, Zürich, 1949
Alvar Aalto. Gesamtwerk, Zürich, 1963 (2d ed. 1965)
C. Faber: Arne Jacobsen, Stuttgart, 1964
E. J. Jelles und C. A. Alberts: Duiker, Amsterdam, 1972
F. Stuessi: Othmar H. Ammann, Basel, 1974
R. A. M. Stern: Georg Howe, New Haven, 1975
P. D. Pearson: Alvar Aalto and the International Style, New York, 1978
S. F. Starr: Constantin Melnikov, Princeton, 1979

There are none concerning E. Owen Williams, Eduardo Torroja, Berthold Lubetkin, Marcello Piacentini, A. W. Shchusev, Albert Speer, the Vesnin brothers, or the Golosow brothers.

Only recently have a few accounts been published that deal with the specific characteristic styles of the 1930s, among them: B. Hillier: The World of Art Deco, New York, 1971; D. J. Bush: The Streamlined Decade, New York, 1975.

Part III

Comprehensive descriptions of architecture between 1950 and 1970 have been pursued at various times, arriving, however, mostly at subjective results. The often preconceived criteria led to restrictions which did not allow the development of an overview resulting from the material itself and the reviewed categories. Thus, the pioneering research of Giedion, Pevsner, and Hitchcock must be considered as inadequate for the epoch after 1950. A relatively objective picture is presented by the Japanese publication: Contemporary Architecture in the World, Tokyo, 1961. Reflecting more the view of the separate countries: M. Major: Geschichte der Architektur, vol. 3, Budapest and Berlin, 1960; C. Jones: Architecture Today and Tomorrow, New York, 1961; B. Champigneulle and J. Ache: L'Architecture du XXe siecle, Paris, 1962; J. Jacobus: Die Architektur unserer Zeit, Stuttgart, 1966; G. Dorfles: L'architettura moderna, Milan, 1972; H. Ragon: Histoire mondiale de l'architecture et d'urbanisme modernes, 2 vol., Paris, 1972.

Geographically oriented accounts of architecture of various countries form valuable collections of material:

G. E. Kidder Smith: Italy Builds, New York, 1955
Z. Dmochowski: The Architecture of Poland, London, 1956
G. E. Kidder Smith: Sweden Builds, New York, 1957
W. D. Howie: Contemporary Architecture in South Africa, Johannesburg, 1958
G. Kavli: Norwegian Architecture, Oslo, 1958
J. H. van den Broek: Guide to Dutch Architecture, Rotterdam, 1959
U. Kultermann: Neues Bauen in Japan, Tübingen, 1960 (2d ed. 1967)
M. Bicher: Architecture in Bulgaria, Sofia, 1961
M. L. Cetto: Moderne Architektur in Mexiko, Stuttgart, 1961
F. Bullrich: Arquitectura Argentina Contemporanea, Buenos Aires, 1963
T. Faber: Dansk Arkitektur, Copenhagen, 1963
U. Kultermann: Neues Bauen in Afrika, Tübingen, 1963
C. Martinez: Arquitectura in Colombia, Bogotá, 1963
G. Gusti: Architectura în România, Bucharest, 1965
F. Merényi: Cento Anni Architettura Ungharese, Rome, 1965
M. Besset: New French Architecture, New York, 1967
A. Galardi: Neue Architektur in Italien, Stuttgart, 1967
P. Trzeciak, ed.: Architecture in Poland. 1945–1966, Warsaw, 1968
E. Tempel: Neue japanische Architektur, Stuttgart, 1969
A. Solokorpi: Modern Architecture in Finland, New York, 1970
C. Moore Ede: Canadian Architecture, Toronto, 1971

Several series of books reveal valuable information about the more recent architecture in individual countries:

G. Tafuri: L'architettura moderna in Giappone, Bologna, 1964
G. K. Koenig: Architettura tedesca del secondo dopoguerra, Bologna, 1965
V. Quilici: L'architettura sovietica contemporenea, Bologna, 1965
G. Piccinato: L'architettura contemporanea in Francia, Bologna, 1966
S. Bracco: L'architettura moderna in Brasile, Bologna, 1967
J. Bachmann und S. von Moos: New Directions in Swiss Architecture, New York, 1968
R. Boyd: New Directions in Japanese Architecture, New York, 1968
G. Feuerstein: New Directions in German Architecture, New York, 1968
V. Gregotti: New Directions in Italian Architecture, New York, 1968
R. Landau: New Directions in English Architecture, New York, 1968
R. A. M. Stern: New Directions in American Architecture, New York, 1968 (2d ed. 1977)
F. Bullrich: New Directions in Latin American Architecture, New York, 1969
U. Kultermann: New Directions in African Architecture, New York, 1969

Other annual publications show selected examples of outstanding individual buildings of the past year in detailed documentation: The yearbook World Architecture published by John Donat, and the yearbook Lotus by Bruno Alfieri, as well as the magazines Architectural Design, The Architectural Review, Casabella, L'architecture d'aujourd'hui, Oppositions, and Perspecta.

Monographs presenting architects who determine the architectural scene after 1950:

H.-R. Hitchcock: Skidmore, Owings und Merrill, Stuttgart, 1962
C. Jones: Marcel Breuer, Stuttgart, 1962
J. Jacobus: Philip Johnson, Ravensburg, 1963
J. Joedicke: Das Werk des Architekten van den Broek und Bakema, Stuttgart, 1963
V. Scully: Louis I. Kahn, Ravensburg, 1963
C. Faber: Felix Candela, Munich, 1964

S. Moholy-Nagy: Carlos Raul Villanueva Stuttgart, 1964
C. Roland: Frei Otto. Spannweiten, Berlin, 1965
H.-R. Hitchcock: Philip Johnson, New York, 1966
K. Bastlund: José Luis Sert, Zürich, 1967
S. Woods: Candilis, Josic, Woods, New York, 1968
U. Kultermann: Kenzo Tange—Architektur und Städtebau, Zürich, 1970 (2d ed. 1978)
S. Moholy-Nagy: The Architecture of Paul Rudolph, New York, 1970
P. Blake: The Work of Harry Seidler, Sydney, 1973
H.-R. Hitchcock: Hentrich und Petschnigg, Düsseldorf, 1973
R. Giurgola and J. Mehti: Louis I. Kahn, Zürich, 1975
John Jacobus: James Stirling. Buildings and Projects, New York, 1975
Kevin Roche: John Dinkeloo, Tokyo, 1975
P. Drew: Frei Otto, Stuttgart, 1976
K. Frampton: Richard Meier, New York, 1976
Kaija und Heikki Siren: Architekten, Stuttgart, 1977
H. Ronner, S. Jhaveri und A. Vasella: Louis I. Kahn. The Complete Works, Zürich, 1977

Monographs about the following architects are not available: Aldo van Eyck, Robert Venturi, Charles Moore, Giancarlo de Carlo, John Andrews, or Rob Krier, as well as an analysis of the late work of Frank Lloyd Wright.

The following are particularly concerned with the architectural efforts between 1950 and 1970: J. Burns: Anthropods, New York, 1972; P. Drew: The Third Generation, Stuttgart, 1972; P. Navone and B. Orlandoni: Architettura radicale, Segrate, 1974; Five Architects, New York, 1975. C. Jencks is searching to connect the old masters and the young generation: Modern Movements in Architecture, New York, 1973, and M. Tafuri and F. Dal Co: Architettura Contemporanea, Milan, 1976, present a basic analysis of the architecture of the period.

Part IV

Comprehensive documentation of the state of architecture after 1970 exists in large numbers. Several works are part of newly written histories of twentieth-century architecture, others are specifically devoted to recent developments. The latter books are to a large degree based on stylistic argument. Among the major publications in both categories are:

Charles Jencks: Modern Movements in Architecture, New York, 1973.
Kenneth Frampton: A Concise History of Modern Architecture, London, 1973
Manfredo Tafuri and F. Dal Co.: Architettura Contemporanea, Milan, 1976
U. Kultermann: Neues Bauen in der Welt, Tübingen, 1976
Charles Jencks: The Language of Post-Modern Architecture, London, 1977
C. Ray Smith: Supermannerism: New Attitudes in Post-Modern Architecture, 1977
Vittorio Magnago-Lampugnani: Architektur und Staedtebau des 20. Jahrhunderts, Stuttgart, 1980
Kenneth Frampton: Modern Architecture. A Critical History, London, 1980
Charles Jencks: Late Modern Architecture, London, 1980
U. Kultermann: Architecture in the Seventies, London and New York, 1980
Paolo Portoghesi: After Modern Architecture, New York, 1980
Charles Jencks: Architecture Today, London, 1982
William Curtis: Modern Architecture since 1900, Englewood Cliffs, N.J., 1983
Michael Mueller: Architektur und Avantgarde, Frankfurt, 1984
Heinrich Klotz: Moderne und Postmoderne, Berlin, 1984
Thomas W. Sokolowski, ed.: Modern Redux: Critical Alternatives for Architecture in the Next Decade, New York, 1986
Heinrich Klotz: The History of Postmodern Architecture, Cambridge, Mass., 1988
Philip Johnson and Mark Wigley: Deconstructivist Architecture, New York, 1988
Charles Jencks: The New Moderns, London, 1990

Peter Cook and Rosie Llewellyn Jones: New Spirit in Architecture, New York, 1991

Taisto H. Maekelae, ed.: Wars of Classification, Princeton, 1991

Dennis Sharp: Twentieth Century Architecture. A Visual History, New York and Oxford, 1991

Geographically oriented documentation of architectural developments since 1970 in different parts of the world follows:

P. Szafer: Nova Architektura Polska, Warsaw, 1972

R. A. M. Stern: New Directions in American Architecture, rev. ed., New York, 1977

H. and M. Bofinger: Architektur in Deutschland, Stuttgart, 1979

Peter M. Bode and Gustav Peichl: Architektur aus Österreich seit 1960, Salzburg, 1980

U. Kultermann: Architekten der Dritten Welt, Cologne, 1980

William Malchev: Bulgarian Architecture, Sofia, 1981

Anne Berty: Architectures Colombiennes, Paris, 1981

Shelly Kappe, ed.: Modern Architecture: Mexico, Santa Monica, Calif., 1981

Amiran Harlap: New Israeli Architecture, London, 1982

Werner Blaser: Architecture 70/80 in Switzerland, Basel, 1982

Leon Whiteson: Modern Canadian Architecture, Edmonton, 1983

E. Bru and J. L. Mateo: Spanish Contemporary Architecture, 1984

Kamil Khan Mumtaz: Architecture in Pakistan, Singapore, 1985

U. Kultermann: Zeitgenoessische Architektur in Osteuropa, Cologne, 1985

H. Suzuki and R. Banham: Contemporary Architecture of Japan. 1958–1984, New York, 1985

Exhibition catalogue: Emerging Voices. A New Generation of Architects in America, New York, 1986

Kenneth Frampton, ed.: Contemporary Spanish Architecture: An Eclectic Panorama, New York, 1986

Christian Norberg Schulz: Modern Norwegian Architecture, Oslo, 1986

David B. Stewart: The Making of a Modern Japanese Architecture, Tokyo and New York, 1987

Jonathan Glancy: New British Architecture, London, 1989

Robert Powell: Innovative Architecture in Singapore, Singapore, 1989

Manfredo Tafuri: History of Italian Architecture: 1944–1985, Cambridge, Mass., 1989

W. Lesnikowski: The New French Architecture, 1990

Botond Bognar: The New Japanese Architecture, New York, 1990

S. Poole: The New Finnish Architecture, 1991

Ivan Straus: Architekture Jugoslaviji, Sarajevo, 1991

Mexico: Nueva Arquitectura, Barcelona, 1991

Hiroshi Watanabe: Amazing Architecture from Japan, New York, and Tokyo, 1991

Jackie Kestenbaum, ed.: Emerging Japanese Architecture of the 1990s, New York, 1991

Documentation and research devoted to the work of individual architects is rather extensive since 1970, and is seen in a great number of publications:

U. Kultermann: Kenzo Tange: Architecture and Urban Design, Zürich, 1970

R. Spade: Paul Rudolph, New York, 1971

John Hejduk, Architekt, Zürich, 1973

Peter Blake: Architecture for the New World: The Work of Harry Seidler, Sydney, 1973

H. R. Hitchcock: Hentrich und Petschnigg, Düsseldorf, 1973

Kevin Roche, John Dinkeloo, Tokyo, 1974

A. Drexler, Ed.: The Architecture of Skidmore, Owings and Merrill, New York, 1974

R. Giurgola and J. Mehti: Louis I. Kahn, Zürich, 1975

W. Curtis: A Language and a Theme: The Architecture of Denys Lasdun and Partners, London, 1976

Kenneth Frampton: Richard Meier, New York, 1976

Emilio Ambasz: The Architecture of Luis Barragan, New York, 1976

Philip Drew: Frei Otto: Form and Structure, Boulder, 1976

A. Savio: L'architettura di Aldo Rossi, Milan, 1976

Noboru Kawazoe: Kenzo Tange, Tokyo, 1976

H. Ronner, S. Jhaveri, and A. Vasella: Louis I. Kahn, The Complete Works. 1935–1974, Boulder, Colo., 1977

Neri Pozza: Carlo Scarpa, Padova, 1978

Peter Blundell Jones: Hans Scharoun, London, 1978

D. Dunster, ed.: Michael Graves, New York, 1979

Nory Miller: Johnson/Burgee Architects, New York and London, 1980

John Pastier: Cesar Pelli, New York, 1980
Christian Norberg-Schulz: Louis I. Kahn: idea e immagine, Rome, 1980
Gerald Allen: Charles Moore, New York, 1980
S. Abercrombie: Gwathmey/Siegel, New York, 1981
Jorge Glusberg: Miguel Angel Roca, London, 1981
Vincent Scully: Robert Stern, London, 1981
Gianni Braghieri: Aldo Rossi, Bologna, 1981
Manfredo Tafuri: Vittorio Gregotti: Buildings and Projects, Milan and New York, 1982
Vincent Scully: Michael Graves, New York, 1982
Peter Collymore: The Architecture of Ralph Erskine, London, 1982
Philip Drew: The Architecture of Arata Isozaki, New York and London, 1982
Svetlosav Raev, ed.: Gottfried Böhm: Bauten und Projekte. 1950–1980, Cologne, 1982
Malcolm Quantrill: Alvar Aalto: A Critical Study, London, 1983
Jan van der Marck, ed.: Arquitectonica. 1977–1984, Miami, 1984
Francesco Dal Co and Giuseppe Mazzariol, eds.: Sarlo Scarpa. 1906–1978, Milan, 1984
Walter McQuade: Architecture of the Real World. The Work of Hellmuth, Obata, and Kassabaum, New York, 1984
Massimo Dini: Renzo Piano. Projects and Buildings. 1964–1983, New York, 1984
Peter Arnell and Ted Bickford, eds.: Charles Gwathmey and Robert Siegel, Buildings and Projects. 1964–1984, New York, 1984
Francis Strauven, ed.: Aldo van Eyck, Antwerp, 1985
O. M. Ungers. 1951–1984. Bauten und Projekte, Braunschweig and Wiesbaden, 1985
Philip Drew: Leaves of Iron. Glen Murcutt. Pioneer of an Australian Form, Sydney, 1985
Mirko Zardini: The Architecture of Mario Botta, New York, 1985
John Hejduk: Mask of Medusa. Works 1947–1983, New York, 1985
Arthur Drexler: Ricardo Bofill and Leon Krier, Architecture, Urbanism and History, New York, 1985
Malcolm Quantrill: Reima Pietilae: Architecture, Context and Modernism, New York, 1985
Eugene J. Johnson, ed.: Charles Moore. Buildings and Projects 1949–1986, New York, 1986
Yukio Futagawa, ed.: Tadao Ando, Tokyo, 1987
Francesco Dal Co: Mario Botta. Architecture. 1960–1985, London, 1987
Arnulf Luchinger: Herman Hertzberger: Buildings and Projects 1959–1986, The Hague, 1987

Wolfgang Pehnt: Lucien Kroll: Buildings and Projects, New York, 1987
Behnisch und Partner: Arbeiten aus den Jahren 1952–1987, Stuttgart, 1987
Patrice Goulet: Jean Nouvel, Paris, 1987
Lamberto Rossi: Giancarlo de Carlo, Architecture, Milan, 1988
Svetlosav Raev, ed.: Gottfried Böhm: Lectures, Buildings, Projects, Stuttgart and Zürich, 1988
William Curtis: Balkrishna Doshi. An Architecture for India, New York, 1988
The Architecture of Arthur Erickson, New York, 1988
S. Hines, R. Haag-Bletter, et al., eds.: The Architecture of Frank O. Gehry, New York, 1988
Kay Kaiser: The Architecture of Gunnar Birkerts, Florence, 1989
Mario Bellini et al.: Emilio Ambasz: The Poetics of the Pragmatic, New York, 1989
Mayne and Rotondi: Morphosis. Buildings and Projects, New York, 1989
Jan Lambot, ed.: Buildings and Projects of Foster Associates, Berlin, 1989
Sarah Mollman-Underhill, ed.: Stanley Tigerman. Buildings and Projects. 1966–1989, New York, 1989
Werner Blaser, ed.: Santiago Calatrava, Boston, 1989
Carter Wiseman: Ieoh Ming Pei. A Profile in American Architecture, New York, 1990
Lucia Funari: Robert A. M. Stern: Modernità e Tradizione, Rome, 1990
Sergio Crotti, ed.: Vittorio Gregotti, Bologna, 1990
Wayne Attoe, ed.: The Architecture of Ricardo Legorreta, Austin, 1990
Kenneth Frampton and Joseph Rykwert: Richard Meier Architect. 1985–1991, New York, 1991
Carolina Vaccaro and Frederic Schwartz, eds.: Venturi, Scott Brown and Associates, Bologna, 1991
Morris Adjmi, ed.: Aldo Rossi Architecture 1981–1991, Princeton, 1991

Specific publications dealing with problems regarding architecture and society in the 1970s and 1980s are:

Chrysalis. A Study of the Relationship between Indian Culture and Form, Montana State University School of Architecture, 1971
A. Tzonis: Towards a Non-Oppressive Environment, Boston, 1972

Giancarlo de Carlo: An Architecture of Participation, Melbourne, 1972

Hassan Fathy: Architecture for the Poor, Chicago, 1973

E. F. Schumacher: Small is Beautiful, London, 1974

B. C. Spiegel, ed.: Citizen Participation in Urban Development, Fairfax, 1974

David Dickson: Alternative Technology and the Politics of Technical Change, London, 1974

Susana Torre, ed.: Women in American Architecture. A Historic and Contemporary Perspective, New York, 1977

Jan Wampler: All Their Own: People and the Places they Build, New York, 1978

E. Graboury: Amerindian Identity, The Architectural Review 8, 1980

Mary Ellen Hombs and Mitch Snyder: Homelessness in America. A Forced March to Nowhere, Washington, D.C., 1982

David Wright and Dennis A. Andrejko: Passive Solar Architecture. Logic and Beauty, New York, 1982

Alberto Perez-Gomez: Architecture and the Crisis of Modern Science, Cambridge, Mass., 1983

Tod Marger: The Critical Edge: Controversy in Recent American Architecture, 1986

Lorenz, Clare: Women in Architecture. A Contemporary Perspective, New York, 1990

Aaron Betsky: Violated Perfection: Architecture and the Fragmentation of the Modern, New York, 1990

Jack Travis, ed.: African American Architects in Current Practice, Princeton, 1991

Colin Davis: High Tech Architecture, London, 1991

Photo Credits

Montgomery, Oldfield and Kirby,
    Lusaka   241
Museum of Modern Art, New York   36, 70,
    125, 127
Andrija Mutnjakovic, Zagreb   238
National Design Institute, C. Staub
    (photographer), Ahmedabad, India   190
Velimir Neidhardt, Zagreb   235
Arnold Newman, New York   174
Tomio Ohashi, Tokyo   198, 202
Satrabandhu Ongard, Bangkok   247
I. M. Pei, New York   249
The Pritzker Prize, Los Angeles   209
Toomas Rein, Tallinn   228
Kevin Roche, John Dinkeloo and Associates,
    Hamden, Conn.   122
Jean Roubier, Paris   107
Abby Sadin, Gwathmey and Siegel,
    Philadelphia   205
Roland Simounet, Paris   224
Henk Snoek Associates, London   180
Vitaly Sokhin, St. Petersburg   227
Stadtbildstelle Leverkusen, Schwarz
    (photographer)   42
Dr. Franz Stoedtner/Heinz Klemm,
    Düsseldorf   5a, 17, 18, 20, 22, 24–27, 30,

35, 38–41, 43–47, 51, 53, 54, 58, 59, 61,
    62, 65–69, 94
Ezra Stoller Associates, Mamaroneck,
    N.Y.   110, 112, 113, 133
Donald Stull, Boston   212
Radovan Tajder, Zagreb   237
Kenzo Tange, Tokyo   250
Thomas Airviews   90
Edward Teitelman, Camden, N.J.   21, 129
Ullstein-Bilderdienst, Berlin   95–98
O. M. Ungers, Cologne   223
György Vadasz, Budapest   232
Steve Van Gorp, St. Louis, Mo.   207
Vasari, Rome   90
Venturi, Scott Brown, and Associates,
    Philadelphia   204, 215
Rafael Vinoly, New York   251
Kari Virta, Helsinki   217
Vitra Design Museum, Weil   222
Albert Winkler, Bern   161
Wu Changfu, Shanghai   247a

All other photographs are from the author's
archives.

Index of Names

Aalto, Alvar, 53, 84–87, 88, 109, 111,
  134–135, 141, 142, 149, 163, 195, 200,
  202, 205, 231
Abdelhalim, Halim, 235
Abercrombie, Patrick, 130
Abraham, Raimund, 116
Abramovitz, Max, 111
Abrossimov, P.W., 101, 102, 151
Adaua, 229
Affleck, Ray, 127
Agostino, Alfredo, 161
Agrest, Diana, 117, 229
Ahsan, Raziul, 239
Aida, Takefumi, 246
Aillaud, Emile, 141
Airas, Timo, 203
Aisenpreis, Ernst, 53
Akiyama, T., 182
Alabyan, Karo S., 71, 100
Al-Bayati, Basil, 235
Alberts, Tom, 204
Albini, Franco, 93, 166, 233
Alen, William van, 14, 15, 17, 79
Alexander, Christopher, 228, 247
Alfon, Santos R., 240
Ali, Habid Fida, 237
Aloisio, Ottorino, 59
Alver, A., 218
Ammann, Othmar H., 81
Anahory, Eduardo, 150, 213
Ando, Tadao, 213, 246, 247
Andrault and Parat, 141
Andrews, John, 110, 117, 129, 130, 241
Angel Roca, Miguel, 229
Anger and Heymann, 174

Anissimov, A., 217
Anselmi, Alessandro, 212
Antič, Ivan, 225
Arai, Alberto T., 155
Archigram, 134
Architects Collaborative (TAC), 187, 189,
  231
Architects' Company Partnership, 132
Architektengroep, 204
Archizoom, 149, 212
Arp, Hans, 61
Arquitectonica, 198
Artaria, Paul, 89
Artigas, Francisco, 155
Arup, Ove, 132, 177
Aschieri, Pietro, 94
Asmussen, Erik, 203
Asplund, Erik Gunnar, 87
Atelier 5, 145, 146, 210, 228
Athfield, Ian, 241
Attolini Lack, Antonio, 227
Aubert, André, 105
Auer, Fritz, 145
Aulenti, Gae, 211, 212
Aurobindo, Sri, 174
Aymonino, Carlo, 149, 212
Azagury, Elie, 167, 168, 230
Azevedo Leao, Carlos, 82
Azuma, Takamitsu, 246

Baburov, A., 150
Backström and Reinius, 135–136
Badran, Rasem, 232
Bakanowsky, Louis I., 198
Bakema, Jacob Beren, 137, 142, 204

Baker, Herbert, 83
Baldwin, F.W., 12, 13, 14
Balladur, Jean, 141
Banfi, Gian Luigi, 93
Banham, Reyner, 8
Barchin, G.B., 67
Barnes, Edward Larraby, 122
Baroni, Berardi, Gamberini, Guarneri,
    Lusanna, and Michelucci, 92
Barragan, Luis, 155, 227
Barsodi, Ralph, 75
Bartning, Otto, 49
Batey, Andrew, 198
Baudizzone, Erbini, Lestard and Varas, 228
Baudot, Anatole de, 23
Bauersfeld, Walter, 56
Beaudouin, Eugène, 26, 103–104, 141
Beckett, Welton, 125
Behnisch, Günther, 145, 209
Behrens, Peter, 4, 9, 26, 30–31, 32, 39,
    42, 69
Bel Geddes, Norman, 69
Belgioioso, Lodovico di, 93
Belgioioso, Peresutti, and Rogers, 148
Beliaieva, A., 218
Bell, Alexander Graham, 12–14, 25
Bellini, Mario, 247
Ben Embarek, Mourad, 168, 230
Benevolo, Leonardo, 62
Ben Miled, Tarek, 231
Bennett, Hubert, 131
Benson, Allan L., 10
Berenson, Bernard, 2
Berg, Max, 55, 56
Bergstrom, G.E., 71, 100, 101
Berkovici, S., 152, 223
Berlage, Hendrik Petrus, 2, 12, 39, 60, 69, 88
Bermudez, Guido, 158
Bernardes, Sergio, 159
Bernardini, Domenico, 94
Bertiga, Jorubena, 239
Bijvoet, Bernard, 15, 64–65, 88
Bill, Max, 142
Bird, Walter, 127
Birkerts, Gunnar, 120, 122, 196
Björn, Malene, 235
Bleriot, Louis, 14
Blom, Piet, 204
Blomfield, Reginald, 45
Blomstedt, Aulis, 135
Bo, Jörgen, 136, 168, 204
Bo Bardi, Lina, 159, 160, 228
Boccara, Charles, 230
Bodiansky, Vladimir, 105, 139, 210
Bofill Levi, Ricardo, 149, 150, 200, 211,
    213, 214, 231
Bofinger, Helge, 209
Bohigas Guardiola, Oriol, 212
Böhm, Gottfried, 144, 200, 205, 206, 209
Bokhari, Abdullah, 235
Bolonha, Francisco, 159
Bonatz, Paul, 98
Bond, J. Max, 197
Bonet Bartran, Pep, 213
Borezki, A.B., 151, 152

Borges, Max, 157
Borisovski, Georgi, 150
Borromini, Francesco, 46
Bosch, Theo, 204
Botta, Mario, 147, 200, 210, 247
Bourbonnais, Alain, 141
Brasini, Armando, 59, 92
Bratke, Osvaldo, 159
Bravo, Jorge, 155
Brechbühler, Hans, 89
Bregman and Haman and Zeidler
    Partnership, 199
Breuer, Marcel, 69, 79, 88, 89, 110
Brinkman, Johannes Andreas, 89
Brinkman, W., 62, 64
Broek, Johannes Hendrik van den, 137,
    142, 204
Brunfaut, Maxime, 89
Bryant and Bryant, 197
Buckminster-Fuller, Richard, 13, 81, 125
Budilovski, 218
Budimirov, Bogdan, 153
Bunshaft, Gordon, 111
Burle-Marx, Roberto, 83, 159
Burnet, John, 88
Burnham and Root, 14, 18
Busignani, A., 33–34
Buszko, Henryk, 220
Büxel, Winfried, 145

Cacho, Raul, 155
Cacoub, Olivier-Clement, 231
Calatrava, Santiago, 210
Calini and Montuori, 147
Calini, L., 175
Cambridge Seven Associates, Inc., 198
Cameron, Chisholm, and Nicol, 241
Caminos, Horatio, 161
Campbell, Wendell J. and Susan B., 197
Campo Baeza, Alberto, 150, 213
Candela, Felix, 91, 156, 157, 166
Candilis, Georges, 139, 166, 168, 210
Cano Lasso, Julio, 150, 213
Cardinal, Douglas, 200
Carlo, Giancarlo de, 148, 212
Carloni, Tita, 147
Carmona, F.L., 156
Casbarian, John C., 198
Castelnau, Eliane, 168
Castiglioni, Enrico, 148, 161
Castro, Fidel, 157
Catalano, Eduardo, 83, 116, 161, 229
Caudill, Rowlett, and Scott, 166, 233
Cekanauskas, Vitautas, 217
Cetto, Max, 155
Cézanne, Paul, 4
Chadirji, Rifat, 164, 166, 232
Chafee, Judith, 187, 197
Chakhava, Giorgi, 218
Chalk, Warren, 134
Chamberlain, Powell, and Bon, 131
Chareau, Pierre, 103
Chashakjan, M.N., 151
Chatchikian, 219
Chaurorn, Nitt, 241

Chemetov, Paul, 211
Chemnitz and Nürnberg, 45
Chermayeff, Peter, 198
Chermayeff, Serge, 88, 116
Chernaivskii, Ilia, 151, 216
Chiantante, Paola, 212
Chiattone, Mario, 59, 60
Christie, Alden B., 198
Chrjakov, A.F., 101, 102
Cirici Alomar, Christian, 213
Clotet Dallas, Lluis, 213
Coates, Well, 88
Coderch de Sentmenat, José Antonio, 150, 212
Colucci, Gabriella, 212
COMTEC, 169
Cook, Peter, 134
Coop-Himmelblau, 210
Corrales, José Antonio, 213
Correa, Charles M., 174, 175, 190, 228, 237, 238
Correia de Lima Costa, Marcelo Luiz, 150, 213
Costa, Lucio, 82, 154, 159
Cox, Richardson, and Taylor, 241
Csete, György, 223
Cubitt, James, 132, 231
Cuijpers, Petrus Josephus Hubertus, 60
Curtiss, G.H., 12

Dahinden, Justus, 142, 147, 168, 169, 171, 210
Dali, Salvador, 91
Daneri, Luigi Carlo, 93
Dannatt, Trevor, 164, 165, 233
Darvich, Djahanguir, 236
Dastuge, Marcel, 105
Davis, Chermayeff, Geismar, and de Harak, 127
Debbio, Enrico Del, 93
Deilmann, von Gerkan and Marg, 209
Deilmann, von Hausen, Race, and Ruhnau, 144
Deklava, Marko, 224
De Klerk, Michael, 60
Desbarats, Dimakopoulos, Michaud, Lebensold and Wise, 127
Devilliers, Christian, 211
Diba, Kamran, 236, 237
Dieste, Eladio, 228
Dieterich, Paul E., 198
Digerud, J., 203
Dinkeloo, John, 118–119, 120, 188
Dischinger, Franz, 56, 57
Dissing and Weitling, 142, 203–204, 205
Dixon, Fenella, 201
Dixon, Jeremy, 201
Djumenton, G., 150
Dobrowolski, Jan, 220
Dobrowolski, Krystina, 153, 220
Doecker, Richard, 95
Doesburg, Theo van, 3, 37, 60–61
Dokic, Aleksandar, 225
Domeniq, Günther, 210
Donato, Emilio, 150, 231

Donato, Enrico, 213
Dondel, Jean-Claude, 105
Dorizo, 218, 219
Doshi, Balkrishna V., 173, 174, 190, 237–238
Doxiadis, C.A., 172
Drake and Lasdun, 132, 169
Drew, Jane, 169, 172
Dudok, Willem Marinus, 60
Duhart, Emilio, 154
Duiker, Johannes, 15, 64–65, 88, 89
Dumont, Alberto Santos, 14
Düttmann, Werner, 144, 209
Dyckerhoff and Widmann, 56, 57

Ecochard, Michel, 164, 166
Eddé, Henri, 164
Edison, Thomas Alva, 9–12
Egender, Karl, 89
Eggers Group, 235
Ehn, Karl, 51, 52
Eiermann, Egon, 142
Eiffel, Gustave, 12, 13, 14, 25
Eisenman, Peter, 127, 193, 194–195, 205, 247
Ekwueme, 169
El Hakim, Mahmoud, 231
El Kafrawi, Kamal, 231, 233
Elliott, Julian, 169, 170, 229
Elmslie, George, 5
Elsässer, Martin, 57
England, Richard, 232
Erdei, Andras, 221
Erickson, Arthur, 127, 199, 200
Ernst, Max, 74
Erole, Pier Luigi, 212
Erskine, Ralph, 136, 200, 203
Ervi, Arne, 135
Esherick, John, 111, 116, 124, 125
Estudio Cinco, 161
Eyck, Aldo van, 108, 137–138, 204, 228
Eyck, Hannie van, 204

Faraoui, Abdeslam, 168, 230
Faravashi, B., 236
Farmanfarmaiyan, Abdolaziz, 166
Farman, Henry, 14
Farrell, Terence, 201
Fathy, Hassan, 168–169, 231
Fayez, Zuhair, 235
Fehn, Sverre, 136, 203
Feininger, Lyonel, 35
Ferguson, James, 5
Ferrer, Miguel, 157
Filenko, L., 218
Finsterlin, Hermann, 47
Finsterwalder, Ulrich, 56, 57, 98
Fisher, Howard T., 79
Forbat, Fred, 49
Ford, Henry, 10, 12
Fort-Brescia, Bernardo, 198
Foster, Norman, 200, 201, 242, 243
Franco, Francisco, 149, 212
Frank, Josef, 52
Franta, Aleksander, 220

Freyssinet, Eugène, 25, 26, 74
Friedman, Yona, 140, 141
Froebel, 5
Fry, E. Maxwell, 88, 169, 172
Fussler, John, 171
Fussler and Cooke, 83

Gabo, Naum, 66
Galvagni, Mario, 148
Gandelsonas, Mario, 117, 229
Gangneux, Marie-Christine, 211
Gantt, Harvey B., 197
Garatti, Roberto, 157
Garatti, Vittorio, 157, 227
Garay, Miguel, 213
Garcia de Paredes, José M., 150
Garcia Lascurain, Sergio, 155
Gardella, Ignazio, 93, 149
Garnier, Tony, 4, 9, 20–22, 23, 26, 27, 58
Gaudi, Antonio, 46, 91, 171
Gavrilin, A., 150
Gazzarolli, Matiaz, 224
Geest, Uwe, 150
Gehry, Frank O., 195–196, 205, 208
Genovese, Roberto Mariotti, 212
Ghiai, Heydar, 166
Gibberd, Frederick, 130
Gibbs-Smith, E., 2
Giedion, Siegfried, 23, 75, 89, 91
Gigliotti, V., 169
Gilbert, Cass, 14
Gillet, Guillaume, 141
Gill, Irving, 18, 20
Gilmore, E.A., 5
Ginsburg, M.J., 67
Gisel, Ernst, 142
Giurgola, Romaldo, 122, 190, 191, 192, 203
Gniedovski, J., 217
Goff, Bruce, 122, 197
Gogowskaja, N.E., 151
Goldberg, Bertrand, 121, 122
Goldsmith, Myron, 188
Golosoff brothers, 66, 67
Gönner and Rhyner, 57
Gonzales de Leon, Teodoro, 227
Gonzales Gortazar, Fernando, 227
Goodhue, Bertram Grosvenor, 20
Gorbachev, Mikhail, 214
Gorbunova, 217
Gowan, James, 133, 134
Grabowska-Hawrylak, Jadwiga, 220
Graeff, Werner, 39
Gramsci, Antonio, 59
Grassi, Giorgio, 212
G.R.A.U., 149, 212
Graves, Michael, 127, 193–194
Greene, Charles Sumner, 18
Greene, David, 134
Greene, Henry Mather, 18
Greene, Herb, 122, 197
Greenough, Horatio, 5
Gregotti, Vittorio, 149, 212
Griffin, Walter Burley, 5, 83
Grigoriants, 220
Grimshaw, Nicholas, 201, 213

Gropius, Walter, 1, 15, 30, 31–34, 35, 37, 38, 42, 47, 49, 52, 69, 73, 79, 80–81, 88, 109–110, 119, 141, 163–164, 175, 187, 189, 190, 231
Grounds, Romberg, and Boyd, 175–176
Grover, Satish, 239
Gruen, Victor, 79
Grung, Geir, 203
Grzimek, Günter, 145
Guardiola, Oriol Bohigas, 150
Guedes, Amancio d'Alpoim, 169, 171, 229
Guedes, Joaquim, 159, 161, 228
Guerrini, G., 94
Guevrekian, 52
Guinard, Carlos, 158
Gunlogsson, Halldor, 136, 204
Gutbrod, Rolf, 164, 209, 233
Gutierrez, Jorge Romero, 158
Gutierrez, Manuel R., 157
Gutnov, Alexej, 150
Gwathmey, Charles, 193, 194

Haan, Herman, 137
Hablik, Wenzel, 47, 49
Habsband, Frances, 198
Hadid, Zaha, 201, 247
Haerdtl, 52
Haesler, Otto, 52
Haeussler, Carlos, 157
Häfeli, Max Ernst, 89
Hajeedar, Haji, 239–240
Halcrow Group, 232
Halprin, Lawrence, 192
Hammad, Bilal, 232
Hansen, Hans Munk, 204, 230
Hansen, Oskar, 153
Hansen, Sophia, 153
Hanson, Norman, 171
Hara, Hiroshi, 247
Hardjoko, Triatno Y., 240
Häring, Hugo, 47, 49, 52–53, 95
Harm, Henry J., 12
Harrison, Wallace, 111
Harrison and Abramovitz, 117
Hasegawa, Atsuko, 246
Häussermann, P. and C., 141
Hayakawa, Kunihiko, 247
Hdshistojanov, 223
Hecker, Zvi, 162, 163, 236
Heilmann, 54
Heimsath, Clovis, 198
Heinle, E., 144
Heinrichs, Georg, 144
Hejduk, John, 127, 193, 194, 205, 207
Helfreich, W.G., 29, 71, 100
Hellden, Lallerstedt, Lewerentz, 87
Hellmuth, Obata, and Kassabaum, 117, 164– 165, 187, 188, 235
Hennebique, François, 22–23
Henricksen, Arne, 203
Hentrich, Helmut, 142, 143, 144, 166
Hernandez, Augustin, 227
Herron, Ron, 133, 134
Hertzberger, Herman, 137, 204, 208
Hijjas, 239

Hilberseimer, Ludwig, 1, 31, 79, 80
Hitchcock, Henry Russell, 109
Hitler, Adolf, 75, 95, 98, 99
Hitzig, Friedrich, 43
Hodgkinson, Patrick, 133, 134, 201
Hodne, Thomas A., 186, 196
Hodne Partnership, 197
Hoffmann, Josef, 2, 4, 26, 52
Höger, Fritz, 44
Holabird and Roche, 14
Holden, Charles, 88
Hollein, Hans, 147, 148, 149, 200, 205,
   209, 210, 236
Holl, Steven, 199, 247
Holzbauer, Wilhelm, 210
Holzmeister, 52
Hood, Raymond, 15, 16, 79
Horiguchi, Sutemi, 83
Howard, Ebenezer, 21–22, 76
Howe, George, 79
Howells, John Mead, 15
Hrzic, Marijan, 225
Huang Xiang-Ming, 242
Hubácek, Karel, 221
Hubacher, Carl, 89
Hughes, H. Richard, 171, 229
Hugo, Victor, 4
Huidobro, Borja, 211
Hussain, Rabiul, 239

Ibrahim, Abdelbaki, 231
Iegerev, U.S., 151
Ihnatowicz, Zbigniew, 153
Islam, Muzharul, 239
Isozaki, Arata, 108, 178, 182, 205, 213,
   244, 246
Israelian, Raphael, 219
Ito, Tooyo, 246
Itten, Johannes, 35, 37

Jacobsen, Arne, 86, 87, 136, 142, 203,
   205
Jaenecke, Fritz, 136
Jaervinen, Kari, 203
Jahn, Helmut, 189
Jain, Uttam C., 175, 237, 238, 239
Jamal, Karim, 166
Jeanneret, Pierre, 172
Jenny, William Le Baron, 14
Jofan, B.F., 29, 71, 100
Johansen, John, 110, 122, 189
Johnson, Philip, 110, 111, 112, 119, 122,
   141, 162, 186, 187
Jones, Edward, 199
Jonov, J.I., 151
Josic, Alexis, 139
Jourda, François-Hélène, 211–212
Judd, Robert Stacy, 20
Jumsai, Sumet, 241
Jurcsik, Karoly, 221

Kahn, Louis I., 53, 122–124, 149, 173,
   174, 190, 192, 196, 236, 237, 239

Kaljundi, Tiit, 217
Kallmann, McKinnell, and Knowles, 111,
   187, 190
Kamal, Fawizah, 240
Kandinsky, Wassily, 2, 35
Karmi, Dov and Ram, 163, 236
Karpinski, Zbigniew, 153
Katstaller, Karl, 157
Kavinde and Rai, 175, 239
Kawaguchi, Mamoru, 182
Kawakami, I., 182
Keck, George F., 79
Keil Amaral, Francisco, 150, 213
Kemmer, Fritz, 98
Ken Yeang, 239, 240
Kévés, György, 152, 221
Khairallah, Samir, 235
Khalid, Ruslan, 239
Khan, Faziur, 188
Kharitonova, S., 150
Kidder-Smith, G.E., 92
Kiesler, Frederick, 236
Kikutake, Kiyonori, 178, 181–182, 228,
   244, 246
Kirkland, M., 199
Kitagawara, Atsushi, 246
Kitbutr, Chulathat, 241
Klee, Paul, 35
Kleihues, Josef Paul, 209
Kliment, Robert M., 198
Klump, Henry, 157
Kochar, G., 219
Kohn, Pederson, and Fox Associates, 187,
   189
Kolchev, Stefan, 223
Konstantinov, Janko, 153, 226
Koolhaas, Rem, 137, 204, 247
Koppel, Eva and Nils, 136
Korchev, M., 67
Korngold, Lucjan, 159
Korsmo, Arne, 87, 136
Kossinsky, A., 219, 220
Kotli, Alar, 151, 217
Koutský, Karel, 221
Kowalski, Z., 220
Kozel, Jan, 221
Kraemer, Friedrich Wilhelm, 142
Kramer, Paul, 60
Krassilnikov and Velikanov, 217
Kravez, S., 66–67
Krawetz, 219
Kreis, Wilhelm, 44
Krier, Leon, 205
Krier, Rob, 108, 146, 147, 205, 209
Kristl, Stanco, 224
Kristofferson, John, 203
Kriukelis, Hlomauskas, 217
Kroll, Lucien, 205
Krushchev, Nikita, 150, 214
Kubassov, W.S., 151, 217
Kulikova, V., 217
Künnapu, Vilen, 217, 218
Kurokawa, Noriaki (Kisho), 178, 180, 181,
   182, 183, 205, 223, 224, 228, 231, 233,
   241, 244, 246

Kurtovic, Ivo, 225
Kuzlianov, V., 217, 219
Kwan, Simon, 242

Ladowski, N., 66
Lagaro Ortiz, Eduardo, 231
Lai Lok Kun, 239, 240
Landsbergis, 217
Lane, Barbara Miller, 98
Lankrs, Peter, 199
Lapin, Leonard, 217, 218
Lari, Yasmeen, 237
Larsen, Henning, 204, 233
Lasdun, Denys, 131, 132, 134, 200, 201
Laul, Anil, 239
Laurens, Claude, 169
Lawrence, D.H., 74
Lawrov, B., 69
Lazarenko, 217
Lazarescu, Cesar, 223
Leborgue, Marcel, 89
Le Corbusier, 1, 2, 3, 22, 26–29, 31, 39,
    53, 69, 73, 74, 82, 83, 103, 104, 109,
    111, 116, 122, 138, 139, 149, 154, 163,
    171, 172, 174, 177, 187, 190, 193, 194,
    210, 224, 231, 237
Legorreta Vilchis, Ricardo, 227
Lenin, V.I., 65, 66, 70
Leonhardt, Fritz, 144
Leonidov, Ivan, 67, 68
Lescaze, William, 79, 88
Levi, Rino, 159
Leykam, Marek, 153
Lezava, I., 150
Libera, Adalberto, 93
Libeskind, David, 159, 247
Liceaga, Alfonso, 155
Lichtblau, 52
Lim Chong Keat, 239
Lim, William, 240
Linazaro, José Ignazio, 213
Lindstroem, Sune, 235
Linek, Jan, 221
Lissitzky, El, 62, 64, 66
Littmann, 54
Llewelyn and Davis, 131
Locsin, Leandro V., 240
Lods, Marcel, 26, 103–104
Loegler, Romuald, 220–221
Loghem, J.J. van, 69, 89
Lohmer, Gerd, 144
Longo, Eduardo, 161
Lonkov, A., 218
Loos, Adolf, 18, 52
Loover, Avo-Himm, 217
Lorenz and Williams, 195
Lotz, Wolfgang, 99
Lubetkin, Berthold, 87
Luca, Julije De, 225
Luckhardt, Hans, 47, 95
Luckhardt, Wassily, 47, 95, 141
Luisi, Franco Per, 212
Lumsden, Anthony, 240
Lund, Kjell, 136, 203
Lundberg, J., 203

Lundy, Victor, 127
Lurçat, André, 52, 69, 103
Lutyens, Edwin, 83
Lyndon, Donlyn, 192

Maaskant, H.A., 89
McAfee, Cheryl L., 197
McCurdy, J.A.D., 12
MacGregor, Luis, 155
Machado, Rodolfo, 116–117, 229
McIntosh, Gordon, 83
McKenzie, Voorhees, and Gmelin, 14, 15
Mackey, David, 150, 212
Mack, Mark, 198, 247
Maclachlan, Roy, 229
Madalena, Sordo, 155
Madhloom, Medhat Ali, 166
Madison, Robert P., 197
Magas, Boris, 153, 225
Maher, George W., 5
Mahony, Marion Lucy, 5
Maillart, Robert, 57, 89–91
Maillou, Riuox de, 2–3
Maki, Fumihiko, 181, 228, 244, 246
Makiya, Mohamed Saleh, 166, 232
Makkor, Igor B., 218
Makovesz, Imre, 152, 221, 223
Maksimovič, Stojan, 225
Malevich, Kasimir, 65, 66, 101
Malhotra, J.C., 175
Mallet-Stevens, Robert, 26
Malone, Geoffrey T., 240
Manevich, 217
Mangiarotti, Angelo, 148
Mann and McNaillie, 9
Manosa, Francisco, 240
Mansfeld, Al, 163, 236
Manteola, Flora, 161, 228
Mao Tse-tung, 176
March, Werner, 96, 98, 163
Marchi, Virgilio, 59
Marcks, Gerhard, 35
Marcos, Ferdinand, 240
Maré, Eric de, 73
Marinetti, Filippo Tommaso, 57, 58
Markelius, Sven, 87, 136
Marot, M., 141
Mars, Vernon de, 79, 111, 116
Martienssen, Rex, 83, 171
Martin, Leslie, 134, 166, 233
Martini, Massimo, 212
Martorell, J.M., 149–150, 212
Martorell, Bohigas, and Mackey, 213
Massey, Geoffrey, 127
Mathur, B.P., 175
Matté-Trucco, Giacomo, 59–60
Matthew, Robert, 131
Matusik, Ivan, 221
May, Ernst, 50, 51, 62, 69, 141, 171
Maybeck, Bernhard, 18
Mayekawa, Kunio, 177, 178, 244
Maymount, Paul, 141
Mayne, Tom, 198
Maziéres, Patrice de, 168, 230
Mehta, Jaimini, 192

Meier, Richard, 126, 127, 149, 193, 205
Meij, Johan Melchior van der, 60
Melnikov, Kontantin, 67, 69, 74
Mendelsohn, Erich, 31, 44-46, 69, 82, 88, 109, 111, 117
Mendez da Vasconcelos, Ernani, 82
Merrill, John D., 111
Meyer, Adolf, 32, 37
Meyer, Hannes, 38, 69
Meyer and Holler, 20
Michelucci, Giovanni, 93, 149
Mies van der Rohe, Ludwig, 2, 30, 31, 38-42, 47, 52, 62, 73, 74, 79-80, 109, 110- 111, 112, 118, 122, 127, 136, 141, 187, 188, 189, 199
Mihelič, Milan, 224
Milani, Pino, 212
Miliutin, N.A., 69
Millares, Hoffmann, and Branco, 158
Miluniy, Vlado, 221
Minangoy, A., 141
Minz, W.O., 101
Miralles, Enric, 213
Miranda, A., 157
Mirheydar, M., 236
Missing Link, 210
Mitchell, Ehrman B., 122, 192
Mjelva, Haakon, 136, 203
Moersid, 240
Moholy-Nagy, Laszlo, 1-2, 3, 37
Molezun, Ramon Vazquez, 213
Mondrian, Piet, 2
Moneo Valles, José Rafael, 150, 213
Montes, Jorge, 157
Montes, Mario, 229
Montgomery, Oldfield, and Kirby, 169, 229, 230
Montuori, Francesco, 212
Moore, Charles, 124, 190, 192, 205, 241
Moore, Lyndon, Turnbull, Whitaker, 124
Mora, Enrique de la, 155, 156
Morandi, Riccardo, 159
Morasutti, Bruno, 148
Moreira, Jorge Machado, 82
Moretti, Luigi, 130, 148
Morgan, Julia, 20
Morgan, William, 197
Morimura, Raymond, 199
Morris, William, 4, 35
Moser, Werner M., 89
Moss, Erick Owen, 198
Mouliar, L., 218
Moustafa, Ahmed Farid, 233
Moya, Hidalgo, 131
Moya, Juvenal, 157
Mueller, Hans, 144
Muller, Peter, 240
Mumford, Lewis, 100
Mumtaz, Kamil Khan, 237
Munir, Hisham A., 166, 231-232
Munnik, Visser, and Black, 171
Murata, Yutako, 182
Muratov, V., 219, 220
Murcutt, Glen, 241
Murphy, C.F., 111, 189

Mussolini, Benito, 91, 92, 147
Muthesius, Hermann, 30
Mutiso, Reuben Musyoka, 229
Mutnjakovič, Andrija, 226
Mutschler, Carlfried, 209

Nagashima, Koichi, 246
Neff, Wallace, 127
Neidhardt, Velimir, 225
Nenkov, 223
NER group, 150
Nervi, Pier Luigi, 92, 93, 109, 111, 116, 117, 147
Netsch, Walter, 111
Neufert, Ernst, 142
Neumann, Alfred, 162, 163, 236
Neutra, Richard J., 18, 20, 79, 111
Newman, Barnett, 187
Nicolosi, Patrizia, 212
Niedermoser, 52
Niemeyer, Oskar, 82, 83, 141, 149, 154, 159, 230
Nikolski, A.S., 67
Nilsen, Jörn, 136, 204
Norman and Dawbarn, 171
Norris, Harry A., 83
Noto, Anna Di, 212
Nouvel, Jean, 211
Novarina, M. and P., 233
Novikov, F.A., 151
Nowicki, Jacek, 153
Nowicki, Matthew, 116
Nuñez-Yanowsky, 211, 214

Obata, Gyo, 188
Oblak, Ciril, 224
Obregon, José M., 157
Odak, Tomislav, 225
O'Gorman, Juan, 155, 227
Olatunde, David, 169
Olbrich, Joseph Maria, 30
Olivo, Marcello d,' 148
Oltai, Peter, 223
Olumuyiwa, Olewole, 169, 229
Omrania, 233
Ongard, Satrabandhu, 241
Ortegas Flores, Salvador, 155
Ortiz Echague, Cesar, 150
Ostertag, Roland, 144
Otaka, Masato, 181, 246
Ott, Carlos, 211
Otto, Frei, 144, 145, 164, 209, 233
Oud, Jacobus Johannes Pieter, 2, 39, 42, 52, 62, 63
Outram, John, 201
Owings, Nathaniel, 111
Oy, Devecon, 230, 231

Paalman, Endel, 151
Paateleinen, Raili, 135, 202
Padula, A. La, 94
Pagano, Giuseppe, 93
Page and Broughton, 235
Pakniya and Moayed-Aahd, 166
Palacios, Augusto, 155

Palmer and Turner, 177, 242
Palui, B.V., 151
Pani, Mario, 155, 227
Pantovic, Milorad, 153
Parkin, John B., 13, 127, 130
Parson, Ralph M., 164
Pascoletti, Cesare, 94
Patel, V., 175
Patrizi, Giampietro, 212
Paysse Reyes, Mario, 228
Peatfield and Bodgener, 171
Pei, I.M., 111, 113, 127, 166, 177, 187,
    188, 199, 211, 240, 242, 244
Peichl, Gustav, 210
Pelli, Cesar, 116, 122, 127, 129, 187,
    188–189, 229
Penttilae, Timo, 203
Peralta Ramos, F., 161
Perco, R., 52
Pereira, William L., 166, 233
Peresutti, Enrico, 93
Peret, Auguste, 138
Perez de Arce, Mario, 161, 229
Perkins, Dwight H., 5
Perkins and Will, 166, 168
Perlstein, Y., 163
Perraudin, Gilles, 212
Perret, Auguste, 25, 26, 69, 105
Petschnigg, Hubert, 142, 143, 144, 166
Piacentini, Marcello, 59, 92, 93, 94
Piano, Renzo, 140, 141, 212
Piccinato, Luigi, 93
Pietilae, Reima, 135, 136, 166, 202, 235
Pietri, Alejandro, 158
Pineda, Fernando, 155
Pinós, Carme, 213
Pirraz, 236
Piszar, Eugenio, 155
Placidi, Corrado, 212
Platz, Gustav Adolf, 45
Plischke, 52
Poelzig, Hans, 30, 42–44, 69
Pokrovski, I.A., 151
Poljanski, A.T., 151, 215
Polk, Willis Jefferson, 18
Ponti, Gio, 93, 147, 236
Pope, John Russell, 79
Popov, A., 150
Popov, I., 151
Porro, Ricardo, 139, 157, 210, 226, 227
Portoghesi, Paolo, 148, 164, 168, 169, 205,
    212, 232
Portzamparc, Christian de, 211, 247
Porumbescu, M., 152
Porumbescu, N., 223
Posokhin, Mikhail V., 151–152, 214, 215
Powell, Philip, 131
Prakasch, Aditya, 175
Pran, Peter, 198
Prasad, Shivnath, 175
Predock, Antoine, 187, 196, 197
Price, Cedric, 133, 134
Prouve, Jean, 105, 141
Pruncu, M., 152
Pruncu, N., 223

Prus, Victor, 127
Purini, Franco, 149, 212

Rafamatanantsoa, Jean, 169
Ramirez Vazquez, Pedro, 155
Ramos, Jorge, 240
Ranalli, George, 198, 199
Rankine, Terry, 198
Rau, Heinz, 163, 236
Ravelomamantsoa, José, 169
Ravnika, Edvard, 224
Ravnikar, Vojteh, 224
Raymond, Antonin, 79, 83
Razzaghi, Y., 236
Rebellon, Josefina, 227–228
Rebori, Andrew N., 79
Rechter, Jakov, 236
Reichlin, Bruno, 147, 210
Reidy, Affonso Eduardo, 82, 159, 160
Reinhart, Fabio, 147, 210
Rein, Toomas, 217, 218
Resnik, D., 163
Revell, Viljo, 129, 130, 135, 161
Rewal, Raj, 239
Rhone and Iredale, 199
Ricci, Leonardo, 148
Rice and Daubney, 241
Richards, I.A., 3
Richardson, H.H., 30
Richter, Hans, 39
Richter, Venceslav, 153
Rickard, Bruce, 176
Ridolfi, Mario, 93
Rietveld, Gerrit Thomas, 52, 61, 62
Righter, J.V., 199
Rimpl, Herbert, 98
Rio, Jorge del, 157
Ritter, H., 57
Roberto brothers (Marcel, Milton,
    Mauricio), 159
Roca, Miguel Angel, 190
Roche, Kevin, 118–119, 120, 188
Roche and Dinkeloo, 118–119, 187, 188
Rodia, Simon, 20
Rodtschenko, Alexander, 65
Rogers, Ernesto N., 93
Rogers, Richard, 140, 141, 201, 247
Romano, M., 94
Romero, Paolo, 157, 158, 227
Romney, Hervin, 198
Roosevelt, Franklin D., 75
Rosanov, 219
Rosenberg, Alfred, 75, 95, 98
Rosenberg, Yorke and Mardall, 132
Rose, Peter, 199
Rossi, Aldo, 108, 147, 148, 149, 200, 205,
    212, 247
Roth, Alfred, 28, 89
Roth, Emil, 89
Rothko, Mark, 187
Rotondi, Michael, 198
Roza, Gustavo da, 199
Rudnev, L.V., 101, 102, 214–215
Rudolph, Paul, 110, 119, 187, 189, 242
Ruesch, H., 57

Ruhnau, Rave, and von Hausen, 144
Rulea, C., 152, 223
Ruskin, John, 4, 35

Saarela, Heikki, 203
Saarinen, Eero, 117, 118–119, 188
Saarinen, Eliel, 15, 79, 109
Sabadke, Manfred, 145
Sabha, Fariburz, 239
Sack, Monty, 171
Sadovsky, S., 150
Saenz de Oiza, Francisco Javier, 150, 213
Saevich, 217
Safdie, Moshe, 117, 129, 130, 163, 190,
    192, 199, 240
St. Florian, Friedrich, 116
Sakakura, Junzo, 83, 177, 244
Salinas, Fernando, 157, 158, 227
Salinas, Raul, 155
Salmona, Rogelio, 157, 228
Salvisberg, Otto Rudolf, 49
Samona, Giuseppe, 93
Samuels, Danny, 198
Samuelson, Stan, 136
Sanchez Elia, Peralta Ramos, Alfredo
    Agostino, and Clorinda Testa, 228
Sanchez Elia, S., 161
Sanchez, Felix, 155
Sánchez Gómez, Javier, 161, 228
Sant'Elia, Antonio, 1, 3, 57–58, 59, 60
Santelli, Serge, 190
Santos, Josefa, 161
Sarger, René, 141, 236
Sauvage, Henri, 26
Savioli, Leonardo, 149
Scarpa, Carlo, 148, 149
Schader, Jacques, 147
Scharoun, Hans, 30, 42, 47, 50, 95, 141, 142
Scheerbart, Paul, 39, 46–47
Scheffauer, Hermann, 33
Schein, Ionel, 141
Schindler, Rudolph M., 18, 20, 79
Schipporeit and Heinrich, 111
Schlemmer, Oskar, 35
Schmidt, Hans, 39, 73, 89
Schmitz, Bruno, 30
Schnebli, Dolf, 147, 210
Schneider-Esleben, Paul, 142
Schott, Ehrentraut, 157
Schulte-Frohlinde, Julius, 95
Schulz, Christian Norberg, 136
Schupp, Fritz, 142
Schupp, Martin, 98
Schwagenscheidt, Walter, 141
Schwanzer, Karl, 147, 166
Schwitters, Kurt, 42
Scolari, Massimo, 149
Scott Brown, Denise, 190, 191, 192, 201, 232
Seidler, Harry, 175, 176, 241, 242
Selfridge, T.E., 12, 14
Semino, Rinaldo, 149
Semper, Gottfried, 1
Sepman, Henno, 151, 217
Serafimov, S., 66–67
Serafinov, 219

Serenyi, Peter, 27–28
Serrano, Francisco J., 155
Sert, José Luis, 91, 111, 141, 154, 164
Severini, Gino, 3
Severini, Renato, 169
Shariatzadeh, Y., 236
Sharma, M.S., 175
Sharon, Arieh, 162, 163, 170, 236
Sharon, Eldar, 170, 236
Shchuko, Vladimir A., 29, 71, 100
Shchusev, Alexej Witkorowitsch, 70
Shechlian, 219
Shibuya, Akira, 182
Shilinskas, R. and A., 217
Shinohara, Kazuo, 244, 246
Shipkov, A. and E., 150
Shirashi, U., 182
Sholtovski, Ivan Wladislawowitsch, 70
Shreve, Lamb, and Harmon, 15, 79
SIAL group, 153, 221
Siegel, Robert, 194
Siladin, Branco, 225
Silvetti, Jorge, 117, 229
Simbirzev, Wassily, 71, 100
Simounet, Roland, 168, 169, 211
Siren, Kaija and Heikki, 135, 147, 209, 232
Siza Vieira, Alvaro, 150, 205, 213–214
Skaarup and Jespersen, 232
Skibnievska, Halina, 153
Skidmore, Louis, 111
Skidmore, Owings, and Merrill, 111, 114,
    117, 164, 166, 187–188, 233, 235, 240, 244
Skoda, Rudolf, 209
Slaato, Nils, 136, 203
Smithson, Peter and Alison, 134, 166
Snowden, Lord, 134
Snozzi, Luigi, 210
Sobotka, 52
Sokhin, Vitaly, 216
Solar, Zelko, 153
Soleri, Paolo, 117
Solsona, Justo, 161, 228
Soltan, Jerzy, 116, 153
Sörensen, Erik Christian, 136
Soria y Mata, Arturo, 21
Šosterič, Milan, 225
Sostres Maluquer, Jóse M., 150
Spear, Laurinda, 198
Speer, Albert, 31, 74, 95, 97, 98–99
Spencer, Robert C., 5
Spreckelsen, Johann Otto von, 211
Šrámek, Jan, 153, 221
Šrámková, Alena, 153, 221
Staber, Johann, 210
STAFF, 228
Stalin, Josef, 29, 100, 101, 214
Stam, Mart, 39, 62, 64, 66, 69, 73
Starck, Philippe, 247
Steiger, Rudolf, 89
Stein, Clarence, 75–76
Stein, Gertrude, 122
Steiner, Rudolf, 53–54
Stijnen, L., 89
Stirling, James, 117, 131, 133, 134, 200,
    201, 205, 228

Stoilov, Georgi, 223
Stone, Edward Durrel, 157, 175
Štraus, Ivan, 226
Strauss, Joseph, 81
Strnad, 52
Stubbins, Hugh, 110, 141, 187, 189, 236
Stucky and Meuli, 145
Studer, André, 168
Studio 7, 224
Studio PER, 213
Stull, Donald, 187, 197, 198
Suarez, Mario G., 157
Sukada, Budi A., 240
Sularto, Robi, 240
Sullivan, Louis, 3, 14, 52, 53
Sung-Yong Joh, 244
Superstudio, 149, 212
Sutedjo, Suwondo B., 240
Suyudi, 240
Swoo Geun Kim, 244

TAC. See Architects Collaborative
Taft Architects, 198
Taillibert, Roger, 205, 211, 232
Tajder, Radovan, 225
Takamatsu, Shin, 246
Takayama, Minoru, 246
Takeyama, Kiyoshi Sei, 246
Talati, Arvind, 239
Tange, Kenzo, 153, 164, 166, 177–178,
    179, 181, 226, 229, 230, 232, 233, 235,
    236, 240, 241, 244, 245
Tao Ho, 242
Tarchanian, 219
Tarnawscy, Jerzy, 220
Tastemain, Henri, 168
Tatlin, Vladimir, 1, 65, 66
Taüber-Arp, Sophie, 61
Taut, Bruno, 15, 30, 42, 46–50, 60, 62,
    65–66, 83
Taut, Max, 15, 42
Taveira, Tomas, 213
Tavora, Fernando de, 150, 213
Tayara, Bourhan, 232
Tay Kheng Soon, 240
Taylor, R.R., 75
Tcherkesian, 219
Tenggara, Akitek, 240
Tengrove and Marshall, 176
Terragni, Giuseppe, 93
Terry, Quinlan, 201
Testa, Clorindo, 161
Thermes, Laura, 212
Thom, Ronald James, 199
Thunstrom, Olof, 87
Tigerman, Stanley, 127, 174, 175, 195, 247
Tijen, Willem van, 88, 90
Timme, Robert H., 198
Tiptus, Boonyawat and Pussadee, 241
Tjahjono, Gunawan, 240
Toelpus, Uno, 151, 217
Tomaszewski, L., 153
Tompkins, Harry, 83
Toro, Osvaldo, 157
Torosian, D., 219

Torre, Susana, 198
Torregrosa, Louis, 157
Torroja, Eduardo, 91
Tränkner, Erhard, 145
Trapman, Jan, 137
Troost, Paul L., 95, 96, 98
Trumbauer, Horace, 14
Tsakok, Paul, 240
Tschernischov, S.J., 101, 102
Tschumi, Bernard, 198, 211
Tschumi, Jean, 147
Tseitlina, 218
Tsien, Billie, 198
Tsirkounov, 217
Tubbs, Ralph, 131
Tukan, Jafar, 232, 235
Turina, Vladimir, 153
Turnbull, William, 242
Turnbull and Whitacker, 192
Tusquets Guillen, Oscar, 213, 247

Ugljen, Zlatko, 226
Uhl, Ottokar, 147, 205, 210
Uliashov, 217
Ungers, Oswald Mathias, 116, 144, 145,
    200, 205, 209
Urbahn, Max, 107, 125
Utzon, Jörn, 136–137, 166, 175, 176, 203,
    233
Uytenbogaardt, Roelof Sorel, 229

Vadasz, György, 221, 222
Vaeth, Hans, 98
Valenzuela, Pablo, 157
Valéry, Paul, 3
Valle, Gino and Nani, 148
Vasilevski, I., 151, 216
Vatovec, Egon, 224
Vegas and Galia, 158
Velde, Henry van de, 1, 27, 30
Venchiarutti and Fairfield, 127
Venturi, Robert, 124–125, 190–192, 201,
    232
Vesnin, Alexander, 66, 67
Vesnin, Leonid, 66
Vesnin, Victor, 66, 67
Viard, Paul, 105
Vicente, Manuel, 244
Vieco, Herman, 157
Viganò, Vittoriano, 148
Villagran de Garcia, José, 155
Villanueva, Carlos Raul, 154, 158, 228
Vincente, Manuel, 190
Vinoly, Rafael, 117, 161, 228, 229, 247
Virta, Kari, 202, 203
Vitellozzi, Annibale, 175
Vitic, Ivan, 153
Vlasov, A.V., 151
Vlugt, L.C. van der, 62, 89
Voisin, Gabriel, 14
Voss, Friedrich, 98
Vreeland, Thomas R., 190

Wachsmann, Konrad, 79, 80–81, 116
Wagner, Martin, 49

Wagner, Otto, 4, 58
Wahed El-Wakil, Abdel, 235
Wakabayashi, Hiroyuki, 246
Walker, Roger, 241
Warchavchik, Gregori, 82
Warjenzov, T., 69
Warren, Miles, 241
Warren and Mahoney, 176
Wasilewski, W., 220
Wassef, Ramses Weissa, 231
Watanabe, Hitoshi, 84
Webb, Michael, 134
Weber, Gerhard, 142, 143, 144
Weber, Karl-Heinz, 145
Weese, Harry, 122, 195, 247
Weidlinger and Salvadori, 157
Weitling, Otto, 136
Werner, Eduard, 33
Wiener, P.L., 154
Wijdeveld, Theo van den, 60
Wilhelm, Günter, 142
Williams, Amancio, 83
Williams, E. Owen, 88
Williams, Todd, 198
Wils, Jan, 89
Wilson, Colin St. John, 200, 201
Wilson, Hugh, 131
Wines, James, 183, 198
Winslow, C.M., 20
Winter, Franz, 28
Wittmer, D.J., 71, 100, 101
Wituchin, D.S., 151

Wohlert, Vilhelm, 136, 168, 204, 230
Wong, Alfred, 240
Wong Tung, and Partners, 242
Woods, Shadrach, 139, 166, 168
Wright, Wilbur and Orville, 2, 5, 12, 14
Wright, Frank Lloyd, 2, 3-9, 14, 20-21,
    22, 25, 26, 27, 28, 30, 33, 34, 35, 37, 52,
    53, 60, 61, 62, 73-74, 75-77, 83, 108,
    163, 197, 231
Wright, Henry, 76
Wright, Lloyd, 20
Wu Changfu, 242

Yamada, Mamaru, 83, 177
Yamasaki, Minoru, 111, 115, 164, 166, 235
Yeltsin, Boris, 214
Yorke, F.R.S., 88
Yoshida, Tetsuro, 83
Yoshizaka, Takamasa, 177
Yuncken, Freeman Brothers, Griffith, and
    Simpson, 175

Zablocki, Wojciech, 220
Zabludovsky, Abraham, 227
Zabolotni, V.I., 101
Zahiruddin, Shah Alam, 239
Zapata, Carlos, 198
Zarak, E., 157
Zekovic, Radosav, 226
Zevaco, Jean Francois, 168
Zevi, Bruno, 46

Index of Places

Aachen, Germany, 31
Aalsmeer, Holland, 64
Abuja, Nigeria, 229
Aegruder-Nelijärve, Estonia, 218
Agadir, Morocco, 168
Ahmedabad, India, 124, 139, 154–155,
    173, 174, 237, 238
Ahwaz, Iran, 236
Al Ain, United Arab Emirates, 233
Albuquerque, New Mexico, 197
Alençon, France, 205
Aleria, Spain, 150
Alessandria, Italy, 93
Alfeld-on-Leine, Germany, 32, 33
Al-Gassim, Saudi Arabia, 233
Algeciras, Spain, 91
Algiers, Algeria, 103, 231
Almeria, Spain, 213
Amiens, France, 138
Amman, Jordan, 164, 232
Amsterdam, Holland, 60, 61, 62, 65, 88,
    89, 137–138, 204, 208
Andalous, Algeria, 230
Ann Arbor, Michigan, 196
Antwerp, Belgium, 89, 103
Apeldorn, Holland, 204
Artek, Crimea, 151, 215
Ashiya, Japan, 246, 247
As-Sarir, Libya, 231
Athens, Greece, 110, 215
Atlanta, Georgia, 193
Aukland, New Zealand, 241

Auroville, India, 174
Avord, France, 25

Bad Friedrichshall, Germany, 144
Bad Hersfeld, Germany, 144, 145
Baghdad, Iraq, 110, 163, 164, 191, 232
Bagsvaerd, Denmark, 203
Bahrem, Saudi Arabia, 233
Baltimore, Maryland, 198
Bangkok, Thailand, 241
Barcelona, Spain, 39, 41, 212, 213
Bari, Italy, 212
Bartlesville, Oklahoma, 108
Basel, Switzerland, 57
Batumi, Georgia, 218
Bat Yam, Israel, 162, 163
Bear Run, Pennsylvania, 76
Beeston, England, 88
Beijing, China, 177, 188, 242
Beinn Bhreagh, Canada, 13
Beirut, Lebanon, 164, 232
Belgrade, Yugoslavia (former), 225, 226
Belo Horizonte, Brazil, 82
Beni-Badhal, Algeria, 75
Bensberg, Germany, 144
Bergisch-Gladbach, Germany, 205
Berkeley, California, 18, 111, 116
Berlin, Germany, 30, 31, 33, 38, 40, 42,
    43, 46, 49, 57, 62, 96, 97, 98, 99, 110,
    139, 141, 142, 144, 192, 194, 201, 205,
    209, 214
Berlin-Britz, 49, 50

Berlin-Kreutzberg, 205, 207
Berlin-Moabit, 30, 31
Berlin-Siemensstadt, 49–50
Berlin-Tegel, 209, 221
Bern, Switzerland, 89, 90, 91, 147
Bexhill-on-sea, England, 88
Bielefeld, Germany, 141
Big Sur, California, 124
Blumberg, Germany, 142
Bocholt, Germany, 205
Bochum, Germany, 144
Bogotá, Colombia, 157, 228
Bogra, Bangladesh, 239
Bojnice, Czechoslovakia, 221
Bologna, Italy, 181
Bombay, India, 175, 238, 239
Bordeaux, France, 26
Borgoricco, Italy, 212
Borgo Ticino, Switzerland, 148
Boston, Massachusetts, 111, 113, 187, 188,
   190, 197, 198
Boumaine du Dades, Morocco, 168
Brasilia, Brazil, 154, 159
Bremen, Germany, 141, 147
Bremen-Vahr, 141, 142
Bremerhaven, Germany, 209
Breslau, Germany, 43, 55, 56, 57, 95
Bridgeport, Connecticut, 193
Briey-La-Forêt, France, 139
Brno, Germany, 39, 41
Broni, Italy, 149, 212
Brunn, Germany, 41
Brussels, Belgium, 139, 147, 151
Bryn Mawr, Pennsylvania, 192
Bucharest, Rumania, 152, 223
Budapest, Hungary, 152
Buenos Aries, Argentina, 161, 228
Buffalo, New York, 7–8, 30
Busto Arsizio, Italy, 148

Cabo Negro, Morocco, 230
Cairo, Egypt, 169, 231
Calcutta, India, 175
Calgary, Canada, 200
Cambridge, England, 88, 134
Cambridge, Massachusetts, 79, 80, 111,
   116, 118, 190
Canberra, Australia, 83, 175, 176
Cape Kennedy, Florida, 125
Capetown, South Africa, 229
Capri, Italy, 93
Caracas, Venezuela, 158, 228
Cartagena, Colombia, 157
Casablanca, Morocco, 25, 167, 168, 230
Castrop-Rauxel, Germany, 204
Celje, Yugoslavia (former), 224
Cesce Budejovice, Czecholovakia, 221
Cesenatico, Italy, 148
Chambery, France, 210
Chandigarh, India, 172, 174, 237
Chandler, Arizona, 79
Changigarh, India, 139
Channel Heights, California, 79
Chantilly, Virginia, 118
Charkow, Russia, 67

Charleroi, Belgium, 89
Chattanooga, Tennessee, 198
Chicago, Illinois, 3, 4, 5, 7, 12, 14, 15, 79,
   80, 110, 121, 122, 188, 189, 195
Chimbote, Colombia, 154
Chorweiler, Germany, 205, 206
Cidra, Puerto Rico, 157
Cincinnati, Ohio, 189, 195
Clichy, France, 105
Coldspring New Town, Maryland, 192
Cologne, Germany, 33, 34, 46, 47, 48, 145
Columbus, Indiana, 192, 194
Columbus, Ohio, 194, 195, 198
Como, Italy, 58, 92, 93
Copenhagen, Denmark, 136, 203
Cordoba, Argentina, 229
Courcourconnes, France, 211
Coyoacán, Mexico, 156
Cuernavaca, Mexico, 156
Cumbernauld, England, 131

Dacca, Bangladesh, 124, 155, 173, 174,
   190, 239
Dallas, Texas, 188
Damascus, Syria, 232
Dammam, Saudi Arabia, 233, 235
Darmstadt, Germany, 30
Delft, Holland, 137, 204
Densapar, Bali, 240
Depok, Indonesia, 240
Dessau, Germany, 37–38, 52, 75
Dharan, Saudi Arabia, 164, 166, 233, 235
Doha, Qatar, 233, 235
Dornach, Germany, 53–54
Drachten, Holland, 204
Dramburg, Germany, 32
Drancy, France, 103–104
Dresden, Germany, 57
Druskininkai, Lithuania, 217
Düsseldorf, Germany, 57, 144, 205

East Hampton, New York, 194
Edmonton, Canada, 200
Elisabethville, Congo, 169
Elkins Park, Pennsylvania, 109
Erevan, Armenia, 219
Essen, Germany, 144
Eveaux, France, 139
Evora, Portugal, 214
Exeter, New Hampshire, 123, 190

Fargo, North Dakota, 193
Farsta, Sweden, 134
Firminy, France, 139
Florence, Italy, 31, 149
Fort Wayne, Indiana, 193
Fort Worth, Texas, 123, 190, 198
Frankfurt, Germany, 50, 51, 57, 62, 141,
   189, 193, 195, 205, 209
Fredensborg, Denmark, 136, 137
Fujisawa City, Japan, 246
Fukuoka City, Japan, 181, 183, 195, 247

Gallaratese, Italy, 149
Garching, Germany, 143

Garden City, New York, 119
Garkau, Germany, 53
Gelsenkirchen, Germany, 144
Geneva, Switzerland, 28, 147
Genova, Italy, 212
Gentofte, Denmark, 86, 136
Gourna, Egypt, 169
Groningen, Holland, 201
Guadalajara, Mexico, 227
Guatemala City, Guatemala, 157
Guben, Germany, 39
Gudao, China, 242
Guelph, Canada, 130

Haarlem, Holland, 89
Habana del Este, Cuba, 158
Hagen, Germany, 31
Hague, Holland, 193
Haifa, Israel, 163, 236
Halen, Switzerland, 146
Hamburg, Germany, 110, 141
Hanagi, Japan, 246
Harbor Springs, Michigan, 126
Harlow, England, 130
Havana, Cuba, 157
Heiligenstadt, Germany, 52
Helmond, Holland, 204
Helsinborg, Denmark, 136
Helsinki, Finland, 135, 202, 203
Hilversum, Holland, 60, 65, 88
Hiroshima, Japan, 178, 246
Hoek van Holland, 62
Hokkaido, Japan, 246
Hollabrunn, Austria, 210
Hollywood, California, 18, 20
Hong Kong, 177, 188, 243, 189. 242
Hourani, Egypt, 231
Houston, Texas, 183, 187, 189, 194
Hull, Canada, 200
Hunstanton, England, 134
Huntington, New York, 192
Hyderabad, India, 237–238

Idrija, Yugoslavia (former), 224
Ife, Nigeria, 170
Imabari, Japan, 178
Imatra, Finland, 134
Inchon, Korea, 244
Indianapolis, Indiana, 119, 120, 188
Irvine, California, 198
Irvine, England, 131
Islamabad, Pakistan, 172, 175, 236
Issyk-Kul, Siberia, 215
Istanbul, Turkey, 42

Jaerna, Sweden, 203
Jakarta, Indonesia, 190, 240
Jeddah, Saudi Arabia, 137, 188, 233, 235
Jena, Germany, 56–57
Jerusalem, Israel, 130, 163, 192, 236
Johannesburg, South Africa, 189
Jyvaskyla, Finland, 84–85

Kaleva, Finland, 135
Kalol, India, 238

Kanagawa, Japan, 244, 245
Kankakee, Illinois, 4–5
Karachi, Pakistan, 175, 237
Karlsruhe, Germany, 204, 209
Karlsruhe-Damerstock, 52
Kassel, Germany, 52
Kerbela, Iraq, 232
Kettwig, Germany, 205
Khartoum, 168, 169
Kiev, Ukraine, 101, 218, 219
Kimihurura, Rwandi, 205
Kitakyushu, Japan, 182, 246
Kobe, Japan, 196
Kobela, Estonia, 217, 218
Kofu, Japan, 178, 179
Krakow, Poland, 221
Kranj, Yugoslavia (former), 224
Krefeld, Germany, 39
Kuala Lumpur, 240
Kufa, Iraq, 232
Kurashiki, Japan, 178
Kurayoshi, Japan, 178
Kyle, South Dakota, 186, 197
Kyoto, Japan, 83, 177

Laensi-Sakylae, Finland, 203
Lagos, Nigeria, 223
Lahore, Pakistan, 237
La Jolla, California, 18, 123
Lake Buena, Florida, 193
Lakeland, Florida, 76
La Plata, Argentina, 228
Las Vegas, Nevada, 197
Legnano, Italy, 93
Le Havre, France, 138
Leicester, England, 133, 134
Leipzig, Germany, 57, 209
Le Mirail, France, 139
Leningrad, Russia. See St. Petersburg, Russia
Leopoldsville, Congo, 169
Liberec, Czechoslovakia, 221
Lidingö, Sweden, 134
Lima, Peru, 157, 228
Lingotto, Italy, 60
Linz, Austria, 147, 209–210
Lisbon, Portugal, 214
Liverpool, England, 201
Ljubljana, Yugoslavia (former), 224
Logrono, Spain, 213
London, England, 87, 88, 131, 132, 133, 134, 191, 201
Los Angeles, California, 18, 19, 20, 21, 79, 189, 193, 195, 196, 198
Louisville, Kentucky, 193
Luban, Germany, 43
Lund, Norway, 203
Lusaka, Zambia, 169, 170, 229, 230
Luxor, Egypt, 231

Madison, Wisconsin, 5, 109, 111, 114
Madrid, Spain, 91, 150
Magdeburg, Germany, 47, 49
Magnitogorsk, Russia, 69, 75
Mainz, Germany, 142, 203
Malmoe, Sweden, 87

Mamaia, Rumania, 223
Manila, Philippines, 240
Mannheim, Germany, 57, 144, 209
Marl, Germany, 137, 142
Marne-la-Vallée, France, 211
Marrakech, Morocco, 230
Marseille, France, 28, 103, 104
Martha's Vineyard, Massachusetts, 198, 199
Mason City, Iowa, 33, 34
Massandra, Crimea, 151, 215
Matsuzaki, Japan, 246
Mazzorbo, Italy, 212
Meaux, France, 139
Mecca, Saudi Arabia, 164, 209, 233
Melbourne, Australia, 83
Mérida, Spain, 213
Mesa Verde, Colorado, 197
Mexico City, Mexico, 155, 156, 227
Miami Beach, Florida, 130
Milan, Italy, 57, 58, 59, 147–148, 212
Milton Keynes, England, 131
Minneapolis, Minnesota, 120, 122
Mishima, Japan, 246
Missasauga, Canada, 199
Mityana, Uganda, 171
Modena, Italy, 149
Mönchengladbach, Germany, 209
Monrovia, California, 20
Mont Anyel, Oregon, 135
Monterrey, Mexico, 156
Montmagny, France, 25
Montreal, Canada, 125, 127, 129, 130, 145, 151–152, 192, 211, 215
Moorhead, Minnesota, 193
Moscow, Russia, 28, 29, 57, 66, 67, 68, 69, 70–71, 100, 101, 102, 151, 152, 214, 215, 216–217
Moshi, East Africa, 171
Mostar, Yugoslavia (former), 226
Muna, Saudi Arabia, 233
Munich, Germany, 96, 98, 141, 142, 144, 145, 209
Munkkiniemi, Finland, 85
Münster, Germany, 144

Namugongo, Uganda, 171
Nanterre, France, 211
Nantes, France, 139
Naples, Italy, 147
Nemours, France, 211
Neubühl, Switzerland, 89
Neuilly, France, 139
New Canaan, Connecticut, 122
Newcastle-upon-Tyne, England, 203
New Delhi, India, 83, 175, 203, 238, 239
New Harmony, Indiana, 193
New Haven, Connecticut, 118, 119, 122, 123, 124, 125, 190, 192
New York City, 14, 15, 16, 17, 78, 79, 109, 110, 111, 112, 115, 116, 117, 118, 119, 122, 130, 147, 186, 187, 188, 189, 193, 194, 198, 199
Niagara Falls, New York, 189, 197
Nianing, Senegal, 229
Nimes, France, 212

Norman, Oklahoma, 122
Norwich, England, 201
Novi Sad, Yugoslavia (former), 224
Nürnberg, Germany, 57, 97, 9

Oakland, California, 119
Oak Park, Illinois, 8, 195
Oberlin, Ohio, 125
Okinawa, 181, 182, 246
Old Westbury, Rhode Island, 193
Olimp, Rumania, 223
Opladen, Germany, 143, 144
Orange, New Jersey, 9, 10
Orbetello, Italy, 92
Orlando, Florida, 125
Orvieto, Italy, 92
Osaka, Japan, 127, 178, 182, 215, 244, 246, 247
Oslo, Norway, 86, 194, 203
Ottawa, Canada, 192
Ouderkerk aan de Amstel, Holland, 204
Oxford, England, 134

Paatsalu, Estonia, 217
Pahang, Malaysia, 240
Paimio, Finland, 85, 88
Pampulha, Brazil, 82
Panama City, Panama, 157
Paris, France, 13, 21, 24, 26, 28, 57, 74, 83, 103, 105, 139, 140, 141, 188, 198, 211, 214
Pärnu, Estonia, 217
Pasadena, California, 18, 20
Peckham, England, 88
Pecs, Hungary, 223
Peenemünde, Germany, 98
Penafiel, Portugal, 214
Penang, 240
Perinton, New York, 194
Petaling Jaya, Malaysia, 239
Philadelphia, Pennsylvania, 79, 123, 124, 191
Philippsburg, New Jersey, 9
Picton, Canada, 199
Piestany, Czecholovakia, 221
Pine Ridge, South Dakota, 197
Piran, Yugoslavia (former), 189
Pisa, Italy, 29
Pitsunda, Georgia, 215
Plano, Illinois, 110
Plattsburgh, New York, 192
Plock, Poland, 153
Pordenone, Italy, 148
Porter, Illinois, 195
Porto, Portugal, 214
Porz-Zurndorf, Germany, 205
Posen, Germany, 43
Potsdam, Germany, 44, 45
Poznan, Poland, 153
Prague, Czechoslovakia, 221
Prague-Chodov, 221
Prague-Zelivka, 221
Pretoria, South Africa, 83
Princeton, New Jersey, 73, 193
Priština, Yugoslavia (former), 226

Providence, Rhode Island, 192
Punta del Este, Uruguay, 228
Purchase, New York, 191
Purkersdorf, Austria, 2

Rabat, Morocco, 230
Racine, Wisconsin, 76, 77
Raincy, France, 25
Raleigh, North Carolina, 116
Ramat Gan, Israel, 163, 236
Ras Lanuf, Libya, 231
Red Deer, Canada, 200
Rehovot, Israel, 162
Reston, Virginia, 194
Rio de Janeiro, Brazil, 82, 103, 159, 160, 228
Riyadh, Saudi Arabia, 164, 165, 166, 188, 204, 233, 235
Rochester, New York, 123
Rödovre, Denmark, 136
Rome, Italy, 21, 56, 59, 93 – 94, 147, 212, 246
Ronchamp, France, 139
Rostow, Russia, 100
Rotterdam, Holland, 62, 63, 64, 88, 89, 137
Royan, France, 141
Runcorn, England, 131
Rye, New York, 188

Sadanska, Bulgaria, 223
St. Dié, 103
St. Gall, Switzerland, 147
St. Louis, Missouri, 46, 116, 117, 188, 190, 192
Saint-Paul-de-Vence, France, 141
St. Petersburg, Russia, 31, 32, 216
Saint-Quentin-en-Yvelines, France, 211
St. Sauveur, Canada, 199
Saitama, Japan, 246
Sänätsalo, Finland, 195
San Bernardino, California, 122, 128
Sandpoort, Holland, 12
San Francisco, California, 15, 18, 79, 81, 116, 124, 125, 181
San Juan, Puerto Rico, 157
San Juan Capistrano, 193
San Rafael, California, 109
Santa Barbara, California, 111, 124
Santa Cruz, New Mexico, 192
Santa Monica, California, 194, 195, 196
Santiago, Chile, 154
São Paulo, Brazil, 159, 160, 161, 228
Sapporo, Japan, 201
Sarem-El-Sheikh, Israel, 163
Sárospatak, Hungary, 221, 223
Säynätsalo, Finland, 85, 86, 134
Sceaux-les-Blagis, France, 141
Scherer, Switzerland, 147
Seattle, Washington, 191
Segrate, Italy, 149
Seoul, Korea, 244
Seville, Spain, 212, 213, 246, 247
Sézana, Yugoslavia (former), 224
Shahsawer, Iran, 236
Shanghai, China, 242
Sher-E-Banglanagar, 174
Shiraz, Iran, 236

Shushtar, Iran, 236
Sibenik, Yugoslavia, 153
Sidi-Bel-Abbes, North Africa, 25
Sinikello, Finland, 202, 203
Sitges, Spain, 149, 150
Skopje, Yugoslavia (former), 153, 178, 224, 226
Slaato, Norway, 203
Sofia, Bulgaria, 223, 224
Split-Pljud, Yugoslavia (former), 225
Stafordville, New York, 190
Stavanger, Norway, 203
Stevenage, England, 130
Stockholm, Sweden, 87, 203
Strasbourg, France, 61
Strickler, Switzerland, 147
Stuttgart, Germany, 39, 45, 52, 141, 200, 205
Sunila, Finland, 85
Surabaya, Indonesia, 240
Suresnes, France, 104
Sydney, Australia, 136, 175, 176, 241

Tägu, Korea, 147
Taichung, Taiwan, 177
Taif, Saudi Arabia, 166
Takamatsu, Japan, 178
Taliesin West, Arizona, 76
Tallin, Estonia, 151, 217
Tampere, Finland, 202
Tananarive, Madagascar, 169, 171
Tapiola, Finland, 134, 135, 136
Tarquinia, Italy, 212
Tashkent, Uzbekistan, 214, 217, 219 – 220
Taveira, Portugal, 213 – 214
Tblissi, Georgia, 218
Teheran, Iran, 137, 166, 236, 237
Tel Aviv, Israel, 163
Tempe, Arizona, 187, 196, 197
Terni, Italy, 148, 212
Thamesmead, England, 131
Tiaret, North Africa, 25
Ticino, Switzerland, 210
Titograd, Yugoslavia (former), 226
Tokyo, Japan, 83, 84, 177, 178, 181, 244, 247
Tombeek, Belgium, 89
Toronto, Canada, 127, 129, 130, 199
Trenton, New Jersey, 123
Tripoli, Libya, 231
Trombay, India, 175
Tromso, Norway, 203
Tucson, Arizona, 197
Tunis, Tunisia, 231
Turin, Italy, 59

Ulm, Germany, 142
Union, New Jersey, 9
University Park, Pennsylvania, 191
Unterdambach, Austria, 210
Urbino, Italy, 212
Ustron, Poland, 220
Utrecht, Holland, 61, 62, 88

Vällingby, Sweden, 134, 135 – 136
Vancouver, Canada, 199, 200
Varna, Bulgaria, 223

Vashi, India, 238
Vela Luca, Yugoslavia (former), 226
Velem, Hungary, 223
Venice, Italy, 139, 149
Verona, Italy, 148
Vevey, Switzerland, 147
Vienna, Austria, 51, 52, 147, 148, 210
Viipuri, Finland, 85
Villeneuve-d'Ascg, France, 211
Villeneuve Loubet, France, 141
Villeurbanne, France, 210
Vilnius, Lithuania, 217
Visiko, Yugoslavia (former), 226
Voronov, Russia, 216

Warren, Michigan, 118
Warsaw, Poland, 153
Warsaw-Mokotów, 153
Washington, D.C., 71, 79, 100, 101, 188
Wauwatosa, Wisconsin, 109
Weber, Switzerland, 147
Weil, Germany, 201, 205, 208

Weimar, Germany, 34, 35
Wellington, New Zealand, 241
West Hollywood, California, 198
Wichita, Kansas, 81, 111, 114
Wilmington, Delaware, 189
Winnipeg, Canada, 199
Winterthur, Switzerland, 147
Wolfsburg, Germany, 141
Woluwe, Belgium, 205
Wroclaw, Poland, 220

Xochomilco, Mexico, 156

Yamagushi, Japan, 246

Zagreb, Yugoslavia (former), 153, 224, 225
Zalaegersteg, Hungary, 221, 222
Zug, Switzerland, 147
Zurich, Switzerland, 89, 90, 91, 137, 147
Zurich-Stadelhofen, 210
Zwolle, Holland, 204